M

THE AUTHOR   Richard
Oxford University. He has wri
and modern, including *Land of*
Companion to Travel in Greece;
the Great and *Legends of Alexander the Great*. He is also the author of the
Traveller's History of Turkey.

He is Publisher for Classics and Archaeology at Routledge, and   orary
Fellow of Exeter University. He is a regular guest
the Aegean, and tries to visit Greece at least once

SERIES EDITOR   Profe   f
the Royal Historical Societ, and   the Lo do   o-
politan University. He has published over 20 books including the biographies
of Joseph Chamberlain, Prince Philip, George VI and Alison Uttley, historical
and military subjects, stories for children and two novels. His most recent books
are the highly praised *Empire: The British Imperial Experience from 1765 to the
Present* and (with Keith Surridge) *The Boer War*. He has reviewed and written
extensively in the national press and in journals and is an advisor to the BBC
History Magazine.

Other Titles in the Series

THE TRAVELLER'S HISTORY SERIES

'Ideal before-you-go reading' *The Daily Telegraph*

'An excellent series of brief histories' *New York Times*

'I want to compliment you ... on the brilliantly concise contents of your books' *Shirley Conran*

Reviews of Individual Titles

A Traveller's History of Greece

'... provides an A–Z cultural gazetteer and an authoritative general history.' *The Weekend Telegraph*

'the beauty of this work is its comprehensive yet still readable nature ... this historical guide will not only be a holiday companion but a constant source of reference about Greek history for years to come.' *Kent Messenger*

'Clearly written, well-structured, and fixing on illuminating and arresting details about events, places, and participants, the book packs a lot into a compact format ... (An) excellent, needed, and rewarding publication.' *Small Press*

A Traveller's History of Turkey

'For informed guidance on the Anatolian peninsula, *A Traveller's History of Turkey* is a whirlwind tour of the key figures in Turkey's history and an excellent portable reference book'.
The Times Literary Supplement

A Traveller's History of London

'... dip into Richard Tames's literary, lyrical *A Traveller's History of London*'. *The Sunday Telegraph*

A Traveller's History of India

'For anyone ... planning a trip to India, the latest in the excellent Traveller's History series ... provides a useful grounding for those whose curiosity exceeds the time available for research.' *The London Evening Standard*

A Traveller's History
of Athens

A Traveller's History of Athens

RICHARD STONEMAN

Series Editor   DENIS JUDD
Line Drawings   PETER GEISSLER

Interlink Books
An imprint of Interlink Publishing Group, Inc.
New York • Northampton

First American edition published in 2004 by
INTERLINK BOOKS
An imprint of Interlink Publishing Group, Inc.
46 Crosby Street, Northampton, Massachusetts 01060-1804
www.interlinkbooks.com

Text copyright © Richard Stoneman, 2004
Preface copyright © Denis Judd 2004
Line drawings Peter Geissler
Maps by John Taylor

The front cover photograph © Peter M. Wilson/CORBIS

Library of Congress Cataloging-in-Publication Data

Stoneman, Richard.
  A traveller's history of Athens/by Richard Stoneman.
  p. cm.—(The traveller's history series)
Includes bibliographical references.
  ISBN 1-56656-533-2 (Paperback)
  1. Athens (Greece)—History. I. Title. II. Traveller's history.
  DF921.S76 2004
  949.5'12—dc22

                                           2003023720

Printed and bound in Great Britain

Contents

Preface

'There is no Greek,' wrote the orator Aelius Aristides, in the middle of the second century AD, 'who would not wish to have been born an Athenian rather than a citizen of his own city.' Although this was perhaps an exaggeration, it did encapsulate a significant truth – that for much of its glorious, antique and modern, history, Athens has been a centre of culture, civilization and of a life style that other, less blessed cities, could only envy.

Among poets who sang its praises, Pindar wrote: 'Oh You, olive shiny and violet crowned, glorious Athens, famous in songs, rampart of Greece, divine city!'

There are few world cities with anything approaching Athens' reputation as a cradle of art, philosophy and political innovation. Just to list some of the names that made the city a beacon of enlightenment and civilization during classical times is awe-inspiring: Socrates, Plato, Aeschylus, Aristophanes, Sophocles, Euripides, Pericles, and Demosthenes. No wonder that it has been such a highly desirable destination for tourists, visitors and students from the time of the Roman Empire to the present day.

No wonder, either, that the British public schools, so dedicated to the training of an elite to rule not only Britain but a world wide Empire, elevated the study of Ancient Greek and Greek culture to the top of the educational tree. Athens and Athenian were terms used freely by the Victorians to signify the highest quality: thus an obviously intellectual, philosophically inclined statesman like Gladstone or Balfour might be dubbed 'Athenian', while a slum-cleared, municipally revived and cherished city like late nineteenth-century Birmingham was sometimes, and perhaps a touch mischievously, described as 'the Athens of the Midlands'. Edinburgh was unquestionably the 'Athens of North Britain'.

Like so many ancient European cities, however, Athens has had a very chequered, even messy, history. This could hardly be avoided in view of the antiquity of its origins and the rise and fall of dynasties and civilizations. Christian Byzantine rule, the Frankish conquest of 1204, the four hundred years of Ottoman domination and the brief but bloody German occupation during the Second World War all left their marks, some of them unsightly and tragic.

Athens, however, has had the spirit and energy to rise above these dislocations and interruptions. The return of democracy in 1974, Greek membership of the European Union, and the rapid growth of mass tourism have all helped to transform the city and save it from the worst excesses of developers and entrepreneurs. As the author of this lucid and comprehensive book writes: 'In 1969 Athens was in many ways a Levantine city, crowded and dirty with too many concrete buildings and too much decay of the finer ones.' Since the late 1980s, however, Athenians have 'transformed the polluted concrete jungle into a city that may be called chic.' Athens now even has a modern and efficient metro.

There is no danger that Athens will fall out of favour as a tourist destination. Its ancient reputation, its recent reforms and development, and its permanent place in Western, even global, culture will ensure that. For those who wish to travel there, Richard Stoneman's fine history, deeply rooted in his own classical education and interests, will be an ideal companion.

Denis Judd
2003

Foreword

Around the middle of the second century AD, the Greek orator Aelius Aristides delivered his *Panathenaic Oration* at a celebration of the annual Panathenaea. The oration, which runs to 73 pages of text (around the half-way mark, Aristides apologises that it is becoming a little long), is an extended celebration of the glories of Athens. As Aristides lumbers towards a conclusion, around fifty paragraphs from the end, he lists the city's advantages: its ample possession of necessities; the beauty of its culture; its capacity for warfare; its climate, art and political constitution; the famed Mysteries of Eleusis. All these combine to ensure that in this unique city the life of man is a fulfilled one. 'There is no Greek', he writes, 'who would not wish to have been born an Athenian rather than a citizen of his own city.'

Most of the terms of this paean recall, in inflated terms, the similar praises of Athens made by Pericles in his funeral speech of 431/0 BC, about six hundred years earlier. A reputation that could endure for six hundred years, and make Athens one of the most admired destinations for tourists and students in the Roman Empire, was already something of a burden for the city to bear. As a result of the Renaissance, western classical education, the Grand Tour, the Philhellene movement and the development of modern tourism, that reputation has been sustained for a further two thousand years.

The reputation is a justified one, for many of the most important advances and discoveries in political thought, philosophy, literature and the visual arts were made in Athens in the fifth century BC. Yet many travellers, from the Middle Ages to the twentieth century, have found it difficult to square that reputation with the untidy and, in earlier times, insignificant city they encountered. The great discontinuities in Athenian (and Greek) history – the abolition of paganism by Christian emperors, the Frankish conquest of 1204, four centuries of Turkish rule, the German occupation and Civil War of the 1940s – have created a city that contains many layers of history above the classical past. Not all are of equal artistic merit, but all are worth the historian's attention as they go to make up a complex and intriguing mixture. In Athens it is easy to look beyond and below the crowded modern city and find substantial traces of three thousand years of history. As the recent Metro excavations have made visible again the pattern of thousands of years of human occupation in this spot, so it is the aim of this book to open the reader's eyes to some of the layers of actions, ideas and achievements that lie below the surface of the present.

Athens has changed greatly even in the thirty-odd years that I have known it. In 1969 it was in many ways a Levantine city, crowded and dirty with too many concrete buildings and too much decay of the finer ones. Since the late 1980s, the calm and prosperity induced by parliamentary democracy and by membership of the European Union have transformed the polluted concrete jungle into a city that may be called chic. Many parts have been pedestrianised and are a pleasure to walk in. Efforts have been made to reduce pollution. Public transport has been improved beyond imagination by the Metro and (in 2004) the return of trams. Restoration has been undertaken not just on the classical monuments but on the nineteenth-century buildings of Plaka and elsewhere, which in the 1970s looked as if they were fit only for demolition. Unauthorised building is on the decrease though it still threatens the Attic countryside. The people and the authorities of Athens have become aware of their history as a totality and are no longer overwhelmed, as Aristides was, by the weight of the all-demanding classical past.

There are many reasons to visit Athens, and I hope the reader will enjoy them all.

NOTE ON SPELLING

No book on Greek history can begin without an apologia for the author's choice of spellings. The Greek and Latin alphabets do not correspond exactly, and furthermore the pronunciation of Greek has changed extremely since the classical period. No one system of transliteration will do for all periods of Greek history.

In general I have preferred familiar English names where they exist (Athens, Thebes, Piraeus, Odysseus as against classical Athenai, Thebai, Peiraieus, Odysseus or modern Greek Athina, Thiva, Pireas or Pireefs, Odysseas or Odyssefs). For familiar classical and medieval names I use the Latin spellings which have become sanctioned by generations of use: e.g. Thucydides, whom I shall never learn to recognise as Thoocky-dee-dees, and Michael Acominatus. For less familiar classical names I tend to use transliterated Greek spellings, e.g. Panakton. For modern Greek names I transliterate according to conventional rules, with k and –on rather than Latin c and –um. Modern Greek has no letters for b, d and g and represents these with mp, nt and gg or gk. I use the simpler western forms for these spellings, though this can lead to ambiguity when d represents, for example, both nt and Greek delta which is pronounced dh. I invite the reader to discover my inconsistencies and to devise a better system if s/he can.

CHAPTER ONE

Mythology and Prehistory: from the Beginnings to the End of the Dark Age

Athens, the capital city of modern Greece and renowned through much of history because of the glories of its classical age in the fifth century BC, was in prehistoric and early times one of the less significant of the Greek states. In comparison with some other parts of the Greek world – the rich and well-watered agricultural lands of Macedonia and Thessaly, the pastoral landscapes of the central Peloponnese, the fish-filled seas of the little island communities, the agricultural plains and good communications eastwards of the Asia Minor coastline – Attica had little to offer. Attica (the peninsula on which Athens is situated) is an exceptionally arid region, with treeless mountains, few rivers and those small ones, ill-adapted for the husbandry and subsistence agri-culture that characterised prehistoric peoples. Its mineral resources were relatively abundant, but it required a more developed society to find a use for, and to exploit, the marble mountains surrounding Athens, the fine potters' clay, or the lodes of silver in the region of Laurion.

What Athens did have to offer, which was of value in prehistoric times, was a remarkable defensive position on the rock that became known as the Acropolis (the 'high city'). Standing on the Acropolis one can look south-west to the coastline (the air was clearer six thousand years ago than it is now), and closer at hand westward to the low hills of the Muses and of the Nymphs, with the Pnyx lying between them. To the north-east is the conical hill of Lycabettus, according to legend thrown there by the goddess Athena in her anger at the daughters of Cecrops (she missed, and it remains where it landed). The horizon is bounded by the four mountains of (from west to east) Aegaleos, Parnes, Pendeli and Hymettus. The Acropolis controlled the sightlines in every

Attica and its demes

direction. Its walls were sheer and for the most part unscaleable; and on its north slope there was a small spring of water, essential for any defensive retreat.

It is hard now to think away the dusty concrete buildings (and a number of fine ones) that surround the Acropolis on all sides, but when the earliest humans to leave traces began to settle around the Acropolis, during the Neolithic period (ca 4000–3000 BC), the region consisted of dry and scrubby maquis like the rest of Attica. However, it was (and is) moistened by the waters of three small rivers: the Cephisus rising in the foothills of Mt Parnes and flowing south to Phaleron; the Ilissus, running from the foot of Mt Hymettus south of the Acropolis through what was, in classical times, an idyllic rural landscape; and the Eridanus, which rises on Mt Lycabettus and runs north of the Acropolis, through the present agora, and then underground by uncertain courses to the sea.

Plato, writing in the fourth century BC, and relying no doubt on imagination and intuition rather than any scientific evidence, described a prehistoric Attica more welcoming than it was in his time (or today):

> But at that epoch the country was unimpaired, and for its mountains it had high arable hills, and in place of the moorlands, as they are now called, it contained plains full of rich soil; and it had much forest land in its mountains, of which there are visible signs even to this day; for there are some mountains which now have nothing but food for bees, but they had trees no very long time ago, and the rafters from the trees felled there to roof the largest buildings are still sound. And in addition there were many lofty trees of cultivated species; and the country produced boundless pasturage for flocks. Moreover, it was enriched by the yearly rains from Zeus, which were not lost to it, as now, by flowing from the bare land into the sea; but the soil it had was deep and therein it received the water, storing it up in the retentive, loamy soil. (*Critias* 111cd)

There may be some idealisation of the ancient past here, but there is an understanding of ecological processes, and we may envisage a prehistoric Attica that offered some conveniences to the prehistoric farmer. We do not know when the cultivation of the olive and grape began, but we may assume that it was early; and the gathering of the matchless Attic honey will have gone on from earliest times.

The earliest settlements around the Acropolis date from the fourth millennium BC, and from about 3000 BC there has been continuous occupation of the area south of the Acropolis until the present day. Occupation at this early date is mainly evidenced by tombs and burials, as the dead were often more substantially housed than the living. During the early Bronze Age (3000–2000 BC) there were settlements at coastal sites including the area of Hellenikon airport, Thorikos, Raphina, Brauron and Marathon, and the inland area of Athens was less used. This may represent a period of peace and freedom from outside threats, allowing people to inhabit exposed coastal areas with little reason to retreat to the fastness of the Acropolis.

Change came around 2000 BC with the arrival of new people whom we may call Greeks. They came from the north and are distinguished by new burial customs and a distinctive style of pottery; they brought with them not only the horse but a new language, Greek. They referred to the people whom they displaced as Pelasgians, Lelegians or Carians, and thought of them as kin to the race of Carians in south-west Asia Minor who continued to live there, speaking and occasionally inscribing their non-Greek language, into the fourth century BC. The pre-Greek language is preserved in many place names, those ending in –ttos, -ssos and –nthos (Mt Hymettos; Halicarnassus in Caria; Corinthos in the Peloponnese) as well as in the word for sea, *thalassa*, indicating that the Greeks arrived from a land where sea was an unknown thing.

The later part of the second millennium, around 1600–1100 BC, saw increased occupation of the area around the Acropolis. (The period is defined archaeologically as Middle Helladic to Late Helladic I.) There was settlement in the area of the Theatre of Dionysus, and as far east as the precinct (to be) of Olympian Zeus. This half millennium was also the heroic age of Greece, when most of the great myths of the heroes such as the Labours of Heracles and the voyage of Jason and the Argonauts were supposed to have taken place. This period culminated in the legendary war of the Greeks against Troy, traditionally dated around 1250 BC. This event, one of the lynchpins of the chronology of their own prehistory that the Greeks of later times constructed, marks the moment when Athens emerges into Greek narratives of the past.

Legendary Athens

Athens is scarcely mentioned in Homer's epic account of the war at Troy. To the Athenians of the archaic and classical ages, when their political greatness and power was already dawning, it was unacceptable to suppose that they had no past worth the mentioning. There were tales of heroes and ancient kings, to be sure. Some intellectuals (we have no idea who) took it upon themselves to structure some of these stories into a more coherent history and to link them to those of the great heroes. By the fifth century BC, from which our extant sources date, these stories were well-established currency both in dramatists like Euripides and in sober historians like Thucydides. But it is important to remember that all these stories first became 'authoritative' about 600 years after the events they purport to describe.

Athena, the tutelary goddess of Athens, a warrior maiden renowned for wisdom and born not from a mother but directly from the head of her father Zeus, was also the protecting goddess of ancient Troy. Troy's safety depended on the protection of an ancient image of Athena known as the Palladium (after one of her titles, Pallas, a word of unknown significance). After the fall of Troy, the Palladium (according to one fifth-century writer, Pherecydes of Athens (FGrH333F4)), was seized by the hero Demophon, the son of Theseus, and brought to Athens.

Thus the crucial link was made between the Athenian past and the great heroic achievement of the Greeks. But this was not, of course, the beginning of the Athenians' story about themselves. That began with their origin from the soil of Attica: they were not indeed siblings of the other Greeks, but had an inalienable claim to their own land from which they sprang. One tradition said that in pre-human times Attica had been home to one of the Titans, Titenios, who alone did not join in the war against the gods. Later, before history began, there had been a king, Ogygus, but after his time the land had fallen into desolation (Philochorus F74). Subsequently a king of Athens emerged named Cecrops. He was an earthborn creature, half man and half snake. At this time Athena and Poseidon (the sea god) were vying for possession of Attica. Poseidon created a spring of salt water on the Acropolis; Athena gave the olive tree (its descendant still grows on the same spot near the Erechtheion). Cecrops declared that Athena's was the more useful gift. The scene was depicted on the lost west pediment of the Parthenon.

The two following kings were deposed in turn and succeeded by Erichthonius, another partly serpentine monster, who had been born in an unusual way. The lame god Hephaestus attempted to rape Athena on the Acropolis, but ejaculated prematurely: she wiped off the semen with a piece of wool and flung it to the ground, where it presently engendered Erichthonius. Athena gave the baby in a basket to the daughters of Cecrops, Herse, Pandrosos and Aglauros (Dew, All-dewy and Glittering) to look after. When they saw what they were supposed to be nursing, they were terrified and jumped off the north wall of the Acropolis. The story is of course not entirely consistent with the story that Athena tried to crush them by throwing Mt Lycabettus at them. Athena took over the baby herself and reared him to manhood. He became the founder of the festival of the Panathenaea.

Erichthonius' son and successor as king, Pandion, was father to Erechtheus, who seems in some respects to be a doublet of Erichthonius. He is mentioned in the *Iliad* (2.544–51). He also had a son called Cecrops, who had a son called Pandion. The doubling of names is a sign that, as often happened, mythographers were struggling to make the legends associated with the individuals fit into the chronology. (A famous case is Sarpedon in Homer, who has to live for three generations to fit the stories.)

Erechtheus was the father of several interesting mythological characters including the nymph Oreithyia (who was carried off by the north wind Boreas, in a famous Attic legend), the nymph Procris (who loved Cephalus), and the woman Creusa who is the heroine of Euripides' play *Ion*. This charming play is about the legendary ancestry of the Ionians, the branch of the Greeks to which the Athenians belonged: they spoke a distinctively different dialect from their opposite numbers, the Dorians, of whom the Spartans were the most notable. Creusa, raped by the god Apollo and having given away the child, is at last reunited with her son, Ion, who is working as a temple attendant at Delphi. Ion later established the Athenians' first constitution, according to Aristotle's *Constitution of Athens*.

Theseus

Erechtheus' successors can be traced in the accompanying table.

The Legendary Kings of Athens (as listed by Castor of Rhodes, FGrHist 250) (The regnal dates are those that Athenian chroniclers might have proposed, if pressed, and have no absolute validity.)

ERECHTHEID DYNASTY

Actaeus
|
Cecrops I (1556–1506) = Agraulos

Erysichthon   Pandrosos   Agraulos   Herse
Cranaus 1506–1497

Amphicton, son of Deucalion 1497–1487

Driven out by **Erichthonius** = ?
|
Pandion 1437–1397 = Zeuxippe
|
Erechtheus 1397–1347 = Praxithea

Procris   Oreithyia   Creusa   others   **Cecrops II** 1347–1307   Pandoros   Metion
=   =   = Xuthus |
Cephalus   Boreas   Ion   **Pandion II** = daughter of king of Megara
(1307–1282)
|
Aegeus = daughter of king of Trozen
(1282–1234)
|
Theseus 1234–1205
|
Demophon 1183–1150
|
Oxyntes 1150–1136

Aphidas 1136–1135   **Thymoetes** 1135–1127
Overthrown by
Melanthos

With Pandion II's son Aegeus we enter the heroic age. Aegeus married Aethra, daughter of the king of Trozen on the north coast of the Peloponnese, and their son was Theseus, the most famous hero of Athens. Theseus, like his older contemporary Heracles, carried out a series of labours which established him as a culture hero, a civiliser. He destroyed the formidable Bull of Marathon; he got rid of several unpleasant bandits who inhabited the route from Athens to the Isthmus. Procrustes had a bed in which he would invite visitors to sleep. If they did not fit, he lopped bits off or stretched them until they did. Sinis used to bend down pine trees and tie his victims' arms to them, then let them spring apart. Sciron used to ask passers by to tie his shoe, and then kick them off a cliff. Theseus gave them all a taste of their own medicine. The stories almost certainly developed late, on the model of those of Heracles: a delightful narration of them is in Bacchylides' eighteenth poem.

But the best known of the legends of Theseus is that of the Minotaur, part of which is told in Bacchylides' seventeenth poem. King Minos of Crete had a wife Pasiphae who was enamoured of a bull. She contrived to have intercourse with it, and produced the fearful monster the Minotaur, a man with a bull's head. This creature was kept in the labyrinth in Crete and had to be placated with a yearly tribute of seven Athenian youths and seven Athenian maidens. The story seems to reflect a period when the great sea power of Crete was exercising some dominance over the lands of the central Aegean. Thucydides in his 'archaeology' (I.4) speaks of the Minoan thalassocracy when 'Minos controlled the greater part of the Hellenic sea'. One year, Theseus was among the party sent to Crete. Falling in love with Minos' daughter Ariadne, he obtained her help: she was a clever girl, and gave him a ball of string so that he could find his way out of the labyrinth after despatching the Minotaur. Needless to say, he succeeded where generations had failed, and returned safely to Athens. Unfortunately, in the excitement of his adventure, which included carrying off Ariadne and then abandoning her on Naxos, he forgot to change his sails, as he had agreed with his father, from black to white to indicate his success. Aegeus, watching out from the south-west corner of the Acropolis, saw the ship with black sails approaching, deduced that it brought news of

Theseus and the Minotaur

the death of his son, and jumped in his despair off the rampart. He fell into the sea (a remarkably long way away), which was thus named the Aegean after him.

Two further legends associate Theseus with a companion. He goes with Heracles to capture the girdle of the Queen of the Amazons (who invaded Attica in legendary times); and he descends into the under-world with Pirithous to abduct Persephone, the Queen of the dead. The latter escapade fails, and is disastrous for Pirithous, who has to stay among the dead; but Theseus at least returns safely to the upper world.

An intriguing feature of Theseus is his outsider status. Unlike the Athenians, who claimed to be born from the soil of Attica, the hero who became central to the formation of their city came from Trozen. It is only his deeds that took place in Attica and the Megarid. Several, such as his rape of Helen (he was 50, she was 7, if the chronology is calculated carefully), are localised at the deme of Aphidna. But his cult is an Athenian not an Attic one, closely connected with the legends, and probably the sixth-century activities, of state formation.

A standard view (Hans Herter) associates the development of Theseus' legend with Pisistratid rule in the early sixth century (see Chapter 2), and derives its popularity in art (vases, wall paintings, sculpture) from an epic poem the *Theseis*, dated to the early sixth century. Theseus, for example, is credited with the foundation of the Panathenaic festival, which was reorganised by Pisistratus in 566. This conflicts of course with the legend that ascribes its foundation to Erichthonius.

But an alternative view (Henry Walker) points out that the legend really gains momentum after 510, in the period of Cleisthenes' democratic reforms, and that Theseus is now presented as an Ionian rival to the Dorian (Spartan) Heracles, as well as a proto-democrat. In truth, Theseus is a role model for all politicians and it is hard to tie his origins to a particular political epoch or group.

His legend is prominent in the literature of the fifth century. Theseus figures in the mythographer Pherecydes' *Attica* (pre 490). In 476/5 Cimon gained political kudos from his discovery and repatriation of the 'bones of Theseus'. Sophocles wrote an *Aegeus* in 468. The contemporary Bacchylides (ca 530–450) devoted two poems to the hero. In the plays of Euripides, in the later fifth century, Theseus is both an epic hero (*Hippolytus*, 428 BC) and a democratic king (*Suppliants*, 422 BC), a role he also plays in Sophocles' *Oedipus at Colonus* (produced posthumously in 401 BC).

Theseus, according to the legend, succeeded Aegeus as king of Athens. Thucydides (2.15) describes the political changes introduced by Theseus (Aristotle classified this as the 'second Athenian constitution':

> From the time of Cecrops and the first kings down to the time of Theseus the inhabitants of Attica had always lived in independent cities, each with its own town hall and its own government. Only in times of danger did they meet together and consult the king at Athens; for the rest of the time each

state looked after its own affairs and made its own decisions ... But when Theseus became king he showed himself as intelligent as he was powerful. In his reorganisation of the country one of the most important things he did was to abolish the separate councils and governments of the small cities and to bring them all together into the present city of Athens, making one deliberative assembly and one seat of government for all.

SYNOECISM

This process, known as synoecism, was characteristic of state formation in the historical period. The story perhaps pushed back events of the early archaic period to legendary times, giving them an air of hallowed antiquity. However, the archaeology does seem to indicate centralisation of Attica, represented by the massive fortification of the Acropolis, by about 1250 BC. The inscribed historical chronicle known as the *Marmor Parium* dates the synoecism of Attica to 1259/8. A festival, the Synoikia, was established to celebrate the event and continued for centuries. The walls, known to the Greeks as Pelasgian work (Pausanias 1.28.3), enclosed an area which also contained the so-called 'Palace of Erechtheus and Aegeus', a Mycenaean palace building. Also from this Mycenaean period dates the staircase constructed 25 metres down into the rock to the spring on the northern slope. There was apparently also a second circuit wall running around the south side of the Acropolis, known to Greeks of classical times as the Pelargikon or Pelasgikon: no trace of this wall has ever been found, though the area it enclosed continued to be so designated into the fifth century BC.

Though Athens had established control early over the neighbouring communities, not least Eleusis and (a more fraught case) Megara, legend reflected the tensions that still prevailed. One example is the story of the war of the prehistoric King Erechtheus against Eleusis under its king Eumolpus. Again, this story shows the struggle the mythographers must have had to build a connected narrative, since Eumolpus was, according to the genealogies, a grandson of Oreithyia, one of Erechtheus' daughters. The legend as told in Euripides' play *Erechtheus* (422 BC?; now preserved only in fragments) ran that Erechtheus could only win the war if he sacrificed one of his daughters to the gods. The play presents the willing sacrifice of the daughter as a heartening example of patriotism.

Many institutions and festivals of Athens had their origin, according to later legends, in heroic times. One of the most important historically was the court of the Areopagus, which in the fifth century had its powers limited to homicide cases. It was supposed to have been established by the god Ares who fixed his spear there in the course of a dispute with Poseidon. In the fifth century, Aeschylus' trilogy *The Oresteia* (458 BC) concludes with a trial of Orestes before the Areopagus for the murder of his mother: the play celebrates the supersession of revenge by law, and the new focus of the Areopagus on homicide alone.

Greeks liked to identify a 'first discoverer' for important cultural advances, and according to the historian Istros Theseus' trainer Phorbas had been the inventor of wrestling (since Theseus was such a good wrestler). A more significant 'invention' was the cultivation of grain, introduced by Triptolemus, son of the legendary king Celeus of Eleusis. Triptolemus was a central figure in the mythology of the Eleusinian Mysteries, which told how Persephone was abducted by the King of the Underworld and had to spend six months of each year (representing winter) in the Underworld before returning to earth in spring. Her mother Demeter's search for her is told in the *Homeric Hymn to Demeter*. Demeter taught the art of corn-growing to Triptolemus. In some versions Triptolemus is identified with his brother Demophon, whom Demeter tried to make immortal by placing him in a fire. Demophon was supposed to be have instituted another Athenian festival, the Choes (pots).

The writers of Attic history began with Hellanicus (ca 480–395). The Atthidographers as narrowly defined were a group of writers in the fourth and third centuries (see Chapter 6), but they were not unique in their interests. Hellanicus' own *Atthis* ran from earliest times to the end of the Peloponnesian War. The later Atthidographers wrote on religious customs, on dialect as well as historical and legendary events. Later historians of Athens also showed much interest in these matters. Around the turn of the first centuries BC and AD, for example, Ammonius wrote four books on Altars and Sacrifices, Crates wrote on sacrifices, and on dialect, Glaucippus wrote on religious affairs, Lysimachides on oaths. Much of what we know or can deduce about the legendary history of Athens derives from these writers. Too often we get only fleeting glimpses rather than a continuous story. There is no context, for example, for the clearly important legend of King Codrus,

MEDONTID DYNASTY

1127–1090   Melanthus
            |
1090–1069   Codrus
            |
1069–1049   Medon
            |
1049–1013   Akastos
            |
1013–994   Archippos
            |
994–953   Thersippos
            |
953–922   Phorbas
            |
922–892   Megacles
            |
892–864   Diognetos
            |
864–845   Pherecles
            |
845–825   Ariphron
            |
825–798   Thespieus
            |
778–756/5   Aischyles
            |
755–753   Alcmaeon. Last life-archon
            |
753–683   Ten-year archons: Charops, Aisimides, Cleidicus, Hippomenes, Leocrates, Apsandros, Erexios
683/2   Creon: first annual archon

who sacrificed himself in battle when the Peloponnesians invaded Attica: his grave was close to Aegeus' at the foot of the Acropolis (Pausanias I.19.6).

The Dark Ages

All over Greece the Mycenaean age, represented by the great palaces of Mycenae, Tiryns, Pylos and elsewhere, came to an end around 1100 BC. The causes are unknown but the end was certainly violent. The cataclysm ushered in a long blank in the archaeological record known as the Dark Ages, which lasted until 750 BC. The recent Metro excavations have uncovered some sub-Mycenaean (11th century BC) graves in the region of Syntagma Square, along the road to the Mesogeia; but little else survives except for some pottery with distinctive geometric designs.

The chroniclers filled the gap with information. Theseus, who had abdicated in old age, was succeeded by other members of his family (see table). The break contemporary with the Trojan War is represented by the new dynasty founded by Melanthus: his successor Codrus (1090–69) was the last king of Athens, and his son was merely archon for life. His successors were also archons – appointed rulers – though the method of appointment is not known. This sytem endured until 683/2 when the first ten-year archon was appointed, and history begins again.

The archaeological curtain rises a little earlier, in the middle of the eighth century. It is a very different scene, and one where, for the first time, we have almost contemporary writings to help us to reconstruct the history.

CHAPTER TWO

The Archaic Period
(750–479 BC)

Athens emerges slowly from the emptiness of the Dark Ages. The archaeological record indicates a slow increase in population from the tenth to the eighth centuries. However, in the ninth and eighth centuries some distinctive developments are visible. Most evident is the emergence of a new style of pottery decoration, Geometric Art, which appears to have been invented in Athens. Characterised by meticulous geometric designs of key patterns, checks, whorls, circles and other motifs in black on an ochre background, this pottery is the first example of the marvellous use the Athenians were to make of their clay resources over the next few centuries. Many of the pots are functional in shape, but they show an artist's pride in their ornamentation and, later, in their massive size. The Dipylon vase of ca 760–50 is the largest of these. In the later part of the period the rigid geometry is interspersed with animal designs and even human figures: one famous example, clearly a funerary urn, depicts a funeral procession with the dead man on a bier and wailing women accompanying it.

Pottery of this period has been found at al-Mina in Syria, indicating a trading network extending beyond the mere locality. A corollary of this is the influence of oriental pottery styles on the pottery of the seventh century. This is first noticeable in the pottery of the great trading city of Corinth, which is decorated with bands of animals both real and legendary including sphinxes, griffins and chimaeras. In Athens, a new freedom of expression is visible in the proto-Attic style, which regularly represents mythological scenes such as the labours of Heracles or the adventures of Odysseus. This new style shows us two things: first, that the corpus of heroic legends that went under the general name of the

Homeric poems is now in circulation; and secondly, the fact that some of the figures are provided with names is of the utmost importance, for this marks the introduction of writing into Greece. Like the sphinxes and chimaeras, the alphabet was a device invented in Phoenicia: it was quickly adopted by Greeks for its transparent usefulness, and was instrumental in the emergence of the first great literature of the western world. It also did wonders for the historical record, because of the Greeks' 'epigraphic habit' – their propensity to record important events and laws in writing, and furthermore to do so by inscribing them on stone, which has enabled their preservation to the present day. The eighth century marked the beginning of history for the Greeks, for later chroniclers used as the basis of their dating the year 776 BC, the 'first Olympiad', when the Panhellenic Olympic Games were first celebrated. (Each Olympiad consisted of four years and dating was by year 1,2,3,4 of each Olympiad.)

The archaeological record indicates that this period of prosperity and achievement was followed around 700 by a decline. Various explanations have been offered for this. One possibility is a severe drought, which would be reflected in the unusual number of dedications to Zeus as rain god about this time, and perhaps in the foundation legend of the cult of Artemis at Brauron, which involves drought and famine. An alternative, economic explanation looks to the rise of the neighbouring states of Argos and Aegina as traders, perhaps eclipsing the former Athenian dominance. This gains support from the known political events in Argos, where Pheidon made himself tyrant (supreme ruler), while Corinth's trade was already earning it its sobriquet of 'Wealthy Corinth'. Another important moment is the introduction of coinage, again an eastern invention, pioneered by the kings of Lydia through whose capital, Sardis, the gold-bearing river Pactolus runs. The first Greek state to mint coins was Aegina, about 625–600 BC. Athens did not produce any coinage until about 570.

A few isolated events are known from the seventh century BC in Athens. According to legend, the kings of Athens after Theseus had continued for several reigns until the kingship was replaced by the archonship (archon means ruler). Now, in 683 BC, according to tradition, the archonship was fixed as a ten-year office instead of one for life. The event signals a move away from autocracy to a more sophisticated and accountable political structure.

About 50 years later, around 632 BC, one Cylon attempted to make himself tyrant in Athens. Throughout Greece in the seventh century, tyrannies were being established. The word does not have the connotation it later acquired, but simply means a sole ruler. Typically, a would-be tyrant was an aristocrat who was able to use the support of one party (often a disenchanted poorer element of the population) to establish a position of absolute power against his rivals. Cylon was the son-in-law of Theagenes of Megara, who was just such a tyrant, and had achieved his reputation by victories in the great athletic contests of Greece (Pausanias 1.28). But in Athens, the great clan of the Alcmaeonids opposed Cylon and, when he seized the Acropolis with his supporters, they besieged him there until hunger and thirst forced him to surrender. The Athenians persuaded them to come out with false promises of safe conduct, but then put them to death, including even some who had taken sanctuary at the altar of the Eumenides. Because of this impiety, a curse rested on the Alcmaeonids which still had political repercussions a century later (Hdt 5.71, Thuc. 1.126–7).

The seventh century was a great age of law-giving in Greece. In part this was occasioned by the foundation of many colonies overseas by Greek states suffering from land hunger: the new colony needed its own laws as it had no ancestral customs, and a law-giver made some. This occurred also in old-established states like Sparta, where Lycurgus was famed as the creator of its laws. In about 621 Athens had its own lawgiver in the person of Draco (Drakon), whose laws were famous for the harshness of their penalties (hence 'Draconian'). Draco is supposed to have said that, having established death as the penalty for lesser offences, he could find nothing harsher for the great crimes such as murder. Though Draco's laws were gradually modified and ameliorated over time, they were re-inscribed on stone in the agora as late as 409/8 BC.

Finally among historical events of this century was the annexation of Eleusis. This gave Athens control of the Panhellenic sanctuary of Demeter and the Mysteries which were celebrated there. The agricultural cult of Demeter (Mother Earth) centred on the annual disappearance of her daughter, Persephone, who was supposed to have been seized by the god of the Underworld while gathering flowers, and her reappearance in the spring with the return of new life to the fields. The cult became more than a simple agricultural festival however; its Mysteries, which were unique in Greece, were celebrated, not like other festivals outside a temple, the home of a god, but inside a meeting hall known as the Telesterion, and they focused on the promise of a blissful afterlife to those who had been initiated in the Mysteries. The detail of the Mysteries remains mysterious because, first, it was a crime for any initiate to breathe a word of what he had experienced, and secondly, because Christian writers like Clement, who did know something of what occurred, rigorously suppressed the information because of its dangerous similarities to Christian rites and beliefs.

Solon

With the figure of Solon (ca 640–558 BC) we encounter the first three-dimensional character in the history of Athens. He rose to prominence because of increasing social tension, characteristic of so many Greek states at this period, which it fell to him to solve. We do not know what his origins were, though tradition had it that he came from a family of modest means, and that he travelled as a merchant in the early part of his life. A poet as well as a statesman, he wrote accounts of his political actions in the same elegant metres he also used for the verses he composed for singing at dinner parties. (This last shows that he belonged to the aristocratic milieu where such things took place.) Large portions of his writings are preserved in Plutarch's *Life* of Solon and in the *Constitution of Athens*, written by one of the pupils of Aristotle and preserved under the philosopher's name. They enable us to see for the first time the actions and motivations of a Greek statesman; but, not surprisingly, there are some problems of interpretation.

The key issue seems to have been the growing economic dependence of the poor on the rich. His main reform was known as the *seisachtheia* or 'shaking off of burdens', which took place in about 594/3 and consisted of the abolition of enslavement for debt. But what form had this taken? Diverse views have been put forward. One view assumes that smallholders were bound to landlords in a sharecropping system. The inferior partners in this relationship were known as *hektemoroi*, 'sixth-parters': but if one takes the obvious interpretation, one sixth is too low for a normal sharecropping proportion. The argument would continue that if the worker defaulted on his share, his body became security for the debt and he became a slave of the landlord.

But it seems unlikely that there were large estates at this period, and thus this kind of feudal relation could hardly have pertained. We know, too, that part of Solon's reforms consisted of tearing up the *horoi* or boundary stones. These, it seems likely, were markers indicating that a proprietor had a lien on the land. The facts fit better with an interpretation according to which independent farmers rented their land from a landowner subject to payment of a rent in kind. It was the challenge of paying this regular sum, particularly in years when the yield was poor, that occasioned the difficulty. The rent of one-sixth of the produce would in a bad year leave the farmer too little to live on. So Solon's reform was essentially the abolition of a kind of clientship. Debts were cancelled and the small farmers put on an independent footing.

Did Solon cancel *all* debts? The evidence is unclear, but in a society where coinage had not yet been invented, certain kinds of debt could not well arise. As most of what we know of Solon's activity relates to property classes, it seems likely that his cancellation of debts was confined to the farmers.

Solon divided the population into four economic classes: the *pentakosiomedimnoi* or 500-bushel men (the wealthy), the *hippeis* (knights, wealthy enough to own a horse), the *zeugitai*, (yokemen), whose land produced between 200 and 300 medimnoi of corn, and the *thetes* or landless poor, who would work as labourers for hire. These classes became the basis for election to public office, and this was the second strand of his reforms. He introduced the procedure of choice of archons by lot (before, archons had perhaps 'emerged' in the way that the leader of the British Conservative Party used to). This process of lot became one of the lynchpins of the Athenian democracy in the fifth century: Solon, in introducing it, put the city on the first steps to that remarkable political system.

He also created a Council of 400 to prepare business for the Assembly and to hear judicial appeals. The Council and the Areopagus were referred to by Plutarch (Solon 19.2) as 'the state's two anchors'. Solon ensured that the Assembly met regularly, and compiled a new code of laws. The Laws of Athens were in later times generally known as the Laws of Solon, even though many additions and changes had been made in the meantime. He thus continued the tradition of great lawgivers of archaic Greece. The laws were inscribed on axones, wooden drums on a spindle, that were set up by the Prytaneion or Town Hall: the location of this at this date is uncertain, but it was probably on the north slope of the Acropolis near where the Church of St Nicholas Rangavas now stands.

He further curbed conspicuous displays of wealth, thus limiting the ostentation and influence of the wealthy. For example, it was forbidden at funerals to 'sing pre-composed laments' – which would have required hiring a bard, like Pindar in the fifth century in less progressive states, to write the laments.

In a word, Solon's aim could be described as 'social justice'. The limiting of aristocratic display and the introduction of lot broke the monopoly of the Eupatrid (well-born) clans on politics and enabled a wider range of talented men to take part in politics. In his poems, he praised above all the virtue of *Eunomia*, 'good laws'. Tyrtaeus in Sparta had also written poems on eunomia; but for the Spartan good government meant discipline, for the Athenian it meant justice. He wrote allegorically in one of his poems (fr 12) of the people: 'By winds the sea is lashed to storms; but if no one stirs it up, it is of all things the most just'. And again (Aristotle, *Ath. Pol.* 12):

> I gave to the people as much esteem as is sufficient for them, not detracting from their honour or reaching out to take it; and to those who had power and were admired for their wealth I declared that they should have nothing unseemly. I stood holding my mighty shield against both, and did not allow either to win an unjust victory.

After his reforms, Solon went into voluntary exile for ten years, to allow his laws time to work and to prevent his being tempted, or requested, to tinker with them in response to circumstances. This action, which was undoubtedly undertaken out of scrupulous honesty, may have had in it the seeds of the tensions that arose over the next generations and led to the seizure of power by Pisistratus and his sons in the 560s.

It was during his travels, in Egypt and the Near East, that Solon acquired the reputation of one of the sages of Greece. As he wrote in a famous line, 'I learn continuously as I grow older'. The best-known anecdote concerns his meeting with the fabulously wealthy Croesus, king of Lydia, who asked Solon whether he had met anyone happier than him, Croesus. Solon's characteristically Greek reply, that one should call no man happy until he is dead, angered the king; but Solon was to be proved right when Croesus fell from his happy situation following the conquest of Lydia by Cyrus of Persia. As he sat with his family on a pyre, waiting to be burned alive by the Persians, he called out the name of Solon three times. Cyrus, puzzled, asked him whom he was referring to. When Croesus explained, Cyrus released his prisoner and treated him with honour; and so, Plutarch writes, 'Solon gained the reputation of having with a single saying saved one king and educated another'. (An alternative version of the story has Croesus remind Apollo of the precious gifts he had sent to Delphi, whereupon Apollo sent a rainstorm which extinguished the pyre – a less morally satisfying tale.)

THE TYRANNY OF PISISTRATUS

While Solon was abroad, renewed political tension and factionalism arose in Athens. There were three main groups involved: the Men of the Plain, the Eupatrids, led by Lycurgus; the Men of the Coast, led by Megacles the son of Alcmaeon; and the Men beyond the Hills (of north and east Attica), led by Pisistratus. It is tempting to see in these divisions distinct economic classes. Plutarch himself says that the Men of the Hills 'included the common rabble of hired hands, with their bitter enmity towards the rich'. The Eupatrids would then be the traditional aristocracy, and the Men of the Coast the new rich, displaying their wealth through artistic patronage (many of the magnificent marble *kouroi* made at this period, perhaps as grave markers, come from Sounion and the region around). But this is surely too neat. For one thing, not all the labouring classes came from north-east Attica (though there must have been a relatively high proportion of poor farmers). It is much more plausible to see the tensions as the result of continuing rivalry between great clans, each of whom built up a power base by representing the interests of a particular group. Pisistratus, then, followed the characteristic pattern of a tyrant's rise to power by enlisting the support of those who had little to lose and driving a wedge between the two opposing parties. He got himself voted a bodyguard by pretending that he had been attacked by enemies, and with them seized the Acropolis. After a short period his rivals drove him out, but then he was restored, as Herodotus tells:

> His rivals falling foul of one another once again, Megacles found himself so harassed that he made overtures to Pisistratus and promised to restore him to power if he would consent to marry his daughter. Pisistratus agreed to the terms which Megacles proposed, and then to bring about his own return to power, they devised between them what seems to me the silliest trick which history has to record. The Greeks have never been simpletons; for centuries past they have been distinguished from other nations by superior wits; and of all Greeks the Athenians are allowed to be the most intelligent: yet it was at the Athenians' expense that this ridiculous trick was played. In the village of Paeania there was a handsome woman called Phye, nearly six feet tall, whom they fitted out in a suit of armour and mounted in a chariot; then, after getting her to pose in the most striking attitude, they drove into Athens, where messengers who had preceded them were already, according to their instructions, talking to the people and urging them to welcome Pisistratus back, because the goddess Athena herself had shown him extraordinary honour and was bringing him home to her own Acropolis. They spread this nonsense all over the town, and it was not long before rumour reached the outlying villages that Athena was bringing Pisistratus back, and both villagers and townsfolk, convinced that the woman Phye was indeed the goddess, offered her their prayers and received Pisistratus with open arms. (Herodotus I. 60)

These events took place around 560, Pisistratus' first seizure of power having been in 566. A collapse of Alcmaeonid support led to a period of exile, from which he returned in 545, defeating his opponents at the Battle of Pallene, and establishing the tyranny for the remainder of his life (he died in 527) and for much of that of his sons, Hippias and Hipparchus.

The 'reign' of Pisistratus was by common consent a Golden Age for Athens. Full employment for the poor who had supported him was secured by a programme of public works. The first Temple of Athena (the predecessor of the Parthenon) was built (parts of its pediments survive, though where it stood is uncertain), as was the temple of Nike. Work was begun on a huge temple of Olympian Zeus in the idyllic region along the River Ilissus. Its monumental scale echoed that of the great temples of Asia Minor, notably Miletus, Ephesus and Samos; but it was not completed in Pisistratus' lifetime – not indeed until the reign of Hadrian nearly seven hundred years later. A number of other rural shrines were also established by the Ilissus, including those of Artemis Agrotera ('in the fields'), Apollo Delphinios (Pausanias 1.19.1) and Gaia, the Altar of Boreas and that of the Ilissian Muses, the sanctuary of the Nymphs and Achelous and that of Pan (Pausanias 1.19.5).

North and north-west of the Acropolis the public area of the classical agora was laid out and its boundaries formally defined. Until now the agora had been situated on the north-east slope of the Acropolis. The new 'classical' agora replaced what had been a domestic quarter and burial ground until then, and offered more commodious space for public buildings than the previous location. The Enneakrounos or public fountain was constructed (where the agora church of Ag Apostoloi now stands), and extensive pipelines and aqueducts were laid: parts have been discovered in the Metro excavations, running along a line from Mt Hymettus, down Amalias Avenue and Syntagma Square towards the Agora. Some of the sections bear lettering of the sixth century. Major civic buildings were erected including a building for the Heliaea or Law Courts for the first time, and probably a council house. A house in the south-west corner of the agora has been cautiously identified as probably the residence of the Pisistratids themselves. Housing was also built for city officials (Arist., *Ath. Pol.* 3.5).

Festivals were established, not least the Panathenaea, celebrated each year in Hecatombaion (roughly July) at the beginning of the Attic year. Its reorganisation is associated with the name of one Hippocleides, archon in 566/5. A processional way was constructed for the procession to follow (one may still walk up it through the agora), slowly pushing forward the great ship that carried the new robe to the goddess on the Acropolis. The procession was described by Himerius (Or. 3.12) at the end of the fourth century AD:

> In this festival the Athenians bring the sacred trireme to the goddess. The ship begins its progress directly from the gates, as if leaving a fair harbour; it moves on from there, as if on a waveless sea, along the middle of the Processional Way, which sweeps down straight and level from the height, and cuts through the colonnades spread out on either side, where the Athenians and other people come to do business. The crew of the ship consists of priests and priestesses, the Eupatrids crowned with golden garlands, the rest with garlands of flowers. The ship itself, high and towering as if on waves, is borne on wheels which bring it on its numerous cross-axles to the hill of Pallas. There one can imagine the goddess looking down on the festival ... The breezes that bear it on come from the shrill sounding of Attic pipes.

Temples were also built in the rural areas of Attica, notably that of Artemis at Brauron, and ones at Rhamnus, Sounion and Icaria. This control of the rural cults of Attica represented, like the establishment of the Panathenaea, an increasing centralisation of rule and an emphasis on national cults and legends. It was probably at this period that the main lines of the Theseus legend were established, and the composition of a now lost epic poem, the *Theseis*, will have crystallised some of the stories.

Athenian religion

This may be a good moment to give a more general account of Athenian religion. Central to religious life were the cults of the civic deities Athena Polias and Apollo Patroos. Like many gods, Athena had other titles too, notably Parthenos. Gods were housed in temples and tended by priests or priestesses whose role was often hereditary. Worship and sacrifice took place before the temple on the altar, often as the culmination of a procession. There were no 'services'. Many of the other Olympian gods also received cult in Athens, but lesser gods were prominent too.

Other civic cults included the important festivals of Dionysus, the City Dionysia, Great Dionysia and Lenaea, at which tragedies and comedies were performed from the early fifth century. These, like the Panathenaea, lasted for several days. By the end of the fifth century there were nine major festivals in Athens: besides those previously mentioned, there were the Asclepieia (420), the Bendideia in Piraeus (late fifth century), the Eleusinia (see Chapter 1), the Olympieia, the Theseia (476/5). Large quantities of sacrificial victims, mainly bulls or goats, were needed for all of these; but this was not the case for another group of festivals that included the Plynteria (washing of Athena's robe), the Thargelia and the Thesmophoria (small piglets were thrown into a pit as a sacrifice to Demeter). There were also a number of family-centred festivals including the Amphidromia, performed five days after the birth of a child, the rites of Artemis at Brauron which marked the puberty of girls, and the Gamelia which marked the entry of wives into a *phratry* ('clan').

Many festivals involved competitions, and these were upgraded after 566. Prizes, originally simple at the Olympic and Pythian Games, became very valuable in the case of the Panathenaic Games, where victors would be awarded huge quantities of olive oil in special Panathenaic amphoras (to the value of one talent in the fourth century).

Brauron girl from the fourth century BC with a hare

The competitions would include athletics, music, torch races and, in the case of the festivals of Dionysus, drama and dance. All in all there were over 60 festival days in the Athenian year. In addition, all the demes also had their own festivals, and there were cult centres for tribes, phratries and families as well. (A table of the major festivals is given in an appendix, p. 355).

All public business in the assembly began with the sacrifice of a pig and prayers. Legal oaths began with vows to the gods and included curses on violators. Speeches in the lawcourts began with prayers. Omens, oracles and divination were widely employed and respected. Complicated rules were aimed at avoidance of religious pollution. All in all, religion permeated every aspect of community life, and scandal was caused by professions of atheism such as that of Anaxagoras (who said the sun was not a god but a large hot stone) or of unorthodox gods like Socrates' 'inner voice'. In the fourth century both Aristotle and Theophrastus were castigated for impiety.

THE ARTS

The literary arts flourished under Pisistratus. The great lyric poets Anacreon and Simonides were guests at Pisistratus' 'court'. In 534, it is said, Thespis first introduced tragic choruses with narrative elements, thus inventing drama. By 510 tragic choruses were dedicated every year at the City Dionysia (in Elaphebolion, roughly March) and performed stories of the heroes. In addition, Pisistratus regularised the performances of the *rhapsodes* (oral performers) who recited the Homeric poems at festivals, with the result that a standard text was established and written down for the first time. It is to Pisistratus that we thus owe the existence of our texts of Homer's *Iliad* and *Odyssey*.

Attic pottery painting reached new heights with the beginnings of the black figure style, again representing many scenes from mythology as well as everyday life. In sculpture, the haunting and mysterious *korai* (maidens) who greet one in the Acropolis museum date from this period. It is surely at this time that many of the patriotic myths of Athens, which we recounted in the previous chapter, have their origin. All in all, Athens was becoming a world-class city. The arts flourished and politically there was peace.

Kore – one of the haunting maidens in the Acropolis Museum

Aristotle (*Politics* 1314a) discusses the various modes of tyranny. After speaking of the vicious tyrant, he goes on to discuss an alternative way of preserving a tyranny, by making it more like kingship. A parallel passage in his *Constitution of Athens* shows that he was thinking of Pisistratus when he wrote the following: 'the tyrant should act in the role of a good player of the part of a king. He must show himself, in the first place, concerned for the public funds. . . . In general, he should act in the role of a guardian, or steward, who is handling public rather than private money.' It was by such statesmanlike qualities that Pisistratus created his Golden Age of Cronos (as Aristotle called it: *Constitution of Athens* 16. 7–8).

But the rivals of Pisistratus and his sons were only quiescent. In 514 Pisistratus' son Hipparchus was stabbed to death by Harmodius and Aristogiton, allegedly as a result of a lovers' quarrel. The surviving Pisistratid, Hippias, was a harsher ruler (Thuc. 6.54–9, *Ath. Pol.* 18), though we have few details of his rule, and most of them do not exemplify his evil qualities. A curious story in Aristotle's *Economics* (II.2.3) tells that he sold off the upper floors of buildings, and their steps and fences, to their owners, in order to increase state revenues: this is apparently an early example of privatisation. It may have been Hippias who first furnished the herms – apotropaic pillars topped with a bearded head of Hermes that stood on street corners and before houses,

The beautiful Attic owls on a silver coin

as familiar a sight as pillar boxes in Britain – with their distinctive phalli. It was probably under Hippias that the beautiful Attic coins, the owls, were first minted.

One aspect of Hippias' tyranny was that the Alcmaeonids were driven into exile. In 510 they returned and, with the help of the Spartan king Cleomenes, deposed him and sent him into exile at Sigeum. Despite the achievements of the tyranny, the two tyrannicides were memorialised in a sculpture group that is one of the greatest monuments of sixth-century art. The following period was one of civil unrest, which reached its resolution with the rise of Cleisthenes.

Cleisthenes

Cleisthenes was an Alcmaeonid, the son of Megacles, the rival of Pisistratus. He was also the grandson of Cleisthenes the tyrant of Sicyon. Following the fall of the tyranny he and Isagoras were rivals for the control of Athens. Isagoras became archon for 508/7 and tried to have Cleisthenes expelled by calling in the Spartans under Cleomenes again: they invoked the hereditary curse of the Alcmaonidae as a reason for removing Cleisthenes, but his programme of popular reforms won him support and he eliminated the power of Isagoras. Cleisthenes then introduced a complicated reorganisation of the social and political structure of Attica. He created ten new tribes in place of the four old Attic tribes, and named each one after a hero. Each tribe was divided into *trittyes* (thirds), each third being drawn from one of the three main geographical regions of Attica (city, coast and inland). Each trittys in turn contained ten *demes* (villages, local communities). The effect was to reduce the old channels of patronage and influence, and to provide each citizen of Attica with a heroic ancestor (after whom his tribe was named) as well as a focus of local loyalty (his deme). Tribal festivals provided the rhythm of daily life and the focus of civic pride. The localisation of politics into the demes also tended, not only to an increase of democracy, but also to a greater influence of the centre (Athens) as distinct from the aristocratic networks of the old tribes. The same effect was produced by the creation of the *apodektai*, the treasurers of state revenues. The reforms were perhaps not entirely disinterested: a distinguished historian, W.G. Forrest, has suggested that what Cleisthenes did was to 'set the demos free, confident that an Alcmaeonid tail would continue to wag the Attic dog'. Be that as it may, Cleisthenes' reforms endured, as did the other major innovation of his ascendancy, the institution of Ostracism. This provided for the possibility, if there was dissension in the city, of an election of one individual to be sent into exile for ten years. If the assembly voted to hold an ostracism, voters would then inscribe the name of the candidate for exile on a potsherd (*ostrakon*), and the individual whose name appeared most frequently (provided there were at least 6,000 votes) was exiled. (A similar system came into use in other Greek cities, too, for example Syracuse, where the names were written on leaves and the institution was therefore known as *petalism*.) There has been scepticism as to whether ostracism was really introduced by Cleisthenes in the reforms of 508/7, since the first known ostracism did not take place until twenty years later. It is puzzling to imagine a lawgiver introducing so new a law without having some immediate purpose; but certainly the Athenians believed that it was part of the laws of Cleisthenes.

A combined attack by the Boeotians and the people of Chalcis in Euboea in 507/6 broke a long period of peace; but their resounding defeat by Athens proved to Herodotus at least that the new equality was a 'good thing' (5.78).

Cleisthenes' new democracy (if so it may be called) continued the Pisistratid tradition of public works. The most important structure was a new temple to Athena, of which only the foundations survive, in the centre of the Acropolis south of the Erechtheum. A number of the pedimental sculptures survive and are in the Acropolis museum. Major public buildings include the Bouleuterion for the meetings of the Boule (Council), on the west side of the agora, as well as the house of the king archon to the north of it; and the area of the agora was defined by boundary stones that emphasised its sacred space and its importance as the centre of the Attic people.

The Persian Wars

The half century of external tranquillity was broken by the irruption of the Persian Empire into the Greek world. The vast Persian Empire, with its capitals at Susa and Persepolis in Iran, ruled Asia as far west as the borders of Afghanistan, and the whole of Asia Minor including the coastal fringe (Ionia and neighbouring regions) which was inhabited by Greeks. In 499/8 the Greeks of Ionia revolted against Persia. The Athenians sent assistance, but in 494 the Greeks were defeated at the Battle of Lade, an island off Miletus; Miletus itself was sacked. The Persian king, Darius, formed the view that his control of the Asiatic Greeks could not be secure as long as Greece itself was free of his control, and determined on an invasion. In 490 the Persian fleet, commanded by Darius' nephew and son-in-law, Mardonius, crossed the Aegean, captured Eretria on Euboea, and then moved to the Bay of Marathon where they drew up their ships at Schoinias. Hippias, the former tyrant who had been exiled, acted as the Persians' guide to Eretria and then to Marathon. Here a pitched battle was fought on the plain, near the great marsh at its northern end. When the Persians advanced, the Athenian centre charged them at a run from over a mile away. Though they were pushed back, the Athenian and Plataean troops on the wings were victorious and encircled the Persian centre. The Persians withdrew to their ships. The Athenians pursued them and set fire to the ships. At the end of the day the Persians had been utterly routed and suffered enormous casualties. (According to Herodotus, they lost 6,400 men and the Athenians only 192.)

The Athenian army was, as usual, commanded by ten generals. One of these was Miltiades, whose father Cimon had been banished from Athens by Pisistratus. Miltiades' son, also called Cimon, was to become an important figure in fifth-century politics.

The Athenians had made their stand alone, except for a contingent from Plataea. The Spartans had not joined the battle, for a reason described by Herodotus:

> Before they left the city, the Athenian generals sent off a message to Sparta. The messenger was an Athenian named Pheidippides, a trained runner. According to the account he gave the Athenians on his return, Pheidippides met the god Pan on Mount Parthenium, above Tegea [north of Sparta]. Pan, he said, called him by name and told him to ask the Athenians why they paid him no attention, in spite of his friendliness towards them and the fact that he had often been useful to them in the past, and would be so again in the future. The Athenians believed Pheidippides' story, and when their affairs were once more in a prosperous state, they built a shrine to Pan under the Acropolis, and from the time his message was received they have held an annual ceremony, with a torch-race and sacrifices, to court his protection . . . The Spartans, though moved by the appeal, and willing to send help to Athens, were unable to send it promptly because they did not wish to break their law. It was the ninth day of the month, and they said they could not take the field until the moon was full. So they waited for the full moon, and meanwhile Hippias . . . guided the Persians to Marathon.

The news of the victory was carried to Athens by a runner, named either Thersippos or Eucles (the accounts differ). The distance of this Marathon run is approximately forty kilometres; a modern marathon runner covers it in three hours or less. The victory at Marathon was a tremendous achievement for Athens, and gave them the justifiable reputation of having saved Greece single-handed from the aggressor. Fifty years later old men could still be asked with respect, 'and did you fight at Marathon?'

The Athenian dead were buried in a huge mound (the soros) 9 metres high, the Plataeans in a smaller mound at Vrana. The Persian dead were buried near the site of the present Church of Panaghia Mesosporitissa, and the Athenians also erected a trophy of the captured weapons here; but Pausanias in the second century AD could find no trace of the Persian burial. The battlefield retained an eerie atmosphere for centuries. Pausanias wrote that 'here every night you can hear the noise of whinnying horses and of men fighting. It has never done any man good to wait there and observe this closely, but if it happens against a man's will the anger of the daemonic spirits will not follow him' (1.32.3).

The decade following Marathon saw new dedications to several of the gods: not only Pan, who could hardly be refused, but also Heracles, in whose sanctuary at Marathon the Athenian army had camped: new games were instituted in his honour. On the Acropolis, work was begun on a new temple of Athena, the predecessor of the Parthenon on the same site; and a great bronze statue of Athena, known as the Promachos, created by the sculptor Phidias and paid for with the spoils of Marathon. According to Pausanias, it was so tall (about thirty feet) that the tip of the spear and the crest of the helmet were visible to sailors approaching from Sunium.

> It was clothed in garments of the same material as the whole statue, namely of bronze. The robe reached to the feet and was gathered up in several places. A warrior's baldric passed round her waist and clasped it tightly. Over her prominent breasts she wore a cunningly wrought garment, like an aegis, suspended from the shoulders and representing the Gorgon's head. Her neck, which was undraped and of great length, was a sight to cause unrestrained delight. Her veins stood out prominently, and her whole frame was supple and, where needed, well-jointed. Upon her head a crest of horsehair 'nodded fearfully from above.' Her hair was twisted in a braid and fastened at the back, while that which streamed from her forehead was a feast for the eyes; for it was not altogether concealed by the helmet, which allowed a glimpse of her tresses to be seen. Her left hand held up the folds of her dress, while her right was extended toward the south and supported her head.

(The statue was removed to Constantinople in the fifth century AD and destroyed in the sack of the city by the Fourth Crusade in 1204: it is to the Byzantine writer Nicetas Choniates that we owe this, the only detailed description of it.)

Outside the city, new temples were begun at Sounion (for Poseidon) and at Rhamnous (for Nemesis). The Athenians also dedicated one tenth of the spoils of the battle in the Athenian Treasury at Delphi: their monument included a series of bronze statues, probably of Attic heroes.

Themistocles

The 480s saw the emergence of one of the greatest politicians of fifth-century Athens, Themistocles. The son of a non-Athenian mother, he shows how far the social matrix of Attica had loosened under the impact of the democratic reforms of Cleisthenes. He was undoubtedly far-sighted in his policies for Athens, though the extent to which he was also looking to his own position has often been debated, and historians both ancient and modern have held widely differing views of his disinterestedness. He is naturally contrasted with both the aristocratic, pro-Spartan Cimon, and the conservative, aristocratic Aristides ('the Just') in the ancient sources.

Themistocles was archon in 493/2 and during his archonship he began the development of Athens' harbour, the Piraeus. He foresaw that Athens's strength could never be as a land power – that would always be the preserve of Sparta – and that Athens must develop sea-power not only for trade (since the land was so harsh and lacking in resources) but for defence and military supremacy. After Marathon, the Persian fleet had been able to anchor at Phaleron, at that time the main harbour. Ten years later, after Salamis, it was still Phaleron to which the fleet retired. But in the meantime, Themistocles had persuaded the Athenian Assembly, in 482, to invest the proceeds of a discovery of a rich lode of silver in the mines at Laurion, not in handouts to the people, but in the construction of a fleet of 100, or perhaps 200 triremes – 'one of the most important events in the history of western civilization', according to the historian Russell Meiggs (1972, 122). He also saw to the development of the naval facilities at Piraeus, which now became the major port of Athens, not least by encircling it with a fortification wall. Critics of Themistocles (such as Plutarch) opined that by this investment in the fleet and harbours Themistocles increased the power and boldness of the demos against the nobility, 'since power now passed into the hands of sailors, boatswains and pilots'. The excessive influence of the 'naval mob' in fifth-century politics became a bugbear of conservative authors.

The retreat of the Persians after Marathon had been only temporary and the Greeks must have expected them to return. Darius died in 486, which provided a breathing space; but in 482 his successor Xerxes set out with a much larger army to reduce Greece once and for all. According to the sources his army consisted of 100,000 men and his fleet of 1,207 triremes (lighter and more manoeuvrable than the Greek triremes). The fleet was supplied by the subject peoples of the Asia Minor seaboard, whose loyalty could perhaps not be counted as secure as that of the free Greeks to their native land. By autumn 481 Xerxes had reached Sardis, the capital of the region. His advance preparations included the construction of a canal across the Athos peninsula (to obviate the danger of a repeat of the events of 492 when Mardonius' fleet was wrecked off Athos), and the building of a bridge of ships across the Hellespont for the army to march over.

The Greeks held a Panhellenic Congress at Corinth, the first occasion on which the majority of the Greek states had met to decide on joint action. The Spartans already had control of most of the Peloponnesian states through their League. The central Greek cities joined the alliance, but the northern states such as Thessaly decided to side with the Persians. In the end northern Greece was lost without a blow. The first resistance to the advance of the Persian army came at Thermopylae. The Spartans seem to have been reluctant to commit troops so far north of the Isthmus, but were constrained to do so in order to keep Athens and the rest of central Greece on side. The heroism of the Spartan defenders at Thermopylae is legendary; but they were outnumbered and in the end slaughtered to a man. The sea battle that took place more or less simultaneously at Artemisium resulted in a Greek victory, hailed by Pindar as the day that 'the Athenians laid a shining foundation of freedom', but the fleet alone could not hold the position.

The Persian fleet advanced in three days in June 479 to Phaleron, and thence to the island of Salamis. Attica was evacuated: 100,000 people were removed in the space of five days. The Persians under Mardonius marched on the near-empty city of Athens. A small force of defenders was quickly disposed of, and they entered the Acropolis, where they plundered and pillaged the treasuries and burnt down the temples. The destruction was supposed to be a retaliation for the Greeks' destruction of Sardis during the Ionian revolt in 498. All the new buildings of the Pisistratid period were destroyed (Hdt 9.13, Thuc. 1.81.3). The Old Temple of Athena, the early Nike temple, the treasuries, all were razed; the korai were damaged, many shattered vases still show the traces of fire. The agora was also wrecked. Seventeen wells were filled with debris. The statues of the Tyrannicides were taken away to Susa, not to be recovered until Alexander's conquest of Persia more than 150 years later.

An oracle had told the Athenians to place their trust in their wooden walls. A minority group attempted to defend the city from behind a wooden stockade, but Themistocles came up with the correct interpretation of the god's words, that the Athenians should rely on their ships to save them. All resources were put into the great conflict with the Persian fleet at Salamis.

The Persian strategy may have been to block the Greek fleet in the strait between Salamis and the mainland. According to Herodotus (8.75.2–3), Themistocles sent a messenger to the Persians which induced them to enter the strait by night, believing that the Greeks were retreating and part of the fleet would defect to them. When dawn broke, they found the Greek ships facing them. The battle lasted all day (24 September 480). 'The Greek ships entirely encircled the Persians, hulls were upturned, the sea could not be seen, so full it was of shipwrecks and slaughtered men' (Aeschylus, *Persae* 418). At the end of the day it the Persian defeat was complete. The Persian garrison on the island of Psyttaleia was massacred. The tragic poet, Aeschylus, who probably fought in the battle, wrote in his play *Persae* that Xerxes, seated on a throne on a hill above the strait, was able to watch the destruction of his fleet and the massacre of his men: 'he groaned aloud, and tore his clothes and shrieked piercingly, then rushed away with his land forces'.

The Battle of Salamis was the final defeat of the Persians by sea. The fleet withdrew to Samos (by spring 479) to guard against the possibility of a general uprising of the Greeks of Ionia. In August 479 the Greek fleet attacked the Persians at Mycale, and – according to tradition on the same day – the last pitched land battle between the opposing forces took place at Plataea. Again this resulted in a Greek victory, which was celebrated in poetry this time by Simonides, in a poem first published from papyrus in 1992. The Persian army began its slow and painful retreat through Greece, and never invaded Greece again.

CHAPTER THREE

Classical Athens: the Fifth Century BC

The Persian War, and the attendant destruction in Athens, marked the end of an era. The period that followed was a new beginning, in politics and also in art and literature. Athens' extraordinary recovery from the Persian sack led to a remarkable development in political institutions – the introduction of direct democratic rule by the citizenry – and to one of the greatest artistic flowerings the world has ever known.

The first priority was to repair the damage caused by the Persians. The leading politician of the time was Themistocles, and he organised the rebuilding of the city wall in 479. The process took less than a year, and in their haste to complete it the Athenians used old blocks and even funerary monuments (Thuc. 1.90.3, 93.2). Parts of this wall have been excavated south of the Acropolis metro station and in the Ceramicus; in 2003 there were also visible some stretches in Kotzia Square, below the National Bank of Greece. The wall was 6.5 km in extent and included in its circuit the Sanctuary of Olympian Zeus. It incorporated 13 gates, most of which can be identified by name. This wall remained standing until it was destroyed by Lysander in 403 (and it was rebuilt by Conon in 394). The circuit changed little throughout antiquity. (Outside it, north of the gate leading to Piraeus, was the place where executed criminals were thrown: one of Plato's characters in the *Republic* [439e] mentions the grisly fascination that drew him to look on such remains.)

The building of this wall was Themistocles' last major act in Athens. In 472 he was ostracised, under that distinctive Athenian custom designed to rid the city of any citizen whom a majority felt to be becoming burdensome. He was condemned to death in his absence in 469, and made his home in Persia from 465. He died in the city of

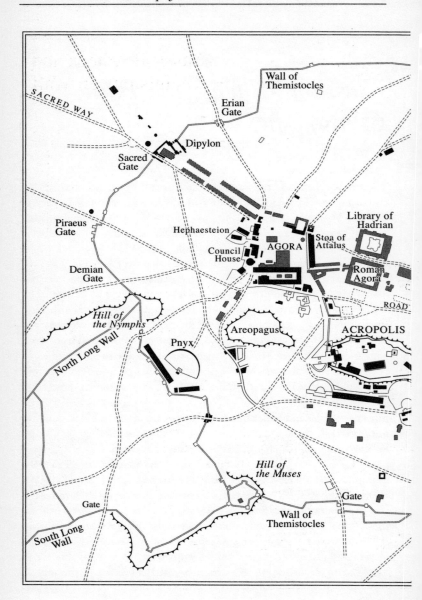

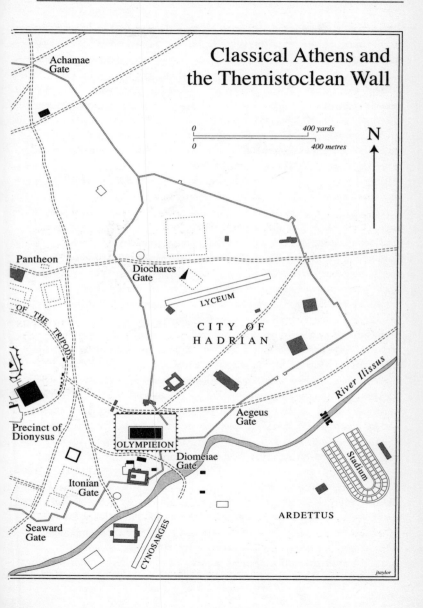

**Classical Athens and
the Themistoclean Wall**

0 ——— 400 yards
0 ——— 400 metres

N

Achamae
Gate

Pantheon

OF THE TRIPODS

Diochares
Gate

LYCEUM

CITY OF
HADRIAN

River Ilissus

Precinct of
Dionysus

OLYMPIEION

Aegeus
Gate

Diomeiae
Gate

Stadium

Itonian
Gate

ARDETTUS

Seaward
Gate

CYNOSARGES

jtaylor

Magnesia on the Maeander. Plutarch says that he had a magnificent tomb there. However, a tomb in Piraeus has been known since antiquity as the 'Tomb of Themistocles' and it is possible that at some later date his remains were brought back to Athens and interred there.

The sanctuaries on the Acropolis, unlike the city wall, were not rebuilt at this time. Following an oath the Athenians had sworn after the Battle of Plataea, not to rebuild the sanctuaries that the Persians had destroyed, as a memorial of their sacrilege, the old temple of Athena, the ancient temple and the shrine of Athena Nike on the Acropolis were left in ruins. Much of the rubble was simply buried (including 14 statues deposited in a mass grave NW of the Erechtheum, which were dug up in 1886). It is not clear where the treasures of Athena were kept, or where the statue of Athena Polias was housed. The former was kept safe in the '*opisthodomos*': but what was this? It should mean simply the back room of the old temple; but that had been destroyed. Perhaps this part of the building remained standing. However, the *opisthodomos* is not mentioned before 434 so it seems more likely that it refers to the back (western) end of the Periclean Parthenon. So the home of the treasure – the deposit safe of Athena's bank – remains unidentified. And the city's most ancient cult statue, the Athena Polias, may well have been housed in the predecessor of the Erechtheion.

More substantial building works in Athens are associated with the name of Cimon. Cimon was elected *strategos* in 479 and soon became the dominant politician of his generation. Wealthy and aristocratic, he was well known for his public and individual generosity – he used to allow the people of Athens to enter the fruit orchards on his unwalled estate, somewhere on the north-west slopes of Philopappos hill, and help themselves to whatever they wanted – and this secured him a considerable following. He continued to prosecute a war against the Persians through the 470s and 460s. He made some conquests in Thrace, and then captured the island of Skyros. Here he discovered some giant bones (Plut 8.5–6) which were soon declared to be those of the hero Theseus. With great pomp and ceremony these were brought back to Athens and deposited in the Theseion (wherever exactly that was: it is not to be located under the building now known as 'Theseion' which was in fact a temple of Hephaestus). Plutarch says that this was the main reason for his popularity in Athens. Cimon's third success was a sea battle at the mouth of the River Eurymedon in about 468 BC.

His public works included the planting of numerous trees in the agora and in the public gardens known as the Academy, turning them into haunts of cultivation and refinement. 'He planted plane trees in the city square, and transformed the Academy from a dry unirrigated spot into a well-watered grove, which he equipped with obstacle-free racing tracks and shady walks' (Plut. *Cimon* 13.7–8). (The Academy was so called because it incorporated a shrine of the hero Hekademos; later Plato established his school there.) Cimon also erected the Stoa Poikile or Painted Stoa, which was adorned with paintings by Polygnotus depicting the great achievements of the Persian War, such as the battle of Marathon. These paintings were still visible in the second century AD when the Roman traveller Pausanias admired and described them. Another building associated with Cimon's name is the Tholos in the agora (ca 470). The Klepsydra (well) on the NW slope of the Acropolis was also built about this time; and he may also have been responsible for the fortification of Eleusis.

The Delian League

Very shortly after the end of the Persian wars the allied Greeks chose Athens to be their leader in future conflicts, and the position was formalised in the formation of the Delian League – so called because its treasury, fed by contributions from all the allies, was on the sacred island of Delos. The architect of the Delian League was the Athenian statesman Aristides, known as 'The Just'. Often coming into conflict with the wily Themistocles, he had worked well with Cimon. According to Thucydides, he caused the Ionians to swear an oath 'to have the same friends and enemies as the Athenians'. Each member of the league had a single vote, though many followed the Athenian lead. Every state provided a contribution of ships, though some commuted this for money. Aristides assessed the amounts due according to the size and prosperity of the state concerned. The first cities to join were the islands of the central Aegea, plus Samos, Lesbos, Chios and possibly Rhodes.

Chalcidice was not far behind. Most of coastal Ionia probably also joined in 478. But the first complete records of membership date from 454 and after, for in that year (and each year afterwards) one-sixtieth of the annual tribute from the allies was made over to the goddess Athena, and the sums paid were recorded on stone. These so-called Athenian Tribute Lists thus enable one to work out (by multiplying by 60) what tribute each ally paid each year.

DEMOCRACY

A great development in the importance of the League for Athens came with the ascendancy of Pericles. Pericles came to power in the wake of Cimon's fall from grace. Cimon went to the aid of Sparta when Ithome revolted, and while he was away a politician named Ephialtes was able to push through some major reforms. The precise nature of those reforms is very uncertain, but it is clear that they represented a great step forward for radical democracy. The most important change seems to have been the abolition of many of the powers of the Areopagus, which was from henceforth primarily a homicide court. The other powers of the Areopagus were transferred to the Boule (Council). Cimon found himself outmanoeuvred and he was ostracised in 461. He returned in 451 but died soon afterwards in Cyprus. Ephialtes, however, was soon murdered.

In the meantime Ephialtes' associate, the much better known Pericles, had become the *de facto* ruler of Athens. His power rested to a considerable extent on the increasing enfranchisement of the male population, a tangible sign of which was the introduction of jury pay in 460s. This meant that even the poorest citizens could take part in trials, and thus the results did not always go the way of the well-heeled. Aristotle, who disapproved, wrote in his *Constitution of Athens* (27.4) 'Pericles' property was insufficient for this kind of service (i.e. the liberality of Cimon). He was therefore advised by Damonides of Oe (who seems to have been the originator of most of Pericles' measures, and for that reason was subsequently ostracised) that since he was less well supplied with private property he should give the people their own property; and so he devised payment for the jurors. Some people allege that it was as a result of this that the courts deteriorated, since it was always the ordinary people rather than the better sort who were eager to be picked for jury service.

Besides the courts, the main organs of the democracy were the Council and the Assembly. The main function of the Council of 500 was to prepare the business for the Assembly, but its powers were extensive. They included powers over magistrates and, later, over the controllers of state contracts (*poletai*), receivers of state income (*apodektai*) and payers for state works (*kolakretai*). The Boule provided committees for many issues and exercised 'ministerial' functions. It met on perhaps 250 or 300 days a year (though the Assembly met on at most 40 days in the fifth century). A standing committee of 50 members, which changed ten times a year, was known as the Prytanies and carried out most executive functions of the Boule. The members of the Boule were selected by lot for one year and the selections were deme-based so that its composition was fully representative of Attica. By the fourth century one was allowed to serve twice in a lifetime, so that up to one quarter or one half of the citizen population might have experience as a bouletes.

The Assembly consisted, in principle, of all the citizens (i.e. adult males) and met on the hill of the Pnyx, which could accommodate an audience of about 6,000: for some decisions a quorum of 6,000 was required. Though leading politicians naturally often dominated business, the Assembly was a sovereign body and did very often make its own independent decisions, though very commonly it will have ratified decisions already effectively approved by the Boule. The decisions that are remembered are the bad ones, like the condemnation of the Arginusae generals (ch. 4), and of Socrates (ch. 5); but the popular voice, despite the protestations of ideological opponents like the anonymous writer known as 'The Old Oligarch', conducted affairs as effectively as any such body can.

This radical or direct democracy, where every citizen was directly involved in and responsible for every political decision, represented a tremendous step forward in human organisation and in the emancipation of human groups from arbitrary political control. But it is important to remember what it did not include. The political body consisted of all adult male citizens. Women were not included, nor the metics (*metoikoi*), the 'resident aliens' who included many of the successful businessmen of the city. A very large class excluded from the franchise was that of slaves. Very few households except the simplest peasants will have been without at least one slave, and prosperous families will have possessed several of these 'human tools'. In a world with limited technology, slaves performed many mechanical tasks including those that are now done by machines. Slaves had no civil or human rights, and their evidence at law was only admissible under torture. Most slaves were war-captives and thus might be intelligent and educated people; men might become tutors or even set up a banking dynasty like the freed slave Pasion in the 390s (he also owned a shield factory); women became maids, cleaners and, not infrequently, free sexual relief for their masters.

WOMEN

Slaves did emancipate women from the drudgery that characterised the lives of modern women before the advent of kitchen machinery. For a woman in a prosperous family, life could be comfortable, though she was expected to lead a quiet and retired life, and to veil herself in public. Much of her life (like that of priestesses in their temples) was devoted to wool work – spinning, weaving – and vase paintings often depict such activities as well as bathing, dressing, hairdressing and sometimes laundry or grinding corn – but never cooking. Sexual scenes are also frequently depicted and it is conventional to assume that the women portrayed here are *hetaerae* (courtesans) or prostitutes.

An orator in the fourth century famously asserted that men have wives for making children, *hetaerae* for entertainment and boys for pleasure. Many *hetaerae* could rise to positions of great influence, such as Pericles' mistress Aspasia.

Many women also engaged in business or professional activities. Midwife and priestess were two revered professions; but there were also vendors of many kinds – fishwives, sellers of oil, bread and vegetables. In peasant families women will, like twentieth-century Mediterranean women, have done at least 50 per cent of the labour including fetching water, child care, looking after the chickens, picking and preserving fruit.

Women also had important religious roles to play in the city. Mourning the dead was their task, even when young. They celebrated the feast of Pots at age three, and were initiated in the rites of Artemis at Brauron at puberty, after which they took part in processions, including the Panathenaea, as *arrhephoroi* and *kanephoroi*. Another girls' festival was the Anthesteria. Grown women took part in the Thesmophoria (sacred to Demeter and Kore), the Adonia (where they planted pots of lettuce which quickly withered, to honour the dying god Adonis), the Lenaea (for Dionysus) and, sometimes, the ecstatic rites of Dionysus (as maenads).

Athenian men feared women who escaped from political subjection. Several of Aristophanes' comedies focus on the intervention of women in the political process. In *Lysistrata* they try to stop war by a sex strike; in *Ecclesiazusae* they take over the assembly; and in *Thesmophoriazusae* much ribaldry is directed at their supposed activities during this women-only festival. Euripides' *Bacchae* is a terrifying picture of women out of control under the leadership of the god Dionysus in his guise as a bull: they roam the mountains, capturing and tearing apart small animals. Vase paintings depict maenads pursued by satyrs. How far these depict reality or simply a carnival scene, or fantasy, cannot be determined; but it seems improbable that many Athenian wives slipped out of an evening to rend rabbits and deer with their teeth on the mountains.

The position of women at Athens was inferior in respect of freedom to those of Sparta. Spartan women could inherit property, Athenian women could not. An Athenian women became '*epikleros*' and had to have a guardian, a male relative, to control the property attached to her. The aim was no doubt to preserve land holdings, for the Spartan system resulted in the constant division of land into smaller and smaller lots, and had a direct impact on the decline of Spartan manpower. Athenian property law made for stability.

LITURGIES

An important and structural feature of the democracy was the institution of 'liturgies' (*leitourgiai*, works for the people). An obligation was imposed on wealthy citizens (some 1,200 in the fifth century) to pay for certain major items of public expenditure. There were about sixty of these annually, plus some extraordinary requirements. The system served the function that graduated taxes fulfil in a modern society. One of the most important annual liturgies was the *choregia*, by which the choregus paid for the training and costumes of the actors and chorus in one of the dramas presented at the festivals of Dionysus. (This could cost around 2,000 drachmas.) The choregi in the fourth century often erected monuments of their contribution, and several of these still stand: that of Lysicrates (335/4 – later known as the Lantern of Demosthenes); that of Thrasyllus (320/19, on the face of the Acropolis above the Theatre of Dionysus); and that of Nicias (320/19, west of the Theatre). Other annual liturgies included the *gymnasiarchy* (training of teams for the torch race, cost 1,500 drachmas in the fourth century), the *architheoria* or funding of a sacred embassy to one of the Panhellenic festivals, and provision of banquets for deme festivals. A major extraordinary liturgy in wartime was the trierarchy, which required the trierarch to build, fit and pay for the crew of one trireme of the Athenian fleet.

Pericles

Pericles dominated Athenian politics for a generation. His chief opponent was Thucydides the son of Melesias (not to be confused with the historian, Thucydides the son of Oloros). Melesias was a distinguished athletic trainer – his pupils had won many victories at the Games – with strong connections to the aristocratic island of Aegina (which Pericles called 'the eyesore of the Piraeus'). However, Thucydides was ostracised in 443 and this began a period of unbroken power for Pericles, who was re-elected *strategos* every year until 429.

Pericles' ascendancy coincided with a change in the character of the Delian League. Persia had ceased to be a threat in the 450s: the last stand-off was when Athens became involved in the revolt of Egypt against Persian rule in 459. The motivation may have been to secure the corn supply, but at all events it was unsuccessful. In 449 it seems that an individual named Callias negotiated a peace with the king. The existence of this 'Peace of Callias' is a major historical quandary, as the evidence for it is contradictory and it may never have taken place. (It may have been invented later as part of an argument.) Whether or not it did, the situation it represents, of a cessation of hostilities, meant that the League had lost its *raison d'être*. However, Athens had already begun to benefit from its primacy in the League and was unwilling to see it disbanded. In the 450s Athens had sent out '*cleruchies*' – groups of settlers – to take over land in the allied states, who thus both benefited their own economic position and were able to keep an eye on the political situation in the host states. In 454 the treasury was relocated from Delos to Athens, and one-sixtieth of the tribute was paid to Athena. In the 440s the Athenians began openly to talk of 'rule' over their allies, and thus the Delian League turned into the Athenian Empire.

The apparatus of empire included garrisons and *episkopoi*, 'over-seers' (the word is that which was later used for Christian bishops); Athens explicitly supported democratic governments in the cities and worked against oligarchic groups, who in their turn would seek the favour of Sparta. Thus the Greek world gradually divided itself into two blocs, democrats in league with Athens, oligarchs with Sparta. Athens kept tight judicial control of its subjects and also practised various forms of economic coercion: for example, cities were not allowed to export corn except to Athens. As early as the 460s Naxos and Thasos had tried to secede from the League and been forced to come back in.

The tension with Sparta led to conflicts in the 460s which are known as the First Peloponnesian War. In 458/7 the Spartans marched into central Greece, but retreated without causing lasting damage. In 456 Athens conquered Aegina, and the Spartan general Tolmides sailed, threateningly but ineffectively, around the Pelopon-nese. This was a kind of cold war which came to an end, soon after the Peace of Callias (449) with an agreement called the Thirty Years Peace (446).

PIRAEUS

The strength of the democracy also derived in part (conservative writers made it a criticism) from the voting power of the citizens of Attica's largest deme, the port of Piraeus. Though part of the Athenian state, it functioned in many ways as an independent city, with its own civic officials and even, it seems, courts. It grew in size and prosperity from the mid-fifth century. Within the Themistoclean fortification walls of 493, the celebrated town planner Hippodamus laid out a city with four broad boulevards (*plateiai*) reaching diagonally down the peninsula, and intersected at frequent right angles by narrow streets (*stenopoi*). Very little of the ground plan or the buildings can be discovered today because of the growth of the modern city above it. But we know that the agora (called the Hippodamian agora) was west of Munychia hill, north of Zea.

Piraeus was the major port of the eastern Mediterranean from 450 to about 320 when Rhodes became dominant. It main function, initially, was to supply Athens' needs, above all in grain. It has been calculated that six grain ships would need to unload daily in the high season to feed the city. In addition, Athens imported iron, tin, copper and timber, and exported silver, oil, wine and honey. However, the port became popular with merchants from the whole Mediterranean, especially the east, and in the fourth century BC the growing number of temples of foreign gods shows how the city adapted itself to the needs of those who frequented it. (The first foreign god to arrive was the Thracian Bendis in 429.)

Athens levied a 2 per cent tax on all cargoes, but its main aim was to secure the corn-supply. The corn dealers were overseen by officials known as the *sitophylakes* (corn-guards). Shortages of grain, especially if caused by hoarding, could lead to riots and, once at least, to a near-lynching (in 386 BC).

Though frequently detached from the city by conquerors, and more than once acting as a base for opposition forces (e.g. in 411 BC), Piraeus remained part of the Athenian state until 229 BC, when it became permanently a separate polis.

Periclean Athens

The result of the security with which Athens controlled her subjects, and to a lesser extent the revenues of Piraeus, was a very considerable flow of wealth to Athens. Pericles was the architect of a policy that put this wealth to work creating the architectural glories of a city that became justly famous for artistic achievement of all kinds. Pericles' critics protested: 'the Greeks regard it as outrageously arrogant treatment, as blatant tyranny, when they can see that we are using the funds they were forced to contribute for the military defence of Greece to gild and embellish our city, as if she were a vain woman adorning herself with costly marble, statues and temples at 1,000 talents a time.' Pericles himself said (Thuc. 2.13.3) that the buildings of Athens were created, not just with the tribute money, but with the other revenues of Athens, including the silver of the mines at Laurion and the proceeds of the always lucrative export trade in the famed Athenian olives.

The buildings for which Pericles was responsible include all the great buildings of the Acropolis and its sculpture and statuary. One of the things that most aroused the wonder of contemporaries was the speed with which the buildings were completed. The Parthenon was built between 447 and 433/2, the Propylaea between 437 and 432 (though it was never quite finished), the temple of Athena Nike was begun in the 430s and completed by 424; the Erechtheum may have been as late as the 420s. In the lower city, Pericles built the Odeion that bears his name; the Stoa of Zeus (430–20); and the temple of Artemis Agrotera (445–35). In addition, major temples were constructed at Eleusis, Sounion, Rhamnus, Thorikos and Pallene.

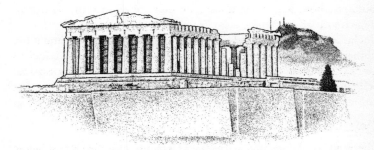

A view of the Parthenon built at the time of Pericles

THE PARTHENON

The Parthenon has been described as 'a victory monument for imperial Athens'. In fact the whole Acropolis, from the temple of Nike (victory) on the western edge to the triumphant Athena Parthenos in the temple itself, with a victory perched in her hand, is a celebration of victory. The Parthenon, the first of these buildings to be begun, is justly admired as one of the greatest achievements of architecture. The architects were Ictinus and Callicrates. The plan itself consisted in a widening of the Older Parthenon, increasing the frontage from six columns to eight, and a slight lengthening as well. But the key to its beauty is a repeated proportion of 9 to 4, which harmonises every dimension in the building, and the added refinement that none of the lines is entirely straight. It was not until the nineteenth century that this 'entasis' was recognised and properly measured: it is a feature that makes the temple seem to float and shimmer, despite its massive proportions and the earthbound drive of its columns.

The second spectacular feature of the Parthenon was the wealth of sculpture that adorned it. Here the master craftsman was the great sculptor Phidias, whose name has become synonymous with the peak of classical art. His was the mastermind that devised the design and detail of the pediments, the metopes and the frieze. But more than 90 separate hands have been identified as working on the carvings. The east (front) pediment portrayed represented the birth of Athena, released from her gestation in the head of her father Zeus (after he swallowed the goddess of wisdom, Metis) by a blow of the axe of Hephaestus. Though the scene is frequent in black figure vase painting, we do not know how it was shown on the pediment as too little is left of the sculptures. The west pediment showed the quarrel between Athena and Poseidon for possession of Attica: the moment when Poseidon created a salt water spring on the Acropolis, and Athena caused an olive tree to rise up beside it, was shown in a vigorous group at the centre of which the two deities start back from each other in a form that has come to be known as the 'Phidian V'. The metopes portrayed the battle of Lapiths and Centaurs, one of the enduring symbols of Greek superiority over barbarians. Most intriguing, and best preserved, is the frieze that ran all the way around the outer surface of the inner cornice, in a position most difficult to see from the ground. Almost all the slabs are in the British Museum, positioned at eye level so that one can appreciate the mastery of their art. But what do they represent? The consensus view has been that the figures are those of the Panathenaic procession carrying the scared robe to Athena. A refinement of this view has been the suggestion that the number of figures is exactly the number of the Athenians who died at Marathon, so that the whole frieze is a commemoration of that victory. However, the numbers can only be made to match by discounting the grooms in the frieze, which is a somewhat suspect procedure. What cannot be in doubt is that all these riders and warriors, youth and maidens, elders and priests, are dedicated to the service of the goddess who dwelt in the temple.

The temple was her home, yes, like any god's temple in ancient Greece. But it is a most unusual temple. It was not the focus of any cult; there is no altar for sacrifice. It housed the statue of the Parthenos, but otherwise it is more of a treasury or strongroom, and a symbol conspicuous for its size as much as anything. In the year 434/3 it contained (among other things), according to a calculation by John A. Camp (81), 'a gold wreath, five gold libation bowls, two nails of gilded silver, six Persian daggers, twelve stalks of golden wheat, two gilded wooden baskets, a gilded wooden box and incense burner, thirty-one bronze shields, seven Chian couches, ten Milesian couches, nine sabres, four swords, fourteen breastplates, six thrones, four stools, a gilded lyre, three ivory lyres, four wooden lyres, and thirteen bronze feet for couches' as well as 'eight and a half boxes of rotten and useless arrows'. This is in addition to the coined wealth delivered as tribute by the allies.

The great treasure of the temple was the chryselephantine (gold and ivory) cult statue of Athena Parthenos, by the master Phidias himself. It stood more than nine metres (30 feet) high, and held in its hand a winged victory about two metres tall. At her left side Athena held a shield with a snake beside it, and on the plinth was carved the story of the birth of Pandora, the first woman. The drapery of the statue was made of gold plate weighing 44 talents. The statue vanished in antiquity but numerous small copies survive to give an impression of what

but for the astounding flowering of literary art that reached its peak in his 'reign' and continued until the end of the fifth century. In large part this was through the investment in the dramatic competitions which formed part of the festivals of Dionysus, the Dionysia and the Lenaea. The theatre of Dionysus had been the site of dramatic performances since the end of the sixth century. The 470s saw the first performances of plays by the first of the three great tragedians of classical Athens, Aeschylus (525–456). In 472 he staged his political play, *The Persians*, an account of the Persian defeat from the Persians' point of view: Pericles was the *choregos*, that is, he paid for the production. Of the plays Aeschylus wrote (between 70 and 90) seven survive, and one of those (*Prometheus Bound*) may be falsely attributed to him. The great themes of Aeschylus' plays are the justice of Zeus and its working out over time and generations. Most of his plays were performed as tetralogies, three tragedies and a humorous satyr-play to conclude. Besides a chorus that danced and sang, there were two speaking actors to take as many parts as were required. Aeschylus made extensive use of spectacle and stage machinery (the *ekkyklema* on which tableaus were rolled out from the stage building, for no violent action was ever portrayed on the stage, the crane for the appearances of gods), and his poetry is magnificent and at times obscure. Some of his plays show a pronounced political engagement, notably the final play of the *Oresteia*, *Eumenides (The Kindly Ones*, i.e. the Furies), where the issue of the blood-guilt of Orestes for the murder of his mother is resolved in a trial before the Areopagus, recently reformed by Ephialtes as a homicide court. Aeschylus' democratic credentials are thus patent in his work.

The second great dramatist of Athens, Sophocles, lived from 496 to 406 and his first production was in 468, when he defeated Aeschylus; his last was in 406 when he dressed his chorus in black in mourning for his younger contemporary Euripides. He wrote more than 120 plays (of which we have nine) and won at least twenty victories. His introduction of the third actor was soon adopted by Aeschylus too. Sophocles has generally been regarded as the most 'classical' of the dramatists. He investigates extreme human situations with unblinking clarity: the working of the gods behind the actions of the heroes, who fling themselves into conflict with the gods and with human norms, is often hidden. Oedipus' relentless and self-destructive drive to discover the truth, Antigone's unbending devotion to the laws of god where they conflict with the laws of man, Electra's monomaniac hatred of her mother who murdered her father and whose revenge is achieved when her brother Orestes returns ('Hit her again!') are portrayed with unflinching gaze, and evoke the 'pity and terror' that Aristotle regarded as the hallmark of tragedy.

The third great tragedian, Euripides (480–406), is infused with the spirit of the age of the sophists, philosophers and teachers who began the investigation of human and related matters on a rationalist basis: Protagoras' dictum, 'Man is the measure of all things' is the leitmotif of their approach. Euripides' heroes seem to encapsulate the problems that might face people in the contemporary world, albeit transposed to a heroic time and scale: *Medea* is an embodiment of the problematic experience of women, *Hippolytus* is a story of love thwarted and religious devotion betrayed, *Troades* and *Hecuba* are portrayals of the horrors of war, by now in full sway in the Peloponnesian War. Some of the later plays, like *Helen* and *Orestes,* are more like adventure stories; and in his last play, *Bacchae*, Euripides returns to the great theme of classical drama, the opposition between a misguided and intransigent mortal and the invincible power of a god who destroys him, in this case Dionysus.

The drama festivals also included Comedy, and of these dramatists the only surviving plays are by Aristophanes (448–380), though the collected fragments of the numerous other comedians fill several volumes. Attic Comedy was a bawdy, hilarious and often ferociously satirical genre which incorporated invective against contemporary politicians and other prominent citizens; literary parody (notably fun at the expense of Euripides in *Acharnians, Frogs* and other plays); pantomine escapism and (always) a concluding celebratory feast and marriage. The chorus consisted of twenty-four dancers, who usually lent their name to the play – *Knights, Clouds, Birds* – and all the performers wore enormous phalli.

PHILOSOPHY

The mid fifth-century was the age of the Sophists. Successors of the great Pre-Socratic philosophers, these men devoted their energy not so much to 'natural philosophy' (to use an eighteenth-century term) as to the science of man. Anaxagoras, a speculator on cosmic matters noted for his shocking statement that the Sun was not a god but a large fiery stone about the size of the Peloponnese, was a friend of Pericles. Most of the major sophists originated elsewhere but came to Athens to find an audience, like Protagoras of Abdera (b ca 485), whose treatise began with the famous statement 'Man is the measure of all things'. Democritus, also of Abdera (b ca 460), the inventor of the atomic theory, may also have visited Athens: he wrote on a wide variety of topics including anthropology, ethnography, morals, physiology and language, and the loss of his works may be one of the greatest barriers to our under-standing of fifth-century thought. Other sophists such as Prodicus of Ceos, Hippias of Elis and Gorgias of Leontini lectured in Athens (for a fee) and have been immortalised as characters in the dialogues of Plato, generally being worsted in debate by Socrates.

Socrates (469–399) was a figure of such immense importance in the development of philosophy that its history is divided into those who came before him (the Pre-Socratics) and the rest. Socrates' key con-tribution was to question everything, to enquire of everyone a *logos* (account, rationale) of their beliefs and behaviour. He also despised those who professed philosophy for money (obviously he could afford to do it without payment) and made many enemies both by his insistent questioning and by his combative style. His preferred pupils were young aristocrats with whom he could engage in discussion in the gymnasium. He also, he claimed, received guidance from a *daimonion*, a divine spirit who directed his actions in moments of difficulty.

Socrates wrote nothing, and this account is based on what we can derive from, above all, the dialogues of Plato, in every one of which Socrates is the (or a) leading disputant. Plato worshipped the memory of Socrates, who was executed in 399, in what was perhaps one of the most unjust acts ever carried out by the democracy, for 'corrupting the young': but it is easy to see how, in the aftermath of the Peloponnesian War, which had been lost in part through the treachery of Socrates' pupil Alcibiades, and had been succeeded by a tyranny in which one of the leading figures was his pupil Critias, the people might have blamed their misfortune on his philosophy.

Plato's Socrates of disinterested, if irritating, speculation, is not the only one we have. Xenophon's writings about Socrates portray a much simpler ethical teacher, rooted in aristocratic values. Aristophanes' *Clouds*, in the most problematic of the portrayals, shows a Socrates indistinguishable from the Sophists he opposed, engaged in pointless cosmic speculation and the construction of deceitful arguments to favour both sides of a case. Which was the real Socrates may never be known, but his importance is at any rate guaranteed by the impetus it gave to the philosophy of Plato, most of whose problems still exercise philosophers today. Socrates' questioning and dialogic approach epitomises the intellectual achievement of fifth-century Athens.

Historians were also active in fifth-century Athens, notably Herodotus, 'the father of history' (480–425). Born in Halicarnassus, Herodotus nevertheless spent some time in Athens and was an associate of Pericles; he was giving readings of portions of his great work in Athens in 446. More important for our story was Thucydides, whose history of the Peloponnesian War will be considered in the next chapter. Most of the literary splendours that have been described above were produced alongside a scene of vigorous construction activity in the city, and as a backdrop to all was an increasingly bitter and destructive war, which through the writing and analysis of Thucydides has come, despite its restricted local scale, to be one of the best-remembered wars in history, and a touchstone for military analysis.

CHAPTER FOUR

The Peloponnesian War

The Peloponnesian War between Athens and Sparta, and their allies, is a microcosm of all great ideological wars that have taken place ever since. Almost everything we know about it, at least in its first stages, comes from the historian Thucydides (ca 460–ca 400). He was the son of Olorus, the same name as that of Cimon's grandfather. He was probably related to Cimon and to the politician Thucydides the son of Melesias. His history of the war runs from its outbreak in 431 to the middle of 411, where it breaks off, though it was intended to continue to 404. He began to write as soon as the war started and his history must therefore be taken as an honest account of events as they occurred. But the greatness of Thucydides lies in the powers of analysis he applied to events and their causes, and his explorations of human motivations,

Thucydides

which he expressed through speeches put into the mouths of the protagonists. His picture of events cannot often be corrected, and for our understanding of the progress of the war we are largely in his hands. Fortunately they are the hands of a master.

The Peloponnesian War, Thucydides wrote, was the greatest of any that had taken place up to his time. His aim was to understand why it took place, and to provide an account which would be of use to politicians in similar situations in the future. His approach has often been compared to that of the Hippocratic writers who flourished in the second half of the fifth century, and whose detailed and unblinking descriptions of the progress of diseases were likewise intended to be of use for diagnostic purposes in later cases – though in the medical case treatment would often be of strictly limited efficacy.

Thucydides' discussion of the causes of the outbreak of the Peloponnesian War in 431 has occasioned an enormous amount of scholarly discussion. In a sentence that is difficult to translate, he wrote: 'In my opinion, the *truest explanation (alethestate prophasis)*, although it was least publicised, was that the Athenians becoming great and instilling fear into the Spartans compelled them to go to war. But *the openly expressed grounds of complaint (aitiai)* on each side, on the basis of which they broke the truce and went to war, were these.' Thucydides then goes on to narrate how Athens intervened on the side of Corinth's colony Corcyra (Corfu) in a dispute over the small city of Epidamnus, and subsequently at Potidaea in the Chalcidice. One problem is that the word that seems to mean cause *(prophasis)* would usually mean 'an excuse', while the word here translated as 'grounds of complaint' is often used scientifically to mean 'cause'. However, the general point Thucydides is making seems clear, that the underlying cause of hostilities was Athens' growth of power and the threat she was perceived as representing to Sparta and her allies.

The immediate causes of hostilities were, as often happens, relatively local disputes, in this case between Athens and Sparta's Peloponnesian ally, Corinth. Athens had broken the terms of the Thirty Years Peace by failing to respect the autonomy of the Greek states. Other factors have been brought into the discussion. Thucydides later tells us that Aegina (formerly an ally of Sparta, now part of the Athenian Empire) urged Sparta to attack Athens in 432. Also, King Perdiccas of Macedon saw that his interests would be served by a reduction in Athens' power at sea.

Furthermore, the comic poet Aristophanes, and Plutarch, both mention at least one 'Megarian Decree', which has been interpreted as a main cause of the war; by this, Megarians were barred from entering and trading in the Athenian agora after they abandoned their alliance in 446. Megara, close to the Isthmus, was an ally of Sparta and an important trading city. The most comprehensive modern discussion has concluded that the importance of this decree has been greatly over-stated, and that it affected only individual Megarian traders; it had no effect on the trading activity of the state of Megara itself, and thus cannot have been a major factor in the outbreak of hostilities. How-ever, the importance of the Megarian decree in the outbreak of the war continues to be hotly disputed.

Regardless of the specific impetus to the beginning of the war, it is clear that Spartan distrust of the growing power of Athens was at the heart of it. The Spartans voted for war despite the caution evinced by their king Archidamus. Many other Greek states were also beginning to dislike and fear the Athenian Empire, and thus there was some goodwill in favour of Sparta. On the broader level, the conflict was one between ideologies: democratic Athens versus oligarchic Sparta, and at an even more fundamental level, Ionian Athens versus the Doric Peloponnese. One historian has recently written that 'the story ... of the whole Peloponnesian war can be seen as a story of liberation betrayed' (Hornblower 155). Thucydides tells us (2.8.4) that the Spartans won much support 'particularly as they proclaimed that they were going to liberate Greece'.

Athens was an unrivalled sea power; Sparta was renowned for its land army. Their strategies thus were liable to bypass each other. Spartan strategy concentrated on annual invasions of Attica, laying waste crops and forcing the population to take shelter inside the walls of the city. Athenian strategy was to remove the Corinthian empire in the north-west, and to harry Sparta with naval engagements which Athens was likely to win. Pericles' declared aim at this time was to hold the empire but not to enlarge it.

The first of the Spartan invasions took place under the leadership of Archidamus in midsummer 431, when the corn was ripe, beginning with a siege of the border post of Oenoe. The Spartans advanced, destroying crops, as far as Acharnae; but the Athenians stayed behind their walls, and after a while sent out a fleet to harry the coasts of the Peloponnese. In the same summer the Athenians expelled the inhabitants of Aegina, the Dorian island which Pericles regarded as 'the eyesore of Piraeus', and installed Athenian cleruchs so that the land was now in friendly hands.

The following winter, a public funeral was held for all those who had died in the summer's campaigning. The bones of the fallen were placed in a tent in the city, then packed into coffins (one coffin for each tribe) and taken in procession to the public burial place. This was the Ceramicus or Potters' Quarter, which Thucydides calls 'the most beautiful quarter outside the city walls'. The state cemetery was on either side of the road to the Academy, in an area made tranquil by cypress trees and the quiet flow of the River Eridanus. Monuments were erected in honour of the dead. A very fine sculptured and inscribed stele for cavalrymen, by tribes, was excavated in 1995 in the Palaiologou shaft during the excavations for the Metro. It probably belongs to a later period of the war (the excavators argue for 409 BC), but no doubt similar monuments were erected in earlier years also. By custom a distinguished citizen was called upon to make an oration in the cemetery honouring the dead. On this occasion the choice fell on Pericles.

Pericles' Funeral Oration is one of the most famous passages of Thucydides' history, and a *locus classicus* for the ideal picture of Athenian democracy. It is a heartfelt expression of pride in the Athenian political and cultural achievement. After praising the ancestors and the recently dead for their preservation of their country, Pericles goes on to speak of 'the constitution and the way of life which has made us great' (2.36).

> Our system of government does not copy the institutions of our neighbours. It is more the case of our being a model to others, than of our imitating anyone else. Our constitution is called a democracy because power is in the hands not of a minority but of the whole people. When it is a question of settling private disputes, everyone is equal before the law; when it is a

question of putting one person before another in positions of public responsibility, what counts is not membership of a particular class, but the actual ability which the man possesses.... We are free and tolerant in our private lives; but in public affairs we keep to the law. This is because it commands our deep respect. (2.37)

Later, Pericles talks of the cultural achievements of Athens:

Our love of what is beautiful does not lead us to extravagance; our love of the things of the mind does not make us soft. We regard wealth as something to be properly used, rather than something to boast about.... When we do kindnesses to others, we do not do them out of any calculations of profit or loss: we do them without afterthought, relying on our free liberality. Taking everything together then, I declare that our city is an education to Greece... Future ages will wonder at us, as the present age wonders at us now.... This then is the kind of city for which these men ... nobly fought and nobly died. (2.40–1)

Thucydides' own belief in the values Pericles portrays shines through the language in which he reports his speech. It presents a moment of (largely justified) pride in an achievement which was not to be sustained for more than a few years. The prodigious outpouring of literary talent continued at the festivals of Dionysus every year throughout the war; but the first human disaster hit the city within two years, with effects much more severe than the annual invasions, of which the longest, in 430, lasted forty days.

The Plague of Athens

The immediate result of the Spartan invasions was shortage of food and overcrowding in Athens. Weapon-making must have increased very considerably, and it may be that the large number of foundry pits found in the Syntagma area, dating from after 450, should be associated with the drive to arm the citizens. In 429 a plague broke out in Athens, no doubt a direct result of the overcrowding and insanitary conditions. Thucydides once again shows his affinities with the medical writers in his description of the symptoms and effect of the plague; unfortunately, despite his precision, no scholar has ever been able to determine just what the disease was. Over thirty possibilities have been proposed, from epidemic typhus to smallpox and measles. A plague pit in the Ceramicus, uncovered during the Metro excavations, has yielded a number of bodies from a mass burial. DNA testing is being carried out in an attempt to determine the nature of the disease.

Whatever it was, its symptoms were alarming.

> People in perfect health suddenly began to have burning feelings in the head; their eyes became red and inflamed; inside their mouths there was bleeding from the throat and tongue, and the breath became unnatural and unpleasant. The next symptoms were sneezing and hoarseness of voice, and before long the pain settled on the chest and was accompanied by coughing. Next the stomach was affected with stomach-aches and with vomitings of every kind of bile that has been given a name by the medical profession ... the skin was rather reddish and livid, breaking out into small pustules and ulcers. But inside there was a feeling of burning ... Many of the sick ... plunged into the water tanks in an effort to relieve a thirst which was unquenchable.

Most victims died in about a week, and doctors fell to the disease in large numbers.

It caused a severe reduction of the population. Bodies were heaped up in the streets, and there was no time or will to carry out proper funeral ceremonies; many survivors would carry corpses around until they found a pyre that another had prepared, add their own dead to it and set it alight. Plague victims were buried not in the Ceramicus but in special cemeteries, and cavalry members had a cemetery of their own. The rule of law broke down as 'no one expected to live long enough to be brought to trial and punished' (2.53).

Old oracles were recalled in attempts to explain the disaster. In an attempt to avert further suffering, the healing god Asclepius was summoned from Epidaurus. He arrived in the form of a sacred snake, and the poet Sophocles was appointed to the task of housing the god (in his basket) while his sanctuary was being built. It stood just west of the Theatre of Dionysus, and was completed in 421/0. The construction of the sanctuary of another healing deity, Amphiaraus, at Oropos at about this time, may also reflect Athenian concern to avert further onslaughts of debilitating disease.

Pericles himself fell victim to the plague and died in the course of 429. For Thucydides, this was the beginning of disaster because those who succeeded him as leaders of the people were 'demagogues', rabble-rousers of lower-class background and less sound political judgment. His successor was Cleon, mocked by Aristophanes as a tanner (i.e. he was an industrial magnate), and Cleon knew how to win the people to his policies with his loud and forceful rhetoric.

Athenian Successes

This first period of the Peloponnesian War was known as the Archidamian War, after the Spartan king Archidamus who led the land invasions. Athens concentrated on naval operations in the west, with a major naval success at Naupactus in 429, while Sparta spent three years reducing Plataea by siege (429–7). Also in 429, the Megarians invited the Spartan fleet to harbour at their own port of Nisaea; the Athenians responded by strengthening the guard on Piraeus.

In 428 the revolt of Athens' ally Mytilene to Sparta caused a major political debate at Athens. The revolt was crushed by military means, and the debate focused on the treatment of the rebels. Thucydides treats the debate as an example of the instability of the political decision-making process under democracy, and the two speeches by the opposing politicians, Cleon and Diodotus, are subtle and penetrating explorations of the politics of power. The first decision of the assembly was for the execution of all adult males and enslavement of the women and children. A trireme was sent out to carry the decision of the assembly to the general in Mytilene, Paches. But on the next day the assembly 'began to think how cruel and how unprecedented such a decision was – to destroy not only the guilty but the entire population of a state'. Cleon spoke in favour of the original decision, but was followed by Diodotus who argued that the Athenians would store up good will for the future by clemency on this occasion. The assembly voted to rescind the decision. At once a second trireme was despatched to countermand the order. The first trireme had twenty-four hours' start (on a journey that even under steam takes 13 hours), but it 'was not hurrying on its distasteful mission' and the crew of the second, by

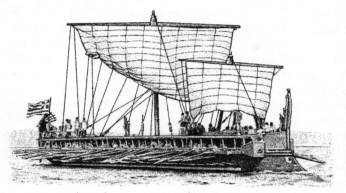

A modern reconstruction of an Athenian trireme

rowing furiously, and taking no breaks but eating on the move and sleeping in shifts, managed to arrive on the shore just as the order for the massacre was being read out. 'So narrow had been the escape of Mytilene.' The land was given to Athenian cleruchs, and the remaining inhabitants had to rent it from the new owners.

There were several major campaigns in the late 420s, the most prominent of which was the campaign by Athens at Pylos and Sphacteria (425). Athens under the general Demosthenes captured the major port of Pylos on the Messenian coast, which was then used as a base for raids and a refuge for Messenian exiles from Sparta. Soon the Spartans under the general Brasidas occupied the offshore island of Sphacteria in order to blockade the Athenians, but Athenian naval superiority resulted in a resounding success and the Spartans were themselves cut off on Sphacteria. Envoys came to Athens to negotiate but failed; Cleon bullied them and sent Demosthenes to conquer Sphacteria. After a siege of 72 days, 292 Spartan prisoners were taken, including 120 officers, and kept as hostages at Athens. The outcome caused considerable amazement as it had been unheard of in the past for Spartans to surrender rather than die fighting. It signalled to the Athenians a loss of morale at Sparta that should be to their advantage.

Nonetheless, the military genius of Brasidas continued to rack up significant victories for Sparta, notably in Thrace since it was possible to get there by land without having to face the Athenian navy at sea. In 424/3 he inflicted a notable defeat on Athens at Delium in Boeotia. Socrates, who was among the hoplites in the Athenian army, later recalled how he had entered a kind of mystic trance on the battlefield and stood immobile for hours listening to the voice of his *daimonion,* the internal spiritual adviser whom he later claimed as the mainspring of his search for wisdom. Later in the same year Brasidas took Amphipolis, an important ally of Athens in the north (whence her timber supplies came). Thucydides, who was commanding troops in the area, was blamed for the defeat and went into exile, which allowed him time to carry out the research for his history.

A year's truce in 423, by which Athens hoped to maintain the status quo and erect fortifications, while the Spartans hoped that Athens would agree to return the prisoners and establish a longer peace, was interrupted when Skione and Mende in the Chalcidice revolted from Athens. Brasidas, who was now receiving funds from the Macedonian king Perdiccas, quickly moved in; the Athenians followed and won the cities back. When the armistice ended after the Pythian Games the following summer, Cleon sailed with troops to win back Amphipolis. A major battle resulted in the defeat of Athens, but both Brasidas and the Athenian commander Cleon were killed in the fighting.

Thus ended the first decade of the war.

THE SICILIAN EXPEDITION

A period of shifting alliances followed. In 421 the Athenian general Nicias negotiated a peace, which was intended to last for fifty years and was known as the 'Peace of Nicias'. In fact it lasted less than six. As early as 418 Athenian troops were involved in a battle at Mantinea, in which the Spartans under King Agis, after ravaging crops, defeated a combined force of Arcadians, Argives and Athenians. But Athens itself was not affected. The years of peace instilled a new sense of confidence into the Athenian people, despite declining manpower and the problem of what to do with the Spartan captives from Sphacteria, who were still being held in Athens.

Confidence was evinced also in their brutal treatment of Melos. This was another episode that showed the claws of the Athenian Empire under stress. Melos was a Spartan colony which had remained outside the Athenian Empire unlike the other islanders. In 416/15 Athens sent a force to subdue them and bring them into the empire. The debate that follows, whether it took place or is an invention of Thucydides – 'the kind of thing that was likely to have been said' – is a magnificent document of political philosophy, outlining in the clearest terms the doctrine of the right of the stronger to rule over others – the 'might is right' creed that is the main topic also of Plato's *Gorgias*. Melos refused to submit, so Athens imposed a total blockade. When Melos eventually surrendered, the people suffered the fate that the Mytilenians had been spared: all the men were executed, and the women and children sold into slavery.

Euripides' shattering tragedy *Trojan Women* (415) seems to reflect the mood of the time, with its emphasis on the horrors of war and the sense that there are no real winners.

In 414 Aristophanes in his comedy *Birds* satirised the megalomaniac empire-building ambitions of his heroes, who set out to escape Athens by building a city in the sky, Cloud-Cuckoo-Land. In this he no doubt had an eye on the activities of the prominent politicians of Athens. Following the death of Cleon, the leading figures had been the demagogue Hyperbolus, exiled as the result of an ostracism he had himself arranged sometime in the years 416–14, the generals Nicias and Demosthenes, and the brilliant but unreliable Alcibiades. Alcibiades, the ward of Pericles and a favourite pupil of Socrates, had led the Athenians into an alliance with Argos against Sparta, which came to an end after the Spartan victory at Mantinea in 418. Alcibiades was full of imperialist ambition and sponsored a plan for a military expedition to Sicily. He and Nicias were appointed to lead the expedition, but before it set off Alcibiades was implicated in the scandal of the mutilation of the herms (ithyphallic figures of the god Hermes which stood at street corners and before houses to bring good luck; large numbers of them were concentrated in the area of the agora) and fled to Sparta, whose cause he supported for the next few years.

The Sicilian expedition was thus left in the command of Nicias, a cautious man who was only a reluctant leader, and who was criticised by Thucydides for excessive adherence to religious observances and fear of supposed bad omens. (He would have preferred to concentrate on the more attainable theatre of war in Thrace.) The expedition set out in 415, with 134 triremes and two fifty-oared ships from Rhodes, carrying 5,000 hoplites. The military preparations and intelligence were inadequate. The allies in Sicily were not as friendly as the Athenians had been led to suppose.

At the same time, conditions at home became more severe as the Spartans, following a suggestion of Alcibiades, set up a permanent raiding post at Decelea in 413: now they could harry Athenian land not just in summer, but all year round. Athens decided to levy a 5 per cent trade tax instead of the tribute in the hope that this would raise more money. Still, both League and city funds continued to be used to wage the war. A number of allies revolted, including the major islands of Euboea, Lesbos and Chios; and both they and the Spartans began negotiating with the Persian satraps of the Asia Minor coast, Pharnabazus and Tissaphernes.

In Sicily, a siege of Syracuse in 414 almost succeeded in reducing the city, but Spartan reinforcements under the general Gylippus arrived (again at the prompting of Alcibiades) and their efforts, combined with inactivity by Nicias, who was seriously ill, reversed the situation. A great sea battle took place in the harbour at Syracuse, which resulted in the defeat of Athens. Demosthenes arrived from Athens with reinforcements, including 73 ships, 5,000 hoplites and large numbers of slingers, archers and javelin throwers. With this land superiority they devastated the Syracusan countryside and mounted an attack by night on the defensive wall on the hill of Epipolae. However, Nicias delayed acting because he believed that an eclipse was an unpropitious omen. A confused battle resulted in further success for the Syracusan side.

Athenian morale was now low and sickness rife. Demosthenes argued for retreat, but Nicias was ashamed to do so and unwilling to make a decision without orders from Athens. A further naval victory by the Syracusans made up their minds for them. The Athenians began their retreat from their land base, but they were hounded by the Syracusans and finally brought up short at the River Assinarus. A massacre took place. Many Athenians were captured, including Nicias, who was executed. Some 7,000 Athenians were imprisoned in quarries where they were exposed to both sun and cold. After about ten weeks, many were then sold as slaves. It was said that some of the Athenian prisoners, imprisoned in the quarries, were able to earn their freedom by their ability to sing famous choruses of Euripides.

The casualty list from the Sicilian expedition has recently been found at the corner of Dipylou and Agioi Asomatoi, but it has not yet (2003) been published. The news of the defeat first reached Athens via a customer in a barber's shop; the unfortunate barber, who spread the rumour further, was tortured for his pains before the news was found to be true.

The Sicilian expedition was a military and political disaster for Athens. Thucydides wrote that it was 'to the victors the most brilliant of successes, to the vanquished the most calamitous of defeats; for they were utterly and entirely defeated; their sufferings were on an enormous scale; their losses were, as they say, total; army, navy, everything was destroyed, and, out of many, only few returned' (7.87). The defeat deprived her of her most noted leaders and led to a severe loss of morale. Thucydides' narrative of the campaign has almost the structure of a classical tragedy, with its sense of inevitable doom attending the actions of a good man out of his depth.

The Oligarchic Coup of 411

The following period, known as the Decelean War, saw a despairing Athens plunging further and further into disaster. The democracy began to lose credibility, and Sparta, through Alcibiades' machinations, now had the wealth of Persia on her side. The satrap Pharnabazus actively supported Sparta, while Athens paid the price for having supported the unsuccessful revolt of another satrap, Pissuthnes, in 414/13. The trierarchs (the wealthy citizens whose public service consisted in building and equipping triremes) had lost a lot of money through the destruction of their ships, and this led them to side with a growing oligarchic movement. The functions of the Boule were taken over by a committee of ten *probouloi*. Several of the demes on the east coast of Attica were fortified, to protect the grain route from the Black Sea: these include Sounion (412), Thorikos (411) and Rhamnous (probably

412). In 411 a coup at Athens resulted in the imposition of an oligarchic government from which the mass of the people were excluded.

The agitation began among the Athenian forces on Samos, who, in contacts with Alcibiades, formed the view that the Persian king, and his satrap Tissaphernes, would abandon their hostility to Athens if an oligarchic government were introduced. The Samian troops sent Pisander to Athens to put things in motion by going around the political clubs. A crucial meeting took place at Colonos, perhaps at the sanctuary of Poseidon Hippios. The rhetoric was about 'restoration of the ancestral constitution', a theme also associated with the contemporary sophist Thrasymachus. (Intellectual concerns were certainly bound up with the political manoeuvring.) Power was seized by a body known as the Four Hundred who asserted that they would then establish a body to be known as the Five Thousand, who would hold the power in Athens. There are two main sources for the sequence of events, Thucydides' unfinished eighth book and Aristotle's *Constitution of Athens*, written a century later. The latter asserts that the Five Thousand did really come into existence, but then says that it existed 'in word only', a view which agrees with Thucydides' insistence on its speciousness. No doubt there were differences among the Four Hundred themselves as to how to proceed: Clitophon moved a proposal for the restoration of the 'Laws of Cleisthenes', and his associate Theramenes was certainly in favour of enfranchising the hoplites. It may have been at around this time that a new Bouleuterion was built in the agora (the archaeological evidence points to a date between 416 and 409).

The constitution of the Four Hundred lasted about four months and they entered into negotiations with Sparta to put an end to the war. A democratic government in exile was formed by the navy at Samos; one of the leaders was Thrasybulus, who was instrumental in the recall of Alcibiades to Athens (407), following the successes he had been responsible for at Kynossema and Cyzicus in 411/10. But in 411/10 the Four Hundred were overthrown under the leadership of Theramenes and Aristocrates, who then introduced a genuine constitution of 5,000. (Thucydides' narrative comes to an abrupt end here and, in addition to Aristotle's political account, we have the much less penetrating military narrative of Xenophon.) There seemed no reason for the continuance of anything less than full democracy, and the full assembly was restored.

ATHENS DEFEATED

The war continued in Asia Minor, where the crown prince Cyrus had now arrived to command the Persian forces. A new Spartan general, Lysander, took command of the Peloponnesian forces, improved the navy, and soon inflicted a defeat on Athens at Notium. Alcibiades was blamed for the defeat and the Athenians elected ten new generals including Conon, who took over the fleet at Samos. He led Athens to a further naval victory, at Arginusae in 406, but this turned into a scandal when the victorious generals failed to pick up the Athenian dead after the battle: all the generals were deposed, except Conon, and were condemned to death by popular decision; only Socrates argued against the decision, and Theramenes was particularly vociferous for their condemnation.

In the following year the Athenians lost the battle of Aegospotami (406/5); their corn supply was cut off, and Alcibiades vanished to Phrygia, where he was shortly afterwards assassinated. Besieged by land and sea,

> they had no ships, no allies and no food; and they did not know what to do. They could see no future for themselves except to suffer what they had made others suffer, people of small states whom they had injured not in retaliation for anything they had done but out of the arrogance of power and for no reason except that they were in the Spartan alliance. They therefore continued to hold out. They gave back their rights to all who had been disfranchised and, though numbers of people in the city were dying of starvation, there was no talk of peace. (Xenophon *History* 2.2.10)

In the end Theramenes undertook to discuss terms with the Spartans. He spent three months with Lysander, 'waiting for the moment when the Athenians, with no food left, would agree to any terms whatsoever' (Xenophon 2.2.16). In the end peace was made on the terms that the Long Walls and the Piraeus fortifications must be destroyed. The fleet was to be reduced and the Delian League was dissolved.

The Dictatorship of the Thirty

The Spartan general Lysander became master of Athens (405). He established a savage dictatorship, known as the Thirty. Prominent members of the Thirty included Critias, a pupil of Socrates. They appointed a council of five hundred, 'and ten governors of the Piraeus, eleven guardians of the gaol and three hundred attendants armed with whips' (Aristotle). The laws of Solon were annulled; some apparently beneficial legal reforms were outweighed by a systematic campaign of putting to death 'those who were outstanding for their wealth, birth or reputation, cunningly removing those whom they had cause to fear and whose property they wanted to plunder. Within a short space of time they had killed no fewer than fifteen hundred' (ibid). Large parts of the Athenian fortification walls were torn down, and the ship sheds in the Piraeus were also dismantled. A more curious action was the reorientation of the Pnyx, which they turned to face inland, 'because they thought that the rule of the sea fostered democracy, whereas farmers were less likely to be bothered by oligarchy' (Plutarch). The speaker's platform now faced the Acropolis. Previously it had been on the opposite side of the assembly area, and the assembled people, seated in the natural slope of the hill, faced the temples of their gods. Now they faced into the hill.

Theramenes tried to resist these moves and insisted on the establishment of the rule of the 3,000 whom the Thirty claimed they had named on a register which was kept secret. The Thirty introduced new laws which enabled them to execute Theramenes (404) and to disarm the rest of the population. They summoned a Spartan garrison of 700 men who occupied the Acropolis.

Thrasybulus, meanwhile, led the democratic exiles to occupy the Attic border fort of Phyle. He then occupied the port of Munychia with about 1,000 troops and defeated the Thirty (May 403). The Thirty retreated to Eleusis. Thrasybulus entered Athens, but the Thirty and their supporters in Athens sent an appeal to Lysander for help. A Spartan force marched out commanded in part by Lysander and in part by the more moderate Pausanias, who according to Xenophon was jealous of Lysander and feared that Lysander would make Athens his personal property. The Spartans camped at Halipedum and set up a blockade of Piraeus. The democrats were forced into the marshes of Halae and had to give way. Thrasybulus then entered into negotiations with Pausanias, who disbanded his army. The men from Piraeus went up to the Acropolis and sacrificed to Athena. Democracy was restored. Many Spartans had been killed in the battle, and were buried at state expense in a special enclosure in the burial ground alongside the road from the Dipylon Gate to the Academy.

A rearguard action in Eleusis was swiftly put down by the execution of its generals, and the rest of their supporters were brought to a peaceful settlement. An amnesty was declared and, according to Xenophon, there was no further civil unrest even up to his own time of writing in the 350s. Soon after the amnesty (ca 400) a new building was erected, the Pompeion, in the space between the Dipylon and Sacred Gates. This was the starting point for the procession of the Panathenaea, and its erection now might be seen as a statement that Athena had regained control of her city and that her people were gratefully celebrating her festivals with new magnificence.

CHAPTER FIVE

Fourth Century Athens

The Democratic Constitution

Although customarily seen as a period of decline from the cultural brilliance of the fifth century, the fourth century in Athens in fact represented the longest sustained period of genuine democratic rule in the city's history. The constitution established after the fall of the Thirty remained in force until after the end of the Lamian War in 322. We are particularly well informed about it because Aristotle devoted the second half of his *Constitution of Athens* to an item-by-item description of its functioning. He reckoned it the eleventh of Athens' constitutions since the legendary beginnings under first Ion and then Theseus. 'The people have made themselves master of everything, and control all things by means of decrees and jury courts, in which the sovereign power resides with the people. The Athenians seem to be right to follow this line, because it is easier to corrupt the few than the many, whether by money or by favours' (*Ath. Pol.* 41).

The franchise included all Athenian males, provided they were of citizen parentage on both sides. The running of the constitution depended on the appointment of officials by lot, except for a few, mainly military, who were elected. The Council of 500 was chosen by lot, fifty from each of the ten tribes. Each month of 36 or 35 days saw the primacy of a different tribe, which was then known as the *prytany*, and its members as the *prytanes*. (The year was a lunar year of 354 days, but for other purposes Athens used a lunar calendar of 12, or in some years 13, months.) The job of the council was to summon the assembly and to prepare its business. It conducted the scrutiny of the nine archons, but the jury court had the final decision if any was to be rejected. It was also responsible for public works including buildings, ship sheds and triremes. The members included ten treasurers of Athena, ten *poletai* responsible for all public leases including the contracts for the mines and taxes, and several other committees of ten including the *euthynoi*, 'examiners', who sat in market hours by the statue of the tribal hero to receive accusations against public officials; if the case was pursued, the *euthynos* handed it to the deme justices or to the *thesmothetae* (lawgivers).

Numerous other groups of officials were appointed by lot, including ten temple repairers, ten *astynomoi* whose duties included overseeing the fees paid to flute girls and the proper disposition of dung heaps as well as the positioning of balconies, gutters and shutters which protruded into the street; ten market magistrates (*agoranomoi*) and ten overseers of the exchange. A group called the Eleven was in charge of the city gaols and of the summary execution of criminals who admitted their guilt (if they claimed innocence, they were brought to trial). The Forty (there were only thirty until after the tyranny of the coincidentally named Thirty) acted as public prosecutors, deciding which civil cases would be brought to trial.

The highest officials of the state were the nine archons: 'the' archon, after whom the year was named, the king archon, whose duties were primarily religious, the *polemarch* (in charge of military matters) and the six *thesmothetae* (lawgivers). The archon appointed the *choregoi* for the tragedies (the choruses were provided by tribes) and was responsible for several festivals and a particular set of lawsuits. The king archon was responsible for the Mysteries and some other festivals, and all lawsuits involving priests or religious matters, as well as homicide cases. The *polemarch*'s duties included arranging the funeral games for the war dead and many cases involving *metics* (resident aliens). The *thesmothetae* appointed the days on which the jury courts were to sit and were responsible for introducing various kinds of suit including bribery, debt, perjury, adultery and others. This interesting mixture of religious and legislative duties shows how intimately the life of the city was bound up with the maintenance of the divine order and the protection of Athena.

Two final important groups of officials were the ten *athlothetae*, responsible for all the arrangements for the Panathenaea and other contests; and the ten generals.

Perhaps the most remarkable feature of fifth- and fourth-century Athens is the important role of the jury courts, each composed of 501 citizens (or in some cases 1,000). Anyone over thirty years old was entitled to be a juror. Aristotle has a fascinating description (*Ath. Pol.* 63–6) of the elaborate procedure for the selection of jurors for each of the courts, involving complicated slot machines, boxwood tickets, black and white bronze cubes, marked acorns and coloured sticks. All this was intended to ensure the absolute randomness of the procedure. There was a time limit on the speakers for the prosecution and the defence, and at the end the juries held a secret vote to determine the outcome. They used two ballots with an axle through the middle, one hollow and one solid. The herald proclaimed that the hollow ballot would be for the first speaker, the solid one for the second, and the jurors deposited one in each of two urns, the first bronze for the votes that were to count, the second wooden for those that were not. The speaker receiving the larger number of votes in the bronze urn won the case.

This system, attacked by Aristophanes in the fifth century as leading to the filling of jury courts with the old and idle who were just there for the jury pay, provided a field of action in the fourth century, as well as the late fifth, for some of the world's first great orators. Lysias, Demosthenes, Andocides, Hyperides, all made their names by forensic oratory, and the courts provided a practice ground for political activity. Their speeches also provide valuable information about the social history of Athens, relations between the sexes, inheritance law, murder and bribery, and other matters.

The Trial and Death of Socrates

Among the first actions of the democratic law courts in the fourth century was the trial of Socrates in 399. Socrates, whose pupils had included the traitor Alcibiades and the tyrant Critias, was brought to trial by Anytus and Meletus on a charge of 'introducing new gods and corrupting the youth of Athens' (Plato, *Apology* 24b). The charge was obviously political in inspiration. The 'new gods' were Socrates' own inner voice, his *daimonion*, of which he often spoke. The charge of corrupting the youth was more serious.

There are two versions of Socrates' speech in his defence, one by Plato and one by Xenophon, resembling each other scarcely at all. In Plato's account, Socrates begins by characterising his opponents as people who misunderstand his work: they see him as a 'wise man' who spends his time pondering 'things above the earth'. (This is essentially the Aristophanic caricature.) He denies the charge of corrupting the youth and insists rather that he improves them. He denies the charge of 'atheism'. Increasing in arrogance as he goes on, Plato's Socrates rejects all the charges, calling at public expense for a reward instead of a punishment and suggesting that the free dinners for life might be a suitable recompense. He insists that he will never give up philosophising, which he regards as a divine mission. He concludes by mentioning his lone refusal to convict the Arginusae generals, and reminds the jury that he once refused an order of the Thirty to arrest a certain Leon.

Xenophon's version is much shorter; it covers the same main points but concentrates more on Socrates' actions in relation to the letter of the charges; it is not a full-blown 'apology' for his way of life such as Plato offers. This Socrates' defence is that his life is not one of wrongdoing. He speaks of his *daimonion*, his divine upper voice (uproar in court). He insists that none of the charges has been proved:

> It has not been shown that I sacrifice to any new deities, or swear by them, or recognise other deities instead of Zeus and Hera and their divine companions. Moreover, how could I corrupt the young by making endurance and economy second nature to them? Death is the prescribed penalty for acts such as temple-robbery, burglary, enslavement and high treason, but even my adversaries do not accuse me of any of these deeds. So I am left wondering how on earth you gained the impression that any action I have done merited the death penalty. (Xenophon, *Defence of Socrates* 25)

Xenophon conludes his account by saying 'Socrates was so arrogant in court that he invited the jurors' ill-will and more or less forced them to condemn him. If anyone in his search for virtue has encountered a more helpful person than Socrates, then he deserves, in my opinion, to be called the most fortunate of all men.'

Socrates was condemned to death by the court. This decision has often been regarded as a miscarriage of justice comparable to the crucifixion of Jesus, and consequently a stain on the reputation of Athenian democracy. It is surely true that Socrates had no political aims or ambitions himself, but simply liked to associate himself with wealthy and handsome young men who would respond to his eristic or question-and-answer method. He did not, it seems, hold any of the views expressed by opponents in his dialogues which were put into practice by Critias and his ilk. So he was condemned by association in a period when the democracy wished to do all it could to prevent a recurrence of the horrors of the rule of the Thirty. He can be seen as a victim of a kind of McCarthyism, a paranoid fear of anything associated with the horrors of the recent past. In condemning him, the Democracy abandoned its own sacrosanct principle of freedom of speech.

Socrates has benefited from the sustaining of his memory by the greatest of his pupils, Plato. While we can know for certain nothing of what Socrates taught, his influence extends through the whole history of western philosophy. Plato was not present at Socrates' death because of illness, but his description of the philosopher's last hours, his discourse on the nature of the soul and the possibility of an afterlife, his calm demeanour as he drank the hemlock and the paralysis gradually spread upwards from his feet until he died, is one of the most moving pieces of writing to come out of antiquity. As in some others of Plato's greatest dialogues, philosophy and speculation, human interest and character drawing, narrative and analysis are combined in prose of matchless limpidity.

Plato

Plato (ca 429–347) belonged to a leading Athenian family, and while his stepfather was a friend of Pericles, two of his uncles, Critias and Charmides, were members of the Thirty Tyrants. Plato made the acquaintance of Socrates in 407 and was deeply influenced by his moral integrity and his commitment to disputation (*elenchus*) as the route to

Plato

understanding. After Socrates' death Plato began work on the series of philosophical dialogues in almost every one of which Socrates is one of the interlocutors. In the earlier dialogues Socrates generally leads the discussion, while in later ones he often takes a back seat. The great question is how far the dialogues represent Socrates' own thought, and to what extent Plato has simply used Socrates as a vehicle for his own ideas. There seems little doubt that the Socratic method is generally Socratic, though it is brought to bear by Plato on many issues that may not have concerned Socrates over much.

The core of Plato's philosophy is a concern for goodness, the search for the nature of the Good and the source of morality. Most famously this concern is expressed in the Theory of Forms, the idea that every existent thing on earth, from tables to moral qualities, are copies of an absolute Form (they used to be called Ideas) of Table, the Good, or whatever 'laid up in heaven'. Things on this earth are a kind of shadow of reality, an idea famously expressed in the simile of the Cave in the Republic, where people on earth are likened to people sitting in a darkened cave, watching a shadow play on the wall in the flickering light of a fire, which they take for reality; on emerging from the Cave into real sunlight, they are dazzled by the first experience of reality.

Some scholars have interpreted this as part of a hermetic doctrine, in which the truth to which Plato was leading his pupils was a mystic truth that could not be written down, and the dialogues are just hedging around the issue. Be that as it may, philosophers have found enough substance in the dialogues to provide matter for debate for more than 2,000 years, and Plato's questions remain alive in modern philosophy.

The second focus of Socratic *elenchus* is the concern for the nature of knowledge and the way to attain it. In early dialogues Socrates uses homely similes such as the bridle maker: whom would you ask to make a bridle but a bridle-maker? Why? – because he has been trained to do it. And so on for all trades with the glaring exception of politician, a calling for which there is apparently no professional training. Plato attributes to this the failure of hitherto existing political systems to produce a perfectly just society.

Most concern has perhaps been felt about the political application of Plato's philosophy: in the *Republic* and later in the *Laws* he develops a political philosophy involving a rigidly hierarchical society. He supposed that the human soul and the state have a similar structure: the soul is a combination of reason, passions and desire, and the task of education, as well as of politics, is to ensure that reason rules the other two as a charioteer rules headstrong horses. In the *Republic*, the rulers are the Guardians. Strict obedience to laws and a strict division of labour are the way to an efficiently functioning body politic. Women are held in common and children brought up communally. Plato was an admirer of Sparta and also of what was believed to be the similarly hierarchical Cretan constitution. His solution for political unrest was the institution of the Good King.

Three times in his life (389, 387, 361) Plato visited Syracuse as a teacher to Dion, the son of the tyrant (absolute ruler) of Syracuse, apparently in the hope of turning Dion into a Just King and Syracuse into a perfect society. But when Dion did achieve sole power the effect was the reverse: he alienated the demos and plunged the city into chaos. After his first visit Plato returned to Athens and established a school in the grove known as the Academy (the sanctuary of Hekademos, where there was a gymnasium). He avoided involvement in democratic politics and established an institution that was to last for almost a thousand years, until the closure of the philosophical schools by Justinian.

Plato also continued the interest of the earliest philosophers in cosmology, and a related part of his thought concerns the immortality of the soul: souls are endlessly reincarnated, and learning is really a process of remembering what one knew in one's past life. A near-death experience, as described in the Myth of Er, is used to bolster this doctrine. Later dialogues focus more on problems of epistemology and still provide difficult conundrums for present-day interpreters.

The most famous of Plato's pupils was Aristotle (384–322), who joined the Academy in 367 at the age of 17 and remained until Plato's death. When Speusippus was appointed to succeed Plato as head of the Academy, Aristotle became first the court philosopher of Hermias of Atarneus (in the Troad) and then tutor to Alexander the Great, returning to Athens only after Alexander had departed for Asia. He became head of the school in the Lykeion (Lyceum, a shrine of Apollo the wolf god, in the area of Rigillis Square).

Much of Aristotle's philosophy is a reaction to Plato's, and many of his arguments may have influenced the development of Plato's own. Aristotle's philosophy is noted for its amassing of facts and examples, which are used in a process of induction to prove general truths. It is a philosophy which accepts the world as it is and aims to understand it, rather than rejecting it as inadequate as Plato often seems to. In particular Aristotle took a great interest in political affairs and philosophy. He and his pupils amassed a collection of more than 100 descriptions of the constitutions of Greek states, of which the *Constitution of Athens* is the only one that survives. Its importance for our knowledge of Athenian history has already become apparent.

The Corinthian War and the King's Peace

After the restoration of the democracy, war with Sparta grumbled on from 395 to 387, a period often known as the Corinthian War because much of the fighting took place near Corinth. One battle in 394 resulted in the death of five Athenian cavalrymen; their tombstone in the public burial ground has been discovered, and in addition a fine relief monument of one of them, Dexileos, which uniquely gives the dates of birth and death of the dead man (414/13–394/3); it is now in the Ceramicus Museum.

The Monument of Dexileos

War continued at sea also, with continuing involvement of the Persians, now on the Athenian side. The Athenian general Conon defeated Sparta in a battle at Cnidus in 394; the lion monument on a headland about a mile east of Cnidus, which was removed to the British Museum by Charles Newton in 1857, though the base is still in situ, may have commemorated this victory. Conon was also able to use Persian money to rebuild the walls of Athens; inscriptions date the sections to the period 393–390 BC.

In 387 a peace known as the King's Peace was in effect imposed on the warring Greek states by Persia. On the Panhellenic scene, this gave the opportunity for a steady growth in the power of Thebes. Sparta, meanwhile, unable to keep up the numbers of the Spartiate elite, went into a decline. Two battles, at Leuctra in 371 and Mantinea in 362, resulted in decisive defeats of Sparta by Thebes, and ended the greatness of Sparta for ever. At Leuctra, 400 of the Spartiates, who now numbered only 1,000, were killed; nearly half the citizen manpower. After Mantinea, the enslaved Messenians became free.

The King's Peace provided Athens with the opportunity for slow economic and political recovery. In 378 Athens established a new maritime league, known as the Second Athenian Confederacy. The enemy continued to be Sparta and the decree for the formation of the league states its aim as 'to force the Spartans to allow the Greeks to enjoy peace in freedom and independence, with their lands unviolated'. The allies included the islands of Chios and Rhodes, the Lesbian cities of Mytilene and Methymna, and the city of Byzantium on the Bosphorus. In deference to the power and quiescence of Persia, all the Greek cities of Asia Minor were declared to be the king's property. Other allies were, eventually, Thebes itself, as well as other leagues such as the Thracian cities, the Chalcidic League and two autocratic states, Thessaly and Epirus under their 'tyrants'. The Confederacy, though it gave Athens primacy, was more egalitarian than the Delian League had been: the allies could veto any Athenian proposal, and 'tribute' was replaced by 'contributions'. The settling of Athenians on allied territory was also forsworn.

The chief architect of the Confederacy was the statesman Callistratus. Despite the declared aims of the Confederacy, his policy was for harmony towards Sparta and hostility to Thebes. Despite the egalitarianism of the new league, war broke out in 357 between Athens and the allies (known as the 'Social War' from Latin *socius*, an ally), partly as a result of the reversion to the policy of cleruchies (in Samos) and partly from the secession of Rhodes, Cos and Chios to the Carian satrap Maussollus. Despite the despatch of Athenian fleets to the trouble spots, Athens had not the resources for a major war. Negotiations ended in the recognition of the independence of Rhodes, Cos, Chios, Byzantium and soon Lesbos. The league was in effect disbanded, and Athens did not again enter on any imperial designs.

Domestic Affairs in Athens

The period after the King's Peace brought Athens the conditions for economic recovery, and this was fuelled in large part by the effective exploitation of the silver mines of Laurion (from 367). The state auctioneers (*poletai*) leased the mines to individuals who would use their slaves to excavate the ore, wash it in great basins, smelt it in furnaces and refine it. Many of the mines as well as the basins and furnaces have left remains in the region of Lavrion, Anavyssos, Sounion and Thorikos. Athenian silver was famed for its purity and its coinage, with the familiar owl on the reverse, was much prized. Thorikos grew considerably in population during the fourth century, as we can tell from the enlargement of its theatre: this indicates that it was not just slaves who were involved in the mining, and that many citizens too found that there was a good living to be made in the vicinity of the mines.

However, the loss of allied income from 355 resulted in poverty at Athens. The situation was redressed by Eubulus, who as a commissioner of public funds devised ways to increase income and to spend the surplus on public works. Eubulus was friendly with Xenophon, who had been in exile in Corinth since 370. In 355 he annulled the decree of banishment, possibly in return for the economic analysis and proposals that Xenophon put forward in his *Poroi* ('Ways and Means'). This was a blueprint for economic recovery, and many of its proposals were certainly implemented by Eubulus. They include offering privileges to *metics* to enable them to create wealth; an income tax; the establishment of hotels for merchants to encourage trade; improvements to the mines and an increase in the number of miners; and the creation of a fleet of public merchant vessels.

Over the next dozen years these measures produced tangible results. Soon, however, the political scene was dramatically changed by the rise of Macedon.

Philip II of Macedon

The northerly kingdom of Macedon had been involved in Greek affairs for a long time. Its kings, though not their subjects, counted as Greeks and were allowed to compete in the Panhellenic Games. One king, Archelaus, had provided patronage and a home to the dramatist Euripides. Beginnning in the 350s, Philip had been increasing its power and expanding its territory with acquisitions in Thrace, notably Athens' important strategic allies Amphipolis and Potidaea (lost during the Social War in 357 and 356 respectively). Such conquests gave him access to the rich timber forests of Thrace and the gold mines of Mt Pangaion, where Philip resettled the city of Crenides and renamed it Philippi (356): these mines brought him 1,000 talents a year, which he used to expand his army and win influence in Greece. In 352 he became ruler of Thessaly and in 348 captured Olynthus. In 346 the Athenians indicated their acceptance of the status quo by making a peace with Philip known as the Peace of Philocrates.

In 346 Philip accepted an invitation to lead a campaign of the Amphictions ('dwellers around') to re-establish their rights over the sanctuary of Delphi, which had been sequestered by the Phocians. The Athenians were in alliance with the Phocians, and this brought Philip head-on against Athens. The war culminated in the Battle of Chaeronea (338) at which Philip defeated the combined forces of Athens and Thebes and became the undisputed master of Greece. In the following year a new league was established, the League of Corinth, which was in effect a league of Philip's Greek subjects. Philip began, aided by the long and often obsequious orations of Isocrates, to develop a plan to lead a campaign against Persia to win back the freedom of the Greeks of Ionia. Only Philip's death by an assassin's hand in 336 put a temporary stop to these proceedings.

Demosthenes

Much of what we know of Philip's career comes from the speeches of his most passionate opponent, Demosthenes (384–322). Trained, like many of the great politicians of the fourth century, as a forensic orator, Demosthenes rose to prominence around the time of the capture of Olynthus with his series of speeches denouncing Philip's activities and insisting that the only recourse of Athens was to resist the rise of Macedon with all its strength. In this policy he was followed by the politicians Lycurgus and Hyperides (another orator), while the cause of accommodation with Macedon was represented by Eubulus, Aeschines, Phocion and Philocrates. Aeschines and Demosthenes were natural enemies: 'Demosthenes drinks water, and I drink wine,' said Aeschines, summing up two completely opposed temperaments. After Chaeronea, Aeschines delivered a stinging attack on Demosthenes following a proposal that Demosthenes be offered a crown at the Dionysia for his constant service to his country; Demosthenes' speech, 'On the Crown' is a long apologia for the whole of his policy to date.

These were years of intense political division between pro- and anti-

Macedonian factions in Athens. Lycurgus conducted more than one prosecution of leading citizens who had 'deserted' Athens in the face of Philip's attack. The most fully preserved is his speech *Against Leocrates*, who took his money and his family to Rhodes, and then to Megara, after the battle of Chaeronea. In 330 he returned to Athens and was prosecuted for treason, but acquitted.

PHOCION

Of the other 'appeasers' not previously mentioned, undoubtedly the major figure is Phocion (402–318). His career spanned almost the entire century; he had begun as an assistant to the general Chabrias in 376, collecting the 'contributions' from the allies, and was elected general 45 times in the course of his life. Incorruptible and conservative, he saw Demosthenes' strident agitation against Philip as unrealistic, and continued to the end of his life to believe that negotiation was the best way for Athens to get along with Macedon. After Chaeronea, he was able to achieve better terms for Athens by negotiation; but, as we shall see, his trust betrayed him in the end. When Philip was assassinated, says Plutarch (*Phocion* 16), 'the people's first impulse was to offer up sacrifice for the good news, but Phocion opposed this. He said it would show an ignoble spirit to rejoice at what had happened, and reminded them that the army which had opposed them at Chaeronea had been weakened by the loss of no more than one man.' He realised that the death of Philip was not the end of the story.

The Age of Lycurgus

From 338 to 324 the statesman Lycurgus (387–324) was in control of the city's finances. His grandfather had been executed by the Thirty, and his early training was in philosophy: so he had impeccable credentials. He succeeded in increasing revenues to some 1,400 talents per annum. The official post from which he did this is obscure, but the results were tangible. Probably he was one of the treasurers of the military fund and maintained his power by personal influence. The *Lives of the Ten Orators* attributed to Plutarch (842F) calls him 'treasurer of the general revenues', which may have been a unique appointment.

Among other things, he regularised the fund known as the *dermatikon*, which produced 6,000 drachmas per annum from the sale of the hides of sacrificed animals. Crime was also reduced by fierce pursuit of malefactors. Lycurgus himself was noted for his probity, his democratic approach and justice, and his austerity of dress.

His building projects included the completion of the arsenal begun by Eubulus, the refurbishment of docks and harbours, the completion of the Panathenaic stadium (330-29) and the rebuilding of the Theatre of Dionysus which now assumed the form we see today, though the actual existing stonework is predominantly of Roman date. Thrones for dignitaries were set up around the edge of the orchestra. He also built a temple of Dionysus Eleuthereus and a stoa to the north of the theatre. He paid attention to the texts of the great tragedians, having definitive editions prepared of the works of Aeschylus, Sophocles and Euripides. Archaeology has revealed the extent of works belonging to this period: the city's thoroughfares were laid out, including a north-south road under what is now Makriyanni Street: it had stone borders and a packed earth surface, and continued in use until the seventh century AD. Fragmentary house remains, and various cisterns and wells as well as the construction works associated with the theatre, have been found from this period.

The area around what is now Syntagma Square was replanned: the Mesogeia road was widened to 7 metres and buttressed on the south. Alongside this road, which was outside the city walls, cemeteries were established in what is now the National Gardens, as well as on the north side of the road for a distance of some 45 metres. The cemetery near Evangelismos was destroyed and the area filled up with pottery workshops and kilns. The gymnasium of the Lyceum was equipped by Lycurgus and here Aristotle established his school: the Lyceum has recently been discovered at Rigillis St, at the back of the Royal Palace. At the same time, the swampy area of the Ceramicus was drained by tunnelling.

Water supply was also a concern, and a new aqueduct was built from Mt Parnes, which can be traced as far southwards as the deme of Acharnae; no doubt it led to the two fountain houses now built by the Dipylon Gate and in the south-west corner of the agora.

Though Lycurgus did not undertake any works on the Acropolis, he devised a new system for inventorying the treasure of Athena. He repaired the statues of Athens and of Victory, and replaced the gold plates that had been removed for war purposes at the end of the Peloponnesian War.

The rebuilding of the Theatre of Dionysus marked a concern for Athens' cultural heritage. The plays of the great dramatists continued to be performed. Aeschylus, Sophocles and Euripides had attained the status of classics. Old Comedy however fell out of fashion, and a new style was established, known as New Comedy, whose chief exponent was Menander (342–292). Gone is the political invective, bawdy and carnival atmosphere, gone the outrageous costumes of the old comic choruses; Menander's comedy is a humorous bourgeois genre, focusing on the romantic affairs of middle-class families and their slaves, and providing the model for Roman comedy as well as much later comedy. Plot is the key: Menander was once asked how he was getting on with a new play: 'Oh, it's finished', he said, 'all I have to do is write the words.' His neat aphoristic style lent itself to excerpting by moralists and anthologists, and until the beginning of the twentieth century that was all that we had of Menander to judge his great reputation in antiquity; but then discoveries of papyri from Egypt produced several almost complete plays and transformed our understanding of his drama, as well as providing much material for social historians of Athens to work on.

The classicising of drama, still put on in competition at the festivals, led to the erection of numerous choregic monuments, celebrating the funding of particular productions by individual choregi. These lined the street of Tripods, a thoroughfare 6 metres wide. One of the few that survive is the monument of Lysicrates, known from the Middle Ages onwards as the Lantern of Demosthenes.

Lycurgus also remodelled the Pnyx, notably creating the three-stepped Speaker's Platform that is still to be seen there; but it seems that the work may never have been completed, since the Theatre of Dionysus now became the favoured venue for public meetings. The sanctuary of Asclepius next to the theatre was also built at this time; and in the agora the temple of Apollo Patroos belongs to the second half of the fourth century, as does the monument of the Eponymous Heroes (the heroes of the ten tribes). New buildings in the north-east corner of the agora were probably law courts, while at the south-west corner a monumental water clock was constructed.

In Piraeus, the buildings were refurbished, perhaps continuing Eubulus' application of the recommendations of Xenophon. Around 330 a new arsenal was completed, the work of Philon, which was much admired in its time. It was some 400 feet long, 50 feet broad and 30 feet high, of limestone with marble details. Inside there were two rows of columns, the side aisles used for hanging up equipment. It had a Doric frieze and cornice. It was destroyed in 86 BC and its location is not known.

Lycurgus' work on the cityscape of Athens was like nothing that had been seen since the age of Pericles. Despite political humiliation and the power of Macedon, Athens was establishing itself as a cultural leader and adapting to a changed environment in a way which would make it a place of pilgrimage for centuries to come. However, international politics was never to leave it alone in quietude, though Athens was from now on more a victim than a leading player.

Alexander the Great and Athens

The international scene was quickly and deeply changed by the accession of Philip of Macedon's son, Alexander III (summer 336). Alexander's first task was to ensure the continuing loyalty of the Greek states. Thebes saw in the change of ruler an opportunity to rebel, and Athens entered a pact with Thebes and sent troops to its aid. However, Alexander arrived even before the Athenians. The siege of Thebes was swift and brutal (October 335): the city was destroyed down to its foundations, the inhabitants massacred or enslaved. Athens had had a narrow escape. Alexander demanded that the city hand over the eight citizens most suspected of involvement in the uprising. They included Demosthens, Lycurgus and Hyperides. Athens refused and entered negotiations, led by Demades and Phocion. The latter, whose influence with Philip was well established, argued (according to Plutarch), that 'if it was peace that Alexander wanted above all, then he should make an end of the fighting, but if it was glory, then he should transfer the theatre of the war and turn away from Greece against the barbarians' (*Phocion* 17).

Whether it was really Phocion who persuaded Alexander to take up his father's planned campaign against Persia, it is certain that his advice chimed with Alexander's own aims. Alexander as a mark of respect sent Phocion a gift, the enormous sum of 100 talents, which Phocion immediately turned over to the Athenian treasury, arguing that he had no need of such wealth for the simple life he led.

In 336/5 the system of training of the young men (*ephebes*) was reformed by the law of Epicrates. All citizens on reaching the age of eighteen must now undergo a two-year period of military training, learning to use the bow, javelin and catapult as well as hoplite shield and sword. The reform increased the number of men eligible for hoplite service by drawing them even from the poorer classes, and thus strengthened the forces available for the defence of Attica's borders. These young men were stationed in their second year at the border forts of Panakton, Phyle, Rhamnous, Eleusis and Sounion.

Nonetheless there was not sufficient employment for all in Athens, and many Athenians became mercenaries. Some entered the service of the Persian king and in due course found themselves fighting against Alexander.

In 334 Alexander set out on his campaign to conquer the Persian Empire and to 'avenge the wrongs against the Greeks', notably the sack of Athens by the Persians in 479. Alexander, who had had Aristotle as his private tutor, was an educated man and, besides carrying his copy of Homer with him everywhere, he was aware of the great cultural achievements of Athens, which he no doubt remembered as long as it was politic to be lenient to Athens. After the battle of the Granicus in 334, his first victory against Darius, Alexander sent to Athens 300 suits of Persian armour. These were displayed in the Parthenon with the inscription 'Alexander, son of Philip, and the Greeks (except the Spartans) dedicated these spoils, captured from the barbarians who inhabit Asia'. He also had fourteen large gilded shields (1.25m in diameter) fixed to the eastern architrave of the Parthenon.

Alexander was never to return to his homeland, dying at Babylon in summer 323. But his eleven-year expedition changed the face of the world, and the Greek states could never act as if he were not there. As Demades said when, a few years into the campaign, there was a rumour of his death: 'If Alexander were dead, the whole world would stink of his corpse' (Plutarch, *Phocion* 22). In his absence, Alexander appointed Antipater as regent in Macedon, and it was his task to ensure that the Greek states remained quiescent in Alexander's rear. Aristotle, with his intimate Macedonian connections, at this time felt it safe to return to Athens (332), where he established his school in the Lyceum.

The first sign of resistance to Macedon came from Sparta, with the revolt of King Agis in 331. Athens nearly joined the revolt, but will have been glad that it did not do so after Sparta was resoundingly defeated by Antipater at Megalopolis in spring 330. Even Demosthenes had argued against involvement. For the next few years resentment grumbled on in Athens without turning into active resistance, and finding its expression in small disputes like that over the Athenian dedications at the oracle of Dodona, to which Alexander's mother, the formidable Olympias, objected as infringing her authority in this Molossian territory.

Despite the prosperity engineered by Lycurgus, the years from 331 to 324 were also a time of crisis because of a severe grain shortage throughout the Aegean. The cause is not known, but the price of wheat rose from five drachmas a bushel to sixteen. Gifts of grain were sent to as many as fifty Greek cities from Cyrene on the North African coast, with the largest shipments going to Athens; and a fleet was despatched to protect the shipments from Etruscan pirates.

In 330 Alexander entered the Persian capital of Susa as conqueror. He sent back to Athens the treasures looted by the Persians from the Acropolis in 480, including the statues of the tyrannicides, Harmodius and Aristogiton. This was a neat propaganda move: the Athenians could hardly object to their return, though the attachment of Alexander's name to the dedication might leave a sour taste in the mouth. In 324, Alexander was back in Susa after his six-year expedition to the east, founding cities in Bactria (Afghanistan) and Sogdia (Tajikistan), and slaughtering his way through Swat and the Indus valley with little permanent result. As King of Kings and the most powerful conqueror history had known, he now demanded that the Greeks acknowledge him as a god. The bill granting Alexander divine status in Athens was sponsored by Demades. This demand occasioned a considerable debate in Athens. Lycurgus indignantly asked 'What sort of god is he when those who *come out* of his temple have to sprinkle themselves with holy water?' At a similar debate in Sparta, one Damis laconically remarked, 'Well, let Alexander be a god if he wants to.' The idea of a man receiving divine honours in his lifetime was still something very new: Lysander had received such honours in Asia Minor, but he was the only precedent. After Alexander it became very common, and most hellenistic kings were honoured as gods on earth.

A further crisis hit Athens with the flight of Harpalus in the same year, 324. Harpalus was the treasurer of Alexander's empire, based in Babylon, where he was responsible for the minting of coinage from the bullion Alexander acquired in his campaign. He devoted his spare time to gardening, importing plants from Greece for the royal parks. (They did well, except that he could not get ivy to grow there.) He also imported two successive mistresses from Athens, Pythionice and (when she died) Glycera, lampooned at Alexander's court, perhaps by the king himself, as 'Queen of Babylon'. When Alexander cracked down on the satraps who had revolted during his absence in the east, Harpalus seems to have felt threatened. He fled with an army of 6,000 men and a treasury of 5,000 talents, probably to Tarsus. But Alexander was moving north. At the same time (March 324) Alexander announced his intention of taking Samos away from Athens and restoring the exiles who had now been gone for forty years. This was a prelude to the promulgation in July of the Exiles' decree, enjoining the return of all displaced persons to their homelands. According to the historian Hieronymus of Cardia, the motive was to ensure that there were supporters of Alexander in every Greek city, to neutralise opposition. Probably as early as May, Harpalus arrived in Attica seeking refuge. At first the Athenians, anxious of the effect their action would have on Alexander, refused to admit him. Harpalus parked his fleet at Tae-narum, and later in the summer returned to Athens with 700 talents. This time he was admitted and put under guard. Alexander showed no sign of taking action to recover his treasure or his fleet, and though Olympias and Antipater demanded his extradition, the Athenians took no action and presently allowed Harpalus to escape. He took up a career as a privateer in Crete and was murdered by his lieutenant Thibron.

His impact continued however, as it was discovered after his escape that only half of the 700 talents he had brought with him were still on the Acropolis. Demosthenes was accused of having received a bribe of 20 talents to drop his opposition to Harpalus' being in the city; Hyperides accused him of being responsible for the disappearance of the rest, who knew where? The Areopagus undertook an investigation and in 323 Demosthenes was put on trial along with Demades and others; Hyperides and Deinarchus led the prosecution. The defendants were found guilty and fined; Demosthenes was unable to pay and was imprisoned, but soon escaped and lived in exile until Alexander's death. Demades also went into exile.

The Lamian War

In June 323 Alexander died suddenly and unexpectedly at Babylon. His death ushered in a period of twenty years of continual strife between the generals who claimed his succession. The immediate result in Greece was that many of the states saw an opportunity to shake off Macedonian rule. In Athens, Leosthenes came to the fore and, with the support of Hyperides and others, persuaded the assembly to vote for war. The opposition to war was led by Demades and Phocion, the latter now nearly eighty years old. The anti-Macedonian mood caused Aristotle to leave Athens: he retired to Chalcis on Euboea, where he died a year later.

Leosthenes became commander in chief of the Greek forces, which inflicted an initial defeat on Antipater and forced him to retreat to Lamia, where he endured a long siege. Leosthenes was killed in the fighting around Lamia, and his funeral oration was delivered by Hyperides: it has been described as 'the last surviving great speech from Athens, the swan song of Greek freedom' (Habicht 39). In simple and eloquent Greek Hyperides praises the commitment of Greeks to freedom and autonomy, which befits a people born from their own land: 'there is no happiness without self-rule' (25). He says that Greece has been destroyed by those who took bribes from Philip and Alexander. Leosthenes and his men, he continues, died in a cause most worthy, and will shake hands in Hades with the heroes of Troy, the tyrannicides Harmodius and Aristogeton, and the great leaders Miltiades and Themistocles (36–39).

In spring 322 Macedonian reinforcements arrived commanded by Leonnatus and lifted the siege of Lamia. Athens took the war to sea, but in two battles at Abydus and off Amorgos the Athenian fleet was destroyed by superior Macedonian forces (July 322). At the same time, Alexander's general Craterus, whom he had appointed to replace Antipater as 'general in Europe', combined his forces with Antipater's under the latter's command. The decisive battle took place at Crannon in Thessaly in August 322. 40,000 Macedonian hoplites defeated 25,000 Greeks and the war was over. Macedon insisted on settling peace terms with each of the Greek states separately, thus dividing the opposition. For Athens, Demades and Phocion led the negotiations. The opposition politicians were extradited and a Macedonian garrison was installed at Munychia. The constitution was amended so that only those with property worth over 2,000 drachmas would have citizen rights: the citizen body was thus reduced at a stroke from 21,000 to 9,000. Demades sponsored the motion for the execution of those who had supported the war, including Demosthenes and Hyperides. Demosthenes committed suicide; Hyperides was hunted down by Antipater's men, and, to punish his anti-Macedonian rhetoric, his tongue was torn out before he was killed.

The installation of the Macedonian garrison in Piraeus in September 322 signalled the end of Athens' independence. At about the same time, Alexander's order regarding Samos was put into effect: the exiles returned and the Athenian cleruchs were expelled. One of the families who returned to Athens was that of the philosopher Epicurus, who was a young man of twenty at the time and was to become one of the most prominent intellectuals of the third century. If Athens' political power was destroyed, its intellectual standing would remain undimmed for some time to come.

CHAPTER SIX

Athens, Macedon and the Coming of Rome
322–86 BC

(i) Macedon takes Control

The new Macedonian rulers quickly installed a form of government more favourable to their needs: a moderate oligarchy based on two classes of citizen, the second of which had no rights to vote or to hold office. The franchise was thus reduced to a little less than half what it had been. The secretary of the council was replaced by a new official, a registrar, in July 321, and a board of *nomophylakes* or guardians of the laws was also created.

The leading politicians were the pro-Macedonian Demades and the elderly Phocion. In 319 Demades and his son Demeas led an embassy to Antipater to request the removal of the Macedonian garrison from Piraeus; however, they were seized and imprisoned on reaching the Macedonian capital, Pella. After a trial before Antipater and his son Cassander, both were executed.

The death of Antipater shortly afterwards at the age of 79 led to an intensification of Athens' difficulties. There was still no one fit to take on the role of king: Alexander's half-brother Philip Arrhidaeus was mentally incapable, and Alexander's son Alexander IV was a child, so the regency must continue. Antipater had named as his successor as regent a general, Polyperchon, and had passed over his own son Cassander, whom he made second-in-command. This naturally led to rivalry between the latter two, and Cassander immediately moved to win support, sending messengers to all the Macedonian forces in Greece demanding they transfer their allegiance to him. The man who brought the message to Athens was Nicanor.

Phocion maintained contact with Nicanor. He 'pleaded the cause of the Athenians and secured lenient and considerate treatment for them: in particular he persuaded Nicanor to sponsor various costly athletic festivals in his capacity as president of the games' (Plut *Phoc* 31). However, Polyperchon used this state of affairs, according to Plutarch, to destroy Phocion. He had little hope of winning Athens over unless he could secure Phocion's achievement. He accordingly sent a letter to Athens announcing the restoration of democracy and called on the citizens to exercise their political rights. Nicanor asked to address the assembly, but the Athenians determined to arrest him when he appeared. However, he was warned of the plan and allowed to escape. Phocion was blamed for his escape. It seems that Phocion genuinely believed in Nicanor's good intentions. He was soon proved wrong when Nicanor's men began to surround the city with a trench.

Phocion now professed himself willing to lead out the Athenians against him, but he was shouted down. While the city was in an uproar and divided, Alexander the son of Polyperchon arrived with an army, 'ostensibly to bring help to the citizens in their struggle against Nicanor, but in reality to seize the city' (Plut *Phoc* 33). Phocion encouraged negotiations between Nicanor and Alexander, but when the Athenians observed this they denounced Phocion as a traitor. Phocion and his supporters fled to Polyperchon's travelling court in Phocis. Polyperchon immediately had one of Phocion's supporters, Deinarchus, tortured and executed; he refused to allow Phocion a hearing, and had him put under guard and sent back to Athens, with orders that the Athenians should put him on trial. The Athenians condemned to death the man of 83 who had been their leading politician for nearly half a century, but those who demanded that he be tortured first were voted down. On Munichion 19 (late May), 318, Phocion and his fellow-prisoners drank the hemlock. Plutarch tells that one of his friends, Nicocles, requested the favour of being allowed to drink the poison first. Phocion agreed, but the poison ran short and the executioner demanded twelve drachmas to prepare some more. Phocion 'sent for one of his friends. He remarked that it was hard if a man could not even die at Athens without paying for it, and told him to give the executioner his fee' (Plut *Phoc* 36). His body was taken beyond the borders of Attica, to Megara, for burial.

If this shameful plot had been intended to secure Athens for Poly-perchon, it failed, for Cassander and Nicanor retained control of Piraeus while Polyperchon had the support only of the city of Athens itself. Athens now became embroiled in the wider war that was developing between Polyperchon and his allies, including Alexander's mother Olympias, on the one hand, and Antigonus, 'general of Asia', Cassander and Lysimachus, satrap of Thrace, on the other. In about August 317 Cassander's troops seized Aigina, Salamis and Panakton. Polyperchon suffered a major defeat at Megalopolis and the Athenians clamoured for negotiations with Cassander. A leading role in the talks was played by Demetrius of Phalerum, a philosopher who had been educated in the school of Aristotle and Theophrastus and whose sur-viving (fragmentary) works show him to have been a good philosopher in his own right. A settlement was soon reached with Cassander. A new regime was instituted, in which the minimum property requirement for full citizenship (1,000 drachmas) was only half what it had previously been. Phocion's name was redeemed and his remains brought back to Athens for state burial. Demetrius was appointed by Cassander as ruler of Athens.

Demetrius of Phalerum

Demetrius (born ca 360) already had a name as a philosopher and scholar. The origins of his family, and his wealth — and hence his rise to political power — are obscure, though it is possible that his family was connected by marriage to that of the general Conon. Perhaps best known to posterity as the man who first collected the fables of Aesop together, he is also important for historians as having made a com-prehensive list of Athenian archons, the basis of chronology. He also wrote on political theory, Athenian law and constitution, philology and even the interpretation of dreams. Closely associated with his philosophical mentors Aristotle and Theophrastus, he had developed ties to the Macedonian royal house. The title he bore as ruler of Athens is not known, and the sources variously refer to him as *epimeletes* (commissar), *epistates* (president) or *prostates* (superintendent). Whatever his title, his power was overriding and conspicuous. By the end of his reign there were 360 bronze statues of him in Athens, mostly equestrian (Diogenes Laertius, *Lives of the Philosophers* 5.75).

Demetrius strengthened the powers of the board of *nomophylakes* (possibly a development of the Eleven, with general powers to apprehend malefactors) and gave new powers to the Areopagus. He also introduced a board of *gynaikonomoi*, whose role was to enforce the proper behaviour of women. He carried out a census which revealed the population of Attica as 21,000 citizens, 10,000 resident aliens (*metics*) and (allegedly) 400,000 slaves – though the last figure can hardly be right.

There is little physical evidence of Demetrius' rule of Athens, though he did oversee the completion of the portico of the temple of Demeter and Kore at Eleusis, and Diogenes Laertius says vaguely that he enriched the city with revenues and buildings. The reason for this dearth is to be found in his remarkable sumptuary laws, aimed at curbing extravagance of all kinds. The aim was not one of money-saving but of preventing ostentation. For example, no one was allowed to hold a feast with more than thirty guests, even for a wedding; funerals were to take place before dawn, and shrouds were to be plain. These provisions recall Solon's restrictions on aristocratic ostentation, such as the singing of composed laments for the dead. In Demetrius' case, it seems the aim must have been to ensure that no one competed visibly with his own luxurious lifestyle. The archaeological effect is seen in his ban on sculptured grave monuments: henceforth there were to be only plain cylinders or slabs to mark the graves of the dead, and the large numbers of these uninteresting objects in the Ceramicus Museum are testimony to the force of Demetrius' edict (Cicero *Laws* 2.66–7).

Liturgies were also abolished, including the *choregia:* Demetrius himself remarked that many a tripod was a monument only to the ruin of the family that commissioned it (fragment 136 Wehrli). Instead one *agonothetes* was elected and his expenses met by the state. The trierarchy was also probably abolished. While such reforms created greater state, and thus 'democratic' control, they also allowed the rich to hang on to their wealth where under the radical democracy they had been forced to spend it for the benefit of the state. The property qualification for citizenship was reduced from 12,000 to 10,000 drachmas, thus extending the franchise. However, land and wealth became concentrated in fewer hands; the poor, unable to take part in political life, also lost their pay for attending the assembly. In part these reforms were possible because Demetrius was an astute manager of the city's finances, bringing revenues back up to the level of the age of Lycurgus. The approach seems also to have been an application of a philosopher's mind to the problem of state administration. Works like Plato's *Laws* and the *Politics* of Aristotle had attempted to blend the contributions of all classes in a 'mixed' constitution that infringed the liberty of all as little as possible. Both had argued for the reduction of funeral expenses and for the firm supervision of women.

Perhaps Demetrius would have developed Athens' role as a cultural centre had he had the opportunity. Certainly he was instrumental after his banishment in persuading Ptolemy I of Egypt to found the Library of Alexandria and the Museum, a kind of royal academy of poets and scholars. But time ran out for Demetrius, an event which, as the author of a work on Chance, he might have anticipated. International politics intervened. Cassander defeated Polyperchon in 316 and in the following year had Olympias executed. He married one of the daughters of Philip II, Thessalonike, thus establishing himself as king in Macedon. He rebuilt Thebes to signal his rejection of actions associated with Alexander (who had once bullied him so cruelly that ever afterwards he shuddered at the sight of an image of the conqueror) and thus won favour with Athens. After his war with Antigonus was concluded in 311 he executed Alexander's wife Roxane and her son Alexander IV, and a year later Alexander's mistress Barsine and her son Heracles.

In 309/8 Demetrius was eponymous archon at Athens and organised the Dionysia of 308, at which he was hailed by poets as 'resembling the sun'. Meanwhile Ptolemy had entered the war on the side of Antigonus and captured a number of Greek cities including Andros and Megara: he was standing at the gates of Athens. Antigonus sent his son, Demetrius, later known as 'the Besieger' (Poliorcetes) with a fleet to Athens. The Athenians mistook the fleet for that of Ptolemy and admitted it to the Piraeus. The new Demetrius at once stormed the city, arrested the philosopher-king and exiled him to Thebes, from where he went to Egypt and became adviser to King Ptolemy I. The ten-year rule of Demetrius of Phalerum was over. The Athenians welcomed the besieger as a liberator.

Demetrius Poliorcetes 307–287

Demetrius quickly made his mark by the 'restoration of democracy'. The city was declared independent, in accordance with his father's 'Proclamation of Tyre' (314) that all Greek cities were to be free and autonomous. The city and harbour were to remain free of garrisons. The census classes and the board of *nomophylakes* were abolished. A donation of grain was promised, as well as timber to restock the harbour with ships. All statues of Demetrius of Phalerum were destroyed (some being turned into chamber pots according to Diogenes Laertius), posthumous honours were offered to Lycurgus, and Demetrius and his father Antigonus were quickly enrolled as part of the Athenian pantheon. Two new tribes were created named Antigonis and Demetrias, and statues of father and son were erected in the agora to join the group of the eponymous heroes: the pedestal had to be enlarged to accommodate them. Additional statues were placed next to those of the tyrannicides. The number of sacred triremes (used in the Panathenaic procession) was increased from two to four, and the two new ones were named after Antigonus and Demetrius.

Demetrius Poliorcetes

Demetrius' personal style was luxurious and designed to reflect his status as a god on earth. From 307 to 301, twenty decrees sponsored by his supporter Stratocles (whom Plutarch called a new Cleon for his vulgarity and boorishness) created new honours for Demetrius and Antigonus as Saviours, Benefactors (divine titles) and also Kataibates, 'he who comes down (i.e. from heaven)'. All Demetrius' decrees were 'to be considered holy' (Plutarch, *Demetrius* 24.4–5). He took up his abode in the opisthodomos of the Parthenon, normally reserved for sacred purposes, and when on Delos in the temple of Apollo there. Plutarch (*Demetrius* 23) says that 'he was entertained, so the arrangement implied, by his hostess Athena, but it could not be said that he was a well-behaved guest or that he conducted himself under her roof with the decorum that is due to a virgin goddess'. Enemies accused him of turning the temple into a brothel. Several courtesans moved in with him, and he pursued boys there as well.

Demetrius valued his services to Athens highly, and imposed an immediate levy of 250 talents as his fee. The money was then spent, according to Plutarch, on soap and cosmetics for Lamia and his other mistresses. Lamia became known as 'the Besieger' herself because of her rapacity.

After a campaign in the Peloponnese in 303, Demetrius returned to Athens and demanded to be initiated into all five grades of the Eleusinian Mysteries at once – a thing impossible since the rites appropriate to each grade were enacted in different months of the year. The problem was solved by the decree moved by Stratocles, that the present month, Munychion, should be renamed, first as Anthesterion and then as Boedromion, so that all the rites could be performed for Demetrius in short order.

One of the most resented of Demetrius' actions was his move against the philosophical schools. The politician Sophocles proposed a resolution that the schools be placed under state control, the immediate result of which was that most of them fled the city. The move was probably particularly aimed at Aristotle's school, the Peripatos, now headed by Theophrastus, which no doubt continued to have strong connections with the Macedonian royal house, now represented by Cassander. The comic poet Alexis praised the move which drove the philosophers 'to perdition', but this probably represents only the usual satirical animosity of the comedians to philosophy, and the popular suspicion that the educators were 'corrupting the youth of the city'. Sophocles was quickly sued by one of Aristotle's pupils on the grounds that his law was unconstitutional: he won his case, and the philosophers returned.

THE PHILOSOPHIC SCHOOLS

The reputation of the schools of Athens was by now considerable. The two that dominated the city at this time were Plato's Academy, under his successors Speusippus, Xenocrates and, at this time, Polemo (followed by Crates); and the Peripatos, so called from the philosophers' habit of 'walking about' while discoursing. (The followers of Aristotle are thus known as Peripatetics.) The two schools continued the philosophical orientation of their founders but with a much broader remit that included most of the subjects that would be offered in a present-day university. The Academy emphasised the concerns of its founder and over time came to be dominated by specialists in epistemology. The Peripatos was more worldly in its orientation, and its scholars were active in zoology, meteorology, botany (Theophrastus' specialism), as well as humane subjects such as rhetoric, religion and political philosophy.

Soon after the return of the philosophers, Epicurus himself returned to Athens and set up a school, known as 'the Garden'. Epicurean philosophy represented a new departure for philosophy, away from traditional objective concerns about the nature of the cosmos to a focus on how to live life well and be happy. The approach has been termed by its leading scholar 'the therapy of desire'. The aim of Epicurus as expressed in his writings was *ataraxia,* 'untroubledness'. The moral drive was based on a thorough-going materialism which derived from the atomic theory of Democritus, denied that the gods, 'if they exist', have any concern with the affairs of men, and asserted that the goal of life is to regulate one's own passions in order to achieve freedom from care. 'The wise man can be happy even under torture'; and in his last letter, written on the day of his death, Epicurus described the agonies of his disease (he had not passed water for seven days) which nonetheless left his mind untroubled and unafraid. Nothing could be a greater travesty than the later perversion of the word 'epicurean' to mean sybaritic, for Epicurus' doctrine was that happiness came from the elimination of desire, not its gratification.

The doctrine of being happy even under torture was shared by the Stoic school also. The first Stoic was Zeno of Citium, who set up his school in Athens about this time, in a colonnade or stoa (hence the name). Stoicism became perhaps the most influential philosophy of antiquity and many of its doctrines were adopted by the Christian fathers. It changed considerably over the centuries, but its essential core was a belief that the world is directed by a divine mind; everything that occurs is for a purpose and is in some sense fated. The task of man is to place himself in harmony with the divine purpose; thus he will achieve inner peace. Stoics seem also to have believed in an eternal recurrence and periodic destruction of the world by fire. They developed a sophisticated logic and physics as well as their ethical and religious doctrines.

A fifth group of philosophers, who did not form a cohesive school, were the Cynics, whose founder was Diogenes, himself a pupil of Socrates' pupil Antisthenes. Cynics took a rejectionist approach to society and pursued lives of extreme privation: the way to escape the limitations of humanity was to be found in living like beasts (which might bring you closer to that other non-human ideal, the gods). Diogenes famously lived in a tub; he threw away his cup when he realised that he could lap from rivers like a dog; and performed his bodily functions in public in the agora. When once reproved for masturbating in public, he replied 'if only I could get rid of hunger so easily, by rubbing my belly'. Cynics were philosophers in the sense that they pursued a particular way of life; but they did not pursue any technical branches of philosophy. They became a prominent feature of cities throughout the Roman Empire, and exercised some influence on the development of Christian monasticism and asceticism.

The Tyranny of Lachares

In 301 the battle of Ipsus brought to an end the wars between Alexander's successors, and established the outlines of the Hellenistic world as it was to continue until the coming of Rome, divided as it was between the Seleucid Empire in the East, Lysimachus' kingdom in Thrace and northern Asia Minor, the Ptolemies' kingdom in Egypt, and Macedon. Antigonus was killed at Ipsus. The Athenians saw in this an opportunity to be rid of his son whom they had welcomed six years earlier, and turned to Cassander for support. It was probably in 300 that a demagogue named Lachares took control of the city, on a tide of unrest associated with a severe grain shortage. He had the support of Cassander, and in 299 Lysimachus made a donation of grain to the city. The opponents of Lachares withdrew to the Piraeus, and they still held it when Demetrius reappeared to re-take the city in (probably) summer 296. In 295 Demetrius, delayed by the loss of his fleet in a storm and consequent refitting, captured the forts at Eleusis and Rhamnus and the islands of Salamis and Aegina, and established a complete naval blockade of Athens. The city was starved into submission. Plutarch tells how Epicurus counted out the daily ration of beans for his pupils, and how a father and son came to blows over a dead mouse. Lachares stripped the gold from the Athena Parthenos and other statues in order to pay his troops; but he could not win and fled to Thebes (295/4).

When Demetrius entered the city the people feared his reaction to their treachery, but he treated the city mildly, though there seem to have been some constitutional changes. Soon after this Demetrius succeeded in making himself king of Macedon by killing one of the sons of Cassander (who had recently died) and driving out the other, who was shortly put to death by Lysimachus. Demetrius built himself a new capital, Demetrias, on the Gulf of Pagasae, which became his residence, though he frequently visited Athens. The Athenians now offered one flattering acknowledgement after another to the new king. The most notable example is the hymn composed for a celebration of the Eleusinian Mysteries in 291 or 290. A poet (perhaps Hermippus) won a competition in hymn-composition with his address to Demetrius:

> Hail, son of Poseidon, most powerful god, and of Aphrodite.
> The other gods are either far distant,
> Or do not have ears,
> Or do not exist or pay no attention to us
> But we see you present, not made of stone or wood,
> But real. We pray to you.

In 290 Demetrius celebrated the Pythian Games in Athens, as Delphi was at the time in enemy hands.

Demetrius' ostentation became ever more marked. Plutarch said that there was 'something theatrical' about him. 'He possessed an elaborate wardrobe of cloaks and hats, broad-brimmed hats with double mitres and robes of purple interwoven with gold, while his feet were clad in shoes of the richest purple felt embroidered with gold.' One of his robes was woven with a design of the universe and all the heavenly bodies. Demetrius' rule represented a significant step forward in the elevation of the absolute ruler far above the level of other mortals.

Independent Athens 287–262

In 287 Athens rebelled against Demetrius, and with the aid of Ptolemy Athenians gained their independence. Demetrius died in 283 and was succeeded by his son Antigonus Gonatas, but Athens was left alone. Little is known of the following 25 years. The city continued to suffer from grain shortages, so severe that in one case, in 286, the Panathenaea was cancelled. There seems to have been some population decline, and many houses in use in the fourth century were abandoned in the third. The towns of Attica show a similar decline, except for some of the fortifications which were renewed in the 260s. A traveller who visited Athens around this time found a shabby place,

> totally dry and ill supplied with water. The streets are nothing but miserable old lanes, the houses mean, with a few better ones among them. On his first arrival a stranger could hardly believe that this is the Athens of which he has heard so much ... Of the inhabitants some are Attic and some are Athenian. The former are gossiping, slanderous, given to prying into the business of strangers, fair and false. The Athenians are high-minded, straightforward, and staunch in friendship. The true-born Athenians are keen and critical auditors, constant in their attendance at plays and spectacles. ... But a man must be aware of the courtesans, lest they lure him to ruin.'

However, he commented, it was possible to enjoy Athens, as long as you brought your own food.

In 279 Athens faced a new terror with the invasion of the Celts from the north. One group invaded Macedonia and killed the king, Ptolemy Keraunos; another, led by Brennus, ravaged Thessaly and headed for Delphi, bent on plunder. The Greeks assembled an army which defeated the Celts at Delphi and drove them back. Pausanias, in describing the campaign, gave the Athenians the pre-eminent role in the fighting, but he, or his source, was clearly basing his account on their achievements against the Persians 200 years before, and the Athenian force of a thousand was merely one of many contingents. One by-product was a reorganisation of the structure of the Athenian army: all citizens from 18 to 59 were to bear arms, and the number of the cavalry was increased from 200 to 300.

These military reforms, and the fortification of the demes, are to be associated with the outbreak of war between Ptolemy (in alliance with Athens and Sparta) and Macedon, in which Ptolemy's stated aim was the 'liberation of Greece', and thus a reduction of the power of Macedon. This is known as the Chremonidean War after Chremonides, one of the important politicians of Athens at the time, who proposed the alliance. Antigonus Gonatas, the king of Macedon, despite Ptolemaic encampments in Attica, succeeded in surrounding Athens. In the course of a long siege, the shrine of Poseidon Hippios, the headquarters of the cavalry near the Academy, was destroyed. In 263/2 Athens surrendered. Macedonian control was re-established, a garrison was imposed, and the ruler appointed by Antigonus was the grandson of Demetrius of Phalerum, also called Demetrius. This was the end of Athens as an independent political entity, though Piraeus was finally reunited with the city.

THE ARTISTS OF DIONYSUS

At this time Athens began to be aware of its literary heritage and to cultivate an image of its glorious past. In 278/7 a building in the theatre was covered in an inscription (IG II^2 2325) listing victorious poets and actors from 485/4 to 278/7. At the same time groups of travelling actors began to emerge, taking the Attic classics to other parts of Greece. These were known as the Artists of Dionysus and grew into powerful guilds who carried out important diplomatic functions, travelling from one religious festival to the next. Athens' reputation acted as a magnet for poets: many of the dramatists of the third century were of non-Attic origin.

THE ATTHIDOGRAPHERS

Another manifestation of interest in the past was the work of the Atthidographers, compilers of chronicles of Athenian history. This group of six historians began with Cleidemos (fl 354–40) and included Androtion (344/3 onwards), Phanodemos (ca 338/7–327/6), Demon and Melanthios in the late fourth century, and Philochorus whose work covers events up to 262. Several of these historians were official *exegetai*, interpreters of sacred law. They built on this expertise to compose histories of Attica from its legendary origins to the present. Unfortunately only fragments of their works survive, quoted in other authors, but from these it is clear that they concentrated on cult origins, obscure myths and customs, but also political events as they came closer to their own times. The work of Philochorus, a true scholar and a religious conservative, was the basis of many later writers' work on Athenian history.

Renewed Macedonian Rule, 262–229

Demetrius was ruler of Athens for seven years, apparently with the title *thesmothetes*, lawgiver. The extent of his control over the appointment of other officials is unclear. There is little information about events in Athens, which was a rather small pawn in Macedon's game. The accounts of the ancient historians dry up around now, partly because the series of local chronicles, the *Atthides*, ceases. There is a marked diminution in political activity, and the *ephebate*, which had now become a corps of volunteers, attracted very few applicants.

Athens was compelled to join in whenever Antigonus went to war, and the city and its territory frequently became a battleground for rival armies. In 255 Antigonus 'granted the Athenians their freedom'. What this meant is unclear – probably very little – but Demetrius the Younger is not heard of again. In 239 Antigonus died and his successor as king of Macedon was Demetrius II, but nothing changed for Athens.

When Demetrius died in 229 he was succeeded by his nine year old son, Philip V. The patent instability in Macedon induced Athens to revolt once again, and Diogenes, an Athenian citizen who had been Demetrius' commander in the Piraeus, handed over the major harbours of Piraeus, Salamis, Munychia and Rhamnous to Athenian control. Diogenes was titled 'Benefactor' and given a special seat at the theatre. A new gymnasium was built and named after him, and for more than a century an annual festival was held in his name. At the same time a new festival, the Aianteia (for the hero Ajax) began in Salamis: it included a regatta, a long race, a torch race, a procession and a sacrifice.

Athens now pursued a policy of strict neutrality. Macedon found itself at war with a new grouping of Greek states, the Achaean League; but Athens declined to join the League to the great annoyance of its leader Aratus and his historian Polybius. This resulted in frequent raids on Attica by Aratus, in 242 and in the 230s. Athens preferred to cultivate the friendship of Ptolemy III of Egypt: in 224/3 he was added to the Athenian pantheon, and a thirteenth tribe was created and named Ptolemais. The gymnasium of Ptolemy was probably built at this time, in honour of this Ptolemy (the alternative is Ptolemy VI). It was later used as a school by Carneades (214/13–129/8) when head of the Academy , and remained in use until AD 267.

A good deal of defensive building took place in Attica in the last decades of the third century, including strengthening of the city walls, refurbishment of the harbours, including Piraeus, and much activity at Rhamnous. The Long Walls, however, which were already practically ruinous, were not repaired. Coinage, which had ceased in 261, resumed in 229, as the mines at Laurion came into operation once more. The coins were of a high standard, and reached even to Arabia, where they were copied by local mints.

(ii) The Second Century BC: the Coming of Rome

Rome had appeared on the Athenian horizon as early as the mid–third century, when the goddess Roma was associated with a new cult of Demos and the Graces. The first diplomatic contact came in 228 when Roman envoys came to explain Roman activities in the Balkans (the

First Illyrian War), which were the beginning of Rome's campaign to isolate and reduce Macedon. In 212 Attalus the king of Pergamon (see below) joined forces with Rome and the Aetolian League to attack Philip V (the First Macedonian War). Rome made peace with Macedon in 206, and the copy of the treaty which is preserved in Livy includes as parties two non-combatant cities, Ilium (i.e. Troy) and Athens. It seems that these two names, of immense historical resonance, were added later by forgery so that when Rome next chose to intervene in Greece, it could claim that it was doing so in defence of the allied cities of Athens and Ilium.

Athenian neutrality ended in 200. In September 201 two Acarnanian youths had taken part in ceremonies at the Eleusinian Mysteries that they were not entitled to. It was surely a genuine mistake, but the Athenians interpreted their action as sacrilege and executed them. The Acarnanians, long-standing allies of Philip, carried out military raids on Attica, and Athens declared war on Philip. The Athenians could not rely on support from their usual ally in Egypt, as Ptolemy IV had died in 204 leaving an heir (Ptolemy V) only six years old, so that a succession of regents, often at war with each other, took control of affairs. Instead Athens had to rely on help from Attalus, from Rhodes (now the greatest trading power in the eastern Mediterranean) and from Rome. Attalus and Roman ambassadors met at Athens in spring 200: Attalus' welcome is said to have been almost as extravagant as that of Demetrius Poliorcetes in 307/6.

> When Attalus was entering the city by the Dipylon, the Athenians stationed the priestesses and priests on each side of the road and then opened all the temples, and, having placed offerings on all the altars, they asked him to sacrifice. And finally they voted for Attalus honours of a type and magnitude which they had hastily voted for no one of their previous benefactors. In addition to other honours they named a tribe for him and put him among the eponymous heroes. (Polybius 16.25.8–9)

Philip V invaded Attica and advanced as far as Cynosarges, which he burnt, as well as the Lyceum, also causing damage at Rhamnous and Brauron. 'He ordered that the sanctuaries of the gods which the Athenians had consecrated in the countryside be destroyed and burned... And Philip did not think it enough only to destroy the sanctuaries and overturn the statues; he ordered that even the individual blocks of stone be broken ... Afterward ... he withdrew into Boeotia and accomplished nothing else worth remembering in Greece' (Livy 31.26.9–13). Fields were burned, massive booty taken, temples and monuments destroyed, tombs uprooted and desecrated. This staggering destruction was largely irreparable and seems to have been the result of vindictiveness rather than any strategic policy.

Philip failed however to take Eleusis or Piraeus, and in succeeding years of the war Attica ceased to be a battleground as the war escalated into a conflict between Rome and Macedon. The Second Macedonian War was prosecuted for the Romans by Flamininus who arrived in Greece in 198, and concluded a peace with Macedon after the Battle of Cynoscephalae in 196, proclaiming the 'freedom of the Greeks' at the Isthmian Games that year. Athens meanwhile carried out a systematic *damnatio memoriae* of the Macedonian rule, abolishing the Macedonian tribal names and destroying statues and inscriptions of Demetrius Poliorcetes and his successors.

THE KINGS OF PERGAMON

The international scene had altered with the rise of new Hellenistic powers, including the maritime power of Rhodes and the realm of Antiochus III in Seleucid territory. The most important was Pergamon, which had become an independent kingdom after breaking away from the territory of Lysimachus in the early third century BC. Its kings, especially Attalus I and Eumenes II, aimed to make their capital a cultural centre to vie with Ptolemaic Alexandria. They established a library second only to that in Alexandria, and developed the use of parchment as a writing material (*pergamenon* in Greek) as an alternative to the Ptolemaic monopoly on papyrus. The presiding deity of the Library and associated cults was Athena, and the kings cultivated links with the acknowledged fountainhead of Greek culture, Athens. Attalus I visited Athens three times in 199 and 198.

George Finlay scorned the influence of the Attalids in Athens: 'In Athens bad government, social corruption, literary presumption, and national conceit, were nourished by liberal donations from foreign princes, who repaid base flattery by feeding a worthless city population' (*Greece under the Romans* 69). But these rulers, like the Athenians themselves, revered the city's glorious past and assisted it in becoming the cultural centre it was to remain now that its political power was gone.

Soon after Attalus I's (241–197) defeat of the Gauls in the 230s, an immense series of sculptures of defeated Gauls was set up in the sanctuary of Athena at Pergamon, and a group celebrating the same victories was also set up at Athens on the Acropolis: 'they represent the legendary war of the giants, the fight of the Athenians with the Amazons, the battles with the Medes at Marathon, and the destruction of the Gauls in Mysia' (Pausanias 1.25.2). Eumenes II, the son of Attalus I, provided Athens with a long stoa to the west of the Theatre of Dionysus, which was designed to provide shelter for those attending the festivals (Vitruvius 5.9.1). The blocks and capitals are of Pergamene marble, carved in Pergamon and shipped to Athens ready for assembly. At the same time a high statue base was erected on the left of the Propylaea (opposite the Temple of Nike) to support statues of Attalus and Eumenes. (This base was re-used in Roman times for a statue of Agrippa). Eumenes' brother, Attalus II, who became king in 159, had studied in Athens under the Stoic philosopher Carneades. His gift to Athens was the stoa that bears his name, on the east side of the Agora, which has been reconstructed by the American School and is used as a museum and offices. It is possible that the stoas of Attalus and Eumenes were both designed by the same architect, as their plans are very similar.

King Antiochus IV Epiphanes of Syria (175–164) also made benefactions to Athens. He renewed works on the temple of Olympian Zeus, which had been left unfinished since the days of Pisistratus. Most of the structure planned by Antiochus was built, at least up to architrave level. It was 110m by 43 m and consisted of a forest of 104 columns: the centre was probably hypaethral (open to the sky). But work was abandoned again when Antiochus died in 164. Though the temple was only completed by Hadrian three hundred years later, the remains that now stand probably belong for the most part to Antiochus' building.

Other kings also made endowments. An unidentified building was the gift of Pharnaces of Pontus in the 180s. A son of the king of

The Temple of Olympian Zeus

Numidia came to Athens to take part in the horse race at the Panathenaea (which he won). These diplomatic contacts, though admira-
tion for Athens surely played a part, may also have had economic
motives. Athens with its port of Piraeus remained an important dis-
tribution centre for grain throughout the Mediterranean, and J. Day
argued in his *Economic History of Athens* that such considerations were
important to the new smaller kingdoms of the late hellenistic world.
The Attic festivals became steadily more international, and these, like
the philosophical schools, attracted many foreigners. The students at
the schools also enhanced civic life by entering the ephebate.

The erection of so many large buildings changed the face of what had
become, in the third century, a rather run-down urban landscape. The
agora itself took on a new articulation and began to resemble the agoras
of the great Hellenistic cities of Asia Minor, regular in form and surrounded with shady colonnades. The Stoa of Attalus was balanced on
the west by the Metroon, which incorporated an archive building and
was remodelled about this time, as well as the older Temple of Apollo
Patroos. With the gymnasia founded in the later third century, these
new buildings gave Athens the face of an ancient town, indeed, but one
with great cultural and educational institutions in a flourishing state.

The 'Tower of the Winds' in the Roman Agora, correctly known as
the Horologium of Andronikos Kyrrhestes, may belong also to the

mid-second century, as the letter forms resemble those on the Stoa of Attalus (though the standard view places it a century later, in the triumviral period). Its octagonal ground plan recalls that of the Pharos of Alexandria, which was likewise decorated with Tritons (the Horologium had one on top, as a weather vane). The eight sides bear sculptures of the eight winds in their appropriate directions, and the whole functioned as a grand weather vane with incorporated sundial and, inside, a water clock.

Rome Conquers Macedon

In 171 the Third Macedonian War broke out: Rome's adversary was now Philip V's successor, Perseus (since 179), who was to be the last king of Macedon. The battle of Pydna in 168 brought an end to Macedonian power and the region came under Roman control. In the autumn of 168, the victorious Roman general Aemilius Paullus made a visit to Athens (Livy 45.27.11–28.1, Plut. Aem. 28.1–2, Polyb. 30.10.3–6). Rome admired the cultural heritage of Athens, and was no doubt impressed by the attention lavished on it by the kings of Pergamon and Syria. The kings, however, began to represent a threat to Rome, and had to be brought down a peg or two; Athens, by contrast, could never win sufficient power to stand against Rome, and could be given more lenient treatment. The Roman senate granted them the restitution of the islands of Delos, Lemnos, Imbros and Scyros, and also awarded them the city of Haliartus, even though it lay in Boeotian territory. Piraeus/Athens also became a free port from 166, a move intended to neutralise the commercial and political power of Rhodes: Rhodian harbour dues sank as a result from one million drachmas to 150,000, and Athens must have seen much of the gain from Rhodes' loss. Athens' position was considerably strengthened, and under Roman protection it, and the rest of Greece, enjoyed peace for almost a century.

ATHENIAN PROSPERITY

Delos was now developed as a trading centre for the eastern Mediterranean. Athenians provided the administrators and rulers, the market overseers and gymnasiarchs, and Athenian cleruchs settled on the island

and became the nucleus of a trading class. Banks and temples were founded. The cults were opened to foreigners and new cults were established including one of the Egyptian Sarapis. A great deal of building work dates from this period of Athenian control, including the portico of 166–50 and the agora of Theophrastus (126–5). Delian and Athenian trade benefited further from the Roman destruction of Corinth in 146 and the creation of Provincia Asia in 133. Many Italian merchants and bankers settled in Delos, as well as traders from Pontus, Syria and Egypt (their dedications to the kings survive), and guilds of merchants from Tyre and Beirut, who brought their cult of Ba'al, identified with Zeus Cynthios. The commodities included not only staples but luxury goods, the silks, spices and perfumes of the east and, not to be forgotten, slaves. Strabo at the end of the first century BC reckoned that 10,000 slaves per day changed hands on Delos.

The second century saw a transformation in the status of Athens which had been begun by the benefactions of the Hellenistic kings. The Parthenon was repaired in 160, the Piraeus theatre in 150; a new statue of Athena Parthenos was dedicated. Such was the prestige of Athens that it was often asked to act as a mediator in inter-state disputes. An inscription of the Amphictyons of 117/16 BC (IGII-2 1134) is a virtual 'panegyric of Athens' (Habicht 278); the people are 'the origin of all good things among mortals; it led men out of a brutish life to gentleness, became the cause of community between fellow-men by the tradition of the Mysteries ... introduced the laws of the god and standards of education, created the competitive festivals of artists and the theatre ... and is recognised as the mother-city of all dramas both tragedy and comedy'. The Panathenaea became an international festival, not just a state celebration.

Athens developed strong links with Delphi in the 140s, and staged elaborate processions there in 138, 128, 106 and 98, which culminated in musical and dramatic performances. Such sacred embassies were a frequent feature of Hellenistic city life, especially in the kingdoms of Asia Minor; inscriptions give us a vivid insight into this particular celebration on the Greek mainland. The guild of the Artists of Dionysus now really came into its own: similar guilds were also established in Alexandria and in Pergamon. They combined the functions of medieval guilds with those of Oxbridge colleges and cathedral dean-and-chapters: their members became immensely powerful and besides their sacred functions they acted as banks, giving loans to members; as ambassadors for inter-state missions; as dining clubs and research centres; and of course as schools for musical and dramatic education. The celebration of the Pythia of 128 included the performance of a newly composed paean to Apollo by the Athenian Limenius. This is one of very few pieces of ancient Greek music to have survived, with its notation: it is inscribed on the south wall of the Athenian treasury at Delphi. Though details of the interpretation of the notation are uncertain, it has nevertheless been reconstructed with sufficient plausibility to allow modern performance and recording.

Athens had minted no coinage from 183 to 164. In the latter year a new series was begun which continued almost unbroken to the year 77 BC. These attractive silver tetradrachms bear a head of Athena on the obverse, and on the reverse the famous Athenian owl that had characterised the great fifth-century coinage. The coinage became a standard throughout the Greek world. The source of the silver is a puzzle, since the mines at Laurion can no longer have been very productive. However, slave revolts at Laurion in 134/3 and 104–100 suggest that the city was attempting to extract the maximum from declining lodes. Another source of silver may have been Macedonian bullion, spoils of the war, that was melted down and re-used.

In the 160s a territorial dispute became the occasion of the first visit of Athenian negotiators to Rome. Athens had laid claim to Oropos on the north-east frontier of Boeotia and Africa; when Rome instructed Sicyon to arbitrate, the Sicyonians rejected the Athenian claim. Athens appealed direct to Rome, and the embassy was composed of the most distinguished philosophers of the day: Carneades of the Academy, Critolaus of the Peripatos and Diogenes of Babylon, a Stoic. The appearance of these eminent intellectuals in the senate was a shock to Rome: Cato denounced their public demonstrations of rhetoric and argument, particularly when Carneades spoke on one side of a debate about the place of justice in international relations on one day, and on the other side the next. This visit was still remembered a century later, when Cicero wrote to his friend Atticus asking for details about it; it had marked an epoch in Rome's own cultural development, and introduced the blunt Romans to the cleverness and sophistication of Greece – the beginning of the process Horace neatly summed up as *Graecia capta ferum victorem cepit*, 'Captive Greece took its savage conqueror captive.'

The dispute over Oropos dragged on for some time, but eventually Oropos was freed from Athenian control in 152. Only a few years later, in 146, a more momentous event was the Roman sack of Corinth. The Roman governor of Macedonia was extending his control to the south and met with fierce resistance from the Achaean League. In the aftermath its chief city Corinth was destroyed; the commander, L. Mummius, looted its greatest art treasures and passed on others to its allies, while lesser works of art were simply destroyed by the soldiery. This shock to Greek relations with Rome did not augur well for the future, despite its presumed benefits to Athenian trade, and Athens was to be directly affected half a century later when she once again chose the wrong side in Rome's war with Mithridates of Pontus.

The bright picture of Athenian prosperity painted above should be set against a startling passage in Polybius' history (36.17), which probably refers to the period after 146. He regards the Macedonian wars as having brought widespread death and discontent, all of which became even worse after Rome assumed control. While Rome could not be blamed for the natural disasters he enumerates – snow, drought, blight of crops – he also refers to a severe decline in population. Many cities became deserted. Economic difficulties led people to kill their new-born children rather than go to the expense of raising them. There should be a law against it, Polybius says. All this suggests widespread suffering in Greece generally, and probably marked class divisions; Athens was, for the time being, one of the lucky ones.

CHAPTER SEVEN

Athens under Roman Rule
86 BC–AD 19

The first century BC opened with Athens positively disposed to Rome. Decrees referred to Rome as 'benefactors of the people', and before 88 BC a special podium was erected in the agora in front of the Stoa of Attalus, for the use of Romans when they visited the city. Not all Romans came to make speeches; before 129 BC Q. Caecilius Metellus attended lectures at the Academy for a prolonged period, and another Roman, Titus Albucius, became an adherent of the Epicurean school and an enthusiast for all things Greek: he arranged a reception for a visiting praetor, Q. Mucius Scaevola, in which all the proceedings were in Greek.

If Rome was well-disposed to Athens, this probably had social consequences within the city. Our sources for the period from 110 to 86 are very sketchy, but it seems that in 106-100 there was some kind of social revolution at Athens. The rich, very probably with Roman support, established an oligarchic government. Appointment to office by lot was abolished, the *euthune* or public examination of magistrates' actions and accounts was abolished. At the same time there was a reform of weights and measures, probably designed to stop the circulation of counterfeits. In 91 this oligarchy developed into dictatorship. A certain Medeius was archon for three years running. Restrictions were placed on public assembly, on the philosophical schools, and on cult activity.

Social tensions in Athens were catalysed as a result of the expansionist policy of Mithradates VI of Pontus. The kingdom of Pontus, in northern Asia Minor, had been established soon after the death of Alexander the Great. When Mithradates VI succeeded to the throne in

Mithradates VI

120 BC, he began to extend his power not only in the Black Sea area and in Cappadocia, but also westwards into Phrygia, where he came into conflict with Rome, who claimed Asia as a Roman province. His army fought westward to the Aegean in 89/8, receiving a welcome from some cities, but subduing others by force. Among the latter was Ephesus, the capital of the Roman province of Asia, where 80,000 Romans were slaughtered in a single day by Mithradates' forces. His successes were striking, and oracles began to predict the imminent fall of Rome.

In spring 88 the news of Mithradates' successes reached Athens and caused great excitement. The Athenians sent a delegation to the king led by Athenion, an Aristotelian philosopher, who brought back letters from the king promising an end to civil strife, a democratic constitution and a solution to pressing debt problems. Roman tax collectors were also never popular. Dazzled by these promises, and seeing Mithradates as the bringer of freedom to all the Greeks, the Athenians threw in their lot with Mithradates and broke with Rome.

The philosopher Posidonius wrote a scathing description of Athenion's arrival in Athens:

> (The Athenians) sent warships and a silver-footed litter to escort him home... Practically the greatest part of the city had poured out for his

reception; and running with them to join them were many other spectators wondering at the paradox of fortune, when the illegally enrolled Athenion is conveyed to Athens on a silver-footed couch with scarlet coverings, a man who had never before seen scarlet on his scholar's gown, when not even one single Roman had insulted Attica with such a presentation of effeminate luxury... The pauper who had held subscription lectures now because of the King farts his way arrogantly through town and country. He was met by the Dionysiac artists, who invited him as the envoy of the 'new Dionysus' to their public dinner complete with prayers and libations. And the man who in earlier days had stepped out of rented accommodation, was escorted to the house of Dies, a gent grown rich with the times from business interests at Delos, a mansion sumptuously fitted out with rugs, paintings, statuary and silver plate. (*History* fragment 36 Jacoby, 253 Kidd; tr. I.G. Kidd)

The population was divided, and many pro-Roman citizens now left Athens, including the head of the Academy, Philo of Larissa, who made for Rome. For people like this, who had benefited from Roman rule, Athenion was no more than a populist tyrant: his supporters, however, included members of all classes, as well as the influential guild of the Artists of Dionysus. His rule soon became a tyranny:

Not many days passed before our philosopher revealed himself as tyrant (displaying the doctrine of the Pythagoreans on treachery). Straight away our tyrant, in defiance of the principles of Aristotle and Theophrastus (how true the proverb that says, 'don't give a knife to a child'), started by immediately getting right-thinking citizens out of the way; and he stationed a guard on the gates, so that many Athenians, worried for the future, escaped by letting themselves down over the walls. Athenion sent cavalry after them, slew some and brought others back prisoners... He started to confiscate the property of many. And he sent out as well into the country men to act like highwaymen against any who were trying to leave; they brought them back before him, and he tortured, racked and made away with them without trial... He created in the city a shortage of even the basic necessities of life, and rationed barley and wheat in small quantities... He imposed a curfew ... with no going about outside even with a lantern permitted. (ibid)

Athenion sent an emissary, Apellicon of Teos, to Delos to take hold of the treasure in the temple of Apollo. However, a Roman squadron pre-empted him and destroyed his forces, cutting down about 600 of them like sheep and taking 400 prisoners. Apellicon fled, but 'Orbius noticed a mass of Athenians taking refuge in farmhouses and cremated the lot, including their siege engines' (Posidonius, ibid). Mithradates' general Archelaus now occupied Delos and the other Aegean islands, and killed all the Romans he could find – it was said as many as 20,000. Archelaus took the treasure and sent it to Athens in the keeping of a force of 2,000 soldiers led by the Athenian Aristion. With the support of these troops, Aristion disposed of Athenion (no source tells us what happened to him) and became tyrant in his stead. Aristion was a philosopher, too, this time an Epicurean, so once again Athens experienced the rule of a 'philosopher-king', which however fell far short of the Platonic ideal. Plutarch wrote with him of contempt (*Sulla* 13): 'his spirit was compounded of licentiousness and cruelty; he had made himself a sink for the worst of the diseases and passions of Mithradates'.

Aristion became Archelaus' second-in-command, and Piraeus the latter's headquarters. When the Roman army under Sulla's command arrived, Athens was in the eye of the storm. Sulla laid siege to the Piraeus with great siege engines which, according to Plutarch, required ten thousand pairs of mules to operate them. Some of the siege engines broke under the onslaught, or were burnt by enemy fire, so that to replace them Sulla turned to the groves of the Academy and Lyceum, the most wooded parts of the suburbs, for timber. He also requisitioned the treasures of Delphi and Olympia to meet his expenses.

Plutarch wrote that Sulla 'was possessed by some dreadful and inexorable passion for the capture of Athens, either because he was fighting with a sort of ardour against the shadow of the city's former glory, or because he was provoked to anger by the scurrilous abuse which had been showered from the walls upon himself and Metella by the tyrant Aristion, who always danced in mockery as he scoffed' (*Sulla* 13). The effect of the siege on Athens was severe. The price of wheat rocketed, and the inhabitants made themselves stews of the herbs that grew wild on the slopes of the Acropolis; they boiled up old shoes and leather water flasks to eat; but all the while Aristion was dancing and joking, and even allowed the lamp of the goddess to go out for lack of oil. He mocked the goddess as much as he did the enemy.

Sulla, at least, was not to be mocked, and soon his troops entered the city. The first place at which the wall was scaled was the Heptachalcon, somewhere between the Piraeus Gate and the Dipylon Gate; the wall was soon thrown down, and at midnight as 1 March began the Roman army poured in, trumpets and bugles blaring, the soldiers shouting out for plunder and slaughter and running amok with swords drawn. 'There was no counting of the slain, but their numbers are to this day determined only by the space that was covered with blood. For without mention of those who were killed in the rest of the city, the blood that was shed in the market-place covered all the Ceramicus inside the Dipylon gate; nay, many say that it flowed through the gate and deluged the suburb' (*Sulla* 14).

Aristion was besieged on the Acropolis but forced to surrender by lack of water. He first burnt the Odeion of Pericles to prevent its huge roof timbers being used by Sulla for siege weapons. Sulla himself fired most of the Piraeus, including the arsenal of Philo (ca 330–29 BC). There was heavy destruction on the western and southern sides of the agora; Roman soldiers destroyed the shields in the Stoa of Zeus Eleutherios which functioned as memorials of earlier wars. The Pompeion was razed, suffering a bombardment of catapult stones (which have been found there), presumably because of its proximity to the city gate. But once the conquest was over Sulla professed clemency and 'forgave a few for the sake of the many, the living for the sake of the dead' (*Sulla* 14).

This clemency did not prevent him from extensive looting, both indiscriminate and deliberate. Besides quantities of gold and silver, the Roman army removed statues of bronze and marble, amphoras and glass. It has been thought that the contents of two ancient wrecks, one near the island of Anticythera and the other from Mahdia in Tunisia, consisted of booty from Sulla's sack, but this cannot be substantiated. Numerous hoards of coins that were buried in this year, and never recovered, testify both to the rapacity of the soldiery and to the loss of life among the Athenians. One cache that escaped the Romans' attention was in a warehouse in Piraeus, burnt during the siege, which contained five life-size bronze statues of gods, probably brought from Delos by Aristion with the rest of the temple treasure.

One of the most notable pieces of booty was the library of Aristotle.

According to Strabo, these books, which had been in the possession of Theophrastus, and augmented by his own collection, had passed to Theophrastus' heir, Neleus. The latter's heirs, 'common people', hid them in an underground place where they suffered from damp, to prevent them from being seized by the King of Pergamum for his library. Much later, they were acquired by Apellicon of Teos (mentioned above as Athenion's emissary to Delos). Being a bibliophile rather than a scholar, Apellicon had copies made, but many of the gaps in the damaged manuscripts were incorrectly restored, so that when published the editions were full of mistakes. Apellicon now died, and Sulla had them taken to Athens where they were copied again. It was not until a generation later that they came into the hands of the Greek grammarian Tyrannion, who was able to have them properly edited. The story is a vivid illustration of the chances and vagaries of the preservation of ancient literature.

Despite the removal of so much loot, Sulla ordered his soldiers not to destroy buildings after the conquest, and took credit in his memoirs for saving Athens from annihilation. Pausanias however said that his cruelty was excessive (I.20.7).

The Sullan Constitution

Sulla's war against Mithradates was concluded in summer 85, and a year later the Athenians were honouring Sulla as a 'liberator' from the 'tyrants' Athenion and Aristion. A new festival, the Sylleia, was established in his honour. In this year he was initiated in the Eleusinian Mysteries.

A new constitution was imposed on Athens. Though it continued to feature the same officials as previously, it became more oligarchic on the preferred Roman model. From this period all known decrees are in the name of the council alone, and not of the assembly as well. The archons became gradually more eminent under Roman rule: the archonships were held by leading citizens and were important as much for liturgies as for any administrative function. There was no thought of restoring selection by lot on the old democratic principle. The eponymous archonship was at one time held by Tiberius Claudius the hierophant 'for a medimnos and 15 drachmas'. The archons seem to have been assimilated in some way to the role held by consuls at Rome. The Council corresponded to the Senate; and the council of the Areopagus became more important in the running of the city than it had been heretofore, though its exact functions, and its constitutional relation to the boule and demos, are obscure.

Athens had become poor as a result of its losses under Sulla. The continued possession of Delos was of little help now that its treasures were gone, and it was no longer a major centre for trade. The availability of slaves had been much reduced since Marcus Antonius (father of the famous Mark Antony) had cleared the seas of pirates in 102 BC. The island was sacked by Mithradates in 69 and only restored in 58, but by then the *negotiatores* had packed up and left. (In the course of time they resettled in Athens.) The Athenians were apparently forced to sell the island of Salamis to make ends meet. They also seem to have lost the control of a number of other islands, which were only restored to them in the 40s by Mark Antony. The Pompeion was repaired in the 60s through a gift of Ariobarzanes II, the king of Cappadocia, but no other rebuilding took place in Athens for 25 years: the post-war cityscape of shattered ruins must have been a pitiful environment, though the major monuments of the Acropolis were undamaged.

At about the same time the Roman governor of Cilicia, Appius Claudius Pulcher, paid for the erection of a magnificent Propylon to the sanctuary at Eleusis. It was adorned with a frieze representing Eleusinian motifs such as grain and baskets, and on the interior wall two splendid Caryatids with baskets of the earth's gifts on their heads faced towards the telesterion. One of these was removed in the nineteenth century by the traveller Edward Daniel Clarke, who found it buried in a dunghill: the inhabitants swore that the fertility of their fields depended on it, but Clarke removed it nonetheless to the Fitzwilliam Museum in Cambridge. Its pair, much better preserved, was excavated later and is now in the Museum at Eleusis.

Athens suffered further depredations from other Roman governors, notably Verres (the object of a series of famous prosecution speeches by Cicero) and Piso. The city was reduced to borrowing from the pirates who were again becoming a menace in the eastern Aegean and were only finally cleared by Sextus Pompey in 67 BC. It seems that sometimes the only thing that kept it going was benefactions by wealthy Romans. Pompey the Great, for example, gave 50 talents in the 60s, a good deal of which went on refurbishing the Piraeus: the harbour was important to the Romans. Another notable benefactor was Titus Pomponius Atticus, the friend and correspondent of Cicero.

ATTICUS AND CICERO

Atticus had arrived in Athens soon after Sulla's sack, at the age of 24. He already had business interests in other parts of Greece, and apparently saw in Athens a favourable arena for his activities. In addition to that, he was plainly attracted to the city for its beauties and its reputation, which resulted in his acquiring the nickname or cognomen Atticus. He spoke Greek like a native. According to his biographer, Nepos, he benefited from the depressed state of the Athenian economy. The city frequently needed to borrow money, and the rates charged by Roman money-lenders were steep. By undercutting them, Atticus attracted business and was still able to make a good profit. He turned his wealth to the benefit of his adopted city and more than once (for example in 50) bought up grain stores and donated them to the hungry city. A philanthropist and also a philosopher, he was drawn to the Epicurean school but adhered to none.

He acted as a host to the young politician and orator M. Tullius Cicero when he first visited Athens in 79. Cicero later wrote, in *de finibus* V.1–2, of their walks in the Academy accompanied by Cicero's brother Quintus and cousin Lucius.

> We arranged to take our afternoon stroll in the Academy, chiefly because the place would be quiet and deserted at that hour of the day. Accordingly at the time appointed we met at Piso's lodgings, and starting out beguiled with conversation on various subjects the three-quarters of a mile from the Dipylon Gate. When we reached the walks of the Academy, which are so deservedly famous, we had them entirely to ourselves, as we had hoped. . . . [Piso remarks] the garden close at hand not only recalls Plato's memory but seems to bring the actual man before my eyes. This was the haunt of Speusippus, of Xenocrates, and of Xenocrates' pupil Polemo, who used to sit on the very seat we see over there.

Cicero was temperamentally more drawn to the Platonic philosophy than Atticus, but the two remained lifelong friends, and Cicero's correspondence with Atticus is one of the fullest and most vivid sources on the politics and atmosphere of the triumviral period.

Cicero attended lectures of philosophers at this time (*de leg.* 2.36), especially of Antiochus of Ascalon, the head of the Academy, and was also initiated into the Eleusinian Mysteries. (But as an old man, he lamented that 'at Athens the learning of the Athenians themselves has long since perished, and in that city there remains only the dwelling of those studies which citizens ignore and only foreign visitors enjoy, captured somehow by the name and reputation of the city' – *de oratore* 3.43.) Nearly thirty years later, in June 51, when Cicero, now an ex-consul and one of the most distinguished men in Rome, was on his way to take up the governorship of Cilicia, he wrote to Atticus of his stop in Athens:

> no private individual or public body has been put to expense on my account or that of any member of my staff. We take nothing under the lex Julia or as private guests. All my people recognize that they must be careful of my good name. . . . I have greatly enjoyed Athens, so far as the city is concerned and its embellishments and the affection the people have for you, the good will they seem to have for me. But many things have changed, and philosophy is all at sixes and sevens, anything of value being represented by Aristus [later head of the Academy] with whom I am staying.

ATHENS IN THE ROMAN CIVIL WARS

Cicero's career coincided with the long period of the Roman civil wars in which two successive triumvirates first combined and then clashed. The first Triumvirate, of Pompey, Caesar and Crassus (formed in 60), developed after the death of Crassus in 53 into the civil war begun when Caesar crossed the Rubicon early in 49. After Pompey's defeat, Caesar became master of Rome and eventually dictator, being assassinated in March 44 BC. His adoptive son Octavian and his second-in-command Mark Antony soon defeated the ringleaders of the assassination, Brutus and Cassius, at Philippi, but quickly became rivals for the succession, and the third member of the Triumvirate, Lepidus, was unable to hold the balance between them. Antony's power base was in the east, above all in Egypt where his liaison with Cleopatra was notorious, and where he styled himself a 'New Dionysus'. The final clash between Antony and Octavian came at the battle of Actium in 31 BC, when Antony's and Cleopatra's fleet was routed. Octavian became master of the Roman world and soon, under the new name of Augustus, the first of the Roman emperors.

These dramatic events had a direct impact on Athens, as on every other Greek city. In 58 a law passed by the tribune Publius Clodius allotted large new provinces to each of the two consuls of the year; L. Calpurnius Piso (Cicero's father in law) was given Macedonia, which was to include Athens and Attica. Athens' sovereignty was simply sidelined and the city became a vassal of Rome. The aim seems to have been, in part, to enable Roman creditors to pursue their debtors in Greek cities more effectively.

When the civil wars broke out in 49, much of the fighting took place in Greece. Pompey's main support was in Greece, and Athens, like other Greek cities, found itself on the losing side as it had in the conflict between Mithradates and Sulla. Athens surrendered immediately after Caesar's victory at Pharsalus. Caesar asked their delegates, 'How often do you expect to be rescued from the ruin you bring on yourselves by the fame of your forefathers?' (App. BC 2.368). The Athenians, let off lightly, dedicated a statue to him. Five years later, in summer 44 BC, the tyrannicides Brutus and Cassius were in Athens to mobilise Greece. Again the Athenians found themselves on the wrong side, even erecting statues of Brutus and Cassius. After the defeat of the liberators at Philippi in October 42 Mark Antony spent the rest of the year in Greece, mostly at Athens. He favoured the city because of its cultured past, and called himself a 'friend of Athens'; he attended the lectures of philosophers and the athletic contests. He added several islands to its territories, including Aegina, Ikos, Ceos, Skiathos and Peparethos.

Throughout the 40s intellectual life continued vigorously at Athens. Cicero's son Marcus studied there under Cratippus, a Peripatetic who had begun as an Academic, and whom Cicero regarded as the best philosopher in Athens; another student was the poet Horace: 'good Athens added a little sophistication [to my Roman education], such as the skill of telling a straight line from a curve, and the search for truth in the groves of the Academy' (*Epistles* 2.2.43–5). Another poet, Propertius, tried to escape an unhappy love affair by a turn of study in Athens: 'In Plato's school and Epicurus' garden I may begin to enlarge my wisdom and reap learned Menander's fruit, and I will undertake rhetoric, the sword of Demosthenes. Of course I will take in the great paintings and please my eyes with the bronzework and the ivory' (*Poems* 3.21, tr. J.P. McCulloch). Ovid, too recalled his student days in Athens as he languished in exile by the Black Sea (*Tristia* 1.2.77–8). By now Athens had the reputation of a city 'from which humanity, learning, religion, crops, justice, laws arose and were spread to all lands' (Cicero, *pro Flacco* 62): its beauty had caused the gods to vie for it, and its antiquity was such that its inhabitants were born from its soil.

In 40 Antony returned to Athens. His wife Fulvia died that year and he married Octavian's sister Octavia, with whom he made Athens his principal residence from 39. When he declared himself the 'New Dionysos' and in that capacity took as his bride the goddess Athena, he was able to avoid bigamy by identifying Octavia with the city's patron goddess. It is said that he required a dowry of six million drachmas from his divine bride. If Antony liked to behave as if he were a Hellenistic monarch, it may be that details of the charges against him are exaggerated by the victors. Athens reluctantly offered honours to Antony's new paramour, Cleopatra, but they were not long to enjoy his favours, as the climax of the war with Octavian approached in 31. Bad omens multiplied: the figure of Dionysus in the Gigantomachy group given by the kings of Pergamon collapsed to the ground; and 'the same storm fell upon the colossal figures of Eumenes and Attalos [near the Propylaea], on which the name of Antony had been inscribed, and prostrated them, alone out of many' (Plutarch, *Antony* 60). After his victory at Actium, Octavian made straight for Athens and distributed grain and other aid. Though Athens had found itself on the wrong side for the fourth time in half a century, it was again treated leniently. Its punishment however included the removal of Aegina and Eretria from its control, and a prohibition on the sale of Athenian citizenship, which had been a lucrative sideline for the city. Antony's request to the victor that he might live out his life as a private citizen in Athens was refused; and he

period Roman leaders had sought influence and support by providing cash for such purposes. Cicero in 51 paid for the restoration of the house of Epicurus; soon afterwards, when Caius Memmius, Sulla's son in law, planned to build a palace for himself on the site of Epicurus' school, Cicero was able to deflect him from his plan at the request of the then head of the school (*Letters to his Friends* 13.1). Atticus' gifts of grain, the construction by Appius Claudius Pulcher of the new Propylaea at Eleusis, and Pompey's gift of 50 talents, have already been mentioned. Also in the 50s, the Odeion of Pericles, which had been burnt by Sulla, was restored by King Ariobarzanes II of Cappadocia. Julius Caesar, in the period of his ascendancy, began work on the Roman Agora, which was completed in the last decade of the century.

Soon after the battle of Actium a small circular Ionic temple was erected in honour of Rome and Augustus on the Acropolis, to the east of the Parthenon: because it names Augustus rather than Octavian, it must date from after 27 BC when Octavian adopted the new title. It was dedicated in the archonship of Areius, which fell between 27/6 and 18/7. It was the first dedication of the imperial cult in Athens, and may have been dedicated at the same time as the Attic decree was passed in 27/6 celebrating Augustus' birthday on 23 September.

The Roman Agora, completed under Augustus, was the largest construction Athens had seen since the Attalid buildings of the second century BC. It reflected the growing commercial importance of Athens and the need for the classical agora to be preserved as a ceremonial and religious centre. The Roman Agora is a large rectangular peristyle court with an Ionic gateway to the east and a Doric one to the west, facing the classical agora. The agora was dedicated, as the inscription on the west gate tells us, in the archonship of Nicias, probably in the year 11/10. It served as the main trading area of Athens, and in the second century AD Hadrian's edict on oil prices was inscribed on the western gateway. The dominant feature of the square at the present day, the Horologium of Andronikos Kyrrhestes, may have been erected at this time, if it is not a century older (see previous chapter). Behind the Tower is the *agoranomion*, the headquarters of the market supervisors. (A dedication to the deified emperor here has led some scholars to interpret it rather as a temple of the imperial cult.) The Roman Agora

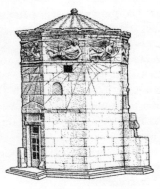

The 'Tower of the Winds'

continued in use as a market through the medieval and Ottoman periods after the classical agora had been built on many times.

The face of the classical agora also changed significantly during the reign of Augustus. The open square was gradually filled up with buildings and monuments, giving it a cluttered appearance resembling that of the Forum Romanum, a kind of archive of significant buildings. The Roman view of city politics did not include large public meeting places for the citizenry. In 15 BC a new *odeion*, or concert hall, was erected in the middle of the agora, where it dominated the entire area by its size. The dedication dates it to 15 BC: it was the contribution of Marcus Agrippa, Augustus' son in law and chief of staff. The building, with a marble paved orchestra, could seat a thousand people, and the exterior was decorated with columns of Pentelic marble. Agrippa received his own monument in gratitude; the statue base of Eumenes and Attalus on the Acropolis, which had been recycled in the 30s for Antony, was used again for Agrippa.

Besides the new building of the Odeion, a number of other buildings were relocated to the agora, chief among them the Doric temple of Ares of the fifth century BC, which had probably stood originally in Pallene (or Acharnae) and had been in honour of Athena, and which was now installed in front of the Odeion. An inscription in it honours Augustus' adopted son Gaius as 'the new Ares'; so this temple too may have been brought into the service of the imperial cult. Parts of the temples of Poseidon and Athena at Sounion were brought to the agora and re-used at this time, and four columns of the Doric stoa at Thorikos were reassembled in the agora (and later re-used again in the rebuilding of the city wall after AD 267). The despoliation of these outlying demes may argue some depopulation at the time. However, the temple of Nemesis at Rhamnous was refurbished, and rededicated to Augustus' wife, Livia, in AD 45/6, soon after her death. In addition, the temple of Zeus Agoraios was moved from the Pnyx (no longer needed for assemblies) to the vicinity of the Metroon.

The lower city was adorned with no fewer than thirteen altars of Augustus, and a statue of Livia as Artemis Boulaia. A double temple was erected as an annex behind the Stoa of Zeus Eleutherios. In addition, statues of prominent Romans sprang up like mushrooms. A later visitor was to remark that on visiting Athens you would find a population of statues more numerous than the flesh and blood inhabitants.

Athenian art and sculpture remained internationally famous. Sculpture of the period shows itself increasingly expert in portraits, a genre popular with the Romans with their cult of ancestors. At the same time there was a lucrative trade in archaising sculpture: Neo-Attic reliefs, replicating the style of the early fifth century BC, were exported in quantity to Italy to adorn the homes of wealthy Romans; some were wrecked before they got there, and there is a good collection in the Piraeus Museum.

One of the most startling events of this period in Athens was the self-immolation of an Indian philosopher called Zarmonochegas or something similar. He came from Barygaza (Broach) and was a member of a delegation to the Emperor Augustus from an Indian king (who sent him some tigers, which Romans had never seen before).

> One of the Indians, Zarmarus, for some reason wished to die, – either because, being of the caste of sages, he was on this account moved by ambition, or, in accordance with the traditional custom of the Indians, because of old age, or because he wished to make a display for the benefit of Augustus and the Athenians. . .; – he was therefore initiated into the Mysteries of the Two Goddesses [at Eleusis], which were held out of season on

account, they say, of Augustus, who was also an initiate, and then threw himself alive into the fire. (Dio Cassius 54.9.7–10)

The spectacle no doubt recalled the similar suicide of Calanus in Babylon, at the court of Alexander. Difficult to interpret, it nonetheless shows that the fame of Athens, and Eleusis, had reached as far as India.

Augustus visited Athens at least twice more before the end of his reign. In winter 22/21 he came to the city but was enraged by the reception the Athenians staged for him: the statue of Athena on the Acropolis, which faced east, turned to the west and seemed to spit blood. It was probably as punishment for this offence that he removed Athens' jurisdiction over Eretria and Aegina, and forbade the sale of citizenship. He refused to stay in Athens but passed the rest of the winter in Aegina. It was probably during this visit also that he met up with the poet Virgil, who was then in two minds whether he should allow his *Aeneid* to be preserved. One wonders if the poet had been influenced by evident anti-Augustan sentiment at Athens in the ambiguity of his portrait of Aeneas. (Horace addressed a poem to Virgil on his departure, a delicate prayer to Aphrodite and the Disocuri, gods of safe voyages, to protect Virgil on his journey, *animae dimidium meae*, 'half my soul'.) The poet and the emperor met for dinner at Megara – what they discussed is not recorded – and took ship for Italy, where Virgil died before reaching Rome.

Anti-Roman feeling seems to have continued in Athens, though the sources are not good. Late authors tell us that there was an actual revolt in AD 13, shortly before Augustus' final visit in 12 for the Panathenaea and the Mysteries. An imperial legate was sent apparently to quell the revolt, which may not have amounted to much. It was perhaps the last gasp of Athenian independence of spirit before knuckling under to the Roman Peace.

CHAPTER EIGHT

The Pax Romana,
AD 19–560

Athens from Tiberius to Trajan

Paul Graindor began his book on this period with the words 'From Tiberius to Trajan, the history of Athens is not marked by any striking event.' This may have been a blessing for the inhabitants, wearied with all too many events in the previous century. The imposition of the Roman Peace, the *Pax Romana*, ushered in several centuries in which civic life was able to develop and prosper undisturbed by internal wars. Virgil, whatever the ambiguities of his Aeneas as a front for Augustus, could see fulfilled the prophecy he had put in the mouth of Marcellus: 'These, Roman, will be your arts: to impose good customs on a world at peace, to show clemency to the defeated and to bring down the mighty.' Roman rule now stretched from the western shores of the European continent to the river Euphrates, and from the Rhine and Danube in the north to the Nile and the Sahara desert in the south. Of this vast empire, the largest and most culturally advanced part was the Greek world that shared the heritage of Alexander and his successors. Throughout Greece and Asia Minor, and even into Syria, Greek cities continued as qusai–autonomous bodies, minting coins and electing their own magistrates. As in the Hellenistic world, inter–city relations were maintained by constant sacred embassies and visits from theatrical and musical troupes to celebrate the festivals of the gods. The unity of this world under Rome was also expressed in religious terms, through the institution of the imperial cult.

Already in the Hellenistic world rulers had begun to receive worship as gods – first Alexander and the Ptolemies, and most notably

Demetrius at Athens when he was hailed as a present helper unlike the distant gods of traditional religion. The Roman emperors needed a way to establish an authority that transcended the civic loyalties of individual cities and enabled them to offer obedience to a higher power. For a Greek polis, the only thing higher could be a god, and thus the Roman emperors officially became gods in the Greek East, though at home they usually put off divinity until they had actually died. (As Vespasian said on his deathbed, 'Oh dear, I think I'm becoming a god'.) Throughout Greece and Asia Minor, temples of the imperial cult were rapidly established: as we have seen, the erection of a temple of Rome and Augustus was one of the first building projects after Actium, and many other temples were soon dedicated to the same use. Every succeeding emperor was to advance the imperial cult further, with increasingly colossal statues of the emperor in question (Domitian's at Ephesus must be a record-breaker), or uncountable numbers of merely life-size statues, like those of Hadrian at Athens.

The emperors of the first century AD did not much favour Athens with their presence, but they had an impact on the urban scene all the same. Most of the cities of the Roman empire underwent parallel architectural developments, not just in the erection of temples of the imperial cult, but in the building of streets and markets on a Roman plan. Claudius made restoration a matter of policy; in part this was reparation for the looting of the previous emperor, Caligula, and made a good propaganda point. Many religious sanctuaries were restored in his reign, notably on Salamis, which had now again become an Athenian possession after the wealthy Julius Nicanor of Hierapolis bought it and gave it back to Athens. Work to improve the ramp to the Propylaea is associated with the name of Tiberius Claudius Novius, an Athenian, in AD 42. A new marble staircase was built on the Colonus Agoraios, in front of the Temple of Hephaestus. These attempts to impose a Roman sense of order on a haphazard street plan were slight in comparison with what took place at, for example, Ephesus; but Ephesus was the capital of the Roman province of Asia, while Athens now had no political standing. (The Roman province of Achaea, in which Athens lay, had its headquarters in Patras.) The area south of the Acropolis became a luxury residential quarter at this time: the Metro excavations in Makriyanni have revealed several houses with atria, gardens and marble statues along the main street to the south.

The Emperor Nero, a Philhellene as well as a megalomaniac, visited Athens on his frequent journeys to Greece, at which he even competed in the Olympic Games. After he had murdered his mother, however, he was afraid to visit Athens for fear of bring pursued by the Furies, who in legend had hounded Orestes for a similar crime and had only been pacified after a trial before Athena who had given them a home below the Areopagus, the seat of justice (Dio Cassius 63.114). For similar reasons he would not visit Eleusis, unlike most other emperors. In 64 he looted a considerable quantity of works of art from Athens and was declared 'the new Apollo', for his own artistic achievements. (There may, however, have been as many as 3,000 statues remaining in Athens even after his depredations.) Nero was responsible for improvements to the Theatre of Dionysus, which was now used not just for dramas but for gladiatorial battles and beast shows. The orator Dio Chrysostom, who lived at the end of the first century, was shocked by this change of use: 'there is no practice current in Athens which would not cause any man to feel ashamed. For instance, in regard to the gladiatorial shows the Athenians have so zealously emulated the Corinthians. . . that. . . the Athenians look on this fine spectacle in their theatre under the very walls of the Acropolis. . . so that often a fighter is slaughtered among the very seats in which the hierophant and other priests must sit' (*Orations* 31.121). Nero left a memento of his visit in the inscription in bronze letters on the eastern architrave of the Parthenon; though it was soon removed after his suicide, the shadows of the letters can still be seen and read.

In the reign of Trajan (98–117) the face of Roman cities began to change again, with the introduction of colonnaded streets. These shady inducements to lingering, and shopping, in the city centre, are well preserved at such eastern cities as Djemila, Gerasa, Pergamon, Ephesus and Palmyra, and in Greece there is a notable one at Corinth. Athens too acquired such a street around AD 100, with the conversion of the Panathenaic Street, now lined with stoas from the Dipylon Gate to the agora (Pausanias 1.2.4, Himerius *Oration* 3.12). The southern colonnade ended behind the Stoa Basileios. In the years 98–102 an Athenian,

Titus Flavius Pantaenus, built the library that bears his name, complete with stoas and peristyle; as part of the exercise the whole area was remodelled, with a colonnade along the street leading to the Roman market, the continuation of a passageway between the northern end of the library and the southern end of the Stoa of Attalus. The exterior stairway of the Hellenistic stoa had to be dismantled, the area between the two buildings was paved with marble and marble facings were placed on the walls. Close by stood a shrine of Trajan dedicated by Herodes Atticus the elder. Such radical remodelling made Athens more orderly and more glorious.

Another major change to the Athenian cityscape came around 114–16, with the erection of the monument of Caius Julius Antiochus Philopappos. Philopappos, a descendant of the kings of Commagene, who had lost their throne in 72, had become an Athenian citizen and a benefactor of the city. The tomb, which stands on the Philopappos hill facing the south side of the Acropolis, dominates the skyline; it was adorned with statues of Philopappos and his ancestors in niches, and stood more or less intact until at least the fourteenth century when Cyriac of Ancona made a drawing of it. The blocks of the burial chamber beneath it were used in the Frankish tower on the Acropolis, demolished in the nineteenth century.

ST PAUL AND CHRISTIANITY

Paul's visit to Athens may be dated to around AD 51 (Acts 17.16–34). He arrived here in the course of his missionary journey across the eastern Roman empire, and, as we are told, made a speech about his new god and was put on trial before the Areopagus. The text tells us that Athens was the most religious city in the world – you could hardly move for statues of gods – yet his teaching was curiously ill-received. Various questions arise. Paul took his inspiration from a dedication 'To the Unknown God' to explain that this was the god whose gospel he brought. Yet no inscription in such terms has ever been found, at Athens or anywhere else in the Roman Empire. (In the Middle Ages, the Parthenon began to be referred to as the 'Temple of the Unknown God', as Symeon Kavasilas wrote to Martin Crusius in the fifteenth century.) If the inscription is not a fiction, it was very well found. The charge of introducing new gods was the same as that of which Socrates had been accused. The location of Paul's discourse is also unclear. Did he preach on the Rock of the Areopagus itself? Or, as is more likely, was he summoned to a closed hearing of the court of the Areopagus in its quarters in the Stoa Basileios? And what was the standing of the Areopagus in the matter? It is one of the few pieces of evidence we have for its function under the Roman Empire; if the story is historical, it appears that the Areopagus was not simply a homicide or supreme court, but had a kind of censorial function. In any case, his doctrine was found 'too absurd to offend' (Graindor) and he was released. According to tradition his audience included one Dionysius, who was converted to Christianity. He became the first bishop of Athens and is known as Dionysius Areopagiticus; he was for many years the patron saint of Athens. His successor as bishop, Publius, was martyred under Trajan and was succeeded by Quadratus who 'brought together the Athenians and rekindled their faith' from apostasy, as Eusebius wrote (*History of the Church* 4.23.6).

Another saint associated with Athens is the Apostle Philip, who is said to have spent two years in the city after the death of Christ. According to the Acts of Philip, the chief priest of the Jews followed him to Athens to engage in argument with him, whereupon Philip caused the ground in the agora to open up and swallow him. The spot was that where the Church of St Philip was subsequently built.

Later, in the reign of Hadrian, Eleusis was the scene of one of the earliest encounters between an emperor and a Christian preacher. Here Marcion (ca 100– ca 165) delivered his 'Apologia' for Christianity in the presence of the Emperor.

Hadrian and Athens

The greatest impact on the Athenian urban scene was due to the Emperor Hadrian (117–138). This cultivated and Philhellenic emperor spent much of his reign travelling continuously about his empire; wherever he went he endowed buildings and monuments, so that all the major cities of the east can boast significant changes dating from his reign. It has recently been calculated that he made more than 210

Hadrian's Arch

'interventions' in over 130 cities. His engineering projects throughout the empire included aqueducts, walls, stoas, granaries and at least twenty temples. Hadrian visited Athens three times, in 117, 124/5 and 132, though he had been eponymous archon as early as 111/12 or 112/13. He lavished especial attention on Athens as the fountainhead of Greek culture, though he also made major benefactions at Smyrna, where he once spent 10 million drachmas in a single day, and at Italica in Spain. His favour to Athens in part took the form of ensuring that his worship there was vigorously prosecuted. No fewer than ninety-four altars dedicated to Hadrian have been found at Athens. Most of his building works belong to his third visit, in 131/2, though a few can be definitely associated with the second visit, in 124/5.

Hadrian extended the boundaries of Athens by erecting an arch east of the Acropolis, with an inscription declaring, on the east side, 'This is Athens, the old city of Theseus' and on the west side, 'This is the city of Hadrian and not of Theseus.' The major monument east of the arch is the Temple of Olympian Zeus. This had been begun by Antiochus IV of Syria in the second century BC (though its foundations and beginnings went back to the fifth century); it was completed by Hadrian and dedicated, probably in his final visit in 132. It contained an ivory and gold colossal statue of Zeus, reviving a tradition of chryselephantine statuary that went back to Phidias in the fifth century BC, and was to be continued by Herodes Atticus in the next generation.

Another important foundation of Hadrian was the Panhellenion. No certain physical trace of the building has been found. A large basilica-like building east of the Roman agora is a likely candidate (there are some fragmentary foundations behind the taverna O Platanos), though an alternative is a small temple with a peristyle court south of the Temple of Olympian Zeus. Its function was as a meeting place of representatives of all the Greek cities. It was the ultimate development of the Hellenistic tradition of inter-city embassies, and in a sense the fulfilment of Isocrates' dream (in the fourth century BC) of a Greek world united under Athens' cultural leadership. An annual festival was associated with it, the Panhellenia, which was attended by cities of the Peloponnese, northern Greece, Asia Minor and even Cyrenaica. In addition there was a quinquennial Great Panhellenia. The *synedrion* of the Panhellenion had the power to issue decrees – but they all had to be communicated to the emperor for approval.

Hadrian also built the Pantheon (Paus. 1.18.9), which has not been identified. Some scholars have argued that it is identical with the Library of Hadrian, others that it is the basilica or temple east of the agora mentioned in the previous paragraph.

Other building works included the refurbishing of the Pnyx – presumably it was permitted again to hold public meetings there, and not in the theatre – improvement of streets and waterworks, notably the construction of an aqueduct which was not completed until the reign of Antoninus Pius, ca 140: it brought water from over 20 km away on Mt Parnes, whence it travelled through an underground tunnel under pressure to a reservoir on Mt Lycabettus, and from there was distributed throughout the city. Many baths buildings were constructed; Athens had more than 24 of them by the end of the second century.

Major works took place in the Theatre of Dionysus. The stage was raised in the Roman manner and its façade and the stage building were adorned with Dionysiac scenes and figures of Sileni, the half animal companions of Dionysus. Many of the seats in the theatre were inscribed with the titles of the priests for whom they were reserved – a vivid illustration of the number of cults active in Athens, since the list of titles occupies many lines of print.

Perhaps the most remarkable monument of Hadrian's reign is the Library of Hadrian. Much more than just a repository of books, it takes the form of a colonnaded courtyard (87 m × 125 m) with one hundred columns of Phrygian marble, resembling one of the imperial fora at Rome, and also Hadrian's own Traianeum at Italica. (Its resemblance to the Forum Pacis has led to the suggestion that it may be the 'Pantheon'.) Most of it is built of Pentelic marble (Hymettian had now fallen out of fashion) and the exterior wall is adorned with projecting columns of green Carystian marble, a new architectural feature. A series of rooms at the eastern end constitutes the library proper, the central one of which housed a statue of the presiding goddess Athena. (There was a similar arrangement in Hellenistic Pergamon.) Here the book scrolls were housed in specially designed niches. The presence of statues of *kosmetai*, trainers of ephebes, suggests an educational purpose for the building. The corner rooms were probably lecture halls, and the colonnades around the reflecting pool provided a space for philosophical discussion and reflection.

Hadrian also gave attention to the sanctuary at Eleusis, building a new Doric temple of Artemis there as well as erecting a number of arches, and a Propylaea that imitates that of the Acropolis. The emperor's bust (it is probably Hadrian, but may be a later bearded emperor) looms large in the centre of the pediment of the gateway. A new bridge on the Sacred Way leading to Eleusis was inaugurated in 125; and a new Pompeion, at the Athens end of the Sacred Way, was built to replace the old one, last restored in the 50s BC.

All these architectural improvements went alongside some important institutional changes at Athens. The constitution was revised, apparently to revive the old laws of Solon and Draco. The precise content of this revival is not known. Among other things a new tribe was created, named after the Emperor, but the number of Council members was reduced from 600 to 500. The Assembly began to meet again on the Pnyx, and decrees were now in the name, not of 'the people' or 'the Council' but of 'the whole city'. Another provision of the constitution is that Council members were forbidden to act as tax farmers. The reference to Solon may refer particularly to Solon's ban on the export of any products except olive oil. Hadrian interested himself in the oil trade, and his oil decree, inscribed on the jamb of the western gate of the Roman Agora, provides that one third of Attica's oil production must be sold to the state. Another decree regulates fish sales, exempting Eleusis fishermen from the 2-obol fish tax when they sell in the market at Eleusis. It became the task of the Areopagus to control profiteering by vendors, particularly at times when there was great pressure on the food supply, such as during the celebration of the Eleusinian Mysteries and other panhellenic festivals. Athens also became the recipient of a grain dole, a unique privilege as no city in the empire apart from the capital, Rome, received such a dole. These measures seem designed to reduce corruption and improve the prosperity of the city. Landholding remained largely in the hands of families (including numerous women), and estates were not formed into enormous *latifundia* as happened in Italy, for example.

Hadrian's measures to beautify and regulate the life of Athens were instrumental in turning it into the intellectual power house of the second century. The library acted as an encouragement to intellectual life, and the guild of the Artists of Dionysus received encouragement. In the succeeding century the philosophical schools became again a dominant feature of the city. While Athens became the Oxbridge or Harvard of the Roman Empire, one paradoxical result of Hadrian's philhellenic activities was that, through his extensive building programme, Athens became a thoroughly Roman city. Graindor concluded his study of Hadrian's Athens by suggesting that it was in fact Hadrian who in large measure created what Gibbon called the 'Golden Age of the Antonines'. A more caustic assessment was that of George Finlay, who saw the Greek cities as being drained of their wealth by the Roman Empire, and 'the most useful public works were neglected, except when a benevolent emperor like Hadrian, or a wealthy individual like Herodes Atticus, thought fit to direct some portion of their expenditure to what was useful as well as ornamental'. The truth, no doubt, lies somewhere in between.

PAUSANIAS

Soon after the death of Hadrian occurred the visit of Pausanias 'the *periegete*'. This visit is perhaps the most important single event for our knowledge of ancient Athens (and Greece), for Pausanias, who is otherwise unknown, was the author of a guidebook in ten books to the whole of classical Greece – that is, the Roman province of Achaea, including Attica, Boeotia, Phocis and the Peloponnese, but excluding Macedonia, north-east Greece and the islands. The visit can probably be dated in the 150s, because the account of Athens in Book I refers to the Odeion of Herodes Atticus as unfinished: it was completed in 160–70, so that at least his Attica book was complete at this time. It is a straightforward account of the buildings and monuments of every major and minor city in Greece, copiously enlarged with relevant historical accounts and mythological associations. It is arranged in the form of itineraries, so that with a few vantage points it is easy to reconstruct his route and to use his text to identify remains that emerge from the ground. His book was first so used by Colonel William Martin Leake, the indefatigable traveller who was sent to Greece in 1799 with the British military mission to Constantinople. In two visits in 1805–7 and 1809–10 he travelled through the whole of Greece reconstructing the topography of the classical world. In 1821 he published his two-volume work *The Topography of Athens* (second edition 1841), which included a complete translation of Pausanias' first book (Attica) plus a detailed discussion of every datum therein. Though since superseded, this work laid the foundations of the study of Athenian topography and thus influenced the course of archaeological exploration.

But what was Pausanias' own purpose? His book tells us nothing about his aims, his education or his connections, though we learn that he came from Ionia, nor about his proposed readership. It seems on the face of it that his book is simply an ancient version of a Baedeker or Blue Guide. Its literary pretensions are few and his historical judgments derivative. Yet a closer look reveals interesting traits. What Pausanias portrays is a Greece without a Roman presence. The historical touchstones are those of classical education ever since – the Battle of Marathon, the glories of Athenian democracy, the tragedy of

Chaeronea. So familiar are these attitudes that it is difficult to realise that Pausanias is one of the first exponents of them. He represents a vision of free Greece, the great classical past with Athens as its summit of achievement. The Roman conquest is something to be ignored – or forgotten – or perhaps to hide in shame. Yet this view of Greece and Athens is one that owed its existence to the attitudes of generations of Romans and the work of emperors like Hadrian. Perhaps it is wrong to make too strong an opposition between the Greek and the Roman view of Greece. An alternative interpretation stresses the religious aspects of Pausanias' work : it is a handbook for pilgrims to the great hellenic shrines. It would be rash to stress one of these views to the exclusion of others. Whether pilgrim or tourist, his readers (for we must assume that he had some) will have been educated Romans who shared his interest in the past glories of Greece (and perhaps had no need to be reminded of a Roman presence which they simply took for granted). But Pausanias' work is a harbinger of a movement of immense importance in the renaissance of Greek culture under Rome, known as the Second Sophistic.

Herodes Atticus

A second figure crucial in the development of Athens as a centre of the second century sophistic movement is the orator L. Vibullius Hipparchos Tiberius Claudius Atticus Herodes. His family, which claimed descent from Miltiades and Cimon and thence from the hero Theseus, had risen to prominence after Sulla's sack of the city. His great grandfather had been an acquaintance of Cicero and had been instrumental in persuading Julius Caesar to lend fifty talents to the city. His grandfather had reached the rank of a Roman knight, but his wealth, reckoned at 100 million sestertii, far outstripped the property qualification for that rank; even a senator was only required to hold 8 million sestertii, and 20 million was already super-rich. This Herodes had been put on trial under Domitian, for uncertain reasons, but it is clear that Domitian wanted to lay hands on his money. The family concealed much of his wealth by burying it on land that he owned; one should not minimise the scale of this task, since 20 million gold

Herodes Atticus

sestertii would weigh about three tons. Herodes was condemned but his fate is not known. In the succeeding reign of Nerva, the next Herodes (born ca 68) appealed to the emperor for a decision on what he should do with some money he had discovered buried on his land. Nerva decreed that he should keep the treasure; and thus the family fortune was restored.

This Herodes (the father of the great Herodes) pursued a distinguished career, being consul twice according to Philostratus, proconsul (governor) of Judaea, a priest of the Augusti under Hadrian and later priest of Olympian Zeus. He also acted as gymnasiarch in Sparta and gave gifts to Corinth. The source of this wealth which he used so beneficially seems to have been banking and land; he owned estates not only in Attica (at Marathon), but on Ceos and in Italy and Spain.

Herodes Atticus, the subject of our story, was born in 103. He was educated in Sparta and Athens and studied with some of the great rhetoricians of the day, including Secundus of Athens. Besides the properties we know he inherited from his father, Herodes also owned a number of marble quarries on Penteli and land from Marathon to Kifissia, at Markopoulo, Vari and Rhamnous, as well as on Euboea and Ceos and in Corinth. The Roman writer Aulus Gellius describes the conversations of the scholars and students at his country house in Kephissia:

> While we were students at Athens, Herodes Atticus, a man of consular rank
> and true Greek eloquence, often invited me to his country houses near that
> city, in company with the honourable Servilianus and several other of our
> countrymen who had withdrawn from Rome to Greece in quest of culture.
> And there at that time, while we were with him at the villa called Kephissia,
> both in the heat of the summer and under the burning autumnal sun, we
> protected ourselves against the trying temperature by the shade of its spa-
> cious groves, its long, soft promenades, the cool location of the house, its
> elegant baths with their abundance of sparkling water, and the charm of the
> villa as a whole, which was everywhere melodious with splashing waters and
> tuneful birds (*Attic Nights* I.2.1–2)

As a young man he was sent on a congratulatory embassy to Hadrian,
but got stage fright and dried up in mid-speech, after which he
attempted to drown himself in the Danube. Fortunately he did not
succeed. He was also connected with the distinguished Gaulish rhetorician, Favorinus of Arles, from whom he inherited both a library and
a slave.

Herodes followed the traditional *cursus honorum* of Roman officials.
He was eponymous archon of Athens in 126/7, at a remarkably young
age, and then proceeded to Rome where he became *decemvir stlitibus
iudicandis* (official with jurisdiction over punch-ups) in 128, quaestor in
129, tribune of the plebs in 131, praetor in 133. In 131/2 he was archon
of the newly founded Panhellenion in Athens, and in 134/5 he was
corrector in Asia, where he got to know the future emperor Antoninus
Pius, paid (with his father's help) for the building of a water supply and
baths in Alexandria Troas, and gave Polemo of Smyrna a quarter
million drachmas after hearing him lecture three times. About this time
Herodes senior died, bequeathing one mina (six drachmas) to every
Athenian citizen per annum for the rest of their lives. The younger
Herodes was enraged at this prodigality and bought himself out with a
one-off payment of five minas per head: the cost of this, with a citizen
population of ca 12,000, will have been 60,000 minas or one thousand
talents.

In 140 he was back in Athens and in charge of the Panathenaic
Games. Where most gymnasiarchs would pay for costumes and feasts,
Herodes decided to refurbish the entire stadium, cladding it in marble

throughout. He also provided the goddess with a magnificent new robe, and 'the ship, as it took its course [along the Panathenaic Way] was not hauled by animals but slid forward by means of underground machinery' (Philostratus, *Lives of the Sophists* 550). It sounds rather like a San Francisco cable car, but no remains of the machinery have been found.) He then went to Rome and became tutor to Antoninus Pius' son, Marcus Aurelius, a post he probably held until 146 and which put him among the highest in the empire. He was consul in 143, and Marcus' other tutor, Fronto, was consul suffect (i.e. consul for the later part of the year, a less distinguished post as the year was named after the first pair of consuls). His other pupils included Marcus' brother Lucius Verus and the orator Aelius Aristides.

He was married by 142 to a lady named Regilla who owned property on the Appian Way (a palace at the third milestone); he gave her a villa of her own in Attica adjoining his own. Returning to Greece he became a master builder throughout the land. He rebuilt the Panathenaic Stadium in marble between 139/40 and 143/4: now used for gladiatorial games, its capacity of 50,000 was as great as that of the Colosseum at Rome. He paid for the rebuilding of the stadium at Delphi and developed a plan to build a canal through the Isthmus of Corinth, which was however never fulfilled. Herodes felt that all his other achievements – his speeches, his honours, his buildings – were only ephemeral; 'but the cutting of the Isthmus is a deathless achievement and more than one would credit to human powers, for in my opinion to cleave through the Isthmus calls for Poseidon rather than a mere man' (Philostratus, *Lives of the Sophists* 552).

One of Herodes' Attic estates has been excavated between Marathon and Oenoe, at a place known as Mandra tis Grias (the old woman's sheepfold): the identification is certain because a number of portraits of Herodes and members of the imperial family were found in the same area early in the nineteenth century; and further inland an arch inscribed as the 'Gate of Immortal Harmony' informs us that it is the boundary between Herodes' estate and Regilla's; the arch also carries poems of mourning at Regilla's death (now in Marathon museum).

Herodes' life was marked by tragedy. His son had died in infancy. After Regilla's death, both his daughters died. He adopted two girls and brought them up as his own; but both were killed when the house they were sleeping in was struck by lightning.

Herodes' most notable legacy to Athens is the Odeion he built in memory of his wife after her death in about 157. It was said that he was responsible for her death, for having ordered his freedman Alcimedon to beat her for some fault when she was eight months pregnant. Regilla's brother brought an action against him for murder; but his defence, besides his innocence, was his patent grief at his wife's death, and he was acquitted. He had his house repanelled in dark Lesbian marble as a sign of mourning; but Regilla's monument remains the Odeion, which is even now used for dramatic performances in the summer. It seems to have been intended as a replacement for the Odeion of Agrippa in the agora, which collapsed about this time. On the south slope of the Acropolis, Herodes' Odeion's semicircular auditorium seats about 5,000 people. Its three-storey stage building rose up to a roof of cedar wood and was adorned inside with statues and reliefs. The wooden ceiling was destroyed by burning during the sack of Athens by the Heruli in 267.

It was Herodes' work as a rhetor or sophist that earned him his reputation in his own day and ensured the preservation of his memory in the biography that Philostratus included in his *Lives of the Sophists*. His writings are lost but his reputation as a teacher was great. His 'Oberseminar' included about ten students and was always concluded by drinks and a meal: his students were known as 'the thirsty ones'. In 174 he was appointed to the imperial chair of rhetoric by Marcus Aurelius. He died five years later in 179 'of a wasting sickness.' Though he expired at Marathon and had left instructions to his freedmen to bury him there, 'the Athenians carried him away by the hands of the ephebes and took him to the city; and every age went out to meet the bier with tears and cries, as would sons bereft of a good father. They buried him in the Panathenaic Stadium' (Philostratus, *Lives of the Sophists* 565–6).

THE SECOND SOPHISTIC

Herodes is one of the most prominent characters in Philostratus' work on the Sophists, which he wrote to preserve the memory of the great teachers of his own and previous generations. Philostratus lived from ca

170 to 205 in the reign of Marcus Aurelius and his successors in the Severan dynasty, and enjoyed the patronage of Septimius Severus' wife Julia Domna, 'the patroness of every art, and the friend of every man of genius' (Gibbon). (Septimius himself had been educated at Athens.) He is one of the most important representatives of the movement known as the Second Sophistic which had its origin in the reign of Antoninus Pius. The characteristics of the movement were an emphasis on rhetorical training and good Attic style. Atticism, the reproduction of the verbal forms and grammatical details of fifth-century Athenian prose, is the hallmark of this movement, which rejected the prevailing *koine* or standard Greek of the Roman Empire (in which the New Testament, for example, is written). The diction is thus artificial; some of the literary forms also seem strange today. One of the most characteristic genres is 'display oratory' – the production of enormously long (and, to the modern reader, often rather tedious) speeches which were given as performances in the theatres and odeia of the Greek half of the empire. Notable exponents of the genre are Aelius Aristides, a pupil of Herodes Atticus and author of panegyrics of Rome, Athens and other cities as well as for a remarkable series of 'Sacred Discourses' describing his illnesses and his personal experiences of the healing god Asclepius. More attuned to modern taste are the biographies of Philostratus, not only of the Sophists but the long work on the first-century wonder-worker and sage Apollonius of Tyana. To this period also belong some of the most popular novels of antiquity, such as Longus' *Daphnis and Chloe*, and the satirical sketches of the Syrian writer Lucian, who passed a good deal of his life in Athens.

Though many of the Sophists worked elsewhere than at Athens, nearly all of them had been educated there. Philostratus' own teacher, Proclus of Naucratis (in Egypt), left his own land because 'he desired to embrace the peace and quiet of Athens'. In this scene of academic tranquillity he prospered and used his wealth well. 'He bought four houses, two in Athens itself, one at the Piraeus, and another at Eleusis. He used to receive direct from Egypt regular supplies of incense, ivory, myrrh, papyrus, books, and all such merchandise, and would sell them to those who traded in such things' (Philostratus, *Lives of the Sophists* 604). He allowed his students free access to his library, and an outright payment of one hundred drachmas would secure admission to all his lectures.

Proclus was surely typical of the many professors of rhetoric who established themselves at Athens from Herodes onwards. Many of them are mere names apart from what Philostratus tells us of them. They came from all over the empire, but with a preponderance from Syria and Arabia.

The first professor of rhetoric at Athens was Lollianus of Ephesus, who also held the office of *strategos*. In this capacity he was at the receiving end of the anger of the people when there was a bread shortage in the city. The people had taken up stones to pelt him when 'Pancrates the Cynic, who later professed philosophy at the Isthmus, came forward before the Athenians, and by simply remarking "Lollianus does not sell bread but words" he so diverted the Athenians that they let fall the stones that were in their hands' (Philostratus 526). On another occasion he solved a crisis when grain was delivered from Thessaly but the city had no money to pay for it, by having a whip-round among his pupils for their fees, and then giving them his lectures without charge.

One of Herodes' pupils was Hadrian of Tyre, who became professor of rhetoric at Athens and in his inaugural lecture announced 'Once again letters have come from Phoenicia'. 'He performed the duties of the chair at Athens with the greatest ostentation, wore very expensive clothes, bedecked himself with precious gems, and used to go down to his lectures in a carriage with silver-mounted bridles... he won over [lovers of Greek culture] by giving games and wine-parties and hunts, and by sharing with them the Hellenic festivals' (Philostratus 587). He later became professor at Rome.

The wealth of these professors is conspicuous. We know that the salary of Apollonius of Athens, as professor of political oratory, was one talent. Chrestus of Byzantium, another pupil of Herodes Atticus, received a salary of ten thousand drachmae. (Yet an officer in the imperial service could receive up to 50,000 drachmas, and the travelling preacher and wonder worker Alexander of Abonuteichos could net 100,000 drachmas in a year.) This salary could no doubt be supplemented by private fees, commissions for rhetorical performances, and political functions such as embassies. Philostratus' *Lives* contain a wealth of anecdote which illuminates the period when Athens turned into a pure university city.

The Second Sophistic has recently been interpreted as a movement in which Greek intellectuals subtly expressed their distance from Roman rule by a kind of 'mental exile': they turned their minds to the glories of the Hellenic past and the purity of the Attic dialect, as a way of expressing their sense of the superiority of Greek culture over the Roman rulers. Yet the examples of these teachers show how embedded they were in the economy and social structure of the Roman Empire: it was Rome that gave them the opportunity to study their past, to write their books and to make their careers. The emperors of the late second and early third centuries nurtured these Greek talents and supported the schools of rhetoric that made Athens a cynosure for the brightest students.

THE SACK BY THE HERULI

The third century in Athens, as in the rest of the empire, was a period of uncertainty and decline and, some historians would say, of crisis. A succession of short-lived emperors in Rome led to a lack of stability; prosperity had led to inflation which became critical towards the end of the century; and the empire was menaced on all sides by barbarian invasions and a growing threat from the revived Persian Empire, as well as secessions by some of its components such as Gaul and Palmyra.

In Athens, there is little evidence of building at this time, though extensive repairs were made to the old circuit wall in the reign of the Emperor Valerian (253–60), as was the case in many other cities. In 267 the Heruli, a tribe from the Black Sea, invaded Ionia and the Aegean islands, and swept into Athens causing extensive destruction. Many buildings in the agora were damaged or destroyed; the Odeion of Agrippa was burned and most of the other major buildings, including the temple of Ares, the Library of Hadrian, the Metroon (with the city archives) and the Stoa of Eumenes were damaged. However, the north-west part of the agora and the Acropolis seem to have been unaffected. A force of two thousand Athenians, under the command of Publius Herennius Dexippus, mounted a counter-attack and drove out the invaders. Dexippus was a scholar and orator who had written on the Successors of Alexander, a general history to Claudius, and on the Scythians. Probably in his 60s, he roused his troops with a speech worthy of Miltiades, echoing with the glory of Greek freedom. The classical past came to the assistance of the defenders and they regained their city.

After the retreat of the Heruli, a new circuit wall (wrongly known as the Valerian Wall after the emperor Valerian) was built around the centre of the city. Its perimeter was much reduced in comparison with the Themistoclean Wall and enclosed an area running north–south from the Roman Agora to the Acropolis. Many buildings were outside it, including the Temple of Olympian Zeus, the Theatre (no longer used), the Odeion of Herodes Atticus, the Pnyx and the Library of Hadrian. Much of it is built from blocks taken from shattered monuments and buildings. It was only completed in the reign of Probus (276–82), as is shown by coins found in the rubble fill. The Library of Hadrian was restored by the prefect Herculius some time before 412, but may have been repaired and in use again early in the fourth century.

Plentiful civic building in Athens in the late third and fourth centuries belies any real crisis in the city's affairs. The Heruli caused no destruction south of the Acropolis, which continued to be an area of luxury villas. Intellectual life among the inhabitants of these villas continued as before. Baths were built in the Olympieion area and enlarged in the fifth century; remains of these, and of Byzantine corn silos, were visible here until the area was cleared for the laying out of the National Gardens in 1833–62. Another bath house was built in the Syntagma area, with its northern edge close to the Hotel Grande Bretagne, and covered an area of 5,500 square metres. To this period also belong the building works and water system uncovered in excavations for the Herodou Attikou metro station, and the remarkable find of an ancient bronze head re-set in stone, perhaps as a protective talisman or ornament in a villa or public building (Pausanias 1.2.4; *The City beneath the City* 201).

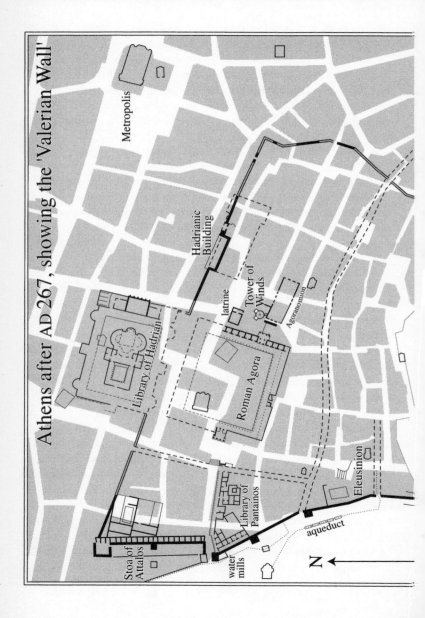

Athens after AD 267, showing the 'Valerian Wall'

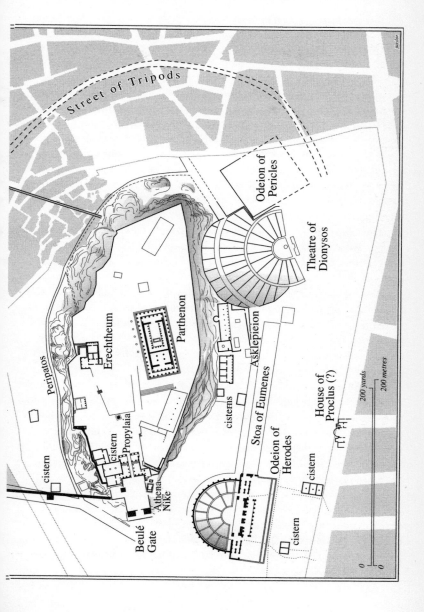

Street of Tripods

Odeion of Pericles

Theatre of Dionysos

Parthenon

Erechtheum

Peripatos

Asklepieion

Propylaia

cistern

cisterns

Stoa of Eumenes

House of Proclus (?)

Athena Nike

Odeion of Herodes

cistern

cistern

cistern

Beulé Gate

cistern

200 yards

200 metres

Jarvior

The Fourth Century

Roman emperors paid attention to Athens during the fourth century because of its great and continuing reputation. Constantine (emperor 306–37) was proud to hold the office of *strategos* of Athens, and he was not averse to receiving an honorific decree from the priest of the Mysteries of Eleusis. The pagan aristocracy was important to him despite his adoption and encouragement of the Christian religion. The role of the *strategos* was, as it had been when Lollianus had held it, primarily a responsibility for provisioning; and Constantine arranged an annual gift of grain to the city. When he founded his new capital of Constantinople in 324, he is said to have taken many statues from Athens to adorn the city. One statue of Apollo was converted to represent the emperor himself; the Byzantine writer Cedrenus says that this had come from Athens, but it is impossible to identify with any known Athenian work, and the information may be false. It seems unlikely that the Christian emperor would have taken any quantity of pagan idols to adorn his new capital.

The Emperor Julian 'the Apostate' or 'the Philosopher' (361–3), who attempted to turn the tide of Christianity and to re-establish paganism throughout the empire, felt a particular affection for Athens. He studied there for a few months in 355, and his initiation in the Mysteries of Eleusis was one of the events that strengthened his adherence to paganism and his rejection of the Christianity to which he had been raised. (An early poem by Constantine Cavafy, of 1896, imagines the young prince testing the 'demons' of the mysteries by making a sign of the cross at them.) 'May the gods who decide all things', he wrote at the end of his *Letter to the Athenians*, 'vouchsafe me to the end the assistance which they have promised, and may they grant to Athens all possible favours at my hands! May she always have such emperors as will honour her and love her above and beyond all other cities!' Julian's brief reign did not allow him time to make any material impact on Athens.

Theodosius I (the Great; 346–95) had a major impact on the religious scene in the empire. In a decree of 380 he declared Christianity the one true religion. Though pagan practices were not proscribed, they were given no encouragement, and a blind eye was turned to the activities of Christian leaders who destroyed the shrines and temples of the Hellenes. There is however little evidence of any impact at Athens, which, as one of the most distinguished cities of the empire, was slow to give up the traditional religion.

A frightening moment for Athens was the invasion of the Visigoths under Alaric in 395. He penetrated the barrier of Thermopylae through treachery and made straight for Athens, bypassing Thebes in his eagerness to arrive at the great city. He hoped for a swift victory because of food shortage in Athens; but, according to the historian Zosimus (5.5–6), the gods decreed otherwise:

> I should not pass over in silence the reason for the city's miraculous pre-servation, because it will excite piety in all who hear of it. When Alaric and his whole army came to the city, he saw the tutelary goddess Athena walking about the wall, looking just like her statue, armed and ready to resist attack, while leading their forces he saw the hero Achilles, just as Homer described him at Troy when in his wrath he fought to avenge the death of Patroclus. These apparitions were too much for Alaric who, giving up his attempt against the city, sent heralds to treat for peace... After accepting the terms and exchanging oaths, Alaric entered Athens with a few men. He was treated with every kindness and, after bathing and being entertained by select citizens and given gifts as well, he went off leaving the city and the whole of Attica unharmed.

He then marched on into the Peloponnese.

Zosimus' account may underestimate the damage done to Athens: Jerome (*Ep.* 60.16) says that Attica was ravaged; but in fact there are few signs of destruction associated with Alaric's raid. Nor does he seem, as a Christian conqueror, to have troubled to destroy pagan images. Such damage as there is is outside the post-Herulian wall in the area of the old agora – the Stoa of Zeus, Temple of Apollo Patroos. It seems that his impact was mainly confined to the Piraeus; and he is generally credited with the destruction of the shrine at Eleusis.

When the bishop Synesius visited Athens a few years later, he wrote to his brother (*Ep.* 136):

> Athens no longer has anything sublime except the country's finest names. Just as in the case of a victim burnt in the sacrificial fire, there remains

nothing but the skin to help us to reconstruct a creature which was once alive – so ever since philosophy left these precincts, there is nothing for the tourist to admire except the Academy, the Lyceum, and, by Zeus, the Painted Stoa which has given its name to the philosophy of Chrysippus. This is no longer Painted, for the proconsul has taken away the panels on which Polygnotus of Thasos had displayed his skill.

Synesius' eyes were plainly closed to the monuments of the Acropolis, still certainly undamaged; but his reference to the schools is appropriate, for these continued to flourish through the fourth and fifth centuries.

THE SCHOOLS OF RHETORIC AND PHILOSOPHY

Athens continued to be an important university town through the fourth and fifth centuries. An account written about 395 (the *Expositio totius mundi et gentium*) says 'Athens has the centres of higher learning and ancient historical monuments and something worthy of special mention, the Acropolis'. The schools of rhetoric continued vigorously in the fourth century, though some Sophists left at the end of the third century: the head of the Academy, Cassius Longinus, answered a call from Queen Zenobia of Palmyra to join her court as a tame intellectual. He corresponded with Libanius, but came to a bad end when Palmyra was sacked by the Emperor Aurelian in 274, as did another Sophist, Callinicus, who was murdered beside the Euphrates in a place subsequently named Callinicum. Vivid light is cast on the activities of the Sophists who remained in Athens by the writings of Libanius, who studied there under Diophantus in the 330s. Besides Libanius himself, and the future Emperor Julian, a number of Christians studied rhetoric at Athens, notably Gregory of Nazianzus (from 348 to 358) and Basil of Caesarea (until 355). The former describes how the students of the rival professors met new students at the harbour and attempted to press-gang them into their favoured lecture courses. The great and independently wealthy rhetorician Himerius, a contemporary and courtier of Julian, began his career at Athens, and included Gregory, his son in law, among his pupils; another philosopher, Iamblichus, was able to use his inherited wealth to rebuild the city walls late in the fourth century.

Many of the wealthy houses south of the Acropolis were no doubt the homes of the professors. A century after Philostratus, Eunapius wrote a work also entitled *Lives of the Sophists*, in which he describes the great Sophists of the late fourth century. One of these was what he describes as the 'poor and humble house' of Julian of Cappadocia:

> There were erected statues of the pupils whom he had most admired; and he had a theatre of polished marble made after the model of a public theatre but smaller and of a size suitable to a house. For in those days, so bitter was the feud at Athens between the citizens and the young students... that none of the Sophists ventured to go down into the city and discourse in public, but they confined their utterances to their private lecture theatres (Eunapius 483).

Julian's pupil Prohaeresius, 'the King of Rhetoric', became one of the most notable figures of Athens, and his classes were distinguished by their ascetic, temple-like atmosphere: the Emperor Constans appointed him honorary *praefectus castrorum* and donated some islands to improve Athens' grain supply. A statue of him was erected in Rome. He lost his job under the Emperor Julian because he was a Christian, but was soon restored, and probably lived out his life in the house he had inherited from his teacher Julian the sophist.

Besides the schools of rhetoric, the fourth century saw a notable revival in the Platonic school. From about 350 to 431 this was led by Plutarchus of Athens, a member of a distinguished family whose grandfather had been chief priest of Attica. His father was the wonder-worker (theurgist) Nestorius who worked miraculous cures and is supposed to have saved Athens from the earthquake of 375 which destroyed Corinth. The buildings of the Academy were restored and extended in the early fifth century, but Plutarchus probably built a new home for the school, the 'House of Proclus'.

The complexion of the Academy was changed by the rise of Neo-platonism, a development of Platonic philosophy which made it rather a creed than a method of inquiry, and was associated with semi-mystical 'theurgic' practices designed to enable the adept to approach closer to the Godhead, 'the One'. The theological sophistication of this 'phi-losophy' seems to have been designed to offer to pagans a subtlety equal to that now being developed by Christian thinkers. Neoplatonism had been founded by Plotinus in Rome in the mid-third century; his pupil

Porphyry had previously studied in the 250s with Cassius Longinus at Athens (Longinus held an annual dinner to celebrate Plato's birthday), and an influential school founded by Iamblichus in Syria produced a number of pupils who brought the new philosophy to Athens. The first of these was Syrianus who succeeded Plutarchus as head of the Academy in 431/2. He was followed by Proclus (410 or 412–485), Marinus (d. 490s) and Damascius, who was in post when the school was closed by Justinian in 529.

Proclus came to Athens from Alexandria in 437. The *Life* by his pupil Marinus described his arrival (10):

> He set off for Athens, escorted as it were by all the gods and good daemons who are custodians of the oracles of philosophy. When he arrived at the Piraeus... Nicolaus, who subsequently became illustrious as a sophist but was then a pupil with the teachers in Athens, went down to the harbour as though to an acquaintance... He led him therefore toward the city, but Proclus, feeling fatigue on the road because of the walk, and being close to the Socrateum [a monument by the place where Socrates had been executed] begged Nicolaus to stop there awhile and sit, and at the same time also, if he could obtain water from anywhere, to bring it to him... Nicolaus caused water to be brought from nowhere else than from that sacred spot... and now noted for the first time that he [Proclus] was sitting in the Socrateum and first drank the Attic water from this place.

Proclus' appearance 'was both grave and formidable, so that one seemed to be gazing on the very face of philosophy itself' (Damascius, *Life of Isidore* 59). When the Christians set about displacing the statue of Athena from the Parthenon (which one is not made clear, but it can hardly have been the Parthenos herself), 'it seemed to the philosopher in a dream that he was approached by a woman of fair aspect, who announced that he must prepare his house as quickly as possible: "for the mistress of Athens", she said, "desires to live with you"' (Marinus 30).

Proclus established himself in the house that had previously been inhabited by Plutarchus and Syrianus: 'it was a neighbour to the shrine of Asclepius, celebrated by Sophocles, and that of Dionysus by the theatre, seen, or if not it became visible, from the acropolis of Athena' (Marinus 29). This house is almost certainly to be identified with a large villa (known as Building Chi) excavated in 1955 on the southern slope of the Acropolis and subsequently covered by the building of Dionysiou Areopagitou Street. It included a large central hall decorated with mosaics and an apse with seven niches, linked to some smaller rooms. An inscription including the word for wisdom was found, as well as statues of Isis, the Mother of the Gods and other gods, and a sacrificed piglet with the sacrificial knife still in its neck. Proclus 'especially refused to eat anything that had life, although whenever there was an occasion which imperatively demanded it, he would taste a little meat for the sake of the rite' (Marinus 19). It seems that here we have the remains of one of Proclus' sacred feasts.

After Proclus' death the school suffered a decline, partly associated with the rise of the school of Asclepiodotus in Aphrodisias. Its fortunes revived under Damascius. When the latter became head of the school in 490 he moved its headquarters to more spacious quarters and, according to the historian Agathias, assembled in Athens the best philosophers from the whole Greek world. The new home of the school has been identified with a superb building complex on the northern slope of the Areopagus, discovered in 1970 and known as 'House C'. It comprises two peristyle courts, each at the centre of a separate section, one public, one more private, and incorporating a fountain house, a nymphaeum with a semi-circular pool and a dining room. The layout strongly suggests a connection with teaching, and the reliefs and statues reflect Neoplatonist theology while the portraits seem to represent ascetic philosophers. The statues were concealed in wells around the year 529, and those that were not hidden were degraded by the new owner: for example, a statue of Athena was re-used as a step.

In the year 529 the Emperor Justinian 'issued a decree and sent it to Athens ordering that no one should teach philosophy nor interpret the laws; nor should gaming be allowed in any city, for some gamblers who had been discovered in Byzantium who had been indulging themselves in dreadful blasphemies. Their hands were cut off and they were paraded around on camels' (Malalas 18.451). The ban on the study of law may be explained as stemming from a desire to concentrate the teaching of jurisprudence in the major school of Berytus (Beirut); but the ban on philosophy and gambling (strange pair!) is more puzzling.

The key seems to be their shared reliance on pagan practices and oaths. The testimony (found only in the often highly fanciful chronicle of Malalas) has been doubted, but it seems sure that the end of Athens as a university city came at about this time, as part of a drive to centralisation of intellectual activity in the Roman (now Byzantine) empire.

The sequel to the closure is also told in only one author, Agathias, a sober historian:

> Damascius of Syria [and six other philosophers] had come to the conclusion, since the official religion of the Roman empire was not to their liking, that the Persian state was much superior. So they gave a ready hearing to the stories in general circulation according to which Persia was the land of 'Plato's philosopher king' in which justice reigned supreme... Elated therefore by these reports which they accepted as true, and also because they were forbidden by law to take part in public life with impunity owing to the fact that they did not conform to the established religion, they left immediately and set off for a strange land whose ways were completely foreign to their own, and determined to make their homes there.

The contemporaries of Plato would have felt the irony in this determination that Plato's philosophy was only to be given free rein in the home of the ancient enemy of Athens, the Persian Empire.

The 'House of Damascius' was now desecrated and may have become the home of the bishop of Athens; for Justinian, though he restored the defensive walls of Athens, as of every other city in the empire, allowed no new building in a city which was to be left unrestored as a symbol of the rejected pagan past.

If Harran now became the home of the philosophy of Plato, a clause in the Eternal Peace of 532 stated regarding the philosophers: 'When these men return home they will spend the rest of their lives free of any fear, as private individuals, never forced to profess belief in anything contrary to their conscience or to change their traditional views' (Agathias 2.30.3). However, Damascius never returned to Athens: he seems to have died in Emesa, in Syria, home of Iamblichus the great Neoplatonist of an earlier generation. The last of the Neoplatonists, Simplicius, probably composed his works on Aristotle in Harran.

CHAPTER NINE

Medieval Athens

(i) The Byzantine Empire

THE CHRISTIANISATION OF ATHENS

The Byzantine Empire officially began with the foundation by Constantine of the Christian city of Constantinople in 324. However, this event had little direct impact on the city of Athens or on Greece in general. More important historical changes began in the fifth, and particularly the sixth centuries. The various edicts of Theodosius II, issued between 408 and 450, outlawing pagan practices had a direct impact both on people's lives and on the urban scene. The classical temples and monuments fell into neglect or were desecrated, and churches began to rise up in their stead. Statues were destroyed or removed: the Athena Promachos was taken to Constantinople in the late fifth century, where it was destroyed by the Crusaders in 1204. The Vandal sack of Athens in the mid-fifth century resulted in great destruction, marked in the archaeological record by a layer of ash. But where the city decayed, the church advanced.

The first churches in Athens had probably been established in the first century, supposedly under the rule of Dionysius the Areopagite, the first bishop of Athens: these were a basilica of which remains have been found near the present-day church of St Luke on Patission St (28 October St), and one on the southern side of Mt Lycabettus. But the first church built in Christian Athens was the tetraconch erected in the fifth century within the Library of Hadrian. More striking were the numerous conversions of temples and other classical buildings into Christian monuments, a process that began now and continued throughout the Byzantine period. The Parthenon was converted from a temple of the virgin goddess Athena to a church of the virgin Mother of God (Theotokos), and in 429 the Athena Parthenos of Phidias was removed and is never heard of again. A martyr shrine of Leonides by the Ilissus was transformed into a basilica in the fifth century. The Monument of Thrasyllus became a chapel of the Virgin. The Erechtheum also became a church early in the sixth century; the Horologium of Andronicus cyrrhestes (Tower of the Winds) was converted into a baptistery, the shrine of Asclepius was reconsecrated to Christianity (sixth century, the first basilica in Athens), and in the mid–fifth century the Temple of Hephaestus ('Theseion') became a church of St George, a function it retained into the early nineteenth century when it served as a burial place for at least one western traveller. It is notable that these churches were built within the city itself; in Rome, the capital of the Christian empire, churches were only permitted to be built outside the walls of the city.

Theodosius' wife Eudocia (married 421) was herself an Athenian, originally named Athenais. She erected the 'Palace of the Giants' in the 420s outside the post-Herulian wall. A statue base of Eudocia has been found in front of it; but it changed its use in the 460s, after Eudocia's death. She may also have built the tetraconch church in the Library of Hadrian.

The Theatre of Dionysus also was consecrated as a Christian place of worship at the end of the fifth century, an act which saw the end of nearly a thousand years of theatrical performances in honour of the pagan gods. (It had been abandoned after 267, but used for assemblies in the mid-fifth century.) Fathers of the Church, such as John Chrysostom in late fourth-century Antioch, had been eloquent in denouncing the licentiousness of the shows they housed. Though the ancient tragedies were still performed, the ribald and hilarious plays of the Old Comedy had not been shown for centuries: in their place were circus acts and pantomimes, in some of which one might even behold the naked limbs of women, as well as the gladiatorial shows that even pagan Greeks had objected to. No doubt the holy bishop protested too much, but this kind of popular entertainment would distract the people's attention from the word of God, as well as being (still) dedicated to a pagan god:

so the theatre had to be closed down and made innocuous by re-dedication to the worship of the Christian God.

In all twenty-two new churches were built between about 400 and 550, many of which are now lost to view. (Richard Chandler, at the end of the eighteenth century, saw remains of one near the seventeenth-century church of Dionysius Areopagiticus.)

The culmination of this process of 'de-paganisation' was the final closure by the Emperor Justinian in 529 of the philosophical schools of Athens. This spelt the end for Plato's Academy as well as the rest of the schools: Damascius, the last scholar of the Academy, abandoned his home for ever, as recounted in the previous chapter. The reason for associating this house with Damascius is that it was not, like the neighbouring houses, allowed to fall into decay, but converted into a Christian building: the pool became a baptistery, the triclinium became a catachumeneum and a cross was erected therein. It may be conjectured that this house became the home of the bishop of Athens – another act of re-consecration of a site with deep pagan associations by Justinian, whom his historian Procopius called 'that greatest of all destroyers of established institutions'. Justinian also removed many columns from Athens to adorn his new church of Aghia Sophia in Constantinople.

FORTIFICATIONS

If Justinian did little to conserve the fabric of the city of Athens, he nonetheless devoted some energy to its fortifications, and to those of the other cities of Greece. Repairs were made to the outer circuit wall of Athens, and to the 'late Roman wall'. But under Justinian a new cross wall was also built, conceding the reduced size and importance of the city of Athens, as well as the insufficiency of its population to defend a city defined by the outer circuit wall. Cemeteries for the first time began to be located within the walls rather than without: the recent excavations for the Metro have uncovered a number of Christian graves of the fifth and sixth centuries in the bed of the Eridanus, in the region of Syntagma Square. This change reflects the increasing valuation put on the sacred dead in Christianity.

THE RURALISATION OF THE EMPIRE

The reduced size and population of the city are part of a larger pattern of historical change that affected the whole of the Roman Empire in the fifth and following centuries. Sometimes interpreted as an 'agrarian revolution', it is better viewed as process of steady ruralisation. Cities lost the political role they had had in the later Roman Empire as centres of administration and – just as important – of consumption. The increased centralisation of Byzantine rule, and the militarisation of the beleaguered empire against invaders from the north, meant that cities could no longer maintain even a pretence of political autonomy. Governors came and went, the city's upper classes lost their political significance, and many more people were eking out a simple life on smallholdings. Somehow, it is not clear just when, the semi-feudal system of the colonate of late antiquity had given place to a peasant-type structure of rural life. Large estates continued to exist, to be sure, but the document of the late seventh or eighth century known as the Farmer's Law reflects a society of independent farmers who own their own fields and cattle, can come and go as they please, can hire labour when they require it, and pay tax on their income.

One result of this, and of the interests of our sources, is that the history of Athens is punctuated by long periods of absolute silence. There is no way of writing a year-by-year account of events in Athens for the next seven hundred years or so. The silence and darkness of these 'Dark Ages' is punctuated by brief flashes when an individual enters the historical record such as the rise to the Imperial throne of two Athenian women (Irene, b 752, Empress 780–802, and Theophano, who married the son of the Emperor in 807). Both of these built churches in their native city: Irene may have built that of the Penniless Saints below the north slope of the Acropolis (Prytaneiou/Erotokritou Streets), and perhaps that of the Pantanassa also.

THE INFLUX OF THE SLAVS

More important for the *longue durée* view of Athens and the rest of mainland Greece in this period is the steady influx of Slavic peoples and their allies. As early as the reign of Justinian, in 539 and 540, tribal movements to the north brought Bulgars and Slavs into the Balkan provinces of Illyria, Moesia, Thrace and Macedonia. Slavonic speakers, practising a mixture of stock-breeding and agriculture, had been settled on the upper Vistula and middle Dnieper for millennia. By about 200 AD the Germanic-speaking Goths were putting pressure on their northern fringes, and mingling with them to some extent. The arrival of the Huns towards the end of the fourth century resulted in a gradual spread of the Slavs to the south, where geography and climate were suited to their way of life, unlike the forests to the west. The Slavs, known to the Byzantine as Sklavenoi, were present on the Danube by the end of the fifth century, and some of them were enlisted in the Byzantine army.

The climacteric of the sixth century, when the Slavs began to move across the Danube into the Balkans, was occasioned by the emergence of a number of new peoples apparently from the remains of the Hun Empire. The obscure Kotrigurs and Utigurs appear alongside the Bulgars, ahead of whom lay a long history and an important one for the Byzantine world. Raiders reached Thermopylae as early as 517. In 528 the Bulgars raided Thrace, and a year later Slavs were doing the same. Soon these peoples were threatening Thessaloniki and Constantinople. This was the motivation for the repair of city defences by Justinian, mentioned above.

In 558 the Avars make their first appearance. These were perhaps a Mongol people: certainly their origins lie in central Asia and their state was ruled by a khagan or king. They swept to the west, and were at first enlisted by the Byzantines to control the other peoples threatening their northern frontiers. But pretty soon the Avars took control of, or made common cause with, the Slavs; and this formidable coalition repeatedly poured into the Balkans and northern Greece. They may have besieged Thessaloniki in 586, and they did besiege Constantinople in 626.

Besides the military threat on the northern border, there was also a more subtle and insidious process going on as the Slavs began to settle in peninsular Greece including the Peloponnese, bringing their agricultural way of life to a land that seemed to have room to spare. It seems that they chose mainly to settle in areas that resembled the lands they were familiar with, riverine plains suitable for arable and stock farming such as were to be found in Macedonia, Thessaly and parts of the Peloponnese. The were not drawn to arid and mountainous regions such as Attica.

The extent of this Slavic infiltration is hard to gauge. In the early nineteenth century J.P. Fallmerayer created a scholarly and national scandal by arguing that the original population of Greece was in effect wiped out or expelled by the invading Slavs, who in the course of the eighth century introduced their own culture and displaced that of their hosts. A Byzantine scholar of the tenth century wrote [quoted in Gregorovius 96] that Epirus, Hellas, the Peloponnese and Macedonia are largely inhabited by Slavs: in Elis, 'even the name of the Pisatans, Kaukones and Pylians exists no more, for the Scythians have all these places in their possession'. One might see here no more than the exaggerated reaction of a native to the arrival of foreign immigrants with their curious cooking practices and smells, and to argue from this to a complete change of racial make-up is a large step. The upshot of Fallmerayer's view was that the present inhabitants would be descendants of Hellenised Slavs and not of the ancient Hellenes. This was a view that could only strike horror into the breasts of the nationalist Greeks of the generations following the War of Independence from the Turks. Now, there is no doubt that a great many place names in various parts of Greece are Slavonic in form, especially in northern Greece. One thinks of, for example, Vizitsa and Macrinitsa on Mt Pelion; and there were many more such names in the Peloponnese until they were re-hellenised in the twentieth century. It is also true that much more mingling of peoples and stocks took place in the marches, such as Macedonia, than many present-day Greeks are willing to admit in the face of possible Serbian and Skopjean irredentism. However, there seems no doubt that Fallmerayer's case was greatly overstated. Even if the Slavs came in considerable numbers, it was the Hellenisation that determined their future development. Nonetheless, it may be possible to see in this 'Slavicisation' another aspect of the ruralisation of the Byzantine Empire, a concomitant rather than a cause of the decline of the classical social structure.

THE THEME OF HELLAS

Beginning in the reign of Heraclius in the seventh century, the administration of the Byzantine Empire was reorganised on a regional basis with the division into military governorships called themes. Each theme was under the rule of a *strategos* or general, sometimes also referred to by the Roman name of *praetor* or *propraetor*. The governor was never appointed to his native province (like Greek policemen today), and acted as the representative of the emperor in all local matters. His staff included a lieutenant-governor (*ekprosopou*), military police and, from about the tenth century, a judge. Other officers held the title of archontes. The soldiers of each theme's unit were maintained by heritable grants of land, and usually the soldier was the tenant himself or his son. The soldiers thus became quite substantial peasants, almost 'small gentry'. While the institution of the themes tended to a more pronounced regionalism in the empire, the landholding system resulted in the break-up of large estates and the diminution of the serf-relations of the colonate. Concurrently, city life became more and more attenuated as the cities became mere administrative and garrison centres: the empire was ruralised. The role of the former city councils was taken over by another Byzantine official, the *vindex*.

The Balkan region was divided into ten themes, and those corresponding to present-day Greece were the theme of Hellas, comprising most of mainland Greece north of the Isthmus, with its headquarters at Thebes, and the theme of the Peloponnese, as well as those of Nicopolis, Macedonia and Thrace.

Though the large estates were mainly gone by the end of the eighth century, they began to return during the ninth and tenth centuries as successful military leaders and important civilians invested their gains in land, reconsolidating the smaller holdings of the peasants and the soldiers. Robert Browning (*Byzantium and Bulgaria* 83–4) describes how this led to the creation of a quasi-feudal system of magnates owning the land and exacting various rents and services from the farmers. The rise of this landed wealth and a different kind of society led in turn to the gradual break-up of themes and a diminution of central government control.

Athens remains almost invisible to history through the early centuries of the Byzantine Empire, though we know that it was theoretically exempt from billeting of soldiers. Its main responsibility was the payment of taxes. That this burden became sometimes oppressive we know from the record of an uprising in 915 in which the governor Chases was stoned to death. The case was not unique, for in the eleventh century the historian Michael Psellus was still complaining of the rapacity of the governor of Attica; and in the twelfth century we hear also of the murder of the governor of the theme of Nicopolis. Psellus in a letter to the praetor (no 186) bewails the decline of Athens and the eclipse of its former glories, thus joining a long line of writers, from Bishop Synesius to Lord Byron, who would sound a similar elegiac note.

In 1018 the Emperor Basil II, the Bulgar-Slayer, paid a visit to Athens. As vindicator of the Greeks against barbarian enemies, he must have felt some frisson of the ancient glory of Athens. He visited the Parthenon, now the cathedral of Athens, whose columns had been linked by low walls dividing them into chapels. 'The mind of Basil,' wrote George Finlay, 'though insensible to Hellenic literature, was deeply sensible of religious impressions, and the glorious combination of beauty in art and nature that he saw in the Acropolis touched his stern soul.' On his orders the walls were adorned with frescoes: some faint fragments of images of saints remain. He also endowed the cathedral with treasures from his Bulgarian spoils.

As early as 727 there had been a general rising of the Greeks against the Byzantine Empire. The rebels went so far as to send a fleet to Constantinople, and to proclaim a new emperor, Cosmas by name; but the rebellion quickly collapsed and the attempt was not repeated. Greece, along with other parts of the empire, sank apparently into a low-keyed servitude, its conditions exacerbated by the effects of an eruption of Thera in 726, plague in 745, a prolonged darkening of the sun in 746 and an atrocious winter in 763. Many Greeks of the middle class emigrated to Constantinople if they could, though Greece remained not entirely devoid of skills; in the 740s it was to Greece that Byzantium turned when 500 cement manufacturers were needed for works in the capital. The elegant and pedantic Byzantines seem to have looked down on the simplicity of the Greeks: as George Finlay, a historian who seldom minces his words or waters down his strong Scottish moralism, wrote,

> the imagination and the taste of Hellas had something in their natural superiority that was repulsive to Byzantine pedantry, while the paganism of classic literature excited the contempt of ecclesiastical bigots. A strong mental difference was therefore the cause of the aversion to Greeks that is apparent in Byzantine society, and its operation is equally visible in the hellenic race. The spirit of local patriotism which has always been powerful among the Greeks kept them aloof from the Byzantine service, so that they really occupy a less prominent figure in the history of the empire than they were entitled to claim. (*History of Greece* 2.319f)

Over the period of Byzantine rule some Greeks were able slowly to develop the talent for commerce which is so conspicuous in modern times. Patras became the leading city of the peninsula, and the Mani was also an important commercial hub in the ninth century. Athens however remained at a kind of subsistence level, lacking even the skilled artisans like the silk workers who were the basis of the prosperity of nearby Thebes. Though the Arab geographer Edrisi, writing in the first half of the eleventh century for King Roger of Sicily, had called Athens 'a populous city, surrounded by gardens and fields', it apparently had little to offer beyond agricultural products. In 1146, when the Normans of Sicily under Roger II entered Greece, they spared Athens and concentrated on the richer prizes of Thebes and Corinth: Athens had no manufactures beyond soap and monks' habits; it was impossible even to find a coachmaker. Plaka was virtually uninhabited. As the twelfth century opened Athens, despite its emerging class of notables and an increased control over its own affairs, must have been a poor place. Saracen attacks during the twelfth century made things even worse.

CHURCHES

The one area in which we can see some positive development in the first part of the Middle Ages is in the church. The Orthodox church maintained its strength as one of the main social adhesives of Greek

Kapnikarea Church

society, and Athens was important as the seat of a Metropolitan. Already in the ninth century some new churches were built, introducing for the first time the distinctive forms of Byzantine architecture to the city. In the tenth and eleventh centuries there was an explosion of church building, and John Travlos has calculated that by 1150 there were forty churches in Athens: eight of these survive in their original form, fourteen more are recognisable, and eighteen have vanished without trace. Some of the most significant are the Pantanassa in Monastiraki Square, possibly originally from the tenth century; the eleventh century Ag. Apostoli in the agora, Ag. Asomatoi off Ermou St, the Kapnikarea of the late eleventh century, Ag. Theodoroi on the corner of Klafthmonos Square (1070), and further out the Omorphoklissia near the Olympic Stadium. In the eleventh or twelfth century were built the Church of St Catherine of Sinai (originally of St Theodore) in Ag. Ekaterini Square in Plaka (possibly on the site of the ancient Prytaneion, or a Roman bath), and that of St John the Theologian (Erotokritou Street). Most of these follow the Byzantine architectural model of an inscribed cross with an apse, and domes set upon squinches.

The eleventh century saw an increase in monasticism, following on the miracles performed by a Cappadocian monk named Meletius. The monastery of Kaisariani on the slopes of Mt Hymettus, an eleventh-century foundation, is one of the most picturesque spots in Attica, though it can hardly have been wealthy when it was established, since we know that the abbot was soon in trouble for allegedly stealing his neighbours' bees. The most important Byzantine building of this period is the Monastery Church of Daphni, a few miles outside Athens on the road to Eleusis. Originally founded in the sixth century, it was entirely rebuilt and completed about 1080. The *katholikon* (church) follows the usual simple plan, but its great glory are the mosaics, the first expression of Byzantine humanism in which the rigidity of earlier work gives place to an angular and energetic style, in which figures begin to move and relate to one another, aided by a compositional skill that integrates the decoration with the architecture, and a sense of colour that enlivens the whole though it is far from naturalistic. Above in the cupola, a grim but approachable Pantokrator gazes down, while around the walls the traditional scenes of the New Testament and the Life of the Virgin are played out. When we think of the austerity and hardship that must have characterised the subsistence lifestyle of the mass of the population of Attica, we can perhaps also suppose that places like this could lift their spirits and might seem a not unworthy use of the wealth of the church.

Other buildings of this period deserving mention are a series of new fortification walls, one around the Acropolis and the other an outer circuit wall of the Acropolis known as the Rizokastro. Their date is uncertain. Travlos hazards that they may belong to the later twelfth century, but that they may be of too good quality for this period of misery following on the destruction by the Saracens. They could be as much as two centuries earlier.

Michael Acominatus

Medieval Athens comes for the first time into closer focus in the life-time of the great churchman, Michael Acominatus, Metropolitan of Athens (probably 1175–1204). Born in 1138 or 1140, he came from Chonae or Colossae in Asia Minor, and his younger brother was the distinguished historian Nicetas Choniates. Michael had been educated in Constantinople, from ca 1157, at the feet of the great Bishop of

Thessaloniki, Eustathios, a man of wide learning and one of the great classical scholars of the Middle Ages (he wrote a voluminous and still valuable commentary on Homer as well as an important history of his times). The date of Michael's accession to the see of Athens is uncertain. He says it was 1175, but his predecessor George Xeros died only in 1182: it is possible that George had retired in 1175.

The Metropolitan's residence was probably in the Propylaea of the Acropolis, close by the 'divine Parthenon', the holy shrine (for Michael) of the Virgin of Mother of God; and during Michael's incumbency it seems to have become something of a cynosure for intellectuals. We are told of students from Georgia in the Caucasus. The Archdeacon of Leicester, John of Basingstoke, travelled to Athens to study there, and brought back with him a number of valuable books, including the *Testament of the Twelve Patriarchs* (now in the Cambridge University Library). The chronicler Matthew Paris tells us that Greek 'philosophers' from Athens also visited England and discussed religious matters at the court of King John.

These flickers of contact between Athens and the west must bespeak a more continuous flame, and it is at this time that Godfrey of Viterbo includes in his *Mirror of History* a number of legends about Athens that show how little was remembered, even in the city itself, of its great past. Minerva was the founder of the city, and Niobe its first queen and lawgiver; Aristotle was a native of Athens; and so on. Now for the first time we hear – from the pen of Acominatus himself – the traditional names of the ancient monuments, the 'Lantern of Demosthenes' and the 'Pillar of Plato'; the latter philosopher becomes a magical protector of the city.

Acominatus is the first author to write at length about Athens for 800 years. Unfortunately he has left us, in his letters and his poetry, no detailed description of the appearance of the city in his time; he was more preoccupied in lamenting the sordid state to which the once great city has descended. Ruined buildings, corrupt priests, attacks by pirates in the 1180s and in 1202–3 and abuse of the praetor's powers are the leitmotifs of his description. When the Byzantine admiral Steiriones came to clear the pirates, it was the Athenians who had to pay with higher taxes.

Our see of Athens was once a populous district, but it is being continually emptied. Nay, it is turning into a Scythian wilderness; and the reason is that we are being burdened with a load of taxation far heavier than falls upon our neighbouring territories. The tax-collectors survey our barren soil with measures small enough to check the prints of fleas. The very hairs on our heads are counted; how much more the leaves of vines and plants. In other regions the taxes are either not enforced or else lowered by the praetors. Yet among us each single tax is levied, indeed more heavily than anywhere else, and that in this farthest limit of the Helladic Province. Only last year we, and we alone, had to pay for the building of a fleet which never got built. And when Panisios Steiriones was ranging the coastal waters, again we alone had to pay, cash down, or ships, and yet again still more money was forced out of us by Sgouros and the Praetor... Now everything in Athens is poor and mean, especially the farm-implements. The great city has become a great ruin. The bellows has failed; there is no iron-worker, no bronze-worker among us, no maker of knives. You cannot look on Athens without tears.... Everywhere you see walls stripped and demolished, houses razed to the ground, their sites ploughed under. Time and its dread ally, envy, have dealt with Athens more barbarously than ever the Persians did. Try your utmost, you would not find a trace of the Heliaea, the Peripatos or the Lyceum; and sheep graze among the meagre relics of the Stoa Poikile. (tr. Kevin Andrews, *Athens Alive*, 44–6)

Some allowance must be made for rhetoric, but the tone of Acominatus' lament is that of a Greek who feels the weight as well as the glory of the classic past. Education and wealth have enabled him to rise above the conditions of the masses and to imagine something better than he finds around him. We see in Acominatus the beginnings of a national consciousness that will, over the centuries, gradually enable the Greeks to break free of their servitude.

Acominatus' position was not all rhetoric. As a notable, an archon, he played a role also in the politics of his time – and not just because the burden of taxation fell inevitably on the rich. (Under Byzantine law a system called *allelenguon* prevailed, by which the rich must pay the taxes that the poor could not provide. Though George Finlay (2.387) saw this as an imposition that prevented proper investment in the land, to the poor it may have seemed an entirely reasonable arrangement.) Under the harsh rule of the Emperor Andronikos, taxation had been considerably increased and its collection strengthened. The leniency of the praetor of Michael's first year, Prosouch, was replaced by the harshness and extortion of Drimys. Michael addresses the new praetor as if he were a second Theseus, and pours out flattery of the emperor in the hope of reducing the burdens placed on the city. When Andronikos is succeeded by his murderer Isaac Angelos, Michael applies to the same treatment to him, comparing him to the tyrannicides Harmodius and Aristogeiton. Similar eulogies greet the visits of other Byzantine officials, Basil the Logothete and Admiral Michael Stryphnos. If in such effusions Michael seems to be the archetypal 'Man for all seasons', his patriotism and love of Athens cannot be in doubt. But rhetoric was not enough. Michael became an ever more isolated figure. We cannot tell from his writings whether there was any kind of council of notables or other administrative body in Athens: he gives the impression always that he alone stands for the city and its past. By this period, however, gradually increasing prosperity had led to the development of a class of notables, or archontes, in most of the Balkan cities, from Dubrovnik to Sparta. The term archon in fact is an Athenian one and we must assume that some such body, however informal, did determine the affairs of Athens as the theme system withered away.

Acominatus' lament also introduces us to another great character of the last days of Byzantine Greece, Leon Sgouros. This wealthy Peloponnesian magnate had made himself the virtual ruler, even the tyrant of the Argolid, with his stronghold at Nauplia. He 'administered his inheritance with bloodshed' (Nicetas Choniates): once, he invited a Metropolitan of Athens to dinner, put out his eyes and threw him off the rock. The ship money he required from Athens was supposed to be directed against the attacks of the Saracen pirates. In 1204 he went so far as to conduct an invasion of Athens, demanding the surrender of an enemy whom he regarded as a particular troublemaker. Michael's intercessions with Sgouros (whom he knew personally) were of no avail, and the latter pillaged and burnt the lower city. Michael did, however, persuade him to abandon his attack on the Acropolis – a resistance which Michael was able to compare with the heroic stand of Dexippus in AD 267. Michael's brother, Nicetas Choniates, in his history of the period, describes how the elderly archbishop reasoned and bargained with Sgouros, 'discharging spiritual threats as though from siege engines'.

> Beseeching God that every horror might be visited on this unholy man who was the cause of burgeoning evils, Michael set up engines of war atop the walls to oppose him ... Confronted by such an adversary, a skilled tactician, a man of great learning and unrivalled in virtue, the enemy Sgouros despaired; realizing that it was of no avail to butt his head against the rocky slopes of the Acropolis, he vented his wrath against the city whose acropolis he could not subdue. He put the houses to the torch and carried off those animals suitable for the yoke and as food.

Sgouros then turned away and turned his attention to Thebes, which he subdued. Such was the state of Attica and the neighbouring region when the Sack of Constantinople by the soldiers of the Fourth Crusade led to a far greater upheaval in Greece.

(ii) Athens under Frankish Rule

THE FRANKISH CONQUEST

'There never was a greater crime against humanity', wrote the historian Sir Steven Runciman, 'than the Fourth Crusade.' Diverted from their journey to the Holy Land by a request for assistance from the pretender to the Byzantine throne, Alexius IV, once the Crusaders entered the city they turned to sack and pillage: precious manuscripts of classical and religious works were burnt, bronze statues and treasures of precious metals were melted down, marble statues were destroyed and buildings defaced, tombs were ripped open. The Crusaders abandoned their plan of marching on to Jerusalem, and instead settled as conquering rulers in Constantinople. Count Baldwin of Flanders was crowned the first Latin Emperor of Constantinople.

The Franks (as the Greeks called the conquerors, from the Arabic word *faranj*, Greek *frangos*, a foreigner) divided up the empire between them and soon extended their rule to Greece, where most of the mainland was assigned to Boniface of Montferrat. However, under a commercial treaty already arranged between Venice and the last Byzantine emperor, Alexius III, the Venetians had secured most of the best commercial cities in the Levant, including in Greece the regions of Lacedaemonia, Patras and Methone, Nikopolis and Arta, and the Ionian islands. They also controlled Athens' near neighbour, the island of Euboea as well as Aegina, Andros and Naxos. Boniface also sold Crete to the Venetians for 1,000 marks in silver. By this treaty Venice became, as it proudly boasted, 'the ruler of a quarter and half a quarter of the Roman Empire'.

The remains of the Byzantine Empire were parcelled out in a complex manner. Besides the Frankish principalities in Greece and the Venetian territories, a rump Byzantine court established itself at Nicaea, from which the Imperial throne would in due course be reoccupied. There was also a separate empire of Trebizond ruled by another branch of the imperial family, and Byzantine rule also continued in the Despotate of Epirus from 1204 to 1340.

Boniface's army rapidly moved south through Greece, passing the Vale of Tempe into Thessaly. Leon Sgouros marched north to face the Crusaders, joining the Emperor Alexius III at Larissa and marrying his daughter Eudocia. But he soon retreated before the invaders, and Boniface installed in Larissa the first Frankish ruler in Greek lands, Guglielmo de Larsa; then Velestino (west of Volos) became the fief of Count Berthold von Katzellenbogen. The Franks quickly drove Sgouros back to his stronghold in Nauplia, capturing and sacking Thebes and then in short order Athens. The impoverished city showed little resistance; the cathedral treasury and library were plundered, the precious metals melted down. In despair, Michael Acominatus fled the city and retreated, first to Aulis, then to Euboea, where he took refuge with his friend Demetrius, the bishop of Carystos, and where he owned some orchards; but after a year's stay he removed again to the monastery of John the Prodromos (Forerunner, i.e. John the Baptist) on Ceos, where he lived out his days lamenting the loss of his beloved Athens, and refusing the offers of bishoprics in Nicaea and Naxos. He made one last visit to Athens in 1215, and died, old and sad, in 1220.

THE DE LA ROCHE DYNASTY

Despite the plunder, the Franks seem to have been welcomed as some sort of liberators by the oppressed population of Athens. Boniface appointed a Burgundian nobleman, Othon de la Roche, as ruler of Athens and Thebes with the unique title Megaskyr, 'great Lord'. Othon took up residence in Thebes, in the palace on the site of the ancient Kadmeia – perhaps as clear a sign as any of the poor state of Athens at this time, since it clearly could provide no dwelling worthy of the Burgundian lord. Military governors were installed in the Athenian Acropolis as well as the Theban Cadmeia.

Boniface pressed on into the Peloponnese, and granted its rule to Geoffrey de Villehardouin, who established his capital at Andravida. The most pressing task was the reduction of Sgouros, and Othon assisted Villehardouin in the siege of Corinth. Corinth fell in 1210, quickly followed by Nauplia and Argos, which were added to the fief of Othon. At the same time, Venice seized Modon (Methone), Koron as well as the islands of Andros and Santorini, and the Ionian islands. Genoa established a Duchy in Naxos by 1207.

The rule of the Franks in Greece was essentially a colonial rule *avant la lettre*. Like their brethren in the Holy Land, the Franks mingled little with the native population, but as a corollary they interfered but little in the established social order. The most important change was the establishment of a Latin ecclesiastical hierarchy. Acominatus was replaced by a Latin archbishop, Berard, with eleven suffragan bishops under him, and another archbishop was appointed in Thebes. The Greek church was in effect driven underground and, like the native churches in contemporary Palestine, preserved the national identity through religious institutions while deprived of statehood. Over the centuries of foreign rule, both Frankish and Ottoman, it was the Orthodox church that maintained the memory of the freedom and glory of the Greeks and, after more than six centuries, was to play an important part in re-establishing a Greek state. The Church of Athens received important privileges from Pope Innocent III in 1208, confirming its ancient exemption from all exactions of the secular authorities, and allowing it to maintain its possessions which included the markets of Negroponte and Athens. The monastery of Daphni was transferred to the Cistercian Order, and a Minorite monastery was established at the foot of Mount Pendeli. Othon was however no great respecter of the church and was willing, when necessary, to sequestrate its income for his own needs. Both he and Geoffrey de Villehardouin, indeed, were somewhat anti-ecclesiastical and both were eventually excommunicated by the Pope.

The non-ecclesiastical lands were distributed in fiefs to the nobles and the natives entered a kind of serf-like status. In Palestine the fiefs could often be commuted for cash, and the burden on the native population was of rents rather than of vassals' service; but in the less monetised economy of Greece this can have been less easy to arrange, and one may imagine that the natives paid their dues in service and in kind. Nonetheless, it seems that the Greeks found the relative indifference of the Franks, living their chivalric life of tournaments and feasting in their baronial strongholds, less oppressive than the constant exactions of the Byzantine tax-gatherers. The nobles of Athens and Boeotia were not of high status and they founded no baronial castles of the kind that rose up in other parts of Greece. There were few native magnates in Greece, the bourgeoisie was virtually non-existent, and the population was already used to a subservient and peasant existence. That was slow to change. Byzantine law continued for the most part to be applied by the new rulers.

However, Frankish rule did open up Greek lands to trade. Trading communes of Venetians (already widespread in the Mediterranean by 1187), Genoese and Pisans were soon established in the major ports of Greece, and this gradually increased the prosperity of the cities. Athens, alas, had little to trade, but Thebes, the capital of the Duchy (as it soon became) of Athens, was famous for its silks and the large Jewish community had created a significant commercial life there. Athens controlled four ports – Piraeus, Nauplia, Atalante (on the north coast of Attica opposite Euboea) and Livadostro on the north coast of the Gulf of Corinth. The Duchy had no fleet, but did engage in a little piracy.

The Franks did not remain at peace with each other for long. Following the death of Boniface, who was captured and beheaded by the Bulgars in 1207, the Lombard kingdom of Salonica attempted to break loose from the empire. The Emperor Henry moved to crush them, and Othon's loyalty to Henry was rewarded by his re-establishment in Thebes, which he had temporarily lost to Salonica. Henry was welcomed in Thebes by the Greek priests with drums and trumpets, and the Latin archbishop escorted him to the cathedral for a service of thanksgiving. Henry then proceeded to Athens – the first emperor to visit the city since Basil the Bulgar-Slayer in 1018 – for another service of thanksgiving in the Cathedral of Our Lady. Peace was re-established and two parliaments were held, in 1209 and 1210, between the feudal lords of Greece. One result of this war was the establishment of greater Venetian power in Euboea. The ruler of Euboea, alarmed at the conquests of the king of Salonica, had offered to become a vassal of Venice for protection; from henceforth Venice received a tribute from the island, and had the right to trade and warehouse goods throughout the island. Venice appointed a bailie, whose successors gradually established Venetian authority throughout the island. Venice had in effect won a territory without the need for conquest.

The kingdom of Salonica came to end after the death of Henry in 1216 and Theodore, the Despot of Epirus, was crowned as emperor, thus establishing a rival to the rump Byzantine empire of Nicaea.

In 1225 Othon decided to return home to his lands in Franche-Comté, and was succeeded by his nephew Guy I. His reign, which lasted until 1260, saw increasing prosperity in the capital of Thebes, and a Genoese settlement was established with a consul. New monasteries were founded in his reign, that of St John the Hunter at Marathon, and another at Phyle on the border of Attica and Boeotia.

In 1246 William de Villehardouin became prince of Achaea. His reign of thirty years was marked by a steady increase in Frankish power. He built the great castles of Mistra, Maina and Beaufort, and laid siege to Monemvasia, an enterprise in which Guy I assisted. Guy married one of his nieces, but this did not prevent him from taking sides with the north of Greece against William when he decided to extend his power northwards. In 1258 a battle between the two armies took place at Megara. Guy was defeated and brought to trial. The Frankish peers quickly decided that there was no one of sufficiently high status to try the high-born Guy, and sent him to France for judgment from King Louis IX. Guy set off in spring 1259, but when he reached France, the king decided that the rigours of his journey had been quite sufficient punishment for his offence and reinstated him as lord of Athens. In addition, he granted him the title, which he coveted, of Duke. Thus began the line of Dukes of Athens whose titles echo throughout the pages of Boccaccio, Chaucer and Shakespeare. Shakespeare's Duke Theseus, in *A Midsummer Night's Dream*, is of course a figment, and shows how little awareness of Greek realities there was in the west; but his chivalric role chimes with the sound of the hunting horns and the flutter of bright pennants that set the imagination of Kazantzakis on fire when he visited Glarentza, envisaging the blond Franks in their 'savage fortress'.

The recovery of Constantinople in 1258 by the founder of a new dynasty, Michael Palaelogus, had implications also for Greece. The new emperor demanded the return of Argos and Nauplia from William, who replied that they belonged to Athens; but William ceded his fortresses in the Morea and made peace with Byzantium.

The Duchy of Athens

When Guy died in 1263 the Duchy of Athens had become the most prosperous state in Greece. The city's finances were on a sound basis: Duke John, his successor, was able to lend money for the pay of troops in the Morea, and a canon of Athens, Nicholas de la Roche, was able to endow a building (probably the belfry of the Church of the Megali Panaghia) in the Stoa of Hadrian. The harbour was improved for traders: about this time it came to be known as Porto Leone (the name is first recorded in 1318) from the marble lion that stood on the quay. The Duchy itself had no fleet, but Venetian and other merchants began to settle there. In 1278 a Venetian merchant ship was attacked by pirates near Marathon, and other haunts of pirates were known at Chalcis and at Sounion. By 1305 Athens was supplying Venice with grain.

Nothing is known of cultural life or education in Athens, though Guy II was able to quote Herodotus. Probably the de la Roches, like their kin in the west, read the medieval romances. But no original literature was produced, nothing comparable with the *Chronicle of the Morea* that recounted the deeds of the Franks in the Peloponnese. The Catalan chronicler Ramon Muntaner stated that better French was spoken in Athens than in Paris. There was no building activity, no art that has survived.

Though the de la Roches had gone increasingly native (Duke John spoke Greek and the wife of his brother and successor, William, was a Greek), the Venetian connection consolidated links with the west. The Pope offered indulgences to any who would make the pilgrimage of 'St Mary of Setines'. Greece was now ruled by a variety of powers: the Burgundian Dukes of Athens, the Villehardouin dynasty of the Morea, now under Angevin suzerainty, the Greeks whose power was increasing in various parts of the mainland, the Orsini in the Ionian islands, and the Venetians in the major trading ports. The increasing prosperity of Greece made it of growing interest to western powers, and this led to the next major turn of fortune in medieval Athens.

THE CATALAN COMPANY

The House of Anjou had established formal suzerainty over the Duchy through the marriage of Duke William's daughter to Charles I of Anjou. Charles planned, among other things, an attack on Constantinople. When William died in 1287 his son, Guy II was a minor and his mother Helen (a Greek) became regent. His coming of age and marriage in 1294 were the occasion of a splendid celebration in full chivalric style. Charles saw Guy's minority as an opportunity to establish closer control over Athens. He transferred the suzerainty of his Frankish dominions to his son Philip of Taranto, who strengthened his Greek links by marrying the daughter of the Despot of Epirus. When Charles attempted to enforce on Epirus their submission to his rule, the ruling Despoina Anna (the mother in law of Philip) showed her adherence to Greek dynasties by marrying her son to the granddaughter of the Emperor Andronikos II. Charles now summoned his son's vassals, Count John I of Cephalonia and Philip of Savoy, the Prince of Achaea (he had married William II Villehardouin's daughter Isabelle in 1301), to assist him. This led to what must have been one of the most colourful events in the history of Frankish Greece. Philip of Savoy, to avoid the summons, invited all the chivalry of Greece to a magnificent tournament at the Isthmus. On the plain where the Isthmian games had once been held, the Dukes of Athens and of the Archipelago, the Count of Cephalonia and the barons of Euboea, the Marshal of Thebes and the Marquis of Boudonitza, all assembled in the spring of 1305 to

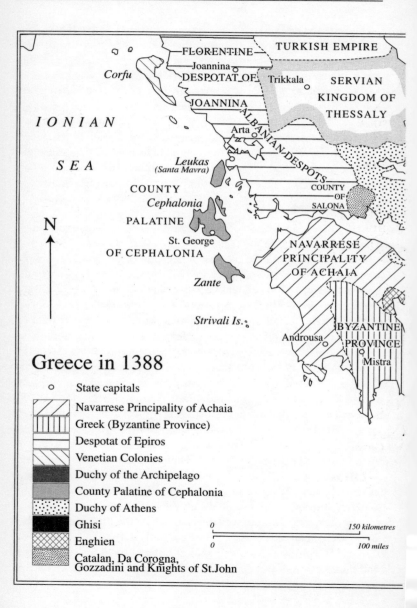

FLORENTINE
TURKISH EMPIRE

Corfu
Joannina
DESPOTAT OF
Trikkala
SERVIAN
KINGDOM OF
THESSALY

JOANNINA

IONIAN

Arta

SEA

Leukas
(Santa Mavra)

COUNTY
Cephalonia

COUNTY
OF
SALONA

N

PALATINE

St. George

OF CEPHALONIA

NAVARRESE
PRINCIPALITY
OF ACHAIA

Zante

Strivali Is.

Androusa

BYZANTINE
PROVINCE

Mistra

Greece in 1388

○   State capitals

⬚   Navarrese Principality of Achaia

⬚   Greek (Byzantine Province)

⬚   Despotat of Epiros

⬚   Venetian Colonies

⬛   Duchy of the Archipelago

⬚   County Palatine of Cephalonia

⬚   Duchy of Athens

⬛   Ghisi

⬚   Enghien

⬚   Catalan, Da Corogna,
Gozzadini and Knights of St. John

0   150 kilometres

0   100 miles

participate in the competitions of horsemanship and warfare of more than a thousand knights. It was the last and glorious flowering of Frankish Greece.

The Sicilian vespers of 1282, representing a crisis in the rivalry of Anjou and Aragon, had paralysed Charles' plans for a war against Constantinople. The peace of Caltabellotta between the two houses resulted in the emergence in the east of the Catalan Grand Company. This formidable army of professional soldiers had been employed by Frederick II Hohenstaufen against the Angevins in Sicily. Their leader at this time was Roger de Flor, an adventurer who had become a Knight of the Temple and thereafter Vice-Admiral of Sicily and a feared corsair. When peace was established the Catalans were unable to return to Spain because they had fought against Frederick's rival for the throne of Sicily, Jaime II of Aragon. Instead they offered their services, with 36 ships and 6,500 men, to the Emperor Andronikos who employed them to control the Turkish threat in Asia Minor. Their activities however quickly led to the plundering of Greek settlements in the area, and eventually Andronikos' son arranged the murder of Roger. Their leader now became Alfonso Fadrique, a natural son of Frederick II, under the nominal command of Frederick's nephew, the Infant Ferdinand. The Company headed into Greece, ravaging Halmyros and Skopelos and threatening Negroponte.

In 1308 Guy II, Duke of Athens, died and was buried in the Cistercian abbey of Daphni, perhaps in the sarcophagus emblazoned with serpents and lilies, which is still to be seen there. With this event 'the most brilliant period in the life of the Abbey' (William Miller) came to an end. Guy's nearest male relative was his nephew Walter (Gautier) of Brienne. Walter arrived in 1309 at Glarentza bearing letters patent from King Robert of Naples and Philip of Taranto and was installed as Duke of Athens. Soon he found trouble brewing in his duchy of Thessaly and decided to employ the Catalan Company to re-establish control. When this was done, he rewarded some 500 of them with pay and lands, and ordered the rest to be gone. Not surprisingly, they refused to go. Walter assembled an army from his Frankish allies in Greece – from Boudonitza, Euboea and Salona, from the Angevins of the Morea and from the Duke of Naxos – in the hope of not only wiping out the Catalans but carrying the campaign to the walls of Constantinople. Estimates of the size of his army varied: a Byzantine source put it at 6,400 horsemen and 8,000 foot, the *Chronicle of the Morea* at 2,000 horse and 4,000 foot, while the Catalan chronicler Ramon Muntaner stated it at 700 knights and an incredible 24,000 infantry from Athens alone.

The Catalan company, with some 3,500 horse and 4,000 foot, and a crowd of Turkish allies, chose their spot for the decisive battle on the marshy plain of the Cephisus in Boeotia. The armies joined battle on 15 March 1311. Walter led the Frankish charge; but as the horses advanced they sank inextricably into the bog, while the Catalans bombarded them with missiles. The Franks were almost entirely wiped out. 'All this noble chivalry' was killed in a single day, wrote Muntaner. Another contemporary observer wrote that not so much as an army chaplain was left to tell the tale. The Duke of Athens was slain and beheaded by a Catalan knife: many years later his head was carried in funeral pomp to Lecce and buried in the Church of Santa Croce.

The Catalans now marched into Livadia, which admitted them without resistance; to Thebes, whence the inhabitants fled; and to Athens, where they quickly made themselves masters of the city. The savage and illiterate soldiers shared out among them both castles and women, acquiring wives, as Muntaner wrote ' to whom they were not fit to hand a washbowl'. 'The luxuries of the Latins were destroyed and squandered,' wrote the Italian G. Villani. This largely leaderless crew of some 7,000 men appointed as their new chief Roger Deslaur of Roussillon, who made his home in the Castle of Salona.

However, the Catalans had plenty of enemies. They were hated by the House of Anjou, since Philip of Taranto claimed the suzerainty of Greece; the Venetians were alarmed at their threatening presence; the Greek states of Neopatras and Arta were naturally opposed; the Pope excommunicated the 'unspeakable band'; and the Byzantine emperor was enraged by their depredations in his dominions. The Catalans decided that they could not 'go it alone' but needed the support of a larger power. They offered their allegiance to Frederick II, who appointed his five year old son Don Manfred the Duke of Athens and sent out as his vicar-general Don Berenguer Estañol, who was succeeded on his death in 1316 by Don Alfonso Fadrique of Aragon.

None of the long succession of titular Dukes in the fourteenth century ever saw Athens, and the vicar-generals were the effective rulers of the Duchy. Alfonso, who married the daughter of Boniface of Verona, lord of Carystus, acquired additional dominions and established a dynasty of his own which ruled Athens for most of the Catalan period: his three sons became rulers of a number of Greek towns.

The new rulers, uncultivated as they were, brought considerable changes to the unfortunate city of Athens. Their official title was 'The fortunate army of the Franks in Romania'. They governed Athens as a corporation, 'la universitat de Cetines', with syndics and a council. The feudal law of Burgundy was replaced by the Customs of Barcelona. The capital, and the High Court, were established at Thebes. Rule was carried out in the name of the feudal lord by his vicar-general, and in each of the three cities of Thebes, Athens and Livadia there was a veguer (vicar) and a castellan – the latter also in the fortresses of Siderokastro and Neopatras. The municipal corporation consisted of prohomens, though how they were appointed we do not know. They chose their attorneys (sindichs) who represented them before the Duke. The style of government was thus transitional between the feudal and the municipal. The wealth of the Duchy was in rents, and the names are known of some fifty Catalan families who owned property in Thebes in the fourteenth century – considerably more than the number of Greek families. The cities dominated the countryside, but we hear no more of the Jews of Thebes and of the manufacture of silk and purple that had been so conspicuous a feature of the city a hundred years before. Even less is known of affairs in Athens.

Greeks had no civic or property rights and were in effect reduced to a state of slavery. They were also forbidden to intermarry. However, these rules cannot have been rigorously enforced, since some Greeks did own property and occasionally occupied important posts such as chancellor of Athens and notary of Livadia, and even sat, late in the Catalan period, on the council of Neopatras. The rule on intermarriage can also not have been adhered to without exception, since the surname Catalanos still persists in Athens.

The Catalans did not interfere with church matters but maintained the Latin hierarchy, with archbishops in Athens, Neopatras and Thebes.

Under the Archbisop of Athens were thirteen suffragan bishops, including Megara, Daulia, Salona and Boudonitza as well as Aegina. Athens remained predominant in ecclesiastical affairs in central Greece. Very few of these prelates, however, were Catalans.

The Catalans had few skills other than warfare, and quickly became known and feared as privateers in the Aegean. In 1310 a treaty between Venice and Byzantium forbade trade with the Catalans, and in 1319 they were compelled to abandon their piracy; but this left the seas open for other pirates, who continued to make life hard for any who lived in coastal communities for another century to come. The Venetians enforced the ban and in 1331 carried out a ruling that all Catalan ships should have one plank removed; recommissioning was forbidden.

In 1331 Walter II, the son of the last Duke of Athens, mounted an expedition from Lecce to reclaim his duchy from the usurpers, but the Catalans refused to emerge from their strongholds to meet his army, and Walter, finding no support forthcoming from the native population, had to abandon the attempt. The main result of this expedition was that the Catalans destroyed the castle of St Omer at Thebes in order to prevent its being used as a base by Walter. A further attempt by Walter in 1340 met with as little success, and he returned to Italy where he became the tyrant of Florence, whence he was expelled in 1343; he returned home to Lecce and in due course died on the field of Poitiers (1356).

A rare glimpse of Athens in these years is afforded by the pilgrim Ludolf von Sutheim, who travelled to the Holy Land between 1336 and 1341. He says of Athens: 'This city, which once was the most noble, is now almost deserted.' He states that 'all its columns' (which is plainly an exaggeration) had been removed to other cities, just as Venice had been built from Troy (a strange idea). He says nothing of any inhabitants he may have met.

Late in the 1340s the Pope, alarmed by the Turkish threat, finally granted recognition to the Catalans. The Turks had been making their presence felt since 1299. In 1326 Osman Pasha captured Prusa (Bursa) and his successor Orhan Gazi (1324–59) conquered Nicaea (Iznik), and in 1346 conducted raids on the Black Sea coast north of Constantinople. Under Murat I (1360–89) Gallipoli was used as a base for raids into Serbia. There was no knowing where the Turkish advance would halt: would they come all the way to Rome?

The history of the Catalans in the 1350s is confused, marked by rivalry between the new vicar-general, Jaime the son of Alfonso and the Marshal Roger de Lluria. The Duchy seems to have been close to anarchy. In 1361–2 the tyranny of the lieutenant Pedro de Pau provoked revolt of the feudatories: he expelled Jaime and attacked Roger, but was killed in a battle at Thebes. Roger de Lluria became the ruler of the Duchy until 1370. In 1363 the Turks occupied Thebes but were driven out a year later by Roger who had employed them for his own ends in a campaign against Euboea.

The 1360s saw the rise of one of the few important named Greeks of the age, the notary Demetrius Rendi (born ca 1330–5). His family, as retainers of the Kingdom of Sicily, were given the right of marriage with Catholics and permitted to purchase land in the same way as the Franks. Such privileges were rare in the extreme. Rendi's daughter later became the mistress of the Florentine Duke Nerio Acciaiuoli. Though Rendi himself is eclipsed after the end of Catalan rule, there is still a church of St John of Rendi between Athens and Piraeus.

In 1369–70 the Catalans began to campaign for union with the kingdom of Aragon-Catalonia. Queen Eleanor, the sister of Frederick III, who had little interest in Athens, offered to buy Athens for 100,000 florins, but the plan came to nothing. Further anarchy ensued on the death of Roger in 1370.

At about this time another threat to Athens arose in the form of the Navarrese Company, a soldier band of obscure origins which made itself master of Thebes and Levadhia but failed to capture Athens and merely ravaged it. The Athenians made a plea to the King of Aragon, Pedro IV, for protection, and at the same time for a more generous tax regime. In 1379 Pedro IV of Aragon annexed the Duchy and remained sovereign until 1388. He ordered remission of taxes to all Greek and Albanian settlers, a move which increased the population of his domain and resulted in the appearance of a number of Albanian village names in Attica. Many villages had become completely deserted. In Eleusis, for example, a number of Albanian Tosks moved in about 1418–25, but they soon moved inland to Mandra for fear of pirates. Though Pedro never visited Athens, he wrote in enthusiastic terms of the beauties of 'the most precious jewel that exists in the whole world, and such that all the kings of Christendom together could in vain imitate'.

The Acciaiuoli

In the meantime the next act in the drama of medieval Athens was being prepared in Corinth. In 1358 Robert II had granted Corinth to Niccolo Acciaiuoli, Grand Seneschal of the kingdom of Sicily, who – as his name implies – had made his fortune in steel. He became the effective ruler of the northern Peloponnese from Cyllene to Trozen. On his death in 1365 his second son Nerio assumed the rule of his domain, and observed with interest the decline of Catalan rule in Athens, about which he was well informed through his mistress Maria Rendi. The vicar-general Rocaberti, hoping to secure his dynasty, had become engaged to Maria, the daughter of the last count, Louis Fadrique. But he then tried to improve his position by repairing to Sicily to seek the hand of another Maria, the heiress of Frederick III and thus Duchess of Athens. In his absence the military command of Athens fell to the gallant Pedro de Pau. Rocaberti's intrigues, however, resulted in his fall from favour with King Pedro and he was removed from his post.

Nerio now contrived a plan to seek the hand of Countess Maria of Athens himself. Being repulsed, he determined that the moment had come to obtain Athens by force. He launched his attack in July 1385, accompanied by 800 Albanian horsemen and a large number of foot soldiers, and by January 1387 was master of the city except for the Acropolis, which was still heroically defended by Pedro de Pau and his troops. Pedro IV was succeeded by his son John I, who reappointed Rocaberti and instructed him to sail to Athens to relieve the defenders. Rocaberti, however, never set sail, and attacks by Turkish pirates on Nerio's troops were insufficient to raise the siege of Athens. By 2 May 1388 Nerio had broken the resistance of the defenders and the Catalans were gone from Athens for ever. They remained in control of Aegina until 1451 and a few families lingered in various parts of Greece (e.g. Zakynthos), but in Athens only the memory of their brutality remained.

The Catalan legacy in Athens was slight in the extreme. There is some Catalan work in the castles of Salona, Livadia and Lamia. They added some fortifications to the Acropolis. An inscription mentioning the Virgin, in Gothic letters, from near the agora gate, is now in the Byzantine museum. Their main legacy is as bogeys in still–current nursery songs that must date back to the Middle Ages.

Athens now fell victim to plague and Nerio quickly withdrew to Thebes. But unlike the previous western rulers, Nerio chose to make his capital the city of Athens, and his palace the Propylaea of the Acropolis. Giovanni Boccaccio, who had been a friend of Niccolo Acciaiuoli, lived long enough to see the establishment of the dukedom and to make it the scene of part of one of the stories in the *Decameron* (2.7), in which the Duke of Athens is 'a handsome, powerfully proportioned youth'. Without the support of a strong home government, and with the threat of the Turks on every side, Nerio found it prudent to make common cause with the native Greeks. Policy seems to coincide, even, with a certain respect for Greek culture, and with an improvement in the standing and influence of the Greek notables. Greek became the official language of government. For the first time since the flight of Acominatus, a Greek archbishop resided at Athens, probably close to the church of Dionysius the Areopagite, and held services in the church which later became the Fethiye Camii, behind the Library of Hadrian. (The Parthenon continued to be the Catholic cathedral of Athens.) Greek became the official language of government and Greek elders, demogerontes, played an important role in the government of the city. At the same time Florentine settlers enhanced the cosmopolitan mix at Athens, among them members of the Medici family who 'went native' under the name of Iatropoulos. But it was not all rosy; the new rulers could not avert plague and depopulation, and no attempt was made to end serfdom.

Nerio's reign also saw the first visit of a westerner to leave a written account of the city, apart from the few words devoted to it by the pilgrim Ludolf von Sutheim in the 1330s (above). Niccolo Martoni, also on pilgrimage, visited Athens in 1394, describing the buildings of the city, and the danger represented by the Turks. The city consisted of about a thousand houses. He visited some fountains, the 'School of

Aristotle', the Castle and the cathedral of St Mary, where he saw a painting of the Virgin made by St Luke, as well as various relics. He also described a Gorgon head on the south face of the Acropolis which was supposed to be a talisman against approaching ships.

The Navarrese, now established in the Morea but having apparently given up Thebes and Livadhia, continued to be a thorn in the flesh of Athens. In 1390 Nerio was taken prisoner by them at a parley called to dicuss the ownership of Argos, which he was anxious to make his own, and only obtained his release by purchasing it with large amounts of the treasure from the Parthenon. In 1389 the Battle of Kosovo had brought an end to the Serbian Empire and within a few years the Turks under Bayazid I had entered northern Greece. Nerio judged it more prudent to pay tribute than to resist, and for his submission the Sultan left Athens in peace.

On 25 September 1394 Nerio died. His will made provision for the restoration of all the treasure that had been taken from the Parthenon to redeem him in 1390, to be funded by the proceeds of his stud farm; and he also endowed a hospital in Nauplia. He also made bequests to the Bishop of Argos and the Archbishop of Athens, and left money for a weekly mass to be said for his soul. But disputes arose from his main dispositions: he bequeathed Megara, Sikyon and Corinth to his younger daughter Francesca, the wife of Carlo Tocco, Duke of Leucadia, and Thebes and Livadhia to his illegitimate son Antonio, whom he had had by Maria Rendi, the notary's daughter. The husband of the slighted elder daughter, Theodore Palaiologos, assisted by Antonio, besieged Corinth and seized the smaller castles. Carlo Tocco, on the other side, called in assistance from the Turks and gained the day; but later he handed over Corinth to the Despot Theodore.

The Greeks of Athens took advantage of the deflection of the attention of Nerio's heirs to invite Turkish assistance to drive out the Latin archbishop, and in 1394 Venice intervened to protect its own territories by driving out the Turks, to whom the Athenians were now paying tribute. The Greek archbishop was imprisoned in Venice, and Venice appointed a governor of Athens. In 1397 the Turks took control of Athens for a period, and they assisted Antonio in driving out the Venetians, following a siege which lasted seventeen months. (The surrender took place in February 1403.)

However, in 1405 Antonio became a vassal of Venice. Though he was not as prompt as they would have wished in paying the tribute, he remained duke for thirty-three years. In 1413 Sultan Mehmet I attacked Euboea, bringing to an end the reign of the Marquis of Boudonitza. Requests by Theodore to the Albanians, and to the Knights of St John, for assistance were unavailing. In 1416 Antonio too was compelled to pay tribute to the Turks, but Venice defeated the Turks at sea and peace was restored for a time by a treaty between the two powers. Through all the succeeding years, and the fall in 1430 of both Salonica and Ioannina to the Turks, Athens was preserved by the diplomacy of Antonio, even when in 1423 an outbreak of plague forced him to retreat to Megara.

Antonio, half-Greek himself, married Greek wives and adopted Greek daughters. He thus continued the process of cultural Hellenisation that had marked the rule of his father. Greeks continued to increase in influence: besides archons, Greeks filled the posts of chancellor and notary. These years saw the birth of two great men, the historian Laonikos Chalkokondyles and his brother Demetrius, who became one of the founding fathers of Greek studies in the west following the Turkish conquest of Constantinople in 1453. It was probably Antonio who added to the Palace in the Propylaea the 'Frankish Tower' which stood until 1875 when it was demolished at the expense of Heinrich Schliemann. Antonio built new walls in Athens and fortified the Klepsydra. New churches were built, including one on the Ilissus bridge, and Ag. Frankos; and the Metropolitan was restored. A temple at Kallirhoe was converted to a church (in the 1670s the Marquis de Nointel celebrated mass there). The Acciaiuoli also had pleasure gardens in the region of the agora and along the Ilissus.

When Antonio died in 1435 his nephew Nerio II occupied Athens and ruled it until 1451, except for an interlude from 1494 to 1441 when his brother Antonio II made himself Duke. At first a Turkish puppet, Nerio was later allied with the Greek despot, a position which put him at a disadvantage when in 1444 the Turks at the Battle of Varna made themselves masters of large parts of Greece. In 1446 Sultan Murat invaded Greece, broke down the Hexamilion wall across the Isthmus that had been built in 1415 by Manuel and so often repaired by the despots, and savagely slaughtered his captives. The onslaught continued under his successor Mehmet II the Conqueror, culminating in 1453 with the fall of Constantinople, an event of incalculable psychological significance for the whole Greek world.

CYRIAC OF ANCONA

The first important moment in the rediscovery by the west of the classical remains of Greece is represented by the visits of the Italian merchant, Cyriac of Ancona (1391–1449 or 1452). Cyriac used the opportunities offered by his trading journeys to collect Greek manuscripts for the Italian humanists who were beginning to discover Greek literature through the good offices of exiled learned Greeks, notably Manuel Chrysoloras. His patrons included Francesco Filelfo (who had married Chrysoloras' daughter) as well as Cosimo de' Medici and Janus Lascaris. But besides manuscripts, Cyriac turned his attention to monuments, copying inscriptions and drawing remains. He travelled repeatedly to Greece. Already in 1427 Filelfo spoke of Cyriac's task of 'restoring antiquity, or rather redeeming it from extinction'. By the end of the 1440s he had visited the Pyramids, the Ionian islands, Epirus, northern Greece and the Peloponnese (especially Sparta and Mistra, where he visited the great scholar Gemistus Plethon, the last Platonist of the Byzantine Empire), Cyzicus and the northern Aegean islands.

It was in spring 1437 that he first visited Athens, twenty-four years after his travels had begun. In his notes on his visit, he refers to the Acropolis by its ancient name for the first time since antiquity. He visited the 'Palace of Hadrian' (Temple of Olympian Zeus), and that of Themistocles, as well as the 'grave of Socrates' (identifications he had no means of challenging). He was told that the Theatre of Dionysus was the Lyceum and that the temple of Nike was the school of Pythagoras. He also saw the Lysicrates monument, the aqueduct of Hadrian, and one of the giants from the Odeion of Agrippa.

But Cyriac did more than just visit. Though he found no library, as he had at Kalavryta and Corfu, he prowled about copying the inscriptions on the Monument of Philopappus (two of which have

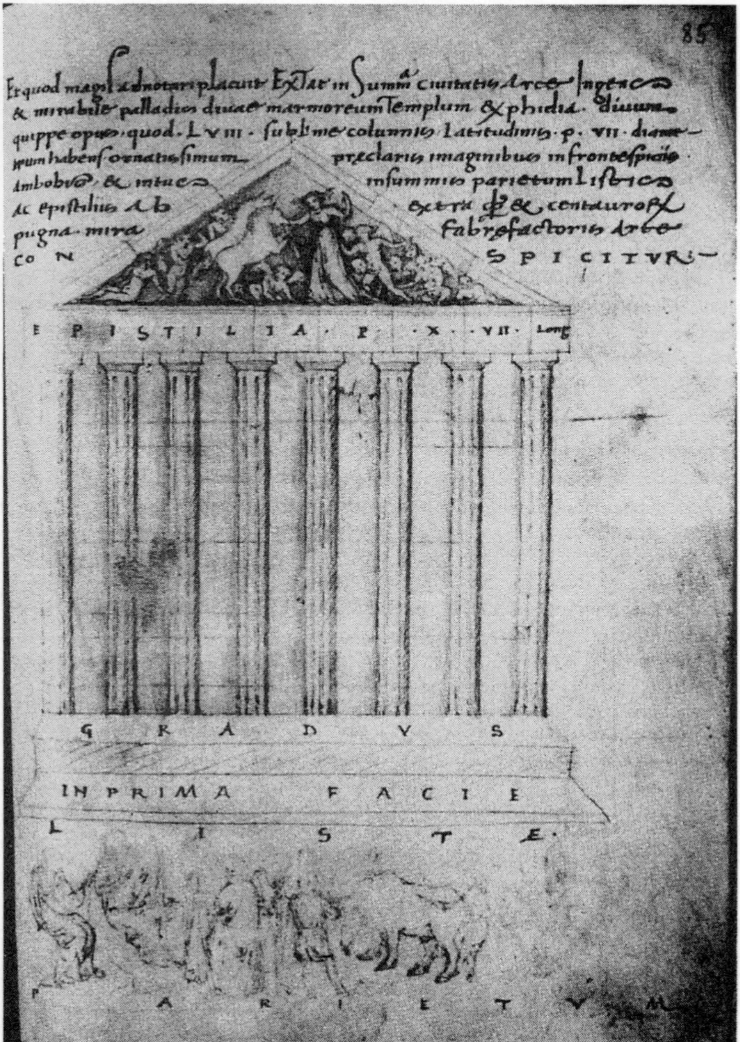

Cyriac of Ancona's drawing of the Parthenon

subsequently been lost) and making drawings of the pediments of the Parthenon: these latter are a valuable record of the appearance of the sculptures before the destruction of 1687, though unfortunately we only have copies made from Cyriac's own sketches, and these are not of high quality. Though his originals cannot have been particularly accurate (the copies show no sign of the metopes or triglyphs), he did his best to record what he thought important, and his copies of inscriptions were honest and careful. It is a tragedy that his own notebooks are lost. If he was not, as Gregorovius called him, a Pausanias reincarnate, his service to archaeologists is of a comparable kind; and his part in the development of the Italian renaissance is a notable one.

The Turkish Conquest of Athens

In 1451 Nerio died, leaving the final act of Frankish rule in Athens to be played in a manner worthy of a Renaissance tragedy. Gregorovius (530) calls it 'a pitiful tragedy of criminal passions and the struggle of insignificant persons for a moment of princely existence'. Nerio's second wife Chiara, the duchess of Boudonitza, had borne him a son, Francesco, who was still a minor on his father's death. Chiara made herself regent of Athens and before long fell in love with a Venetian noble, Bartolomeo Contarini, whose father had been governor of Nauplia. Contarini, knowing where his best opportunity lay, poisoned his present wife and made himself the first man of Athens. However, the son of Antonio II, Franco, had found a position at the Sultan's court, and was perhaps complicit in an Athenian move to have Contarini arraigned before the Sultan. The latter ordered the sinful pair to be deposed. Francesco disappears from history. Franco now arrested his aunt Chiara, and had her imprisoned in Megara, where she was shortly murdered. According to a picturesque legend (as William Miller describes it), Franco strangled her with his own hands in the monastery of Daphni.

Contarini reappeared with a fleet to rescue his wife, but was too late. The Sultan seized the pretext of the miscreancy of Franco to march on Athens himself. An army led by Omar, the son of the governor of Thessaly, attacked the city in May 1456. A comet on the twenty-ninth, the third anniversary of the capture of Constantinople, appeared to presage disaster, and on 4 June Athens fell into the hands of the Turks. As always, the Acropolis held out for longer, and the constable appealed for help to Venice and even to Alfonso V of Aragon, still in name the Duke of Athens. An offer of lands in Boeotia, with Thebes, persuaded Franco to give up his claim to Athens, and to resign it to the Turks. The Latin archbishop departed with the duke, and was compensated with the archbishopric of Lepanto, which he held from 1461 to 1483. The Frankish domination that had lasted more than two centuries was over.

The aftermath for the Acciaiuoli was grim. Franco was killed, his sons were taken away and became janissaries, and his widow, the daughter of the Byzantine noble Demetrius Asen, was taken by Mehmet to Edirne where she became the wife of Amiroutzes, the betrayer of Trebizond. But he, according to a contemporary source (the *Ecthesis Chronica*), died while playing dice and went straight to hell.

The fall of Athens was lamented in poetry, though little of it is of high quality (Gregorovius 535). The neighbouring territory of Euboea (Negroponte) fell to the Turks in 1470 after a fierce siege. The Euripus ran red with blood, and after the city was taken the bailie was sawn in half by the conquerors. Only the Venetian colonies remained of the Frankish presence in Greece.

In 1458, following his conquest of the Morea, Mehmet II spent four days in Athens, where he admired the sights and offered special privileges to the monastery of Kaisariani, whose abbot, it is said, handed him 'the keys of Athens'. He examined and admired the Acropolis, Chalkokondyles wrote, 'with the eyes of a scholar, a philhellene and a great sovereign'. 'How much', he cried, 'do we not owe to Omar, the son of Turakhan!'

CHAPTER TEN

Ottoman Athens

(i) From the Conquest to 1687

The Turkish conquest of Athens was swift and complete. Few attempts were made by western powers to win the city back, and these were only fleeting. Turkish rule lasted in Athens, and in the rest of mainland Greece, for nearly four hundred years. Athens was one of the last parts of Greece to fall under Ottoman rule.

One brief attempt to recover Athens was made almost immediately, by the Venetian commander Vettore Cappello. He captured the lower town, fired a few ships, and explored the sites of the city. He left a written description of his visit, in which he reported that the Tower of the Winds was being used as a church, and he enthused over the monastery of Daphni. But he contented himself with this brief skirmish, and sailed away leaving Athens still firmly under Turkish control.

The Acropolis of Athens was made out of bounds to all non-Turks immediately after the conquest, and became the seat of the garrison and military command. The disdar (military commander) had his palace in the Propylaea, and the Erechtheion was converted for use as his harem. Omar, the conqueror of Athens, settled in the district now known as Patissia. (The word comes from Padishah, Omar's title.) Plaka, which had been uninhabited since the eleventh century, became home to the Albanians whom the Turks employed as guards.

TURKISH ADMINISTRATION

Despite the brutality of the Turkish conquest of many parts of Greece, and despite the reputation for cruelty that lives on in the common speech of present-day Greece, Turkish administration was in many ways more favourable to the native Greeks than Frankish power had been. In particular, the Orthodox Church and its institutions benefited from the change from Frankish to Turkish rule. No longer sidelined as a schismatic sect, they were regarded as the representatives of the religion of the native population. The Ottomans, as Muslims, respected the religion of other 'peoples of the book' or monotheists (though being puzzled about how the Trinity fitted into monotheism), and allowed them liberty of worship. This was in contrast to their attitude to heathen peoples, who must be converted to Islam or suffer the penalty, often of death.

The Turkish governmental structure was the same as in other parts of the Ottoman Empire, which stretched to central Asia and to Egypt. Athens was a part of the *sancak* of Evripos, which was under the command of a *sancakbey*. Above him was the pasha of the Morea (with four *sancaks*) who in turn owed allegiance to the *beylerbey* of Roumeli. (The larger islands and the Asia Minor coast were in the charge of the *Kapudanpasha*.) The power of the pashas was limited by the land-holdings of the veterans which were known as *timars*: they were not hereditary and the *timariot* owed his allegiance to the Sultan and not to the governor. There were about 1,600 *timars* and 300 larger estates or *ziamets* in Greece under Mehmet II.

Athens itself was in the charge of a governor or *voyvode* who was appointed annually; he purchased his appointment, and then recouped the cost by the imposition of taxes. He had a considerable staff of up to thirty people. Other officials of Turkish rule were the *kadi* (judge), the *mufti* (the official responsible for the Orthodox Church), and the *disdar* (the military governor of the Acropolis). The cavalry or *spahis* were under the command of the *spahilarağa* and the Janissaries under the *serdarağa*.

The Greek population was subject to variety of taxes, not all of which applied equally to Turkish or Muslim subjects. These included the *tzaki* or (in Greek) *kapnikos*, literally a chimney tax; the *ocak* or hearth tax, the *haraç* or poll tax and, most resented of all, the *devşirme* or child tribute, by which one in five male children was requisitioned to go to Constantinople and enter the ranks of the elite slave army loyal only to the Sultan himself. This latter tribute was only abolished late in the seventeenth century. In 1645 Athens was able to purchase the privilege of attachment to the Sultan's harem, because of the affection of Ahmet I for a favourite slave, an Athenian woman called Vasiliki. As a result, from now on all taxes were controlled by the Kizlar ağa, or Chief of the Black Eunuchs. This insulated the city to some extent from the depredations of local governors, as the Kizlar ağa became their patron and court of appeal against abuses.

From the beginning conditions favoured the growth of Greek institutions. The loose style of control in the Ottoman empire permitted subject peoples to maintain their own institutions of local government, and thus the Greek population quickly achieved a social hierarchy as well as a system of administration. The Christian population was represented by the *demogerontes*, elders of the people, drawn from the twelve highest ranking families, or *archontes*. These originally held their meetings in their houses, but soon founded the *kouseyio* in a building in the Upper Bazaar. The derivation of the name from the French *conseil* suggests that the institution must already have existed, perhaps in rudimentary form, under Frankish rule.

The next status group was the *noikokyraioi* or landowners, of whom there were twenty-four families. They were addressed as *kyr* (lord) and could be recognised by their pointed red shoes. Below these were the *pazarites*, merchants and stall keepers, and lastly the *zotarides*, the smallholders. Merchants had a number of guilds and had their names prefixed by the honorific *mastro-*. Slavery had finally died out under the Franks, and peasants were left to enjoy more of the fruits of their labour than under Frankish rule.

The city itself at this time consisted of eight districts, two of which, Plaka and Psyrri, still preserve their names: the others were Kottake, Monokaloufti, Roumbi, Boreia ('northern'), Gerlada ('garland', a Catalan name) and Kolymbos. The city grew considerably in size until in 1671 it was six times the size of the Frankish city and contained 2,053 houses, of which 1,300 were inhabited by Greeks, 600 by Turks, 150 by Albanians, and three by 'others'. The total population was about 10,000, three-quarters of whom were Greeks. There is not a single Frank now to be found in the city. Also notable is the absence of any

Jewish population, in contrast to other cities such as Thebes and Thessaloniki. (However, in 1588 a German apothecary named Reinhold Lubenau of Königsberg was guided around the city by a converted Jewish physician named Abraham Sfortius who had studied at Padua.)

The growth of the city did not involve the erection of any distinguished buildings, for the Turks as well as the Greeks found new uses for the existing ones. The only exception to this generalisation are the mosques. Besides the Parthenon, which, formerly a Catholic cathedral, had quickly been converted into a mosque, there were four: the Fethiye Camii or mosque of the Conqueror near the Tower of the Winds, built in 1458 to honour the visit of Mehmet II (still extant); the Küçük Camii (Little Mosque) further up the northern slope of the Acropolis; the Tzistaraki Mosque or mosque of the column, built in 1759 by the *voyvode* Tzistaraki, which still stands in Monastiraki Square; and the Yeni Camii (New Mosque) in the Upper Bazaar. Around these four latter mosques the district of Plaka developed into a bustling market area, divided into the Lower Bazaar, in the region of Monastiraki, the Upper Bazaar corresponding to the interior of the Library of Hadrian (with some hundred shops), and the Grain Market (Staropazaro) in what had been the Roman agora. Plaka became the location of the *voyvodalik* or governor's office, which was in the southwest corner of the Library of Hadrian, and of the Demogerontion, in another corner of the same monument. The customs office and court were also situated around here, as well as cafés, hamams or baths and inns. (The hamam of Abit Effendi still survives at Kirristou 8.) Daily, weekly and annual markets were held here: grain, oil salt and produce could be bought any day of the week in the grain market; a weekly market in the Lower Bazaar, on Sundays after church, purveyed fish, meat, live animals and firewood; a horse fair was held at the Theseion. By the eighteenth century the stock in the bazaars had developed beyond the needs of a subsistence economy to include silks, wine, books and caviar (all observed by H.W. Williams in 1820). Greek merchants set up establishments in Venice, Livorno, Trieste, Bucharest, Vienna, and the objects of their trade came back too to Athens.

Besides the mosques, a few new churches were built. Most significant was the monastery of the Capuchins, who established a mission

The Bazaar (after a painting by Edward Dodwell)

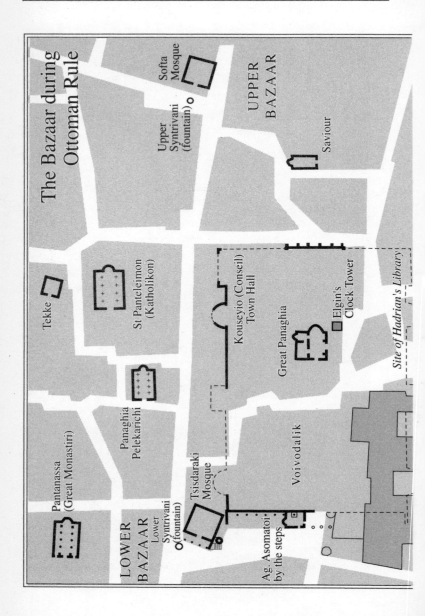

The Bazaar during Ottoman Rule

Softa Mosque

Upper Syntrivani (fountain)

UPPER BAZAAR

Saviour

Tekke

St Panteleimon (Katholikon)

Kouseyio (Conseil) Town Hall

Great Panaghia

Elgin's Clock Tower

Site of Hadrian's Library

Panaghia Pelekarichi

Voivodalik

Pantanassa (Great Monastiri)

LOWER BAZAAR

Lower Syntrivani (fountain)

Tsisdaraki Mosque

Ag. Asomatoi by the steps

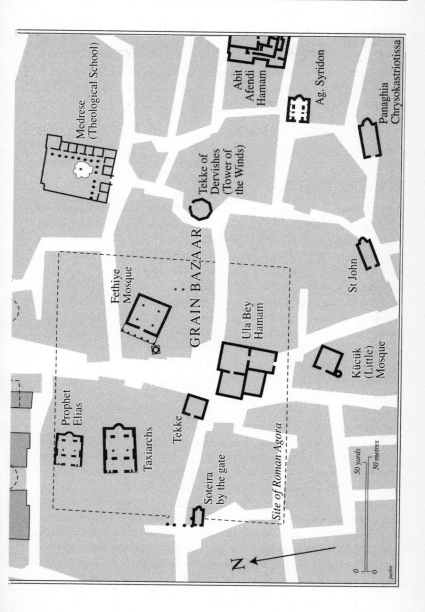

in Athens in the 1660s; but their premises consisted of the 'Lantern of Demosthenes' and the land adjoining it. Several Byzantine churches also vanished during this period, including the Soteira, that of Profitis Elias and that of the Taxiarchs. Other Muslim establishments included the re-use of the Tower of the Winds as a *tekke* for the use of the Whirling Dervishes. Opposite its entrance a *medrese* or theological school was built in 1721.

The southern part of the Rizokastro wall was also preserved, now under the name of 'serpentze'.

Western Travellers

In all these two centuries there is scarcely a single specific historical event to be narrated. Despite slow urban growth, in physical appearance the city seemed very little different in the 1680s from the way it had looked in the 1480s. The city had been almost forgotten in the west until the Renaissance began to stimulate some interest in what had become of the most glorious city of antiquity. Few travellers stopped at Athens. The pilgrim route to the Holy Land passed the city by. In 1537 one Jehan de Vega, cruising past Sounion with a French fleet, reported seeing the columns of 'Aristotle's School'. In 1573 the German humanist Martin Crusius (Kraus) was writing to a correspondent to ask if Athens in fact still existed. In 1610 the splenetic Scots traveller William Lithgow stayed briefly in the city and described it as 'from slaughter'd Athens now a village left'.

Fanciful names of ancient monuments became the stock in trade of the self-appointed ciceroni of Athens when western travellers began to come in greater numbers in the seventeenth century. One of the first was Nicolas du Loir, who travelled in the party of the Venetian ambassador to Venice in March 1641. The party visited Athens while based at Negroponte, accompanied by a certain M. Venizelly. Du Loir, who had been studying his Pausanias, was able to see the Parthenon, correctly described as a temple of Minerva, and was told of the mosque therein, and a chapel with an inscription 'to the Unknown God'. He also saw the 'temple of Theseus' and nearby a large marble lion formerly used as a fountain. The party visited the Long Walls and were shown the 'School of Zeno' to the south of the Acropolis (actually the Theatre of Dionysus), as well as a 'temple of Pan' with two standing columns, above the theatre (a misreading of Pausanias). He identified the octagonal temple (not in Pausanias), i.e. the Tower of the Winds (which a few years later another visitor, the German J.G. Transfeldt [1648–85], identified as the School of Socrates), and the 'Lantern of Demosthenes', which he refused to believe was Demosthenes' study, and was distressed to find a beggar woman encamped in it. The Gate of Hadrian is correctly identified as is the Temple of Olympian Zeus; then follows the 'theatre' (actually the stadium), the 'Lyceum of Aristotle' (the two columns of the aqueduct of Hadrian which were visible well into the eighteenth century), and he mistakenly locates the Academy of Plato in the vicinity of the 'Temple of Artemis' (now vanished) by the Ilissus.

SPON AND WHELER

Other observers of the antiquities of Athens include the Jesuit J.P. Babin, who had prepared a pictorial map of Athens which was published in 1674 by the antiquary Jacob Spon (1647–85). An even more important document from that year was the result of the visit to Athens by the French ambassador, the Marquis de Nointel, fresh from success in renegotiating the capitulations (trading agreements) with the Ottoman Empire. Nointel made a grand processional entry into the city and was enabled to visit the Acropolis itself. An enormous painting now in the National Gallery in Athens depicts his visit, and he described it himself:

> I can assure you that no one has enjoyed all the means which were at my disposal to examine all its artistic treasures; one may say of those which are to be seen in the castle, around the temple of Minerva, that they surpass even what is beautiful in the reliefs and statues of Rome. I entered for the first time, in procession and to the sound of cannon, into the treasury where these marvels are kept, and I returned incognito five or six times to admire them better and to study the beautiful drawings which my painter made of the most beautiful of them, which contain up to two hundred figures, beyond and above the natural, in high and low relief, some entire and some mutilated. There are men, women and centaurs, battles and victories of the

J.P. Babin's map of Athens

latter, triumphs, sacrifices, and if it were possible for me to express the rich confusion which such beautiful order, such fine composition, and the expression of such varied passions have left in my soul, I should undertake it with pleasure.

The painter he mentions was probably his court artist, Jacques Carrey, and the detailed drawings of the Parthenon pediments that survive are usually attributed to him: they remain indispensable evidence for the appearance of the pediments before their damage at the hands of the Venetians in 1687 and by Lord Elgin's agents in 1801.

Spon himself visited Athens in 1676 in the company of the Englishman George Wheler (1650–1723), and was hospitably entertained by the French consul Jean Giraud. Giraud, who was married to a lady of the Palaiologos family, had himself made a study of the topography of Athens, and acted as cicerone to many foreign visitors. Spon was able to benefit from his researches to produce the most reliable account of the monuments so far. In this he came into direct conflict with a charlatan named Guillet de la Guilletière, whose *Athènes Ancienne et Nouvelle* (1675), based on a visit of seven days, incorporated a reproduction of Babin's map with over one hundred identifications of buildings, some correct, but many barely plausible or clearly wrong. Guillet had followed up his account, which seems to have been a kind of bestseller, with an even more fraudulent account of the antiquities of Sparta, of which there was almost nothing left and where he had never been. Guillet had, for example, called the Monument of Philopappus an Arch of Trajan (when it is not even an arch), mentioned the Stoa Poikile and referred to something called the Lantern of Diogenes. He also mentioned the lion near the Parthenon earlier noted by du Loir.

Spon's much more reliable account was given currency, not only by his own book, but by that of George Wheler, which is in part a translation or reworking of Spon's French original. It is an important document of early archaeological exploration of Athens. Guillet, for all his scholarly faults, gave a more gossipy account of present-day Athens from which emerges some of the flavour of life there at the time. Led from one site to the next by a janissary, they were at length taken to see a Greek schoolmaster:

We desired no better, and were upon thorns till we were with him, but alas, how we were disappointed, (who expected nothing but the sublime notions of Plato, Zeno and Aristotle), when the Janizary told us he was a mechanick; how were we surprised to consider a man of that quality should succeed in the place of such excellent persons. We found about thirty young lads sitting upon benches, and their master at the head of them, teaching them to read; he rose up when we came, and received us very civilly, in which, to give them their due, that Nation is not sparing.

The meeting was followed by a visit from two learned monks and a meal of 'a kind of sausage made up with eggs and the belly of a fish they call cephale, and we pollard', followed by neats' tongues and accompanied by 'blackish wine'. The story continues with a long speech by one of the monks about the decline of Athens from its former glories: if this seems to prefigure the laments of the European Romantics over 'Fair Greece, sad relic of departed worth', it may for all that reflect a consciousness among educated Greeks of the period that their nation had been made for better things – a consciousness which was to be one of the roots of the movement for independence in the late eighteenth century.

EVLIYA ÇELEBI

A notable contrast with these accounts of Athens is provided by a contemporary Turkish traveller, Evliya Çelebi, whose account of his wanderings throughout the Ottoman Empire was published in 1667. His description is long and repays reading in full: only a few passages can be excerpted here. It begins from an intellectual milieu totally different from that of the western travellers, sons of the Renaissance as they were. For Evliya, Athens was founded by King Solomon, and the palace here built for the Queen of Sheba with whom he visited the city on a pair of flying thrones. Solomon's son Rehoboam improved the city, as did his great great great grandson Philip of Macedon, the father of Alexander the Great. Pythagoras, Plato, Hippocrates, Aristotle, Galen and their friends spent their long lives (340 years, though in truth 800 would not be long enough to make Pythagoras a contemporary of Galen) seeking for a Remedy against Fate; failing to find it, Plato abandoned philosophy and wandered away to Budapest where he died.

From these flights of scholarship Evliya proceeds to an account of the Parthenon. (As a Turk, he was allowed access to the Acropolis.)

Were we to describe every form and feature of this place, our writing would fill a whole book and the mind of man could not encompass it. It is like some impregnable fortress not made by human agency. Only when looking at these sculptures by Aristos would anybody say that they are human works, and say no more. For every one of these figures seems to be dowered with a human soul ... the painter painted every form of terrible monster and ghastly temptation — demons, devils, wild beasts, enchantresses and angels and dragons and antichrists and Cyclopes and creatures of a thousand shapes and crocodiles and elephants and camelopards and owls and centipedes ... and furthermore the Cherubim and Seraphim [the list goes on].

After the Parthenon, Evliya describes the Propylaea , which he calls the 'school of the famous doctors', and which was at this time used as a powder magazine. 'Descending by the north flank of the citadel, we come into the cool town of Athens, which gives the impression of a fantastic garden.' (Evliya also sees Kifissia as a 'Paradise garden', inhabited half by Greeks and half by Turks.) He describes the three mosques then existing, plus

seven small neighbourhood mosques, a seminary, three children's schools, two oratories of the dervishes, three pleasant baths — of Oula bey, of Hadji Ali and of Abit Effendi — two galleries of shops ... no covered bazaar ... seven thousand houses, tile-roofed and built of stone, like forts. Nowhere are they mud-roofed or built of mud-brick and wood. Each house has its own cistern... All the streets are clean, their surface of beaten sand. Nowhere in this town are there stone-paved streets because there is never any mud.

Evliya also mentions three hundred churches of 'image worshippers'. Fantasy takes over again as he describes the antiquities, including the 'Palace of Belkis' (i.e. the Queen of Sheba: the Temple of Olympian Zeus), the 'Tent of Plato' (Tower of the Winds). Inside the latter is a

Tomb which the infidel Greeks revere as the tomb of Philip ... In the apex of the roof is a tall rod. In ancient times they say that it supported a mirror of the world like that on Alexander's lighthouse, which could reflect all the enemy host advancing on the city from whatever side. Its place is still there, but the mirror is lost. They also tell how in those times the philosophers did such magic works that neither did a plague ever strike this town nor was it ever visited by snakes or centipedes or scorpions or storks, crows, fleas, lice, bedbugs, mosquitoes or flies, until the night when the Prophet, the Beloved of God, was born, and all the ancient spells were nullified. Yet today there are in Athens no centipedes or mosquitoes.

The Bombardment of the Parthenon

This bug-free, mud-free idyll in the cool gardens of Athens, so vividly – if perhaps erroneously – evoked by Evliya, came to an abrupt end when revived western interest in the city once again took military form. Venice lost its possession of Crete to the Ottomans after a thirty-year siege in 1669. In 1683 the Ottomans were only narrowly driven back from Europe at the siege of Vienna. This perceived Turkish threat to Europe led to the creation by Venice, Rome, Austria and Poland of a Holy League against the Ottoman Empire in 1686. The cosmopolitan army raised by Venice was commanded by the sixty-six year old Francesco Morosini, a veteran of the defence of the Cretan capital Candia (Iraklion).

Morosini's army swiftly conquered the Peloponnese and moved against Athens. The Greek notables regarded the westerners as, on balance, likely to be liberators despite their Catholic faith, and arranged to admit them. The Turkish defenders retreated to the Acropolis. The women and children of the leading families took refuge in the Parthenon, which now functioned as a mosque, as well as being, like the Propylaea, a powder magazine. Though the strategic value of Athens was slight, its reputation made it a desirable prize, and Morosini determined on the capture of the Acropolis. He set up four light cannon, two heavy cannon and four mortars on the Hill of Philopappus. The bombardment began on 24 September 1687. On the third day a missile penetrated the roof of the Parthenon, which, like the Propylaea, was used as a powder magazine, and caused a tremendous explosion which caused the central columns of the hitherto intact buildings to be blown outwards. The roof and two-thirds of the cella walls collapsed, as well as the pronaos and the metopes and frieze slabs in the centre of the north and south walls. 'In this way', wrote a member of the besieging force, Cristoforo Ivanovich, 'that famous temple of Minerva, which so many centuries and so many wars had not been able to destroy, was ruined'.

The siege continued for several more days. Ivanovich goes on:

In the meantime, Field Quartermaster General Dolfino, heedless of his own safety and often exposing himself to musket fire in order to speed up the work of the cannons and the bombs, sought to press the fortress ever more strongly and to force the Turks to surrender. Mutoni [the artillery commander], informed by a Greek that some women of the Aga Khan [?] had withdrawn into a house, directed fire at it, and a bomb made such a slaughter of them that the fortress, terrified and still despairing of the aid that had fled, agreed to show the white flag and to surrender: this was at 10.00 pm of [the 28th].... The terms of their surrender were ...: they were to leave all their weapons in the fortress, leave with their women and children and with those possession that each could carry from the fortress to the sea in a single trip, and to hire three foreign vessels for their embarkation and voyage to Smyrna.

The evacuation was carried out by 24 October: 2,500 people left including the garrison of 500. Some German troops remained in the newly liberated city. One mosque was quickly converted for use as a Lutheran church, another for the Catholics. However, the Venetians soon found that they could not hold the city, because of the difficulty of fortifying the road from Piraeus, and on 31 December they decided to evacuate Athens. Morosini considered destroying the walls of the Acropolis fortress before departure, but decided against it. However, he did try to remove some sculptures from the Parthenon pediment, which fell to the ground during the operation and were smashed (16 March 1688); so they were left where they were. Morosini was more successful with the huge marble lion that had stood for centuries on the shore at Piraeus and given the port its name of Porto Leone; he removed this to Venice (with three others), where it still stands by the Arsenal.

With the Venetians' departure, 662 Greek families also evacuated Athens; 500 souls went to the Argolid, others to Corinth, Aegina and

Tinos. The Turks returned to Athens and tried somewhat half-heartedly to strengthen the city's defences, by repairs to the Acropolis and by building the wall known as Hypapandi, protecting the north flank of the entrance to the Acropolis. The Acropolis was quickly inhabited again, and travellers reported seeing about 200 houses on the rock.

On his return to Venice, Morosini was elected Doge. In July 1688 the Venetians laid siege to Negroponte, but without success. A similar failure attended their attempt on Monemvasia in 1689. By 1690, the Turks had recovered all the territory they had lost, except the Morea which was ceded to Venice by the Treaty of Carlowitz in 1699: the Ottomans did not recover it until 1718 (the Treaty of Passarowitz).

(ii) The Growth of Philhellenism

Life slowly returned to normal in eighteenth-century Athens. Prosperity gradually improved under the conditions of peace established by these two treaties. Greek officials began to acquire more power within the city. For example, Alexander Mavrocordatos became Dragoman of the Fleet, and in 1716 his son Nicolos became the first Phanariot (Greek) *voyvode* of Wallachia. The Monastiraki Church was also rebuilt, perhaps as early as 1678. Most of the international events of the eighteenth century made little impression on the Ottoman backwater that was Athens, but underneath the surface there continually grew a national consciousness that began to find expression in the 1790s in the revolutionary songs and plots of Rhigas Velestinlis (executed in Belgrade 1797).

THE SOCIETY OF DILETTANTI

An important feature of the middle of the eighteenth century was the return of the western travellers. The rediscovery of classical architecture was part of a complex cultural movement that became known as the Greek revival. In architectural terms it began with the decision of a London dining club of aristocrats who had visited Italy, known as the Society of Dilettanti, to send an expedition to study the architecture of Athens 'for the improvement of the arts in England'. Two architects,

James ('Athenian') Stuart and his younger companion Nicholas Revett, drew up a detailed proposal: 'Athens, the mother of elegance and politeness, whose magnificence scarce yielded to that of Rome, and who for the beauties of a correct style must be allowed to surpass her, has been almost completely neglected, and unless exact drawings from them be speedily made, all her beauteous fabricks, her temples, her theatres, her palaces will drop into oblivion, and Posterity will have to reproach us.' The pair were despatched in 1750 to Athens, where they finally arrived only in March 1751. They spent almost two years in the city, but the only record of their activities are the four volumes of the *Antiquities of Athens*. Only the first volume was published before Stuart's death in 1788, and the supplementary volume appeared only in 1830. Their work set new standards of accuracy in architectural drawing. The first volume was devoted to the Doric portico which they rightly identified as the entrance to the Roman Agora; the Ionic Temple on the Ilissus (now vanished); the 'Tower of the Winds'; the 'Lantern of Demosthenes' and the Library of Hadrian. Their reason was, according to Stuart, that 'we selected such buildings for our proposed publication, as would exhibit specimens of the several kinds of columns in use among the ancient Greeks; that if, contrary to our wishes, nothing more should be demanded of us concerning Athens, those who honoured us with their subscriptions to that volume, might find in it something interesting on the different Grecian modes of decorating buildings.'

It was not always easy for the artists to get access to the monuments they wished to draw. The Tower of the Winds was in use as a tekke of the Whirling Dervishes, and the ground around it had risen some fifteen feet since antiquity. One of the inhabitants of the area nearby obligingly pulled down his house to enable them to get a better view of the building, and they also obtained permission to break up the floor, from which they removed 2,700 cubic feet of earth before revealing the original marble pavement.

Their work on this, and on the 'Lantern of Demosthenes', bore fruit on their return home in a number of architectural commissions. Among the earliest were Stuart's own architectural adornments at Shugborough (Staffordshire), including an Arch of Hadrian and a

Lantern of Demosthenes (1764), as well as Doric temples here and at Hagley Park by Stuart and at West Wycombe by Revett. Other architects followed suit: Inwood's Church of St Pancras in London incorporates the Caryatid porch of the Erechtheum and James Wyatt's Radcliffe Observatory in Oxford is a copy of the Tower of the Winds. Lanterns of Demosthenes became so popular (spreading by the end of the century to Perth in Scotland, and in the next century to Nashville's State Capitol, to the Philadelphia Merchants' Exchange and even to Sydney's Botanical Garden) that the Palladian architect Sir William Chambers, was moved to contemptuous utterance: 'the celebrated Lantern of Demosthenes, is in reality not quite so large as one of the sentry boxes in Portman Square: its form and proportions resemble those of a silver tankard except that the handle is wanting'. The Tower of the Winds was no better: 'to vulgar eyes [it] resembles exactly one of the dove houses usually erected on gentlemen's estates in the country of England, excepting that the roof is somewhat flatter and there is no turret for the pigeons to creep in and fly out at, but we are assured that a more nice observer will be greater pleased with its elegance and extraordinary beauty'.

Volume II of the *Antiquities* illustrated the Parthenon, including 30 plates depicting the whole frieze, the Erechtheum, the Odeion of Herodes Atticus (miscalled the 'Theatre of Bacchus'), the Choragic Monument of Thrasyllus and the Propylaea. Though publication was after Stuart's death, the drawings were obviously being used as architects' models not only by Stuart but by contemporaries well before that. The work of Stuart and Revett remains a valuable record of the state of the monuments of Athens in the eighteenth century.

The travellers, however, say little about the life of the inhabitants of the city. They returned just before the epidemic or plague which devastated the city in April 1759. The plague arrived from Crete, and was popularly blamed on the activities of Tzistaraki. The latter, as governor of Athens, built a new mosque (the only dated mosque of Athens) known as the Tzistaraki Mosque (1759). To build this he destroyed one of the columns of the Temple of Olympian Zeus to obtain marble dust for mortar, even though this was forbidden by law. The Pasha of Euripus, his superior, began to take action against him, which ended in the expulsion of Tzistaraki. The mosque, however, was built.

Further epidemics of plague occurred in 1789 in which 1,200 Greeks and 500 Turks died; and in 1854 when an outbreak of cholera was regarded as the result of the collapse of another column of Olympian Zeus in a storm in 1852.

HADJI ALI HASEKI

The next window we have on to the history of the city concerns the tyranny of Hadji Ali, known as Haseki (the term means 'royal body-guard'). His incumbency as *voyvode*, beginning in 1775, signalled the start of 'twenty dark years' for Athens. The events of his reign are known to us in detail because of the account written by an eye-witness, Panaghis Skouzes, whose account was written in 1841 though not published until 1902.

Haseki came from central Anatolia and rose to eminence through the favour of the Sultan's wife. In 1772 the state land of Athens was sold at auction and bought by the Sultana, who gave it to Haseki, first to receive the taxes imposed under the new code of laws of 1760 known as the Malikiane. Once Haseki became *voyvode* he immediately began building works and money-lending. The Athenians petitioned to have him removed, but he soon returned, worse than before. Three times in all the Athenians sought to have him removed, and twice he returned, before they got rid of him for good.

After the first return, his first task was to build a wall around the city, in response to raids by the Turco-Albanians in 1778. This was known as the 'Haseki Wall' and can still be traced in places. It was said to be more like a garden wall than a fortification, but it was sufficient for his purposes. It was four cubits (six feet, two metres) high, and was constructed of stones from old or ruined buildings: the entire Ilissus bridge was demolished for stones. The temple of 'Demeter' on the Ilissus, and the aqueduct of Hadrian, also disappeared at this time. The wall had seven gates, corresponding in position to the ancient ones, and 22 towers, one every 200 paces. Its circuit was two hours' walk. It was built by corvee labour, but still it had to be paid for. 'When the work was finished' (writes Skouzes), 'he presented the Athenians with a bill of

42,500 piastres, and they paid it. But alas that wall became a prison for the Athenians. He set guards at the gates, and the people suffered many things until 1784 when the scourge of his oppression was unendurable.'

Haseki's regime was an orgy of tyranny and extortion. His rule relied on the support of the *kocabaşis* or headmen (*demogerontes* in Greek), a hereditary office: he had these in his pocket and was able to extort goods and tribute from the people at will. Many tried to escape the city, acting as if they were simply going out to their fields or leaving dressed as women. The second attempt by the Athenians to be rid of Haseki came in 1785, when he was put on trial, along with the headmen, and condemned by the Porte: an anathema was pronounced on him, and under a new *voyvode* the situation began to improve. The names of his victims were inscribed on a column of Olympian Zeus.

But in 1789 he returned, and began taxing the people at such a rate that soon there was nothing left to tax. With the proceeds he acquired vast olive groves and built himself a kiosk. Those who would not pay were beaten or hanged. The threat of the falanga and impaling was constantly before his victims; those who tried to escape the city were imprisoned, often in cells too small to stand up in.

Relief came for the Athenians when his patroness the Sultana died and Haseki found himself, from 1791, in constant conflict with the Pasha of the Euripus. He gradually lost favour in Constantinople, and the Athenians brought a suit against him. Haseki learnt of the mission to Constantinople, and invited the abbot of the monastery of All Saints in Athens, its instigator, to drink coffee with him. The abbot, realising that the coffee was poisoned, managed to drink only a sip: 'outside he managed to vomit up what he had drunk and called a doctor to his house, but his beard fell out and his teeth were damaged'. The petition nonetheless found favour in Constantinople, and in 1795 Haseki was banished to Cos, where he was beheaded. His head was brought back to Constantinople and placed on display at the palace gate. 'After that', writes Skouzes, 'all the Athenians came back again, and Athens began to recover and prosper. Every year they elected new headmen and began to establish schools.'

By the end of the eighteenth century Athens had become a moderately substantial city, with a population of some 12,500, three-quarters of them Christians. Haseki's city encompassed a million square metres, and contained government buildings (the *voyvodalik* was in the Library of Hadrian), the law courts, council house and customs buildings (also in the Library of Hadrian) as well as numerous mosques (including one in the Olympieion), 117 churches, three schools and a *medrese*, a '*phrontisterion*' founded in 1720, two hans or inns, three hammams; but no hotels or restaurants until 1810. Scarcely any houses remain from this period: 96 Adrianou is one of very few surviving Turkish houses. Their sites were usually irregular and perpendicular to the street, with a courtyard and awning or verandah before the house itself. Turkish burials largely took place in the area west of the Acropolis. Late in the eighteenth century new schools were founded in Athens by the Greeks of Venice, and the first Greek newspaper began to circulate in 1791.

Lord Elgin

The impact of the work of Stuart and Revett in England had led to a greater awareness of classical sculpture and architecture, which in turn resulted in a desire among some westerners to acquire choice specimens for themselves. The process began with Sir Richard Worsley in 1785, who visited Greece with an attendant artist and took home some marbles, later to become famous as the Museum Worsleyanum in the Isle of Wight. In 1794–6 J.B.S. Moritt of Rokeby travelled in Greece and collected a few marbles for his home. Lord Sligo collected a large number of vases, and Lord Nelson shipped home an altar from Delphi on behalf of Sir William Hamilton.

All the westerners who visited Athens made the acquaintance of the remarkable French antiquary Louis-Sebastien Fauvel. Born in 1753, Fauvel had set off on his first Greek tour in 1780; in 1784 he was taken on as a professional artist by the Comte de Choiseul-Gouffier to accompany his residence in Constantinople and to provide the illustrations for his sumptuous *Voyage Pittoresque en Grèce*. Fauvel acquired antiquities on Choiseul-Gouffier's behalf, as well as making casts and becoming an expert on the antiquities in his own right. The French Revolution forced the Count to flee to Russia, and in 1792 Fauvel found that he no longer had an employer; but he stayed on in Athens and in 1795 began to receive a small stipend from the Institut des Arts. Besides collecting antiquities, studying inscriptions, and drawing sculptures, Fauvel prepared a detailed and valuable plan of contemporary Athens. He also did a great deal of useful topographical work, and made a plaster scale model of Pausanias' Athens. His notes and drawings were lost in the rising of 1821; most of his finds, drawings, coins, marbles, vases and terracottas were dispersed or returned to France and sold. The Bibliothèque Nationale acquired his relief plan of Attica. But without any official status, Fauvel's explorations could only be small scale. It was his fate to have his achievements pressed into the service of others, and to see those with greater wealth make finds and acquire collections that he could not hope for.

Of these the most remarkable was undoubtedly Lord Elgin. The Scottish peer became the ambassador to the Ottoman Empire in 1799 and quickly developed the idea of 'benefiting the arts in England from the study of Greek architecture and sculpture'. He also hoped to acquire some choice items to adorn his home of Broomhall near Dunfermline. His first step was to hire a painter to record the antiquities of Greece. He found that he could not afford J.M.W. Turner, but in Naples he took into his employ Giovanni Battista Lusieri, a painter the hallucinatory precision of whose works amazes the beholder – his painting of the Philopappus Monument appears like a photograph, so detailed is it – but who, perhaps not surprisingly, completed very few works.

Alongside Lusieri Elgin sent to Athens a team consisting also of Elgin's secretary William R. Hamilton, his chaplain, Philip Hunt, a cast maker and two draughtsmen. They arrived in May 1800 and were to continue their work there for ten years. It was not until February 1801 that the team was admitted to the Acropolis, taking with them the only cart in Athens: it had once belonged to Fauvel, who was now in prison as an enemy alien as a result of the Napoleonic Wars. But as soon as the team had set up their scaffolding and cast-making equipment, a scare concerning the French fleet gathering at Toulon caused the Disdar to close the fortress again. He would only open up for a *firman* (authorisation) from the Sultan. Thus did Lord Elgin acquire the famous *firman* on which the dispute over the legitimacy of his removal of the Parthenon marbles has rested. The *firman* itself informed the *voyvode* of Athens

> ...it is our desire that on the arrival of this letter you use your diligence to act conformably to the instances of the said ambassador as long as the said five artists dwelling in that place shall be employed as going in and out of the citadel of Athens which is the place of observation; or in fixing scaffolding around the ancient Temple of the Idols, or in modelling with chalk or gypsum the said ornaments and visible figures; or in measuring the fragments and vestiges of other ruined buildings; or in excavating when they find it necessary the foundations in search of inscriptions among the rubbish; that they be not molested by the said Disdar nor by another persons; nor even by you to whom this letter is addressed; and that no one meddle with their scaffolding or implements nor hinder them from taking away any pieces of stone with inscriptions and figures.

Nor hinder them from taking away any pieces of stone with inscriptions and figures. . . . Lord Elgin had perhaps envisaged no more than the excavation of some small reliefs, along with coins and other antiquities. But Hunt, when asked by the House of Commons Select Committee in 1816: 'Do you imagine that the *firman* gave a direct permission to remove figures and pieces of sculpture from the walls or temple, or that that must have been a matter of private arrangement with the authorities of Athens?' replied: 'That was the interpretation which the Voyvode of Athens was induced to allow it to bear.' Elgin may then have been surprised when he visited Athens for the first time in April 1802. He could not be expected to feel the shock of the spoliation of the pedimental sculptures, the metopes and the frieze like the traveller Edward Dodwell who saw it in progress: 'instead of the picturesque beauty and high preservation in which I first saw [the pediment], it is now comparatively reduced to a state of shattered desolation'.

Another traveller, John Cam Hobhouse, wrote,

> A curious notion prevailing among the common Athenians, with respect to the statues, is that they are real bodies mutilated and enchanted with their present state of petrification by magicians who will have power over them as long as the Turks are masters of Greece, when they will be transformed into

their former bodies. The spirit within them is called an Arabian, and is not infrequently heard to mourn and bewail its condition. Some Greeks in our time conveying a chest from Athens to Piraeus containing part of the Elgin Marbles, threw it down, and could not for some time be prevailed upon to touch it, again affirming, they heard the Arab (i.e. the enchanted spirit within the sculpture) crying out and groaning for his fellow-spirits detained in bondage in the Acropolis. The Athenians suppose that the condition of these enchanted marbles will be bettered by a removal from the country of the tyrant Turks.

The Marbles in due course made their way to England, though some were sunk off the island of Cythera and not recovered until 1804. When Elgin left Constantinople in January 1803 he had spent nearly £40,000 of his own money on 'benefiting the arts in England'. He did not arrive back in England until 1807 (having being imprisoned by the French until 1806), and immediately arranged an exhibition of the sculptures in Park Lane.

The artists flocked to the show and were ecstatic. Flaxman, Fuseli, Benjamin Robert Haydon, Benjamin West, were overwhelmed by the experience; their art would never be the same again. The connoisseurs however were less impressed. In particular, the leading light among the Dilettanti, Richard Payne Knight, scornfully told Lord Elgin, 'You have lost your labour, my Lord Elgin. Your Marbles are over-rated: they are not Greek: they are Roman of the time of Hadrian.' This completely wrong judgment influenced the reception of Elgin's offer for sale to Parliament, who offered £30,000, less than half what Elgin calculated as his expenditure to date. Elgin refused to sell. Further trouble came in the form of the attack by the poet Lord Byron in *The Curse of Minerva*, which condemned not only Elgin's removal of the sculptures and his vanity, but the alleged gullibility and foolishness of the Marbles' admirers. Byron, who had arrived in Athens in 1809, had not seen the Parthenon in its pre-Elgin state; but his satirical genius found in the unhappy lord a suitable object for its exercise, and neither his private life nor his offences to Minerva (Athena) are spared.

The sculptures remained in the courtyard at Burlington House until they were finally acquired by the British Museum in 1816. Elgin retired to a somewhat reduced existence in a wing of Broomhall. With the growth of acquisitive mania in the museums of the nineteenth century, the British Museum came to realise what a prize it had acquired, and the sculptures were soon appreciated as one of the masterpieces of the greatest age of the arts. Throughout the nineteenth and twentieth centuries they remained one of the greatest treasures of the British Museum.

Elgin, realising what Athens had lost by his acquisitions, made an effort at compensation by the erection of a clock tower in the marketplace at Athens in 1814. A painting by the Bavarian officer Ludwig Köllnberger (not a very expert artist, to be sure) shows a plain rectangular tower with a pointed roof. This tower was demolished in 1884 after a fire in the bazaar.

The Athens of Lord Byron

The occupation of Italy by Napoleon's troops in 1796 meant that, along with France, the traditional destinations of young aristocrats on the Grand Tour were 'out of bounds'. Instead, the young men in search of formative experiences turned further east, to the lands ruled by the Ottoman Empire, a friendly power, and in particular to Greece, whose history was already familiar to them from their reading at school. On arrival in Athens they were assured of a welcome from the resident antiquary, Fauvel, as well as from Elgin's artist Lusieri, who remained in Athens until he died in 1821, and from the British consul, Spiridon Logotheti. The latter put up several of the visitors to the city, which still lacked a hotel of any kind: even the Elgins stayed with him. One of his first guests was John Tweddell, who reached Athens in December 1798 and was accompanied by a French artist Michel François Preaux, who fulfilled the function of the modern traveller's camera in recording the sights seen. Tweddell however did not live long; he fell ill and died in July 1799, and was buried in the Theseion.

More fortunate was a young scholar, Edward Daniel Clarke, who embarked on a tour of the larger part of the Ottoman Empire in 1799 and wrote it up in several fat volumes. He left Cairo for Greece in October 1801. Through Logotheti he was introduced to several Greek families, and attended a ball to celebrate the betrothal of a young couple. Clarke was extremely amused by the Greek dancing, but failed to impress when an English dance was played to redress the balance. He found the Greek girls and women strange, and writes about them as if they were another species. Though he disapproved of Elgin's activities on the Acropolis, he had no compunction about removing a very fine Caryatid from Eleusis. He tells us that it was buried in a dunghill and that the people relied on its magic powers to maintain the fertility of their fields. Nonetheless it was soon on its way to England, and is still to be visited (along with a bust of Clarke himself) in the lower gallery of the Fitzwilliam Museum in Cambridge.

Next came Edward Dodwell and William Gell, arriving in Corfu in May 1801, and at Athens a little later. They stayed with the Makri family in Ermou street (where Byron was later also to stay), and though this was only a brief visit, Dodwell was back again in 1805. Both Gell and Dodwell were talented artists, and Gell did important topographising work in Greece (Byron called him 'rapid Gell'). Dodwell stayed longer and created some of the most detailed and evocative views of contemporary Athens , which were produced as paintings and also published as a book of engravings. They include views of the Bazaar and of the Capuchin convent, where the Lantern of Demosthenes now came into a use as a lodging house, most famously by Byron.

Lord Byron himself arrived in Greece, accompanied by J.C. Hobhouse, in September 1809. Byron's reputation in England had become so scandalous that he felt it necessary to leave, and romantic Greece was the destination he lighted upon. Travelling first through Epirus, they encountered the famous and ferocious tyrant, Ali Pasha of Yannina, and also the industrious British Resident, William Martin Leake. Leake was to travel in his time in Greece over every inch of the country, topographising and looking for ancient remains. His many volumes are still an indispensable source and reference for modern archaeologists, and his two-volume *Topography of Athens* is the fullest account of the city at that time.

Byron and Hobhouse arrived in Athens on Christmas Day 1809. They lodged, as others had done, with the Makri family in their pair of houses on a site fronting on to Agias Theklas Street (now occupied by a house built in about 1840). Three generations of women lived there; the youngest, Teresa Makri, caught Byron's eye and achieved immortality as his 'Maid of Athens' ('Maid of Athens, ere we part/ Give, oh give me back my heart'). He was equally drawn to the fifteen year old Nicolo Giraud, the son of the French consul. Lusieri was a regular member of their circle, and other English travellers were also drawn to the circle of the famous poet. Among them were John Galt, who wrote an account of his visit; Lord Sligo; and the group of architects centred on Charles Robert Cockerell, who was to achieve fame as the excavator of the marbles of the Temple of Aphaia in Aigina (now in the Glyptothek in Munich) and the builder of the Ashmolean Museum in Oxford.

When Teresa Makri's mother formed the (not unnatural) idea that Byron was going to marry her daughter, he decided it was time to move and took up residence in the Capuchin convent, where the Lantern of Demosthenes functioned as a small library. Here Byron wrote some of the greatest of his early poems, including *Childe Harold* and *The Curse of Minerva*, as well as some of his loveliest lyrics (not least the 'Maid of Athens'). *Childe Harold* not only created the Philhellenic fervour that was later to fuel the participation of idealists from England, Germany, France, Switzerland and elsewhere in the War of Independence; it also led to a kind of fame for the handsome poet that is now the preserve of pop stars and Hollywood actors.

Hobhouse wrote his own account of his travels in Greece (1809). Like the rest, it focuses mainly on antiquities; the Greeks provide at most local colour. His description of Athens notes 400 Turkish houses, over 500 Greek and over 300 Albanian, the latter in the quarter east of the Acropolis. He counted 36 churches and over 100 chapels. Wheat and barley were grown on the Pnyx and Mt Lycabettus, and women also went there to gather green herbs. Small gardens were maintained in the villages of Halandri and Kifissia. Eleusis, says Hobhouse, 'is a miserable village of thirty mud cottages'. He imparts the information that most of the money-lenders at Athens were Franks – charging interest of up to 20 or even 30 per cent. He did also – like John Galt – register the growing self-awareness of the Greeks and the possibility that they might some day soon rise against their Turkish rulers.

'Attica swarms with travellers,' Hobhouse wrote. These included Americans as well as the European nations. Nicholas Biddle, the son of a Philadelphia merchant, visited Greece in 1806. Most of his letters concentrate on topographical and archaeological matters, but he has something to say also of conditions in Athens: 'Athens is favored in its govt and might do well if the Greeks were not so jealous of each other... The Turks are just numerous enough to keep the Greeks in awe without being dangerous.' His view of the Greek people remains distinctly anthropological, however:

> I have seen few objects so disgusting as a Greek woman – their dress and manner is enough to shock licentiousness itself. [Clarke had reacted in the same way]. There is only one part of it, the letting the hair hang over the shoulders which is tolerable... The peasantry are very prettily dressed... With regard to society there is in fact none among the Greeks. What is society without females? And what kind of intercourse is that between a set of men without any information, whose only employment is to smoke? There is no such thing as an assembly of the sexes, a danse, a theatre, music. The country is in that respect barbarous.

THE PHILOMOUSOS ETAIREIA

Biddle had undoubtedly failed to penetrate those circles of Athenian society where intellectual matters were discussed. It is true that the most important Greek thinkers and activists were elsewhere, among the Phanariot community in Constantinople, or else in studious exile in Paris like Korais; but in 1813 the Philomousos Etaireia was founded, a society of Greeks devoted to the enlargement of a national consciousness among the Greeks. It was funded by an English Philhellene, Frederick North (later the Earl of Guilford), who also restored some buildings in Athens. Among other things it undertook to find Greek names for the main political institutions of Athens. The *Kousegio* became the *Bouleuterion*, the *Kocabaşis* became the *Archons*, the *Koinon* (Community) was renamed the *Demos*. The society also restored schools, among other practical works.

This society represented the culmination of an intellectual revival that had begun in the 1770s with the work of Adamantios Korais. Born in Smyrna in 1748, Korais spent much of his life in Paris, where he worked as a classical scholar and re-edited the classics for a modern Greek readership. He believed in education as the route from 'enslavement' to the Turks. He campaigned to reinstate a 'purified' Greek language based on the *koine* of the Roman Empire. His efforts were successful in large part because of the prosperity created by the great Greek merchants of the Ottoman Empire, who had benefited from the difficult conditions of the Napoleonic period to reap rich rewards. As Richard Clogg writes:

> They endowed schools and libraries, and subsidised the publication, principally outside the boundaries of the empire, of a growing, and increasingly secular, body of literature aimed at a specifically Greek audience. During the last quarter of the eighteenth century seven times as many books were being published as during the first. In the twenty years before 1821 some 1,300 titles were published. Perhaps most important of all, the subventions of merchants enabled young Greeks to study in the universities of western Europe (*A Concise History of Greece*, 26).

Alongside Korais' intellectual work, the revolutionary writings of Rhigas Pherraios (or Velestinlis 1757–98), began to waken Greek national consciousness. Kolokotronis later wrote that it was the impact of Napoleon that made the nation (and others) realise that they need no longer be subjects of the Turks. The efforts of the Greek nationalists, largely invisible in Greece itself, combined eventually with political

Rhigas Pherraios

movements from the neighbouring principalities and, last but not least, with the growth of Philhellene consciousness in Western Europe, to create the conditions for the Greek revolution of 1821 which resulted in Greece's liberation from Ottoman rule.

(iii) The War of Independence, 1821–1832

Western travellers, while recognising the strength of Greek desire for independence, regarded it as highly improbable that they would achieve it, at least without foreign aid. Sir William Gell had scorned the idea of a Greek rising, while Hobhouse stated that it would be impossible without help from the west. The first movements, however, came from the north. The foundation of the Philiki Etaireia (Friendly Society) in Odessa in 1814 had provided a forum for discussion of ways and means to revolution. It acquired adherents by claiming that the Tsar supported its aims and activities – but the leading pro-Russian politician, John Capodistria, was never involved with it (though his brothers were). In March 1821 Prince Alexander Ypsilantis, the leader of the Philiki Etaireia, led a rising from the Danubian principalities of Moldavia and Wallachia, and crossed the River Pruth with his troops. He received little support in Romania, and his expedition failed. However, in the same month the Metropolitan of Patras proclaimed the rising in the Peloponnese (25 March). Risings elsewhere were co-ordinated by Ypsilantis' brother Dimitris. Leading Greeks arrived from abroad, including the Phanariot Alexander Mavrokordatos, and others emerged from the provinces, among them Petrobey of Mani and George Koundouriotis of Hydra.

Because of the incapacity of the overall direction from Ypsilantis, the direction of the war fell into the hands of leaders of irregulars, former *klephts* (bandits) who had learned their trade in the service of Ali Pasha of Joannina, the first leader on Greek soil to break away from Ottoman rule. (He was executed in February 1822.) Prominent among these were Theodore Kolokotrones, whose field of operations was the Morea, Odysseus Androutsos, based in a cave on Mt Parnassus, Markos Botsaris at Suli (later killed at Karpenisi), Gogos in Epirus and Karais-kakis at Mesolongi.

In April 1821 Greeks in the Morea began to massacre the Turks around them, with their wives and families, and Ottoman troops marched in to quell them. The horrors of this massacre drove at least one Philhellene, Thomas Gordon, to abandon the cause. The Turks in revenge hanged Patriarch Gregorios on the gate of the Patriarchate in Constantinople, on Easter Day 1821, and also massacred the people of Chios in March 1822. Early successes by the Greek insurgents included the victory at Valtetsi (April 1821) and the capture of Monemvasia (August 1821), but these gains were lost as in-fighting developed.

From the beginning of the revolution a provisional government operated in Greece, with a National Assembly at Epidaurus from late 1821; but many different policies were in play, ranging from the hopes of the diplomat Capodistria for an independent state guaranteed by the fellow orthodox state of Russia, to the westward-looking aspirations of Alexander Mavrokordatos, and the wheeler-dealing of the Minister of War, John Kolettis. The constitution proclaimed early in 1822 was largely the work of Mavrokordatos. The western powers were involved at a political level from the first, as it was in their interest to see the Ottoman Empire weakened, but much of the funding for the revolution came not from official sources but from the Philhellenes. Idealists from Britain, Germany and many other countries, prompted by what they had learnt in school of the Greek ideal of liberty, flocked to the Greek cause and brought it heroism and – those who could – money. But again their aims were various. It was the lack of a strong strategic and policy-making arm on either side that ensured the war dragged on for so many years.

The theatres of war included the Morea, Roumeli and Mesolongi. Most of the population of Athens fled to Salamis; but in 1821 Athens became directly involved in operations as, on 23 April, the Turkish forces retreated to the Acropolis taking with them eleven prominent Greeks as hostages. The Athenians, accompanied by Albanian villagers from Mt Parnes, blockaded the Acropolis. From July to November 1821 Omer Vrioni, the pasha of Ioannina, attempted to relieve the siege, engaging in 'Greek-hunts' in the environs of the city, until he was put in command of operations in East Roumeli. The Greek blockade resumed. Mortars and ammunition were provided by Kolettis and a French officer, Olivier Voutier, supervised the bombardment, which was as ineffective as the mining operations that followed. However, the Turks neglected to secure their water supply, and relied on the Serpentzi wall for defence, with the result that on 21 June 1822 the Greeks forced the Turkish garrison to capitulate. During the fighting the Capuchin monastery was burnt down, this freeing up the 'Lantern of Demosthenes' for later excavation. The Turks and their families were imprisoned in the ruins of the Library of Hadrian (the *voivode*'s palace). However, within three days an Athenian captain named Lekkas incited the Athenian people to murder the prisoners. Four hundred men women and children were massacred, while the Athenian *demogerontes* and *archons* did nothing. Fauvel and Gropius, the French and Austrian consuls, however, did all they could to save the prisoners. More than 300 sought asylum in the French consulate and were in due course evacuated from Piraeus. Lekkas later fell into the hands of the Turks, and was impaled at Negroponte in 1827.

In September 1822 a conference was held in Athens. The delegates assumed responsibility for East Roumeli and rejected the official government body, the Areios Pagos. Odysseus Androutsos now became commander of the Acropolis, a move which eroded further the power of the Areios Pagos.

By the end of 1822 Nauplia was in Greek hands, thanks to Kolokotronis: Dramali's expedition against Corinth, Argos and Nauplia had been defeated and slaughtered at Dervenakia by Kolokotronis' troops. Khurshid Pasha had been defeated in Greece, but the self-declared state still had to fight for its survival, and it still had no established constitutional basis. Kolokotronis, fighting always for his own position and advantage as well as for Greece, refused to admit the members of a new National Assembly, who therefore met at Astros in December 1822. This assembly elected George Koundouriotis President of Greece.

Lord Byron at Mesolongi

In summer 1823 Botsaris was killed at Karpenisi, though the outcome was a Greek victory. In the same season Lord Byron arrived at Cephalonia as the financial agent of the Greek Committee in London, to support Mavrokordatos' cause. Support in England had been growing since August 1822 when George Canning became Foreign Secretary. The government was talking an active and positive approach, and the Lord Mayor of London had subscribed substantial funds for the Philhellene cause. Byron brought glamour and fame, as well as substantial funds of his own and a bright prospect of help from the west. He threw himself into the cause of Greek independence, for which he was ready to die a soldier's death. On 5 January 1824 he arrived at Mesolongi, which, besides being Mavrokordatos' base, had become a symbolic target and was repeatedly besieged by the Turks until it finally fell in April 1826.

At Mesolongi Byron shared a house with Mavrokordatos and Colonel Leicester Stanhope. Here he waited for an army under Sir Charles Napier, and personally funded the war effort for several months, becoming increasingly disillusioned about his Suliot troops, who had become ungovernable since Botsaris' death. But before Napier could arrive, Byron had died of fever, thus becoming a national hero without ever lifting a weapon against a Turk. The aid he brought was not only financial but psychological. The war had a hero to whom none could object.

Only Koundouriotis, as President of Greece, was authorised to spend the English loan, so Kolokotronis finally gave way and admitted him to Nauplia. However, civil war now broke out among the Greek factions, and continued all summer. The Turks meanwhile continued the war on three fronts. In 1824 the Sultan embarked on a new strategy, of attacking Greece at its edges rather than sending troops into its midst. Ibrahim Pasha of Egypt led a force against the Morea; fighting also continued in East Roumeli and at Mesolongi. In addition, a navy was sent to harry the coasts, against which the Greeks, a nation of seamen, fought effectively. In this campaign the island of Psara was reduced to smoking ruins.

While Byron was still waiting in Mesolongi, Colonel Leicester Stanhope set out for Athens, reaching the city on 2 March. He did not trust Mavrokordatos' ambitions for a democratic Greece, and thought the *klepht* leader Odysseus the man of the future. Odysseus, as commander in northern Greece, was now effectively the ruler of Athens, though his headquarters continued to be the cave on Mt Parnassos.

Stanhope established a museum in the Parthenon as well as setting up a press, schools and even a newspaper, the *Ephemeris Athinon,* published by G. Psyllas. But these admirable projects sat ill with the state of anarchy that prevailed in Greece, even in Athens. An Athenian tax collector was murdered. The troops had little interest in democratic institutions and wanted, under Odysseus' influence, to see the city become a *capitanlik* of *armatoles.* (An *armatole* was a 'good klepht', one whose methods and way of life was identical to that of brigands, but who was in the service of the government.) As the intrigues of the soldiery continued, the shopkeepers formed a motley garrison of the Acropolis and invited Prince Dimitris Ypsilantis to take command of the Acropolis. However, the soldiers would not admit him and insisted on maintaining Odysseus in the role (2 September).

Odysseus now took over the revenues of Athens and created a provincial assembly there. He also built a wall to enclose the well below the north wing of the Propylaea. His methods of command were brutal: two alleged traitors (in fact supporters of the Greek government) were executed, and a third, a priest, was walled up in a small tower specially built for the purpose.

In February 1825 Odysseus found his interests threatened by the government of George Koundoriotis, who, under the influence of the Rumeliot Minister Kolettis, was sidelining him in favour of junior officers, and decided to throw in his lot with the Turks. However, his party was soon surrounded and in April he was forced to surrender to his former lieutenant Iannis Gouras, who was now in control of Athens. He was imprisoned in the Frankish tower on the Acropolis. On the morning of 17 July his body was found at its foot, and it was put about that he had fallen in an attempt to escape: but everyone knew that he had been murdered.

THE SIEGE OF THE ACROPOLIS

Gouras' rule in Athens was an oppressive one. His heavy exactions were designed to provision the Acropolis, but led the peasantry to despair. Things became even worse when the Acropolis was besieged in summer 1826. The context for the new Turkish campaign is complex, and can be outlined as follows.

In 1825 Ibrahim had captured Navarino. In May of that year a regular force arrived under the French Colonel Fabvier, which was supposed to instil some order and discipline into the Greek armies. Kolokotronis sacked Tripolis (he boasted that 159 besiegers got through 48,000 animals when they captured the city), but the rest of the Peloponnese was soon overwhelmed by Ibrahim's marauding troops. The west became increasingly horrified at the wholesale destruction of cities, crops and orchards meted out by Ibrahim. In April 1825 a new siege of Mesolongi began, which continued until April 1826, when the remaining inhabitants slipped out and left the undefended city to the troops of Reshid Pasha.

The reorganisation of the Greek and Philhellene forces saw Lord Cochrane become commander of the fleet, while Frank Abney Hastings played an important advisory role. Thomas Gordon also appears on the scene again. In summer 1825 the government fell, but in summer 1826 the new National Assembly at Epidaurus gave the adventurer Sir Richard Church supreme command of the Greek armies, and Cochrane the command of the navy.

Meanwhile in the Ottoman capital the 'Auspicious Event' of May 1826, as the Turks called the abolition of the Janissaries, led to increased strength for the Sultanate. The first move the Sultan determined on was an attack on Athens. This was an important strategic objective, because it was clear that the Greeks, with foreign support, might well win the war; but if Athens could be captured, an emerging Greek state would inevitably be confined to the Peloponnese only.

During the early summer of 1826 Reshid's army, fresh from triumph at Mesolongi, advanced on Athens. He quickly captured Sepolia, Patissia and Ambelokipi, and on 28 June established his headquarters at Patissia. Troops occupied the Hill of the Muses, and batteries were set up on the Pnyx and by St Demetrius' church. A force of 4,000 *armatoles* arrived from Eleusis, where Karaiskakis' troops had their barracks, but Reshid forced them to retreat into the Acropolis. A siege began which was to last until June 1827.

The position of the Greeks in the Acropolis was not comfortable, and over the summer there were a few desertions. On 13 October Gouras was shot during a night exchange of fire – the Turkish marksman aimed at the flash of his rifle. The event drew attention to the precarious position of the defenders and stimulated the government, now located on Aigina, into action. Generals Fabvier and Gordon made some unsuccessful attempts to interrupt Reshid, while Karaiskakis took up a position at a place on the Sacred Way called Haidari. From here he was able to cover a Greek force led by Grigiottis as they entered the Acropolis. Grigiottis now took command. Another of the chief leaders, General Makriyannis, though wounded three times on a single day in October, made his way to Aegina (29 November) to lay out the situation and to request assistance and powder. The government agreed to send troops, but had its own ends to pursue as well: it soon (February 1827) split into two rival assemblies based at Hermione and Aegina.

On 12 December Fabvier and 650 men landed at Phaliron and made their way almost unmolested to the Acropolis. Once here, however, the Greek irregulars prevented him from leaving again: it seems that the government in Aegina wanted to keep him employed there.

George Finlay judged that the right strategy at this time would have been to cut Reshid's supply-line from the north. Instead, General Gordon, remembering Thrasybulus, occupied Munychia. Here he was attacked by Reshid on 11 February 1827 until Frank Hastings (now a general) sailed into Piraeus and diverted the Turks. The Bavarian general Heideck now attacked Reshid's rear from Oropus. Despite this three-pronged attack, supported from the sea by Miaoulis, the Greeks and their allies were unsuccessful.

It was at this juncture (March 1827) that General Sir Richard Church (whom the Greeks had preferred to Napier) and Admiral George Cochrane arrived to command the Greek army and navy respectively, confirmed in their appointments by a now unified Assembly at Trozen. The leaders determined to attack Reshid's supply-line, and Hastings led an expedition to destroy the powder magazines at Volos. Karaiskakis took up a position with three thousand men at Keratsina in the plain of Piraeus, while Church assembled an army of ten thousand at Piraeus itself. In addition, Cochrane assembled a small force of Hydriots.

The assault was undermined by the differences of the commanders. After a skirmish in which 300 Ottoman Albanian troops had taken refuge in a monastery, Cochrane was for storming their stronghold, while Church secretly entered into negotiations. When the Albanians emerged, they were mown down by the Greeks, at whose orders is not clear. More than 200 were murdered, an action which caused General Gordon to resign his command and Reshid to swear vengeance. Karaiskakis attempted unsuccessfully to stop the slaughter. The Greeks now pushed forward to Athens, but they lacked an effective leader. Karaiskakis was mortally wounded in the fighting on 4 May.

On the evening of 5 May Church moved his position (with 2,500 troops) to Analatos at the eastern end of Phaliron bay. 'Tomorrow', exulted Cochrane, 'we will dine on the Acropolis.' But the forces, scattered over a four-mile front with their backs to the sea, were prevented from reaching Athens by the swift action of Reshid who launched a cavalry attack. A massacre ensued. 1,500 Greeks died, as well as 22 of the 26 Philhellenes taking part, and 240 were taken prisoner, all of whom were beheaded except General Kalergis, who survived to become the hero of the constitutional revolution of 1843.

On 5 June the Acropolis capitulated. The garrison of 2,000 marched out, prompting unfavourable comparisons with the heroes of Mesolongi. The superior tactics of Reshid had won him the victory, and later honours in Constantinople. Reshid was master of all that part of Greece that had been Karaiskakis' domain; but he never penetrated south of Megara.

By the end of the summer of 1827 Greece was exhausted. Famine was prevalent. Without foreign aid, the Greeks looked set to be exterminated. The Treaty of London of 6 July determined a limited autonomy for Greece; but Mehmet was preparing a new fleet, and the war was set to continue. Then, on 27 October took place the deciding event of the war, the Battle of Navarino. Ibrahim's new fleet was moored in the bay of Navarino (Pylos), and was surprised by the allied navy under Admiral Codrington. The latter exceeded his orders in mounting an attack, but he was determined to put an end to Ibrahim's atrocities. It was a decisive defeat for the Porte. Sixty of 89 ships were destroyed, 6,000 men were killed and 4,000 wounded. Ibrahim remained in the Peloponnese for another year, but in October 1828 he finally departed and the French took over the castles of Modon, Koron,

Navarino and Rhion. The fighting ended in March 1829, but the Turks did not cede all their territory until September of that year, when the Russian capture of Adrianople led to the Treaty of Adrianople (September 1829); and the Sultan only recognised the Kingdom of Greece in July 1832. The frontier was fixed at a line from Arta to Volos.

The New Kingdom

Throughout the last years of the war the western powers had been engaged with the problem of what, constitutionally, was to follow the war. In 1826 a possible solution had seemed to be that Greece should be an independent state, tributary to the Porte, with the Turks expelled from the land. Other possibilities such as a federal republic, or a presidential state, gave way to the determination to find a king for the new state. On 14 April 1827 Capodistria was appointed President for a term of seven years, with a base first at Trozen, though Nauplia soon became the capital. The first choice of a king was Leopold of Belgium, who at first accepted the invitation and then reneged (May 1830). The interregnum continued.

Meanwhile Capodistria's presidency seemed to many to be turning into a tyranny, and some feared that he would never step down. His absolutist tendencies meant that no rule of law was developed in the new state, schools were founded but soon became barracks; secret police abounded; and the press was silenced. A rising by Miaoulis ended in a ferocious sack of Poros by government troops. The end came as the result of a feud with the Mavromichalis clan of Mani. On 9 October 1831, as he was entering church in Nauplia, Capodistria was assassinated by two members of the Mavromichalis family.

The anarchy that ensued was scarcely kept in control by the governing committee that emerged, consisting of Capodistria's brother Agostino, the Vlach John Kolettis (the former physician of Ali Pasha) and Kolokotronis. The latter two hated each other and Agostino was a nonentity. But the perilous situation came to an end when the Powers came up with the idea of Otto (Otho in Greek), the younger son of King Ludwig I of Bavaria. He was still only 17 years old in 1832. The Great Powers acted as guarantors of his throne, and sent ministers to his court. Otho was officially recognized as king of Greece on 4 October 1832. Ludwig provided him with an army of 3,500 Bavarian troops, and on 1 February 1833, Otho landed at Nauplia to a rapturous welcome.

CHAPTER ELEVEN

The Reign of King Otho
1833–1862

Otho's arrival represented a new start for Greece. The eighteen year old king was accompanied by three regents: Count Armansperg, the law professor Georg Maurer and General Carl Heideck. In addition, the kingdom was guaranteed by the three Protecting Powers: England, France and Bavaria. The regents set vigorously about the task of creating a new and workable state. Maurer created an effective law code, but other measures were less successful. The regents, in absolutist mode, created a policy of centralisation, so that for example *demarchs* were no longer locally elected by chosen by the king from a list prepared locally. George Finlay mordantly observed that a policy of centralisation could not be expected to work in a country that had no roads. A road-building programme was announced but never under-

Otho and Amalia

taken. In addition, factionalism continued. The regents worked closely with Kolettis, who became a powerful minister, while the Capo-distrians under Kolokotronis felt excluded and even founded a secret society, the Phoenix, to resist the government: its members were arrested in September 1833. Brigandage became rife. In 1834 Britain persuaded Ludwig to recall Maurer and Abel, with the result that Armansperg wielded absolute power from August 1834 until February 1837.

One pressing matter was the choice of a capital. Though Nauplia had been the capital under the presidency, and Otho had landed there in February 1833, many other possibilities were canvassed, including Megara, Piraeus, Argos, Syros and Tripolitsa. Kolettis even declared that only Constantinople would do. In the end the choice fell on Athens. Otho entered Athens on 23 May 1833, and his arrival was celebrated with a service in the Theseion – the last Christian celebration ever to be held there. Athens was officially declared the capital on 29 June 1833 and the transfer took place in December. From this point on, Athens becomes the political centre of the Greek state, and it becomes a delicate business to distinguish the history of Athens from that of Greece. Major political events of national or international importance took place in Athens. The focus of this book will be resolutely on urban history, with the political scene providing no more than a backdrop for the architectural, social and cultural development of Athens, and for major political events that affected the city and its population directly.

Athens in 1831 was a city in ruins. It had a population of barely 4,000. Horses were stabled in the Theseion, as Alexander Rangavis recalled in 1862; the Temple of Olympian Zeus was a lime kiln, and camels browsed where twenty years later the university stood. By 1840 the population had reached 25,000, and by 1853 it was nearly 31,000. By the latter date a substantial number of distinguished buildings adorned its handsome streets. All this reflected a frenzy of building activity and a flood of population to the new city. The villages also grew. Eleusis, which had been used as a barracks in the war, now saw the building of a whole village with blocks from the ancient site.

The Building of Athens

Work had begun on a new town plan for Athens as early as 1831. (Capodistria had sponsored nine new town plans throughout Greece; there were forty such under Otho, and 111 under his successor George I.) The two architects responsible for creating a plan for Athens were Stamatios Kleanthes and Gustav Eduard Schaubert of Breslau, who had both been students with the great Berlin architect Karl Friedrich Schinkel. They had become acquainted with Heideck in Rome, and in 1830 had arrived in Aigina where they were appointed the official state architects of Greece. Though their plan for Athens underwent several modifications, an important feature was the grid plan, which stood as a rejection of the higgledy-piggledy Ottoman city. The initial plan was rejected as too grand and expensive, and requiring a level of expropriation of private property for which the state would find it impossible to pay compensation. Though many buildings would have had to be demolished, the larger part of the city was to be built to the north and east of the existing town (mainly the Plaka area). The proposed demolitions led to rioting in Athens as people anticipated becoming homeless yet again; so in 1835 the plan was revised by the Bavarian architect Leo von Klenze, who was now in charge of architectural restoration on the Acropolis. The layout of present-day Athens is the result of the work of these three architects. An article in the newspaper *Athena* in 1834 accused Kleanthes and Schaubert of producing a plan that looked more like that for a garden than for a city: 'in designing the streets, they did not overlook any geometric shape . . . they drew several triangles, squares, hexagons, polygons, trapezoids, rhomboids etc, so that the professor of mathematics Mr Negres, when he teaches geometry, does not have any need of geometric shapes, having in mind the plan of our city.'

One of the most important decisions to be made was the site and plan of a palace for the king. (This received attention even before the small matter of roads.) The original plan provided for a palace on Omonoia Square; this was later moved to Agios Athanasios, near the Theseion, abandoned because it was malarial. A maverick plan by Schinkel for the conversion of the entire Acropolis into a royal palace was fortunately soon abandoned. (One can see what it would have looked like from the detailed plans and elevations Schinkel prepared, and from the plans, also unexecuted, for a palace at Oriana which incorporated some features of the Acropolis.) Klenze's plan to locate the palace in its present site overlooking what was to be Syntagma (Constitution) Square was selected, and in 1836 building was begun. The choice of architect was made by King Ludwig, and he chose the German architect Friedrich von Gärtner, who had already designed several buildings for Munich and had worked on the Hermitage in St Petersburg. The palace was completed in 1842: it is now (2003) the Parliament building.

While Otho was waiting for the completion of his palace, he lived in two adjoining new houses (1834 and 1835) at 5–7 Paparrigopoulou St – the building is now the Museum of the City of Athens – and from 1837 to 1843 in the 'Old Parliament'. The latter building was then used as the Parliament until 1854 when it was destroyed by fire. A new building on the site by F. Boulanger (1858–75) also served as Parliament until 1935 (when Parliament moved to the Palace in Syntagma Square), then as Ministry of Justice until 1962, and it is now the National Historical Museum.

Gärtner was also responsible for the layout of the Royal Garden behind the Palace. 15,000 plants were imported from Genoa as well as from distant parts of Attica such as Sounion, and Evia, to stock the

The Royal Palace

garden with a flora that far outstripped that of the arid centre of Attica. In 1854 the Royal Family opened the gardens to the public, and in 1923 it was redesignated as the National Garden.

Seldom since antiquity had a king begun with a clean slate like this for the construction of a city to memorialise his reign. Ludwig Steub wrote in the second edition of his *Bilder aus Griechenland (Pictures from Greece*, 1885), 'it seems to me now like a fairy tale, that half a century ago a Bavarian prince should have gone to Greece as king'. Otho's kingdom was in many ways a fairy tale, just as based on fantasy, and as unrelated to political reality as the very different regal fantasies of his nephew Ludwig II, the Swan King, in Bavaria. Like the Philhellenes, Otho found more reality in the glorious history of classical Greece than in the present-day squalor. He treated Greece as a playground and his frivolity in the end cost him his throne. His disregard for the people meant that he and his architects could ride roughshod over the people who were rendered homeless without compensation in the new building programme. But the result was one of the finest assemblages of neo-classical architecture in Europe. Much of it, alas, fell into a sad state of disrepair in the post-war years, as a result of neglect and demolition, but the great public buildings still stand proud among the traffic and bustle of the city. In the 1990s an intensive programme of restoration rescued a great many of the neo-classical buildings of Plaka, from cafés to apartment blocks, but some still await a saviour.

Much of the neo-classical face of Athens was created, not by Cleanthes and Schaubert, but by two Danish brothers, Christian Hansen (1803–83) and Theophilus Hansen (1813–91). While studying in Rome, the elder Hansen had come to know the great neo-classical sculptor Bertel Thorvaldsen, and had decided to visit Greece to see the origins of classical style. He fell in love with the country on arrival in August1833: 'Greece is very beautiful. (It) ... seemed to me a totally different world ... But the country is very difficult to traverse, because there are no roads, and also one gets depressed by the completely ruined villages ... and the completely wild and uncultivated land.'

The neglect of the land was also soon remedied. George Cochrane, the nephew of Admiral Cochrane, remarked in his *Wanderings in Greece* (I.285) that in 1836 the drainage dykes of the plain, which had become completely choked during the war, 'are now opened and ... where at the same period of last year [1835] I should have been walking six inches deep in water, it was now perfectly dry, and fitted for cultivation'.

Hansen arrived at an opportune moment, for the new kingdom needed architects, and before the end of 1834 he had been appointed architect to the Greek Royal Court. He became a close friend of Kleanthes and Schaubert, and also learnt much about archaeology from Klenze and from Ludwig Ross (of whom more below).

Hansen's first building in Athens was the Mint (1835–6) on Klafthmonos Square (demolished in 1939). Its style was essentially vernacular, with Byzantine details. In the same years Kleanthes built the Megaron Rallis, the first of the neo-classical buildings of Athens. But the oldest building from the kingdom is by neither of these: it is the Makrigianni military hospital, later barracks, by Wilhelm Weiler. This blend of Byzantine brick with neo-classical forms is close to the Akropoli metro station: it is now the Acropolis Study Centre and is not currently open to the public.

In 1839 Hansen had the important commission to build the new University of Athens. The Otho University had been inaugurated on 3 May 1837 and housed in the residence of Cleanthes on the north slope of the Acropolis (now the museum of the history of the University of Athens), a fine Ottoman house with a large courtyard. Studies began in October with a total of 52 students and 75 non-matriculated auditors, who ranged in age from teenagers to veterans of the war and 'snowy-haired old men'. In 1839 the rector raised a subscription to build a new university: the largest part of the funds was provided by Baron Sinas. Hansen's plans were approved in May that year. The building stands on Panepistimiou (University) Street. The first wing took two years to build, and classes began there in 1841 while the scaffolding was still up. The building was completed in 1851 though its decoration occupied a further twelve years. The simple and noble proportions of the building, with a central ionic portico flanked by two wings and decorated in the polychrome style which architects had just begun to realise had been characteristic of ancient buildings, set a standard for further public buildings in Athens.

Hansen was kept busy.

I have also built two private houses. In addition I have converted some churches into courtrooms and a Turkish school into a prison [the *medrese* near the Tower of the Winds], and have practically completed a big building with shops [later a silk factory: see Ch. 12]. Moreover I have executed a lot of drawings, the most important of which are a plan for the city of Corinth, projects for several theatres, a church in Piraeus, a meat-market in Athens, a prison, a Protestant church, a bath at Thermia, a lighthouse in Aegina and others.

He also built a Catholic church in Piraeus, and, with Schaubert, designed the Anglican church in Athens, a neo-Gothic structure in granite with a Byzantine bell tower. (Robert Byron expostulated at the importing of so much Scottish granite to Greece, 'the finest marble country in the world. But there is no salvation in marble'.)

In 1838 Hansen was joined in Athens by his younger brother Theophilus, who stayed until 1846. They designed a number of buildings jointly, but Theophilus' first work was his own design for the Observatory (1842–6) on the Hill of the Nymphs, a largely neo-classical structure of four symmetrical porticos, topped by a dome (not Greek style, but a necessity for an observatory). His mansion for the Demetriou family in Syntagma Square (1842–3), a rectangular construction with a two-storey arcaded façade, was the family home until 1856; the French School then leased it until 1873, at which time two Greek entrepreneurs bought it and converted it into Athens' finest hotel, the Grande Bretagne. (It was extensively reconstructed in 1958, and given a remarkable facelift in 2002–3.)

Together the brothers designed the neo-Byzantine Eye Clinic (begun 1850 and completed by the Constantinopolitan architect Lysandros Kaftanzoglou in 1852) and the Academy (1859–87). The Academy was built on land donated partly by the municipality and partly by the Petraki monastery. A contemporary newspaper article (in *Aion*) scorned the extravagance of the project: 'We have no ships, no army, no roads, but soon we will have an Academy. Turkey, beware!' (Building ceased on the abdication of Otho in 1862 but resumed in 1876.) The building stands alongside the University in a triad of buildings completed by the National Library, another work of the two brothers (1885–92). It is a triple doric temple, and the reading room in the central building resembles the cella of a temple. This group of buildings forms an ensemble comparable with anything in Munich or Berlin.

The existing churches of Athens were not neglected. By 1838 twelve of them had been restored, and six new ones were built. Work began on the Cathedral in 1840, and in 1842 the foundation stone was laid by the King and Queen. Four architects were involved in its design: Theophilus Hansen, Franz Boulanger, Dimitrios Zezos and Panagiotis Kalkos. It is designed, like almost all Greek churches, on a Byzantine model, and incorporates stones from seventy-two demolished Byzantine churches of Athens. (One that was saved was the Kapnikarea, which interrupts the straight line of Ermou Street: Otho's father, Ludwig of Bavaria, had the good taste to ensure that it was spared destruction.) The Cathedral was dedicated on 21 May 1862.

The Catholic Cathedral was originally planned by Klenze in 1844 but redesigned by Kaftanzoglou in 1858 and completed in 1887. Other important buildings of this period include the Arsakeion girls' school. This restrained neo-classical building, whose facade recalls a Macedonian tomb, was endowed by Apostolis Arsakis (1792–1874) in 1846 and designed by Kaftanzoglou. It remained a girls' school until 1930 when the school was moved to Psychiko and the building became a law court: it is now the Court of Appeal. The Church of St Irene (1847, corner of Aiolou and Athinaidos Sts) is another work of Kaftanzoglou. It is of basilica form, with a dome, and the west porch combines a classical pediment with a triple arcade like a Byzantine narthex.

Besides all this monumental architecture, the more functional buildings of the city underwent vigorous development. Existing buildings were re-used: Elgin's clock tower became a guard post, the Turkish *medrese* became a prison: the plane tree used for hangings remained in the courtyard until 1911. The Fethiye Camii, which had been named the Church of Dionysius the Areopagite for five months after Morosini's attack in 1687, had become a school in 1824, then a prison and a barracks, and in Otho's reign it found glory as a military bakery.

By 1833 there were at least 100 shops in the Monastiraki area. The first hotel was established in 1832, the Hotel d'Europe on Ermou street: Alphonse de Lamartine stayed there when he visited Athens. There was a German library on the ground floor. (The Italian manager and his Austrian wife each had only one eye.) Its prices became so high that the Bavarian community clubbed together to establish another, and in 1835 a third was established, the Aiolos (by Kleanthes) on the corner of Aiolou and Dexippou: it is still there, though no longer a hotel.

Brown's store on the corner of Ermou and Athinas, in the heart of the Maltese quarter, supplied English goods at Maltese prices. A considerable foreign colony grew up: French hairdressers, Italian tailors, German pipe sellers, English textile merchants, Armenian money-changers. Edmond About, whose book of 1856, *Le Roi des Montagnes*, was unpopular in Greece because of its exposure of the scandal of brigandage (see pp 251–3), also wrote a not wholly complimentary account of Greece, *La Grèce Contemporaine,* describing his visit in 1852. The open-air life of Athens fascinated him, not least the professors' lectures given on the lawns before the university buildings. The bazaar, he wrote,

> is perhaps the most frequented spot in the city. In the morning, all the citizens, whatever their rank, go to do their own shopping. If you wish to see a senator carrying two kidneys in one hand and a lettuce in the other, go to the bazaar at eight o'clock in the morning. . . . They go from stall to stall, inquiring the rate for apples, the price of onions . . . At eight in the evening, in summer, the bazaar takes on a magical atmosphere. This is the hour when the workers, the domestics, the soldiers come to provide themselves with a supper. Between seven and eight the gourmets partake of a sheep's head for six sous; sober men buy a slice of red water-melon or a large cucumber which they eat delicately, like an apple. The merchants, amid their vegetables and fruits, hail the purchasers with loud cries; large lamps, full of olive oil, shed a beautiful red light on the heaps of figs, pomegranates, melons and grapes. In this confusion, every object seems brilliant; discordant sounds become harmonious; one does not notice that one is splashing through black mud, and one scarcely smells the nauseating odours with which the bazaar is infected.

In 1839 the Oraia Ellada (Beautiful Hellas) café was established at the crossroads of Ermou and Aiolou – 'the central address of the church of the people', as Hans Christian Andersen called it – and others rapidly followed. The Oraia Ellada was the starting point of the march to demand Otho's abdication on 10 October 1862. In the cafés the newspapers that were read included the *Athena* and the *Agathangelos*.

The educational level of the population rose with the establishment of schools as a deliberate government policy. There were soon ten schools in Attica. One of them, in Athens, run by the Reverend Hill, was funded by the revenues from monastery lands (though the Greek clergy were suspicious of too much education). George Cochrane reported enthusiastically (*Wanderings in Greece* II.197–206) that there was 'hardly a child in Athens above the age of six, who does not know how to read, write and (if a girl) to work with the needle'.

Piraeus

Athens' port underwent a similarly vigorous development. A road was built from Athens to Piraeus in 1834–5 by Bavarian soldiers. A horse-bus plied the route, and set off whenever it was full. But soon a traveller arriving at Piraeus might find up to fifty carriages waiting there, and perhaps a few camels as well. The journey from Piraeus to Athens took an hour and a quarter, and travellers arrived covered from head to foot in dust.

Kleanthes and Schaubert's plan for Piraeus created the outline of a distinguished city, and in 1837 the Military Academy was moved there from Aegina. New customs warehouses were built by Kleanthes. The importance of the city grew throughout the nineteenth century. Its neo-classical buildings, though fine, were never as distinguished as those of Athens, and they have suffered sad dilapidation in the last hundred years. In 1840 there were moves to amalgamate the port with the city of Athens, but this never took place. Though intimately linked to the capital, the very different character of Piraeus has ensured it a separate urban development.

HIGH SOCIETY

Count Armansperg created a glittering court life in Athens, which was enjoyed and described by many of the German visitors to Athens. F.G. Welcker, a classical scholar, arrived in 1842 (at the age of 50) and stayed until the following year. He came away from one of the frequent balls declaring that he wished never to leave Athens. Not only the king, but the ambassadors, entertained frequently, and Welcker attended memorable receptions at the Prussian ambassador's and at the Austrian Prokesch von Osten's. The English representative, Sir Edmund Lyons, looked somewhat askance at the merry-making. Classicists were always held in high esteem at Otho's court, and in February 1842 Welcker and Ludwig Ross, the Oberconservator of the Acropolis, attended an intimate dinner with King Otho and Queen Amalia where Welcker was able to press his idea for excavations in the Theatre of Dionysus. 'No court', he wrote, 'could be more lovable or generous.'

George Cochrane described a ball at the Bavarian Minister's residence. Coffee and tea were served; a polonaise was played; and then 'the inimitable band struck up an exquisite German waltz, and the King of Greece, having chosen a Grecian lady for his partner, commenced waltzing. This example was soon followed, and about twenty couple were seen revolving round, with as much agility and grace as I ever observed in the saloons of Paris or London' (*Wanderings in Greece* I. 248).

Other visitors included Prince Pückler-Muskau, a colourful German aristocrat with an African mistress, who developed a plan to reinstate the Olympic games at Olympia on the model of a Munich beer festival, and made a point of acquiring antiquities for his collection. He found that Athens made 'a comic impression': a quarter antique, a quarter Turk, a quarter Modern Greek and a quarter Bavarian. Otho's scientific adviser, Georg Brandis, arrived in 1837 with his entire household including his house tutor, Ernst Curtius, who was later to achieve renown as the excavator of Olympia and one of the most distinguished German classicists of the late nineteenth century. Another classical scholar was Carl Otfried Müller, like Welcker one of the first to combine knowledge of antiquities with philological skill in the explication of ancient literature: he toured Greece in 1840, copied numerous inscriptions in Athens and was fêted at a dinner on a summer evening in the Academy garden. In July he was at Delphi, where he hung upside down in the blazing sun to copy a long inscription; he developed a sunstroke and fever, and six days later he was dead. He is buried on the hill of Colonus.

Another remarkable figure was the Duchesse de Plaisance, who moved to Athens after the fall of Napoleon. Her winter mansion, the Villa Ilissia, has now (since 1930) become the Byzantine Museum. She owned most of Mt Pendeli, where she began the building of a Gothic palace (never completed): in the 1940s Rex Warner found it with 'high walls dripping with moisture; there was moss among the brown crevices. . . . Near the castle is the tomb of the Duchess's daughter. The two ladies are assumed to have found a lover or lovers among the more uncivilized inhabitants of the mountains and there are stories which illustrate both rivalry and affection' (*Views of Attica* 1950, 138f). The daughter predeceased the Duchess, and the latter was famous for keeping her body pickled in brandy.

ARCHAEOLOGY AND CONSERVATION

From the first moments of the kingdom, the conservation of antiquities assumed a high importance. In May 1834 the regent Georg Maurer drafted an act (based on the Italian legislation for Rome) which created the institution of the Greek archaeological service and the establishment of museums throughout the Greek state. It laid down guidelines for the excavation and preservation of antiquities, and ensured that all finds would be the property of the Greek state. The first director of the archaeological service was Ludwig Ross.

Ross (1806–59), a North German who had arrived in Greece in 1832 – stepping ashore on Hydra in a morass of rubbish, dead fish and rotting vegetables, among which pigs rooted, grunting, and naked children played – took up residence in Athens in Kleanthes' house on the Acropolis. One of the other guests, a German architect named Lüders, caused a sensation as the bitter winter set in by building out of some pieces of metal the first stove ever seen in Athens. (Nor were there any glass windows in Athens until 1850.) Ross quickly got to know the foreign residents including the Austrian Consul Gropius, the Munich philologist Friedrich Thiersch, and the Scottish Professor Black who had married Byron's Maid of Athens, Teresa Makri. He toured Attica with the Cambridge scholar Christopher Wordsworth, of whom his companion Richard Monckton Milnes wrote: 'Wordsworth never believes he has gloated long enough on any antiquity whatever, and loves an old wall with a passion more intense than that with which any of Rio's Italian heroines burnt for their unseen lovers.' The excursion was somewhat marred by an attack by bandits, in which Wordsworth was stabbed in the neck – fortunately not fatally.

In August 1833, when Ross was ready to leave Greece, he was offered the post of Unterconservator or deputy keeper of antiquities. He stayed, and worked with Klenze for the next year on the plans for the excavation and restoration of the Acropolis. When work began in August 1834 he was promoted to Oberconservator. The Rock became his dominion, and at evening, he could climb with a visiting colleague to the west gable of the Parthenon and admire the sunset, while his servant brought a bowl of coffee and pipes. In January 1835 eighty labourers began work on the destruction of the Byzantine, Frankish and Turkish buildings, to reveal the classical architecture in its original splendour. The Frankish tower, however, remained, until it was demolished at the expense of Heinrich Schliemann in 1874. This work released all the blocks of the Temple of Athena Nike, which was reconstructed in its original spot on the south-west corner of the Rock. Although the work cost 50,000 drachmas, Ross was able to recoup much of this by selling the non-classical blocks to builders. Even at this time, there was opposition to the destruction of the medieval remains from General Heydeck, who found them picturesque: but for a committed classical scholar, there was no real choice.

The Parthenon was restored as far as possible, beginning with the re-erection of all the columns on the north side, to create a fine view from the city. The undistinguished mosque was removed from the interior of the building. The precision of the reconstruction earned him plaudits all over Europe. Some other digs took place in other parts of Greece, but Athens was the focus, and the Peloponnese was relatively neglected.

Ross founded a museum on the Acropolis to house the finds, and was embarrassed by visits from Prince Pückler-Muskau, and from Count Armansperg's daughters, requesting gifts of finds for their own collections. The rumours led to machinations against Ross; he was forbidden to publish any of his archaeological discoveries abroad: all artefacts were the property of the Ministry, and his reports were to be made to the Minister alone. Ross resigned his post; but in 1837 he was offered a professorship at the University, which he held until 1843 when the Greek rebellions against Bavarian rule forced him to leave for good.

Work on Greek antiquities was not the exclusive preserve of the foreigners. In 1837 the *Arkhaiologiki Etaireia* (Archaeological Society) was founded, under the leadership of Alexander Rangavis (1810–92) and Kyriakos Pittakis (1798–1863). The latter was the most learned Greek of his day. He had been interested in antiquities since the War of Independence, when he had used his topographical studies to solve the problem of lack of water during the siege of the Acropolis by finding the ancient well. He published important work on the topography of Athens as well as forming a collection of inscriptions published in the *Arkhaiologiki Ephemeris* (Archaeological Journal) from 1837 to 1860. He guarded the stones of Athens with passion. Klenze described how

> Shortly before my arrival, half a figure from one of the newly-recovered, magnificent frieze sections of the Parthenon was knocked off by an Englishman before Pittakis' very eyes and taken away; and once I found myself in the Parthenon, Pittakis came up to me, calling for help, because some officers of an American frigate in Piraeus were on the point of hacking down the magnificent ornaments of the Erechtheum and carrying them off.

The Society's funds were not great, but they were able to undertake several digs in Athens – at the Theatre of Dionysus (1840–1), the Tower of the Winds (1838–9), the Thrasyllos Monument, Propylaea and Erechtheum, and also the lion at Chaeronea (all 1839–40). In 1837 the chance discovery of the Monument of Euboulides fixed the location of the ancient agora, but no excavation was possible until 1861, after St Koumouroudes became secretary in 1859 and revived the Society's fortunes. In 1884 a fire destroyed many of the houses in the area and laid the ground clear for digging.

The Coup d'Etat of 1843

In 1843 Greek opposition to Bavarian rule, and particularly to Otho's autocratic ways, came to a head. The Queen was particularly unpopular with the Greeks because of her Catholicism; her failure to produce an heir had also attracted comment. Demands for a constitution became ever more strident and were supported by the Powers, notably England under Palmerston's leadership. In September 1843 Makriyannis and other leaders carried out a revolution. General Kalergis, one of the few officers involved in the siege of the Acropolis in 1826 who had not been executed by Reshid, went to the barracks and united the troops behind him with cries of 'Zito to Syntagma – Long live the Constitution'. He led the troops to the palace and conducted a discussion with the king through an open window. Otho refused to believe that his orders would not be heeded, but on the morning of 15 September he admitted the deputies of the Council of State to the palace and signed the papers creating a constitutional monarchy. A National Assembly was formed: Kolettis and Mavrokordatos were its leading figures, and Greece embarked on a new historical path.

Inevitably this quiet revolution put brakes on many of the projects that Otho had supported. Baron Sinas withdrew the funds he had provided for the construction of the Academy, which was only completed in 1887, eleven years after Sinas' death. The rate of new building slowed – but how much had been achieved in ten years! The remaining nineteen years of Otho's reign had much less impact on the Athenian scene.

In 1849 tension was created by the Don Pacifico affair. Don Pacifico, a Maltese Jew and a British citizen, had attempted, with other Jews, to prevent the traditional Easter Monday burning of Judas in effigy in Psyrri Square in Athens. In reprisal, a mob attacked Don Pacifico's house and ransacked it, nearly setting it on fire. The British government under Palmerston did not take lightly such affronts to its citizens. To this cause of complaint were added various grievances of other British citizens (some of the Ionian islands), in particular the matter of a piece of land bought by the historian George Finlay from a Turk in 1840; by 1847 this had been enclosed, without notice and without compensation, in the Royal Gardens, and Finlay wanted redress. Palmerston's response was to send a fleet to blockade the Piraeus, and from January to March 1850, no ships, even those carrying local traffic, could enter or leave Piraeus – a grave blow to Greek trade, and a cause of severe food shortages in a hard winter. The blockade was so strict that Sir Thomas Wyse, the British Minister in Athens, even prevented the delivery of a shipment of potted plants to Queen Amalia, which were a gift from an Egyptian Greek. They all died, and she was furious. The blockade ended when Pacifico agreed to a reduced sum in compensation, and Finlay's claim was also negotiated to his satisfaction (though with much expostulation at the impossibility of suing the Greek king).

British severity towards Greece was also actuated by a continuing suspicion of Greek international alliances, which came into the open with the outbreak of the Crimean War in October 1853. Greece leant to the side of Russia and hoped to make territorial gains at the expense of Turkey, even sending troops to the north. Britain, with a much larger French contingent in addition, blockaded Piraeus again, this time for three years, from May 1854 to February 1857. British and French troops occupied Athens, banqueting on the Acropolis; and the French conducted some unauthorised excavations at Piraeus, in the temple of Artemis at Munychia, whence a large number of antiquities were sent to France and disappeared via dealers into private collections.

The blockade of Piraeus could not keep out one enemy, the cholera, which broke out in June 1854. The city was isolated too late and the epidemic spread to Athens, where ten per cent of the population died before the plague was quelled at the end of 1854.

BRIGANDAGE

Throughout the 1850s brigandage became more widespread in Greece. (Already in 1833 Ludwig Ross's party had been attacked in Attica.) Wyse reported to his government 82 cases in a single year. One case involved the Duchess of Plaisance, a friend of the Greeks and a provider of much employment in the building of her country estates on Mt Pendeli. Her friends outnumbered her enemies, and as soon as news of her capture spread – although she had already tranquilly written out a cheque to the bandits – the entire village of Kalandria turned out to rescue her. Other distinguished residents were similarly affected, such as the daughter of Nicholas Boudoris, a senator, who was seized from her home on Evia on Christmas Day 1825 and marched blindfolded on a donkey for three days through the mountains; it was two months before a reduced ransom was paid and she was freed. Francis Noel, a cousin of Lady Byron, was another landowner on Evia whose home was heavily plundered at this time.

Brigandage became more widespread after the granting of the constitution in 1844, and Kolettis (and other politicians) actively encouraged it in order to terrorise the population and bend them to their will. The opening of the jails at the outbreak of the Crimean War (1854) and the interregnum of 1862, gave further stimulus to the brigand bands. By 1870 the phenomenon had developed into something like a Mafia, with certain politicians and local magnates patronising particular bands. Edmond About, who wrote somewhat scornfully of Greek conditions in the 1850s, made this social phenomenon the subject of his 1857 novel, *Le Roi des Montagnes*. The government seemed unable to prevent the outrages, and the impetus to put down the brigands once and for all only came with the tragic Dilessi Murders of 1870.

This was a major international incident. On 11 April 1870 a group of English tourists departed for Marathon; on the way they were intercepted and taken prisoner by a band of twenty brigands led by the brothers Dimitrios (Takos) and Christos Arvanitakis. The brothers demanded a ransom of £25,000 and a full amnesty (the terms varied somewhat as the negotiations continued). One of the party, Lord Muncaster, was sent to convey the demands to Athens under promise to return to captivity. The British Minister, Edward Erskine, bungled the negotiations; the Minister for War, General Soutsos, was in communication with various brigand bands; the opposition leader George Koumoundouros may have been complicit with the band; while Prime Minister Zaimis was adamant that no amnesty could be offered. A retired officer, Basil Theagenis, was sent to negotiate with the band accompanied by a party of troops. The band had by now moved with their four prisoners to Oropos in Boeotia. Francis Noel had become involved in the affair, urging the prisoners to write to Athens, an action which led to his later being accused by the Greeks of complicity with the brigands. On 21 April the band moved north across the Asopos, while Theagenis' troops moved to surround them. At some point a shot was fired by the troops; immediately the butchery began. The first of the prisoners, Edward Herbert, was cut down and then shot; Edward

Lloyd fell some four hundred yards further on. As the band and their two remaining prisoners ran for their lives, brigands now falling to government fire, both the prisoners were shot dead from behind by their captors.

The disaster developed into an international incident. Press and public in Britain and elsewhere were outraged. Some Greeks put part of the blame on the English, as did John Gennadios in a pamphlet about the affair. But the government was forced to take the matter seriously, and the affair represented the beginning of the end for the brigands. After Takos was shot dead by Greek troops near Lamia in September 1873, the scourge effectively expired.

INTERREGNUM

Our narrative has taken us beyond the end of Otho's reign. On 25 January 1858 Otho celebrated twenty-five years of rule, but his popularity, briefly restored by the occupation, was waning. In May 1860 university students held a riotous demonstration against the king, and in February 1861 there was an assassination attempt on Queen Amalia. In February 1862 there was a rebellion of the garrison in Nauplia, followed by risings in other ports, which took a month to suppress. There was increasing discontent because of the royal couple's failure to produce an heir. This meant that, if Otho were to die, his throne would pass to a brother or cousin; yet the constitution provided that his successor must be of the Orthodox faith, which would plainly not be the case. In October 1862 the king and queen set out for a tour of the kingdom. In their absence there were revolts in Vonitza, Patras and finally Athens. On 10 October a crowd marched from the Oraia Ellada coffee house to the palace. The prison was broken open, German houses in Athens were attacked and the Acropolis museum pillaged. On 23 October Otho's rule was decreed at an end. He returned by sea to Piraeus but was not admitted; the commandant of Piraeus was murdered by his own troops when he attempted to allow the king to enter. On 24 October Otho left on a British ship, HMS *Scylla*, never to return.

An interregnum followed while the Protecting Powers – who accepted the Greeks' right to get rid of Otho – struggled to find a replacement candidate. The Greeks favoured Prince Alfred, Queen Victoria's second son, but the Powers eventually settled on the young Prince George of Denmark, who acceded to the throne on 30 March 1863 at the age of seventeen, and arrived in Athens in October the same year, covered in dust after the ride from Piraeus to Athens. In the meantime rival factions had struggled for power and the army had gone out of control, committing public outrages in the streets of Athens. The situation degenerated into civil war with the Minister of War, Koronaios, along with Aristides Kanares and Grivas, occupying the Royal Palace and their opponents, the sixth battalion under Leotzakos in the Plaisance mansion. The ministerial party concentrated their forces in the National Bank and on the Acropolis. Fighting broke out on 1 July and about forty people were killed, but the foreign ministers arranged an armistice the following day. A new ministry was elected and on 5 July the army left Athens, leaving the National Guard to maintain control. The anarchy came to an end with the arrival of the new king, and in November a new constitution was promulgated with increased civil liberties and an increased measure of local government. Greece was now for the first time a true constitutional monarchy.

CHAPTER TWELVE

The Reign of King George
1863–1913

Economic Development

The reign of King George provided opportunities for steady economic and social development in Greece. This was despite political turmoils including a major revolt in Crete (1866), the atrocious Turkish repression of Bulgarian revolt in the 1870s, war against Turkey in 1897 and the beginning of discontent over Macedonia at the beginning of the 1900s. Inns, newspapers and shops multiplied and flourished in the capital. The Prime Minister Charilaos Trikoupis (1832–96, PM 1882–96) made systematic efforts to modernise Greece, introducing parliamentary reforms as well as commissioning new buildings such as the National Library (Theophilus Hansen, 1884, completed 1902). Athens was by no means quiet, however: Trikoupis' main rival, Theodore

Charilaos Trikoupis

Deligiannis, who was prime minister three times, was assassinated on the steps of the Old Parliament on 31 May 1905.

The influence of the Phanariots began to recede, and the new stability of the country led many of the expatriate Greek merchants to establish themselves in the capital. Shipping grew rapidly, especially after 1880 and the end of the Russo-Turkish war, and the Greek fleet tripled in size between 1900 and 1914, to become the eleventh in the world in size, with 2 per cent of the total tonnage. Greek merchants were spread all over the Black Sea and the Mediterranean: in Smyrna, half the population was Greek. Chiot families such as Rallis, Lemos and Hadjipateras were particularly prominent in the shipping business, and famous dynasties from other islands include the Embirikos and Goulandris.

Industrialisation proceeded apace in the capital region. One of the first areas affected was the district that became known as Metaxourgeio, close to ancient Colonus. A plot of land was sold by Prince George Cantacuzenos as early as 1833, and the land was developed by Christian Hansen as a commercial block. In 1854 it was bought by the silk firm of Athanasios Domoutis, and for nearly twenty years it resounded to the noise of steam-powered looms and the songs of the female workers. Domoutis spent part of his wealth on the support of widows and orphans. France was the chief customer for the fine silk. The factory's closure in 1875 put 500 people out of work, and the building declined, functioning as a shelter for refugees in 1944. In the 1990s it was at last restored for residential use.

A powerful working class developed, with its own culture which was to come into its own in the early years of the twentieth century. In 1882 measures were introduced for the protection of workers, for example miners; many workers, from miners to shop assistants, had to work in unsafe and unhygienic conditions. Shop hours were long, from 6 am to 6.30 pm and hygienic facilities minimal.

The completion of the Piraeus railway in 1895, the establishment of the tram to Faliro (1885–90) and the opening of the Corinth Canal in 1893 contributed immensely to the growth in importance of Piraeus, which came to be known as the Manchester of the Orient.

Piraeus started a vigorous programme of industrialisation with the establishment of flour mills, cotton manufacturing and the growth of factories for silk, soap, furniture and alcohol. Other industrial enterprises included the Kanellopoulos soap factory in Eleusis, and the manufacture of explosives was localised in Psychiko. Businesses dealing in women's clothing became plentiful. In 1883 a businessman named E. Poulopoulos established a hat factory and soon persuaded the Prime Minister, Trikoupis, to place a tax on foreign hats, which naturally worked to his advantage. The rise of clothing shops was a major change since formerly women had made all the clothes for their families.

In 1870 a Bavarian entrepreneur, Karl Fuchs, established a brewery (the name was hellenised as Phix) in the Ardittos region: he called it Metz after the battle in the Franco-Prussian War, and this became the name of the district. Between 1870 and 1888 the district became home to several theatres, cafés, music cafés and brothels.

URBAN DEVELOPMENT

The Demarcheion (City Hall), a restrained neo-classical building by Panagiotis Kalkos, was erected in 1872, and became home to the administrations of several influential mayors. From 1883 to 1887 Demetrios Soutsos was mayor: he was eventually fined because of the collapse of public services under his regime. From 1889 to 1914 Spyridon Mercouris (the grandfather of the actress Melina Mercouri) brought major improvements to the city scene. Many streets were paved and squares improved. The imminence of the Olympic Games in 1896 (see below) sparked a major clean-up of the city. Voulis and Adrianou streets were home to butcher's shops and the streets were awash with the detritus of slaughter as well as with simple sewage. Many gardens had become no more than rubbish tips. Mercouris saw to the cleaning of the streets and the planting of cypresses, planes, palms, mulberries and oleanders, as well as the beautification of the major squares (Omonoia, Kolonaki, Kanningos, Plakas and Loudovikou) with trees. In 1896 a corps of street cleaners was formed, and 2,000 gas lamps were erected, the number of which soon increased to 2,700.

These decades also saw the establishment of many important public organisations, ranging from the Parnassos Literary Society (1865) to the Association for the Protection of Destitute Women (1872). Queen

Queen Olga

Olga was particularly involved in good works: she established the Orphanage in Plateia Eleftherias. It is now the Municipal Art Gallery, but the reception counter at which the unfortunate mothers would deliver their unwanted children is still to be seen, and some of the sadness of the orphans seems still to suffuse the building. Olga also founded the Evangelismos Hospital (1883). The monastery at Daphni, which had been a barracks since 1854, briefly became a lunatic asylum from 1883 to 1885, before reverting to use as a sheepfold.

One new building had a more sombre origin. The church of Ag. Sostis was built in Falirou Avenue (now Syngrou) to mark the spot where an assassin had made an attempt on the life of the king on 14 February 1898.

Ernst Ziller

The architectural development of both Athens and Piraeus continued apace with the completion of the Academy by the Hansen brothers (1859–87), the Polytechnic by Lysandros Kaftanzoglou (1862–80), the National Library by the Hansens (1885–92) and the Zappeion Exhibition Hall by Theophilus Hansen and F. Boulanger (1874–88). Numerous churches were built and the wide streets were turned into elegant boulevards lined with fine buildings. Trees were planted along the avenues, and, less visible, but just as important, sewage works were undertaken. City planners looked to the Paris of Baron Haussmann as a model, and the modernisation of the city was seen as a route to the modernisation of society.

A new generation of architects gave a more western touch to the prevailing neo-classical idiom. Many of them were Greeks, but perhaps the greatest impact was made by a German, Ernst Ziller (1837–1923), who had studied in Dresden and then been a pupil of Theophilus Hansen in Vienna. In 1861 he supervised the completion of the Academy building, and in 1868 he settled permanently in Athens, becoming a professor at the Polyechnic from 1872 to 1882. He dedicated his life to the beautification of the city. He continued the established neo-classical tradition with such distinguished structures as the Municipal Theatre (begun in 1857 by Boulanger, completed 1888 and demolished in May 1939) and the National Theatre on Ag. Constantinou Street, the Alexander the Great hotel in Omonoia Square (1899) and the Bangeion opposite (1890), the Cadet School (1889–94) and a palace for Prince Constantine (1891–7). Several other hotels were built on Omonoia Square at the same period, including the Excelsior (now a branch of the National Bank) and the Plaza. Another important building was the Vasilis Melas mansion in the south-east corner of Kotzia Square (1883–4): this was repaired after a fire in 1900, and became the central post office, and subsequently a bank. Ziller also built the Stathatos Mansion (1885), which is now part of the Goulandris Museum, and his style is reflected in works that are not by him such as the Psychas Mansion (now the French Embassy) and the mansions on the corner of Irodotou and Alopekis (now an art gallery).

After a destructive earthquake in 1894 Ziller designed many stronger but less ostentatious buildings. He was also responsible for the restoration of the ancient Stadium in 1896 for the Olympic Games, and for the mansion built for himself by Heinrich Schliemann (1822–90), the excavator of Troy and Mycenae. This was called Iliou Melathron ('Palace of Troy', 1870–81) and stands at 12 Panepistimiou Street; it was sold to the Greek state in 1927, functioned as the Areios Pagos or Supreme Court until 1994, and is now the Numismatic Museum. Its colonnaded Italianate exterior houses a series of palatial marble halls decorated in the Pompeian style.

Ziller's career was very successful but he died poor. His splendid town house in Mavromichali Street, just above Akadimias, adorned on the façade with caryatids, is in a ruined state that all but obliterates its former grandeur.

Ziller's major enterprise was the National Archaeological Museum. The project was opened to tender before 1860, but none of the submissions was deemed satisfactory by the Ministry of Education. In 1860 Klenze's pupil and associate Ludwig Lange undertook a design, which was begun in 1866 on a site donated by the Tositsa family. By the time it was completed in 1889 it had been substantially altered by Panagiotes Kalkos and Ernst Ziller. Originally envisaged with a long colonnade of twenty columns and short wings, topped by a central pediment, it was completed with a short flat-topped central colonnade of four columns and two long wings of smaller columns, twelve on each side, each completed by a pedimented temple-like block. The layout of the halls within was somewhat simplified. The interior has been somewhat modified in recent years, but the exterior remains unchanged.

FASHIONABLE SUBURBS

Ziller also worked in Piraeus, and made his home in Munychia. He laid out the Boulevard Socrates, a grand avenue of neo-classical mansions of ship owners, merchants and professionals, none of which exists today: the street has been renamed Avenue of the Heroes of the Polytechnic. Suburbs of Piraeus such as Terpsithea, Pashalimani and Kastella (Munychia) all filled up with neo-classical houses. One must look upwards to enjoy the antefixes of upright tiles along the roofs of the old houses of Piraeus, a frisky touch compared with the staider grandeur of Athens. (Many houses in Plaka have similar details, however.) Gas lighting was introduced in 1872, electricity in 1904.

Neon Phaleron was defined as a distinct urban district in the 1860s and from the 1880s it became the centre of Athenian social life of the Belle Epoque. Echoing fashionable models as dissimilar as Brighton and Vienna, it blossomed with hotels, baths, a theatre, a bandstand, bathing huts and a cycle track. The Charakopos mansion of the late nineteenth century became home to the Benaki family in 1910 and was turned into a museum in 1931. Piraeus and Neon Phaleron became a centre of artistic activity in the 1880s: the German-trained maritime painter Constantine Volanakis recorded the harbour's life with its steam-sailing ships, its ladies with parasols and its fishermen and hawkers. In the next generation Yiannis Tsarouchis (b. 1910) painted the changing scene.

Another suburb that developed at this period was Kifissia. In antiquity the centre of the district was the cave of the nymphs, and Herodes Atticus had one of his many villas here. From 1885 it was linked to Athens by the steam train known as 'The Beast'. Many of the mansions standing here were built by Ziller. So numerous are these fashionable dwellings that Osbert Lancaster in the 1940s described Kifissia as 'an architectural museum'. The Hotel Melas (1870) was one of the first in Greece. Deligiannis had a house here. Popular locales were the Platanos and the Alsos. King George acquired the estate at Tatoi near here which continued to be a residence of the Greek royal family until the end of the monarchy.

Another major architectural achievement of the end of the nineteenth century is the First Necropolis. The large and often splendid tombs in this cemetery represent one of the finest assemblages of neoclassical tomb architecture and statuary to be found anywhere in the world. Many famous citizens and others are buried here: the tomb of Heinrich Schliemann is among them, but the majority are the resting places of distinguished bourgeois. The tombs are an anthology of neoclassical detail and echoes of Roman and Greek tomb sculpture: angels with reversed torches, mourning figures in classical draperies, winged victories, replicas of buildings such as the Lysicrates monument, tempietti with crosses on top; pyramids, broken columns and urns – all bespeak the harmonious merging of classical symbols of mourning with Christian statements of hope. Many of the artists can be identified, but as many more of the tombs are anonymous, and carry the memory only of their occupants. The necropolis is always busy with visitors to the family tombs as well as those who come to admire the architecture.

PAINTERS

The nineteenth century saw the emergence of Greece, and especially Athens, as a theme for painters. The picturesque ideal gave place to romanticism, and an important school of Bavarian painters was established in the reign of Otho. Most important of them was Carl Rottmann, whose achievement can be described as the discovery of Greek light. 'How I shall paint blue in Greece!' he wrote. His pupil Ludwig Lange worked in a similar style but with more emphasis on genre scenes. Carl Heydeck, the regent, was also a significant painter. One result of all this Bavarian activity was that the next generation of Greek painters studied in Munich. Important representatives of Greek painting of the second half of the century are Nikolas Gyzis (1842–1901), Vikentios Lantsa (Venice 1822–Athens 1902), Polychronis Lembesis (1878–1913) and Iakovos Rizos (Athens 1849–Paris 1916). Most of these are noted painters of the Athenian scene, and their work has achieved increasing recognition in the last twenty years. Two major maritime painters are Constantine Volanakis (Crete 1837–Piraeus 1907) and Theodore Vryzakis (1814–1878).

In 1848 Edward Lear undertook his first tour of Greece, arriving on 2 June. 'Surely never was anything as magnificent as Athens!' he wrote in a letter to his sister. 'The town is all new – but the poorer part of it, what with awnings, & bazaars & figures of all possible kinds is most picturesque.' Of the Acropolis he wrote that it was 'really the most astonishing monument of a great people I have yet seen. Poor old scrubby Rome sinks into nothing by the side of such magnificence.' He picked up a touch of malaria, but was off to Constantinople by 4 August. Lear fell in love with Greece, and returned repeatedly to tour northern Greece in 1849, Corfu in 1855 and 1862–3, and Crete and Athens in 1864. By this time he was jaded and disillusioned and Athens did not hold the charm for him that it had fifteen years before: it was pervaded with a 'queer analytic dryness of soul & mind & atmosphere' (whatever he meant by that), and he decided against making a permanent home there.

ARCHAEOLOGICAL ACTIVITY

The work of the archaeologists, interrupted in the later years of Otho's reign, resumed in the 1860s. An important feature was the establishment of the foreign schools and institutes of archaeology. The first of these was the French school, established as early as 1846. In 1874 the

German Archaeological Institute was established, in 1881 the American School of Classical Studies and in 1886 the British School of Archaeology. All these acted as a base for students of their nations and for archaeological activity, though most of their excavation took place outside the capital. Work in Athens continued to be conducted by the Archaeologiki Etaireia. Their excavation at the Theatre of Dionysus in 1862 was followed by the discovery of the Ceramicus, the ancient potters' quarter and cemetery area, in 1863. Work had begun on the construction of the new Piraeus Street in 1861 and the Society oversaw the excavation and expropriation of land. When the first grave stelae were found in 1863 it was realised what lay here; excavation continued until 1913 under the direction of the Society, and was then taken up by the German school. The eastern part of the area, along the Sacred Way, was covered by soil dumped from these excavations and the ground further disturbed by the building of the vegetable market in 1902; the area has only been properly laid bare as a result of the excavations for the Ceramicus Metro Station.

In 1874 the Frankish Tower on the Acropolis was demolished at the expense of Heinrich Schliemann, who had recently made his home in Athens with his Greek wife Sophia. Further work of the Society included the Asclepieion in 1876, the Stoa of Eumenes in 1877–8, the theatre at Zea (Pashalimani) in 1883–4 and the Odeion of Pericles in 1900. The discovery of the Monument of Euboulides in 1837 fixed the location of the classical agora; an excavation was carried out in 1861, but on 9 August 1884 a fire in the bazaar area destroyed many of the buildings, including the Megali Panagia and the barracks, and gave the opportunity for more extensive clearing and excavation. The fire was contained by the ancient city wall and did not spread to other parts of the city. The clock on the tower donated by Lord Elgin as a thank-you for the Parthenon Marbles stopped at two minutes to two, and in 1885 the tower was demolished. (The remains are in the National Historical Museum.) The Library of Hadrian and the area of the Roman Agora were laid bare and became an archaeological area, free of further building. Ground water prevented deep investigations. Monastiraki Square and Pandrosou Street, being undamaged, became the new centre of the bazaar. In 1891–2 Wilhelm Dörpfeld, the archaeologist whom some called Schliemann's greatest discovery, and who had worked with Ernst Curtius at Olympia, supervised the beginnings of the excavations for the Piraeus Railway.

In 1886 excavations were begun at the Temple of Olympian Zeus, and continued until 1907. Outside Athens the Society excavated at the Amphiareion of Oropus, at Thorikos, at Rhamnous and at Eleusis. In the last decade of the nineteenth century works were directed by Panagiotis Kavvadias and Georg Kawerau, and included the somewhat unfortunate restoration works on the Parthenon and other buildings by Nikolaos Balanos: these made use of iron clamps to hold the stones together, but the iron has had a damaging effect on the blocks it was intended to preserve.

Along with these archaeological works came an increase of scholarly activity and interest in the more recent Greek past. The great folklorist Nikolaos Politis (1852–1921) embarked on his herculean task of gathering and publishing Greek folk songs, Greek popular traditions and superstitions, and all the relics of a traditional way of life that seemed to be vanishing in the gradual transformation of Greece into a European country.

The invention of photography offered a new way to record, not just the contemporary urban scene, but the archaeological remains. The work of photographers such as Francis Bedford (b. 1816), Felix Bonfils (b. 1831, in Athens 1870 and later), J. Pascal Sebah (b. 1838, in Athens ca 1870) and William Stillman (b. 1828 Schenectady, d. 1901, in Athens 1869 and later) provides an indispensable – and also beautiful – record of the appearance of (mainly) Athens at the end of the nineteenth century. Bonfils' panorama of Athens, around 1870, shows a still small city lying to the north side of the Acropolis, and also the Frankish Tower, still standing on the Acropolis. Stillman's photographs of the Parthenon and the Erechtheum provide a valuable service to present-day archaeologists who need to ascertain the appearance of the buildings before the restorations of the later nineteenth century. His use of 'Dallmyer's rectilinear lenses' meant that his were 'the first photographs deliberately to demonstrate the distinctive characteristics of the classical form' (R.A. Tomlinson, *The Athens of Alma-Tadema* 39). These photographers are also testimony to the increased importance of

Greece as a tourist destination: the Baedeker guidebook for 1881 is one of the first to cater for this new interest, and some of Bonfils' photographs include the clientele, as well as showing clearly the chairs and tables of the restaurant charmingly established among the columns of the Parthenon.

The Olympic Games of 1896

A symbol of the modernisation of Greece, but with its links to the past still indissoluble, was the re-establishment of the Olympic Games in Athens in 1896. The ancient Olympic Games had been held at Olympia every four years from 776 BC to their abolition as a pagan festival in AD 395. The idea of holding a modern Olympics originated with the poet Alexander Soutsos. As early as 1837 King Otho had proposed establishing a festival with athletic events, and in 1842 Soutsos had written to Otho suggesting that these should be 'Olympic Games'. The scheme echoed the plan of William Penny Brookes of Much Wenlock in Shropshire, who may be counted the founder of the international Olympic movement: the Much Wenlock Olympic Games began in 1850 and became an annual event. Soutsos' movement gathered momentum with the enlistment of Evangelis Zappas, who from 1856 bombarded the king and his ministers with proposals for an Olympics. Zappas, born in 1800, had fought with Markos Botsaris in the War of Independence and subsequently made a fortune in Bucharest. Part of his wealth went into building the exhibition hall, the Zappeion. The Zappas Games took place in 1875, but they were, in the words of their historian David C. Young, 'a fiasco. The Olympic committee spent almost no money to prepare the stadium... In the spectator areas thornbushes and rocks remained uncleared.. Crude wooden benches were set for paying spectators, but even some of these broke when used.... Disorder reigned.' The Games lasted a total of two and a half hours, and the events were interspersed with band music – polkas and Offenbach. J.P. Mahaffy, an Irish professor of classics who was never at a loss for an acerbic comment, wrote contemptuously of the whole proceedings, and incidentally started the untrue claim that the ancient Olympics had been an event for amateurs. Nothing could be further from the truth.

A generation later, the baton was taken up by Baron Pierre de Coubertin: enthused by Brookes' Olympics, in 1890 he began to develop plans for their re-establishment on an international scale. The first site mooted for an 1896 celebration was London, and it remains unclear exactly how Athens came to be chosen. It was proposed at the Olympic Committee meeting in Paris in June 1894, and in 1895 Prince Constantine created an organising committee. Funds were the main problem. Zappas had left money in his will for future Games, but this had been squandered in Romania. By June an offer of funds had been secured from George Averoff, an Epirote Greek living in Alexandria. Plans for the rebuilding of the stadium by A. Metaxas were approved, and some of the events, including the fencing, were scheduled for the Zappeion itself. The stadium (by Ziller) was completed in spring 1896, and a statue of Averoff stood at its entrance. John Gennadius, who had scorned the proceedings, now changed his tune to that of enthusiastic support. The Games took place in April, involving athletes from most of the countries of Europe as well as from America. Many events were won by the Americans, but there was great joy on 10 April when a Greek, Spyridon Louis, was declared the winner of the Marathon, with its symbolic echo of the great classical past of Athens. He crossed the finishing line at the Stadium two hours, fifty-eight minutes and fifty seconds after leaving Marathon, and his victory was marked by the release of a cloud of white doves. The following days included events in wrestling, swimming and cycling; a sailing contest at Neon Phaleron was cancelled because only Greeks turned up. There was also a performance of Sophocles' *Antigone*, a torchlight parade, a firework display, and a banquet in the palace. (Dress was declared 'informal', so one American athlete came in his running shorts; Spyridon Louis wore a fustanella.) The ten days were a great success. For a time it was mooted that all subsequent celebrations should take place in Athens. Though this did not take place, the Games, with all their symbolism of international friendship, which still take place every four years, owe their re-establishment to the success of the Athens Games of 1896.

The New Century

The twentieth century opened in a mood of optimism in Athens. People were still enthusiastically running mini-Marathons all over Plaka, and practising their discus-throwing at the taverna O Platanos. In 1899 a party was held in the Zappeion gardens to mark the beginning of the new century. In March 1901 the new vegetable market opened in Athinas Street which was hailed as the finest such building in Europe. In the same year 175 new public lavatories were built in Athens, and in August 1902 electric street lighting was introduced. Also in 1902 the mayor introduced a new rubbish collection service: the city was divided into seventy regions, with seventy cleaners, seventy carts, and smart uniforms. The plan worked and this city of 150,000 population ceased to be fragrant with accumulated and rotting rubbish.

A radical plan for the remodelling of the city centre was devised by the architect Bernardakis, but there was no political will to carry it through, and it was ignored, perhaps ultimately to the advantage of many historic buildings.

A darker note was sounded by the riots that took place in November 1901 over the translation, sponsored by Queen Olga, of the Gospels into Modern Greek. The students from the University marched on the Cathedral, the Bishop was forced to resign, and the Prime Minister was stoned, before the uproar died away. The fracas showed the depth of the Greeks' attachment to the Orthodox Church and its traditional forms, for the language of the New Testament, though it was the basis of the *katharevousa* that had been developed by Korais, was already something like a foreign language to the speakers of the vernacular. But such concerns were soon overshadowed by the more momentous events that ushered in the age of Venizelos.

CHAPTER THIRTEEN

From the Balkan Wars to the Civil War
1912–1949

The Age of Venizelos

Greek political life in the first decades of the twentieth century was dominated by the charismatic figure of Eleftherios Venizelos. Born in Crete in 1864, he studied at Athens University and returned to Crete to play a prominent role in the Cretan insurrection against Ottoman rule of 1896–7. He acquired a reputation as a revolutionary leader, to which was added a gift for great eloquence and a deep understanding, fostered by study, of Greek history and contemporary politics. He was leader of the Cretan Assembly when union with Greece was declared in 1905, though this union was not actually completed until 1913. The stage was set for his advance to play a central role in Greek politics.

In northern Greece momentous events were taking place. In the

Eleftherios Venizelos

1890s Bulgarian nationalism had led to the formation of the Macedonian Committee. One branch of this movement was the International Macedonian Revolutionary Organization (IMRO), a terrorist organisation whose outrages reached a peak in the years 1901–3. The western powers intervened in an attempt to force the Ottoman government to institute reforms, but in 1908 events overtook them with the revolution of the Young Turks in Constantinople (officially the Committee of Union and Progress), which led to the overthrow of the Sultan, the abolition of the caliphate, and the eventual benign dictatorship of Kemal Atatürk.

In 1908 the Cretans again proclaimed their allegiance to Greece but were thwarted by an international force of marines, who tore down the Greek flag in Chania. This affront to Greek nationhood caused such an explosion of revolutionary fervour in Athens that a military coup took place. In May 1909 a group of dissident officers forced the resignation of the government of Dimitrios Rallis. Their political experience was limited, but soon they summoned Venizelos from Crete to take charge. Venizelos persuaded the king to summon a National Assembly to revise the constitution, which came into force in 1911. The Military League dissolved itself and Venizelos became Prime Minister for the first time in October 1910, with 80 per cent of the seats in Parliament held by his party. He was Prime Minister a number of times before his final tenure of the office in 1928 and was the central figure in Greek politics even when out of office.

Venizelos instituted a number of reforms which recognised the changed character of Greek politics and society as a result of the industrialisation of the later nineteenth century and the growth in particular of the Greek merchant fleet. A progressive income tax replaced many of the indirect taxes which formerly had fallen with disproportionate weight on the poor; laws against trade unions were repealed; a minimum wage was introduced, as were sick pay, pensions and workplace insurance, and elementary education was made free and compulsory.

WORKING-CLASS CULTURE

These reforms reflected the conditions in the major cities of Athens and Piraeus, where the traditional peasant way of life had been entirely superseded by the growth of an urban working class. This working class brought with it its own distinctive forms of popular culture, some of them emanating from the long-established port city of Smyrna. Already in the 1890s a distinctive feature of life in Piraeus and in the working-class suburbs of Psyrri, Theseio and Metaxourgeio were the popular singers who would perform in bars to the playing of the oud, laouto or sandouri, often surrounded by the fumes of hashish, a relaxation which had spread from the prisons to the harbour proletariat. The songs were Turkish, and dancers performed to the music. A newspaper report (*Acropolis*) in August 1891 commented:

> In the area to the east of Munychia, wherever there is a little coffee shop, the common people gather in stifling disorder from the very early evening hours and spend their time there enjoying the cool of the evening in happy idleness. Oh, those oriental songs and dances... The dances are those of Arabia and Turkey, and they are performed by a graceful young woman from Smyrna called Eleni. First she hooks her castanets over the longest fingers of each hand, and then ... she begins the Arabic dance: how her body twists, rolls, arches and curves...

Increasingly Greek words and themes prevailed. In the 1920s this tradition of bar music grew into the *rebetika*, which in their mood and themes sometimes recalled American blues, and which like American blues developed in turn into the distinctive popular music of 1950s and 1960s Greece. Accompanied by the baglamas, the singers told of prison, unemployment and street life. Among the representatives of the latter were the *manges*, or 'hard men' who strutted the streets, a pistol in one pocket and a set of worry beads protruding from the other. Though serious efforts were made to stamp out the *manges* in the 1890s, they provided one of the stock types in the Karagiozis theatre which developed in the same period.

Karagiozis (Turkish Karagöz) is the central figure of a series of plays performed in a shadow puppet theatre, which seems to have arrived in Greece in the 1850s. The cunning and witty Karagiozis, with his double-jointed arm, is a type of the Greek trickster of all ages from the heroes of Aristophanes onwards. His companions include Stavrakas, the hard man, several of the generals of the War of Independence, Barba-Yorgo (a shepherd in a fustanella), the long-beared Hajiavatis in red boots, and even the hero Alexander the Great (who fights a dragon in one of the plays). The plays are performed out of doors, and the puppets are manipulated against a screen by the concealed operator. The dialogue is full of ribaldry and topical allusions (again recalling Aristophanes). The plays continued to be performed in Plaka in the 1970s, but have perhaps now altogether died out.

Other entertainments of this kind also took place in the Monastiraki area, which became the haunt of conjurors and acrobats. Since independence this area had provided the starting place for the carnival celebrations, and the new popular entertainments simply continued the tradition. The character of the shopping area here also changed with the building of the new agora, the Megali Paranga, in the 1880s. Monastiraki Square became home to sweet shops, tobacco shops, pharmacies and shoe shops. From 1895 there was a secondhand market on Sundays in the Plateia Demoprateriou (Anavrysteriou), and secondhand clothes shops, the property of Jewish families, in the area of Agioi Asomatoi, near the synagogue in Melidoni St. The area towards Avissinias Square became known as Yousouroum after one of the Jewish merchants. Sellers of milk in copper buckets patrolled the streets, as did vendors of halva and koulouria (ring-shaped bread rolls); shoe cleaners sat in wait along the streets.

The electrification of the Piraeus railway in 1904 also had its impact on Monastiraki Square. Horse carriages continued to wait in ranks for hire near the station entrance. Even more significant for transport were the trams. Horse-drawn trams had been introduced in New York in 1832 and first reached Athens in 1882. There was also a steam tram service to Faliron. One of these unfortunately exploded near the Hadrian Gate on 13 May 1907, killing five people. In 1908 the network was electrified. There were now 16 lines covering a total distance of 65 kilometres. The extension of the tram service to Patissia opened up this elegant district of *archontika* (mansions), and numerous restaurants opened along its route, among them the renowned Alysida.

The First World War

International politics continued to have a major impact on Greece and on Athens with the outbreak of the Balkan Wars in 1912. In the First

Balkan War the Balkan League (Greece, Serbia, Bulgaria and Monte-negro) took arms against Turkey. An important outcome, ratified in a treaty of 30 May 1913, was that Salonica became Greek. The Second Balkan War soon broke out over just this fact, and involved Greece and Bulgaria as antagonists. The Treaty of Bucharest of 10 August 1913 ratified Greek victory and territorial gains in Thrace.

On 18 March 1913 King George was assassinated by a madman in Thessaloniki, and was succeeded by his son Constantine, universally known to his people as Tino. The outbreak of the First World War in 1914 brought tension in Greece as Venizelos strongly favoured the Allies, while Tino, who was married to the Kaiser's daughter, leaned in his sympathies towards the Germans. Tino twice compelled Venizelos' resignation in the course of 1915; in 1916 Venizelos established a provisional government at Thessaloniki. This government declared war on Germany and Bulgaria.

There was anarchy in Athens. Venizelists were under constant threat. The Anglo-French secret police had to protect the supporters of Venizelos, and a period of terror in December 1916 saw the slaughter of many of the Venizelists by reservists who supported the king.

By the end of 1916 the Allies had forced Greece to co-operate in its war aims by enforcing the disarming of the fleet and the surrender of control of the railway line to the north. Early in 1917 Constantine abdicated in favour of his younger son, Prince Alexander, and on 12 June he left for Switzerland. Venizelos was reinstated as Prime Minister (26 June), and on 28 June Greece entered the war.

Greece played only a small part in the war and its troops were not engaged until it was almost over. But Athens became a hub of espionage and counter-espionage, and a communications link in the Galli-poli campaign. The activities (some might call them antics) of the British secret service in Athens are brilliantly described in Compton Mackenzie's memoirs, *First Athenian Memories* and *Greek Memories*. Mackenzie was undecided whether Venizelos was to be seen as a Pericles, a great patriotic statesman, or merely a Themistocles, a wily and unreliable politician. The classical terms of reference are notable; but Venizelos might have entertained equal doubts about his western allies. After his uncompromising championship of the Allied cause in the war, he expected that the break-up of the Ottoman Empire would bring direct territorial gains for Greece. As early as 1915 'the Ministers of the Entente were empowered to offer Greece in return for co-operation against Turkey territorial acquisitions in the Vilayet of Aidin'. The Greeks, and even the British (though not the French) took this to mean that Smyrna would be given to Greece.

On 14 May 1919 the Greeks occupied Smyrna. At the Treaty of Sèvres (10 August 1920), the Turks signed an agreement that Greece was to have Smyrna and its surroundings, as well as the whole of Thrace, the Gallipoli peninsula, and some other territories. But when Venizelos sent an army to claim these gains, the chief of staff, Metaxas, warned that it would be no easy task to hold them. The expected western support did not materialise. In January 1920 the new Turkish parliament proclaimed a new Turkish state and rejected all foreign claims. Kemal Atatürk determined that the Greeks would be expelled from Asia Minor.

The Asia Minor Disaster

The Greek crisis was compounded by an assassination attempt on Venizelos at the Gare de Lyon in Paris by several naval officers on 31 July 1920, by the death of King Alexander in October 1920 following a bite from his pet monkey, and by Venizelos' loss of the election of November 1920. King Constantine returned in December, and the western powers looked less warmly on Greece than they had done up to now. The Greek army was severely defeated in two pitched battles against the Turks in 1921, and in August 1922, after the decisive Battle of the Sakarya, the Turks drove the Greeks into the sea at Smyrna. The city was burnt, terrible slaughter and atrocities took place in the city, and more than 150,000 refugees poured into Greece, mainly from Asia Minor but 20 per cent of them from Pontus. This episode, which the Turks refer to as the War of Independence, and the Greeks as the Asia Minor disaster, had a profound impact on Greece, especially on its big cities.

Refugees were sheltered in tents on the archaeological sites, beside the Theseion and in the National Theatre. Shelters of all kinds sprang up from Kaisariani to Kallithea and Nea Smyrni. Even the elegant Kifissia was filled with the suffering refugees. 11,870 'accommodation units' were created in the suburbs of Nea Ionia, Vyronas, Hymettos, Kaisariani and Nea Smyrni. Psychiko too was enlarged at this time. Over the year numbers of the refugees grew to over 1.2 million.

> In Athens people slept on the streets, in a royal villa, in the ruins of the Parthenon, in the theatres. Every velvet-lined box in the National Opera housed a family; other refugees slept in the orchestra and on the stairs. Makeshift camps sprawled for miles along the beaches. Abandoned auto-mobile tyres were cut up for sandals. Pots, pans, even sewing needles became collectors' items. With the approach of winter pneumonia, tuberculosis, malaria and trachoma reached epidemic proportions. Virtually every refugee was ill. . . . By December pestilential diseases among the boatloads of refugees arriving from the Pontus were so virulent that the Greek government was forced to call a halt to emigration from that area. Ship after ship, crammed to the gunwales with human freight, rolled at anchor in the stormy seas, flashing out essentially the same distress signal: 4,000 [5,000 . . . 6,000] REFUGEES. NO WATER. NO FOOD. SMALLPOX AND TYPHUS FEVER ABOARD. (M.H. Dobkin, *Smyrna 1922*, 214f)

Gradually a 'bleak wilderness of suburbs' (Kevin Andrews) rose up on the far side of the Ilissus from the city, to house this vast quantity of Greeks who had lost their homes. As early as 1918 city planners had been working on ideas for planned growth of the city. The Englishman Thomas Mawson had been engaged to draw up a plan, but all this went by the way under the impact of the Asia Minor disaster. It was to be another 65 years before a systematic plan for the city's rapid growth would be implemented.

The political fallout was immense. General Pangalos declared martial law in October 1923 and forced the flight of the king in December. Constantine was succeeded by his son George II, and in 1924 Venizelos was once again elected Prime Minister. But in April 1924, when the country voted for the establishment of a republic, Venizelos resigned, and a series of military coups followed.

> Ambitious generals, disgruntled colonels, captains of all sorts and politicians distrusting each other, wanted to rule. For four years (1924–1928) Greece

was a land of transitory dictatorships, of *coup d'etats*, of abortive *putsches* and rebellions. By the end of this period, Greece had more generals than pieces of cannon, more admirals than warships, generals pensioners at the age of thirty-five, captains máde colonels by a stroke of the pen, and so forth, until nobody knew who was with whom, what army unit was loyal and what not, from where would spring the next *coup d'etat* and with what object in view. (D. Alastos, *Venizelos* 235)

Some attempts at economic improvement were made under the dictatorship of General Pangalos, who made himself President on 18 April 1926. Besides attacking short skirts and hanging embezzlers, he inaugurated the Academy of Athens (25 May 1926), with financial help from Emmanuel Benakis and others. In the same year the Gennadius Library was founded (see below). Gifts from Benakis also helped to establish an aeroplane factory in Phaliron.

The end of Pangalos' dictatorship in August 1926, when he was imprisoned on Crete, led to a confrontation in the streets of Athens. The democrats under Ntertiles and Napoleon Zervas marched down Vasilissis Sofias (then Kifissias) Avenue to Syntagma Square and the Ministry of War (now the Foreign Ministry, on the corner of Vas. Sofias and Akadimias). Cannon stationed in Rigillis Square fired on the demonstrators, the first casualties being the Ambelokipi tram and Zervas' horse. Eventually Ntertiles was able to reach the Prime Minister and engage in talks, and the armed crisis ended.

Venizelos returned for the last time in 1928 to introduce further social and economic reforms. Now elderly, he was less effective than before, and his efforts were hampered by the beginning of the Depression in 1929. A new feature on the political scene was the growth of the Communist Party (KKE) founded in Greece in 1918. On 6 June 1933 an attempt was made to assassinate Venizelos as he drove back to Athens from a dinner party in Kifissia. His car was punctured with as many as 120 bullet holes as the assassins chased the car for three miles down the street. He escaped unhurt, but his wife and his chauffeur were wounded and one of his companions killed. The assassins were never captured and the question of who was behind the attempt remained open. Suspicion fell on the police themselves, on the Prime Minister Rallis and on General Metaxas:

there were many rightist groups who wished to see an end to this popular politician.

Venizelos' last political act was somewhat aberrant, when he joined in the abortive rising of General Plastiras against the dictatorship of General Kondyles. He was sentenced to death in his absence (he was in Paris) but presently amnestied.

In the last years of his premiership Venizelos built a villa for himself in Athens on land at the foot of Mt Lycabettus which his wife had purchased from the National Bank of Greece in 1928. His wife commissioned the architect Anastasios Metaxas, a distinguished practitioner in the neo-classical style (he also designed the Benaki Mansion as the Benaki Museum), to design the house, which was built in 1930–2. Much of the interior furnishings came from Britain, and the garden was laid out in the English style. When Venizelos died in Paris on 18 March 1936, his widow offered the house to the British Government for £46,000, and it is now the British Embassy.

Athens in the 1920s

Despite the political dramas and chaos, Athens experienced significant social changes in the 1920s. These years saw the arrival of the first motor cars, the first radios, the first cinemas and the new dances of the tango and Charleston. Women also sought new freedoms with mixed bathing, women's athletics and agitation for the vote. The bulk of the population lived not far above the poverty line, on bread, olives and onions. The enormous increase in population led to sickness; tuberculosis and malaria were rife, as well as an outbreak of dengue fever in August 1928. Electricity remained rare and in the settlements there were often not even lamps. The cost of living rose steadily though incomes did not. Hardship was alleviated by the market gardens that many citizens owned in the suburbs of Sepolia, Kallithea and elsewhere. The potatoes of Patissia were prized as were the cherries of Kifissia, and Maroussi and Chalandri were prolific in vegetables.

Smart Athenians started to flock in the summer to Glyfada, Voula and Vouliagmeni: previously fashionable Phaliron had become unaffordable. The Trouville dancing bar was one of the first to boast electric light.

Many also began to holiday in Loutraki, or to patronise the hotels of Kifissia. Kifissia had begun to attract tourism in the 1890s, after the establishment of the steam train from Athens in 1885. This was known as 'The Beast', and continued to run until 1935 when the line was electrified. Prime Minister Deligiannis loved and beautified Kifissia. The mayor of Athens, Michael Melas, had established there the Hotel Melas, one of the first in Greece. The 1920s were the golden age of Kifissia tourism. Tobacco merchants from Kavalla and Constantinople patronised its hotels. There were dances, parties and excursions. The Cecil Hotel (1924) was favoured by the politicians of the People's Party including George Papandreou, and the Royal Family, while Venizelos preferred the Pentelikon (1928) and took a whole floor for the summers.

An important amenity of Kifissia was its water. The spring Kefalari was bountiful with water from the underground reservoirs of Mt Pendeli. But Athens consumed three-quarters of the water that ran from Kefalari, and many citizens relied on private wells. However, it was the water of Kifissia that saved Athens in the drought of 1927.

Late 1926 saw a crisis in the Athenian theatre. Travelling troupes had been deprived of a large part of their circuit by the expulsion of Greeks from Smyrna and Constantinople, and found it hard to make ends meet in the cities of the mainland. In addition, the theatre tax increased to 30 per cent. By way of compensation for the people, cinemas opened in great numbers. The first film in Athens had been shown in the open air at Kolokotroni Square: the audience were so rapt in the action that they stoned the screen! Film showings became regular events from 1900, and there were open air cinemas in Syntagma Square and the Zappeion Gardens. The first regular cinema to open was the Panorama in 1907, and the first 'talkie' was shown at the Astir on 19 January 1930. A showing of *Battleship Potemkin* at the Olympia in 1927 was banned but eventually permitted. Almost twenty cinemas opened in that year, at least three showing mainly Rudolf Valentino. In 1928 the Greek film industry made its own hesitant beginnings: one of the first was Orestes Laskos' film, *Daphnis and Chloe*.

Athens was heavily remodelled in the 1920s. The rapid and undisciplined spread of housing caused by the refugee crisis and the increase in the working-class population (there was a further influx after the

Corinth earthquake of 1928 destroyed every building in that city) was ameliorated by the building of the planned suburb of Psychiko, by the Housing Society 'Cecrops'. Funded partly by the industrialist G. Esaias, and designed by the architect Alexander Nikoloudis, it became the finest suburb of Athens. Besides its many villas there was the American College (founded by Benaki, opened 25 May 1929) and the Arsakeion Girls' School. Other garden suburbs included Ekali, Nikiforos, Ilioupolis, Voula, Holargos, Filothei and Koufou; but vast tracts in between were left to grow without any controls.

In 1927 Omonoia Square was remodelled. First built in 1840 as Otho Square, the olive and fig trees had been cut down to make an open space. Oaks and pines were planted. The first cafés opened in the 1860s, and in 1864, after the expulsion of Otho, the square was renamed Omonoia (Concord). In 1905 the oaks were replaced by palm trees; in 1909 the square was asphalted. In 1927 the palms in turn disappeared in favour of the new railway station linking the Athens–Piraeus line with the Kifissia line. (In 2003, Omonoia Square is again being completely remodelled – but there are still no trees.)

Villa building continued. Notable examples are the neo-classical Maximou mansion of 1924 (now the Prime Minister's residence), the Acropol Hotel (1925) and the Beaux Arts Sarogleion Mansion of 1928 in Rigillis Square. The Gennadius Library, a neo-classical and eclectic building by the architect Stuart Thomson, was dedicated and donated to the American School of Classical Studies in April 1926. It houses the library of John Gennadius, formerly Greek Minister in London. Its unmatched collection on Byzantine and modern Greek history, on early travellers, as well as its numerous prints and paintings, are one of the most important resources anywhere for students of Greek history. The impressive mansion of the Confederation of Greek Archaeologists at the junction of Ermou and Pireos also belongs to this period.

Athens in the 1930s

The Wall Street crash of 1929 had reverberations in Greece. The Athens Stock Exchange closed in October 1929. By 1930 the economic situation was terrible. Bankers committed suicide, others were lynched. A strike in Piraeus in April 1929 continued to ferment through the summer, accompanied by suspicious fires.

The economic difficulties of the late 1920s encouraged the growth of the Communist Party of Greece (KKE) and led to crisis in April 1932. Following General Plastiras' unsuccessful military coup of March 1935, the army continued to agitate against the inclusion of communists in the government, and King George appointed George Metaxas commander-in-chief to quell their unrest. Parliament was dissolved (April 1936) and in August Metaxas became dictator of Greece with the support of few except the king.

Against the background of these political developments Athenian life stagnated. Metaxas tried to modernise the country but introduced few changes apart from the trappings of Mussolini-style fascism, while a drastic clampdown on civil rights of all kinds ensured that society ceased to develop. Some public works were undertaken, including the laying out of the grove of Pangrati in 1935. In 1937 the river in Kipseli was covered over to create gardens. Other gardens included the landscaping of the hill Strefi. Many roads were asphalted. The trams were painted green in 1939, and in 1940 sixty new yellow trams were introduced, with leather seats and automatic doors. Despite the increased number, Athenians could still be seen hanging on to the outside of trams at all angles, 'like bunches of grapes'.

Despite the political repression, it was a busy and lively city. Henry Miller, who visited Athens in the 1930s, described his impressions in *The Colossus of Maroussi*:

> Even in the heart of the city sometimes, where the most fashionable, ultra-modern apartment houses are to be seen, the street is nothing but a dirt road. One can walk to the edge of the city in a half-hour. It is really an enormous city containing almost a million inhabitants; it has grown a hundred times over since Byron's day ... The Athenians practically devour the newspapers; they have a perpetual hunger for news. From the balcony of my room at the Grand Hotel I could look down on Constitution Square, which in the evening is black with people, thousands of them, seated at little tables loaded with drinks and ices, the waiters scurrying back and forth with trays to the cafés adjoining the square ...

> I shall always remember the walks through Athens at night under the autumn stars... Somewhere beyond the 'ammonia' region [he means Omonoia], in a forlorn district whose streets are named after the philosophers, I would stumble about in a silence so intense and so velvety at the same time that it seemed as if the atmosphere were full of powdered stars whose light made an inaudible noise.

In this stay Miller came to know some of the artists and men of letters who were bringing Greece onto the international stage: George Seferis, later winner of the Nobel Prize for literature; the modernist painter Ghika; the larger-than-life intellectual George Katsimbalis; the poet Nikos Gatsos (1916–96), who after his 'mysterious and magnetic' poem *Amorgos* of 1943 wrote only songs (many of them set to music by Mikis Theodorakis). Men like these were to create in their generation a remarkable flowering of the arts in Greece.

There were developments in the city's architecture as well, notably the erection of a few French-influenced buildings in a heavy Renaissance style – notably the Bank of Greece at 21 Panepistimiou (1930–8) and the block surrounded by Panepistimiou, Amerikis, Stadiou and Voukourestiou Streets, which won first prize in the Panhellenic architectural competition of 1926/7 and was completed in 1938. The entrance to the First Necropolis (1939) is another notable creation of this period. International modernism also made its mark, notably in the Ford showroom in Syngrou Avenue (1934–5) and a number of schools in various parts of Athens. In 1938 the National Theatre was demolished because it was deemed too shabby to repair.

Archaeological work resumed after the hiatus of the First World War. The Archaeological Society continued its excavations in the Agora, which had begun in 1912, and in 1921–2 they worked on the Lysicrates Monument and the Odeion of Pericles. But funds ran low after 1924, and it was only after a hiatus that excavation began at Marathon in 1936. The German Archaeological Institute began work on the Ceramicus during the 1930s, and the American School began its long connection with the agora excavations: by 1941 ten volumes of reports had appeared as well as numerous ancillary volumes.

Athens in the Second World War

Such cultured pursuits came to an end with the arrival of the Second World War in Greece. For the first two years Metaxas maintained neutrality for Greece, but on 15 August 1940 (the Feast of the Dormition of the Virgin) the warship *Elli* was torpedoed by the Italians. On 28 October 1940, Italian provocations culminated in an ultimatum to Metaxas, even as Italian troops were crossing the Albanian border into Greece. Metaxas' refusal of the ultimatum has gone down in history as his heroic utterance of the word '*Ochi* – No', by which Greece became the only country to enter the war voluntarily on the Allied side. The refusal is commemorated as '*Ochi* Day', 28 October.

The city began to prepare for air raids, and blacked out the lights at night: but the raids on Athens never came. However, an air raid on Piraeus on 20 January killed many, especially among the refugee population. Soon after this, on 29 January 1941, Metaxas died. 'Never was a tyrant more mourned' (G. Kairophylas) – for he had redeemed himself by his honourable and heroic response to the threat of war. The constitutional void was filled by a colourless government appointed by the king. British and Australian troops began to use Piraeus' facilities. The nation's gold was removed from the National Bank to Crete. Measures were taken to protect the antiquities: vaults were dug underneath the National Museum.

On 5 April 1941 the German forces began their attack on Yugoslavia and Greece. Bombing of Piraeus began on 6 April and lasted for several days. In an air battle over Athens on 19 April the British downed 22 German planes. But the German advance was swift and they arrived in Athens on 27 April 1941. All doors and shutters were closed as the Nazi troops marched in and the government surrendered. On 23 April the king and his government retreated to Crete. At 8.45 a.m. on 28 April the Nazi flag was flying above the Acropolis, and German officers were able to stroll among the antiquities and regale their cultured taste with the enjoyment of the treasures they had studied in their first-class classical educations.

Several prominent Athenians committed suicide as soon as the German conquest was apparent. Prime Minister Koryzis took his life on

17 April, and on the day the troops entered Athens the prominent writer Penelope Delta, the daughter of Emmanuel Benaki and friend of Venizelos, took poison. The guardian of the Acropolis would not endure the German ascent of the Rock, and threw himself over the north face, close by the church of St George of the Rock: a plaque commemorates his death.

The German staff set up their headquarters in the basement of the Grande Bretagne hotel. A curfew was imposed and SS guards patrolled the streets. A puppet government was appointed under Tsolakoglou. Archbishop Chrysostomos refused to swear in the new government, and was immediately replaced by Damaskinos. The latter remained in office throughout the occupation and did his best to moderate the excesses of the German rulers.

For the Greeks, it was the beginning of three-and-a-half years of terrible suffering. Athens was perhaps worse affected than the rural areas. There had been shortages of food already in 1940. Now the shortage quickly became a famine. An American diplomat wrote at the end of 1941 that 'a prosperous and industrious city, almost . . . without physical change, has become the abode of hordes of destitute, starving people' (Mazower 23). The Germans simply looted everything they could find – from vehicles, tables and chairs to the contents of warehouses – took whatever food they needed from the inhabitants and sent hundreds of tons more of fruit and other foodstuffs to their troops abroad. The restaurants Panhellenion and Averoff became *Soldatenheime* where German officers could enjoy every delicacy in the sight of the starving Athenians. The Germans failed to make any arrangements to restore food supplies or any kind of normal economic activity in Greece. They claimed that it was Italy's responsibility. 'The Germans have taken from the Greeks even their shoelaces', complained Mussolini, ' and now they pretend to place all the blame for the economic situation on our shoulders.' The puppet government of Tsolakoglou was quite unable to take action.

The city people, without the resources of smallholdings, were hardest hit. The thousands of displaced persons from Asia Minor still lived in shanty towns, and their humble jobs fell away as the occupation continued, leaving them with no resources whatever. The bread ration, which was 300 gm per day at the time of occupation, was down to 100 gm per day by November. Soup kitchens and other forms of assistance were set up in Athens as well as in major cities like Thessaloniki and Volos by charitable and religious organisations, but they reached less than a quarter of those who needed their assistance. By July all forms of public transport had also ground to a halt. Rationing extended to more and more foodstuffs, and meat was unobtainable after September. Many were driven to gather wild grasses and weeds from the countryside and cook these in a pretence of a meal. (The detail recalls the situation during the siege by the Romans in 86 BC.) If a soldier spat out an olive pit, a dozen children would rush to seize it and suck it clean.

Maria Callas, the great soprano, who had been born in New York in 1923, had been studying at the Athens Conservatory since 1937. Though she continued her studies (and braved the curfew to do so), most of her waking hours were spent scrounging for food. She later wrote: 'For the entire summer [of 1941] I had eaten only tomatoes and boiled cabbage, which I was able to find only by walking for miles and miles into the country to persuade the people there to give me something to eat.' Some women could improve their lot by befriending Italian or German officers, and Maria's mother had an affair with an Italian officer; but in autumn 1941 she also sheltered two British officers who had escaped from prison.

A hot dry summer was followed by an unusually harsh winter. It snowed in Athens, there was no fuel to heat the houses. People were weakened with malnutrition and photographs show how a great many individuals simply fell down in the street, never to rise again. 'The pavements were littered with the light bodies of the dead', Kevin Andrews wrote in *The Flight of Icarus* (1959). In scenes resembling Thucydides' description of the plague, corpses were left to lie in the streets for hours, and many could not afford any sort of funeral. The dead were often buried secretly so that the living could continue to use their ration cards. Deaths in Athens and Piraeus in the year following October 1941, at 49,000, were more than three times the previous year's figure. In Greece as a whole, 300,000 died. In December 1941, a thousand people in Athens died every day.

Collecting the dead during the famine of the winter of 1941

Many believed that the starvation was part of a deliberate German policy of extermination of the inhabitants; the Axis powers blamed the British sea blockade for the famine. Soup kitchens were established in Athens and Piraeus, and 400,000 portions were served daily. Relief ships began to make their way to Athens in October: the Turkish ship *Kurtuluş* delivered its first shipment in October 1941, to be followed by four more before 5 January 1942. In early 1942 Great Britain.agreed to the establishment of a relief force for Greece. In January 8,000 tons of grain arrived from Port Said, and by June there were shipments from Argentina, Sweden and the USA, and later from Canada, so that absolute starvation was averted. This assistance, added to the efforts of the Red Cross and other organisations, ensured that the famine came to an end and the next winter was less horrendous than that of 1941.

The Germans effectively controlled only the towns and cities. Demonstrations took place in Syntagma Square on 28 October (*Ochi* Day) 1942 and 1943, but were dispelled by the Gestapo using tanks and water-cannon. Every wall in Athens became a site for the inscribing of resistance slogans. The increasingly politicised resistance took to the mountains and were sustained secretly by the people of the villages. The main resistance organisation was EAM, the Greek Liberation Front, and its military wing ELAS, the Greek Popular Liberation Army. Their tactic was guerrilla warfare, local attacks on German troops and installations. At an early stage special troops from Britain arrived to participate in, and sometimes direct, these operations. Though they achieved little in direct military action, there were some major successes such as the blowing up of the Gorgopotamos viaduct (November 1942), which cut the Germans' main supply-line; this however gave the Germans the excuse to turn off the electricity supply to trams and offices in Athens on the grounds that the deliveries of fuel to generate it had been cut off.

The continual fighting in Greece delayed the German campaign against Russia, arguably having a determining influence on the course of the war. But the price paid by the Greeks was high. The German forces responded to every insurrectional act with punitive raids on villages, and massacres of civilians. More than 1,000 villages were empty at the end of the occupation. An example from Attica is the ambush at Pikermi of two German officers in a car travelling from Athens to Rafina on 22 July 1944. Both were killed, and the partisans fled to the wilds of Mt Parnes. In revenge the Germans hanged 56 innocent men of Pikermi, 27 of them from a single branch of a large pine tree. In addition, they burned down the neighbouring village of Koropi.

Some of the details of these massacres come from reports written by the young Kurt Waldheim (later Secretary-General of the United Nations) in his office in Athens: for example, 'In reprisal for the attack recently perpetrated in the Larisa area, 2 villages burnt down, 65 suspects shot in flight' (Mazower 191). Many civilians were also taken as hostages for eventual execution.

In February 1943, when the Germans threatened to take Greek workers to Germany, the popular response was violent. The Ministry of Labour was burnt down, the carabinieri were ordered to shoot to kill, and only the intervention of Damaskinos, who threatened a general uprising if the order were not rescinded, contained the situation. Further violence attended a strike on 22 July 1943, when 20 were killed and 100 wounded in Omonoia Square. On 25 August 1943 a fire in the Kallithea tram station resulted in the destruction of ninety-three trams. It was probably an accident caused by an electrical fault, but the Germans threatened to seize fifty hostages and take them off to the torture chambers in Merlin St. Again the intervention of Damaskinos calmed the situation and the German contented themselves with announcing that they had 'captured the perpetrators'.

One of the main centres of German power was the SS–run camp at Haidari close to Daphni on the road to Eleusis. Established in September 1943, this was a transit camp for those awaiting deportation (which by this time included Italian soldiers, following the Italian abandonment of the Axis), as well as a holding camp for prisoners awaiting interrogation and hostages awaiting execution. Primitive conditions (lack of beds), shortage of all but the most basic foods (bread and beans) and absence of sanitary facilities were added to beatings, whippings and maulings by dogs to torment the prisoners. Many died of their sufferings; several thousand were executed; others were fixed as human shields to the front of trains to prevent the resistance blowing them up.

Among the thousands who passed through Haidari were many Jews. The plight of the Jews of Greece was particularly bad. Jews had been numerous in the Ottoman Empire since the seventeenth century, though Athens' was not one of the larger populations. About 70,000 lived in Thessaloniki. Of these, about 2,000 were alive at the end of the war. All in all, about 90 per cent of Greece's Jewish population was deported and exterminated. The attack on Jewish establishments began immediately after the occupation and developed into more serious persecution in Thessaloniki by July 1942. In late 1942 Adolf Eichmann sent an aide to take direct charge of 'cleansing' Greece, including Athens (which was in the Italian zone), of its Jews. By August 1943, nearly 50,000 of Thessaloniki's Jews had been sent to Auschwitz: almost all were gassed on arrival. The next month, Germany took control of all of Greece and operations began in Athens.

Eichmann's deputy, Dieter Wisliceny, summoned the Grand Rabbi of Athens, Elias Barzilai, and demanded a list of all the Jews in the city. But overnight EAM/ELAS spirited Barzilai away to the mountains; this ruse gave many Jews time to escape to the mountains. Of an estimated 8,000 Jews, only 1,200 were ever registered by the Germans. A new tactic put into effect on 23 March 1944 was to round up all the Jews at the synagogue in Melidoni Street. The doors were suddenly slammed shut and close on 1,000 people were held at gunpoint; later that day they were herded onto trucks, sent to Haidari and thence to Auschwitz where they were killed.

The savagery of German rule and reprisals led to an intense politicisation of the Greek resistance. EAM/ELAS became increasingly, and bitterly, at odds with the right-wing collaborationist government in Athens. Guerrilla activity became fiercer, and by the end of 1943 EAM/ELAS had many armed men in the cities – street fighters in civilian clothes who bore little outward resemblance to the fierce and ragged, but uniformed, *andartes* in the mountains. Order in the cities was maintained by the government's gendarmes and the Security Battalions, formed by the Prime Minister John Rallis at the behest of the Germans. Direct clashes between left and right began in March 1944 in the area of Kokkinia, when EAM groups attacked forces of gendarmes. Though Germans were not involved in the confrontation that followed, this changed on 13 March when the entire gendarmerie of 2,000 men, with SS support, converged on the northern suburbs of Nea Ionia and Kalogreza for the first of the 'bloccos', as they were known. These were round-ups of the entire population of an area: identity cards were checked, and suspected communists were arrested and then sent to Haidari and then kept as hostages or despatched to Germany. On 13 March, eighteen men were executed on the spot by the orders of the head of the Special Security Branch, Alexandros Lambou. Meanwhile, houses and shops were ransacked. Another mass execution took place at Kaisariani, on 1 May (Easter) 1944, when the Germans executed 200 men.

Through the summer months of 1944 a heroine of the resistance, Lela Karagianni, rescued allied soldiers and spirited them away in a boat, which she had bought by selling her jewellery, to the Middle East. But in September she was betrayed by a colleague under torture. She was captured by the SS, tortured for three days and executed on 7 September.

Executions became increasingly frequent in the next months throughout Athens and Piraeus. During 1944, thousands of men were taken to Haidari and then deployed as forced labour for the German war effort. Every morning corpses were to be discovered outside the

Security HQ's torture chambers in Stournara Street. EAM responded with murders of suspected informers, but this spurred the security forces to mass executions in the German manner, which left rows of corpses dangling from trees along the main boulevards of Athens. Though most of the fighting took place in the poorer quarters, it was not safe to walk in the National Gardens at night. The scale of round-ups and executions became ever greater through the summer. 'The situation in our land', said George Papandreou, the head of the Greek government in exile, 'resembles hell. The Germans are killing. The Security Battalions are killing. The guerrillas are killing. They kill and burn. What will remain of our unhappy country?' He went on to blame the activities of the left-wing guerrillas for the creation of the Security Battalions in the first place.

The Civil War

By the end of August the Germans were getting ready to leave Greece as the allies closed in on them. On 4 October 1944 British forces landed at Patras and began to advance towards Athens, and on 18 October George Papandreou arrived at Piraeus. German rule was over, but a terrible legacy remained. Inflation was rampant, with the price of bread 122 million drachmas a kilo. 1,700 villages had been destroyed and roads, railways, bridges and other communications reduced to nothing. Wheat, tobacco and fruit production had shrunk catastrophically. Piraeus was working far below capacity. Unemployment was widespread. In addition to this extreme economic crisis, the killing continued. Left and right had been so polarised by the events of the war that neither could reach an accommodation with the other, and it was a more than heroic task to re-establish order. EAM joined the government of national unity of August 1944, and the British General Ronald Scobie was placed in command of the Greek resistance forces, with direct control of Athens and the back-up of a British expeditionary force of 10,000.

Throughout November there were shooting and gun battles in Athens between ELAS supporters and members of right-wing bands. The royalist 'Mountain Brigade' was returned to the city of Athens, a move that was seen as provocation by ELAS. ELAS, with the support of the KKE, refused to demobilise as long as the Brigade remained in Athens. Gradually ELAS moved its men closer and closer to Athens until on 16 November Scobie forbade the entry into Athens of any armed men.

On 2 December EAM ministers resigned from the government. On the next day a large EAM demonstration took place in Syntagma Square, to be followed by a planned General Strike on 4 December. A government ban on the demonstration was in vain. Suddenly the crowd began to charge at the police squad in front of the Palace. At this moment, a man in military clothing, who many suspect was an *agent provocateur*, rushed out from the police lines shouting and shooting into the crowd. The police opened fire and a dozen demonstrators were killed. The American Ambassador McNeill described the scene:

> It was the greatest demonstration that Athens had ever seen. Perhaps sixty thousand persons jammed the Square, and other thousands stood outside. The excitement was indescribable and the anger which exuded from the crowd seemed almost palpable.... Young girls, scarcely more than fourteen years old, paraded with the hems of their skirts dipped in blood from the pools on the street.... Banners in English exhorted British soldiers not to interfere in Greek affairs, and reproached General Scobie and Ambassador Leeper for what they had done.

These events, known as the '*Dekemvriana*' were the beginning of the so-called 'Second Round' that started the country's slide into Civil War. The course of events was to a considerable extent decided by the determination of the British Government, headed by Winston Churchill, that Greece must on no account fall into the Communist sphere of influence. The Greek government resigned and Scobie took total control, demanding the withdrawal of EAM/ELAS from Athens. But the left continued to attack government and other buildings (a mansion by Ziller in Ambelokipi was blown up at this time, and many landmarks destroyed), and though the British, aided by the Italians, stood their ground in Athens, they found themselves besieged in the centre of the city, with no access to any ports.

The problem was to be resolved in part by constitutional means, and Britain at last persuaded King George to accept the regency of Archbishop Damaskinos. In pursuit of this aim Churchill personally visited Athens on 26–28 December. On 5–6 January 1945 ELAS retreated from Athens and Piraeus; but as they went they carried out mass executions and took 30,000 civilian hostages with them from Attica alone. Many of these hostages died but more were spirited away to Albania or other communist countries. Acts of terror carried out by the extreme right, based in the Makriyanni barracks south of the Acropolis, added to the woes of the country.

On 12 February an agreement was signed at Varkiza and ELAS demobilised. But the Varkiza amnesty was never implemented, and in spring 1945 the government and militias, such as the right-wing 'X' gang of George Grivas, hunted down leftists. All members of ELAS were regarded as criminals and subject to punishment. In June the most notorious of the *andartes*, Aris Velouchiotis, was seized and killed by government troops, and his head put on public display in Trikkala.

Elections were finally held on 31 March 1946. The government that assumed power was a right-wing one, and it was bent on vengeance for the crimes of the left. King George returned to Greece on 27 September 1946, but died in March 1947 and was succeeded by his brother Paul.

The bitter 'Third Round' of the Civil War lasted from 1946 until 1949. It devastated the entire country, and set families against each other at all levels of society, engendering feuds which took more than a generation to fade. The exclusion of the left from politics led to various kinds of violence, from the Royalist rally of 29 August 1946 which drove the leftists back as far as the Stadium, to the constant terror in the suburbs resulting from grenade throwing, no one knew by whom. When a ferry was wrecked off Euboea with 35 political exiles on board, foul play was suspected but never proved. A fire at an army barracks on 5 July 1947 exacerbated fear of the left, whether with good reason or not. Violence became so ingrained in Athenian society that children would play at parading the heads of their enemies like the *andartes*.

Fear of the left led to fierce repression. Demonstrations were banned and the police saw leftists as their enemy. Many were imprisoned on the island of Makronisi where they were supposed to become 'reformed'.

One prominent leftist was the gifted composer Mikis Theodorakis (b. 1923). In January 1949 he was imprisoned on Makronisi and tortured but, unlike many of his fellow prisoners, survived and was released. He completed his studies in 1950 and went on to win international prizes for his music during the 1950s.

In 1948 assassination of leftists became commonplace. Certain supposedly inflammatory songs were banned, and Athenians had to report to the police where they spent the night. A mass execution at Averoff prison in February 1948 caused public uproar.

On 1 May of that year, the Minister of Justice, Christos Lada, was murdered in front of the Parnassos Club by an airman with a grenade. The motive was uncertain: was it a protest against a law returning homes to their real owners following the occupation, and the consequent dispossession of their present inhabitants? Was it an expression of the anger of the *nouveaux riches*? Or was it revenge for the many attacks of the right on the left? The nature of the terror was that one could never be certain who was responsible for the outrages.

Gradually the regular army improved its organisation and fighting ability. The defeat of the communist rebels began to look assured by spring 1949, and on 16 October ELAS formally announced an end to the military struggle. The refugees began to return almost immediately, and reconstruction began.

CHAPTER FOURTEEN

Athens from 1949 to the present

Athens in the 1950s

The first signs of a new stability in Greek life were associated with the beginning of the political career of Constantine Karamanlis. Born in Macedonia in 1907, and educated as a lawyer, he had entered politics in 1935, though had abandoned it again when Metaxas assumed the dictatorship. He had become Minister of Transport on 7 May 1948 in the reshuffle following the murder of Lada, and six months later he became Minister of Social Welfare (18 November 1948 to January 1950). He quickly developed the improvements that had already been made in the years following the occupation, when, for example, Glyfada had been reforested (most of its trees had been cut down for fuel in the desperate times of the occupation). In his first ministry, Karamanlis quickly took charge of the electricity supply. Marshall Plan aid, which had enabled the Corinth Canal to re-open, also gave $6 million for the Athenian electricity supply, with the result that restrictions on its use were lifted by April 1949. The first electric cookers reached Athens.

Karamanlis was also responsible for the increasingly dilapidated buses of Athens, which had begun to replace trams in 1947. By July 1948 there were 70,000 motor cars in Athens (in 1946 the number had been less than 4,000), and measures were taken for the decongestion of Omonoia Square. Karamanlis also oversaw a programme of road-building, which among other things improved access to the remote areas still held by the rebels, and thus hastened the conclusion of the Civil War.

As Minister of Social Welfare, he had to oversee the repatriation of some 700,000 refugees from the Civil War, beginning from July 1949. By 30 November nearly half a million had been returned to their homes, and some two-thirds of agricultural land abandoned during the war was now back in cultivation.

Archaeological activity at the end of the 1940s was naturally limited. As early as March 1946 Anastasios Orlandos began the *anastylosis* (re-erection of columns) of the Parthenon; and in August 1947 the sculptures of the Parthenon and the National Museum were removed from the 'tombs' in which they had lain hidden throughout the war.

Normal social life had to some extent returned in 1945, as can be gauged from the fact that a 'British Institute' (later to become the British Council) was established in Athens at that time. Rex Warner, its first director, charmed by the exoticism of Athens, affectionately described the urban scene in Plaka:

> All kinds of objects will be on sale. There will be strings of boots, sandals and shoes, strings of sausages and of brightly coloured vegetables. There will be meat roasting on spits, ironwork and jewellery, brilliant blankets and rugs, bottles and, in carnival time, great masks, false noses and paper streamers.

[The scene did not greatly differ in 1969 when I first visited Athens.] Dancing bears, too could be seen in Athens at this time, though they are long gone now. Buses also piqued Warner's observation:

> Both on the journey and while waiting for the bus to start there will often be entertainment of some kind or other. Perhaps there will be a band of picnickers who, on taking their seats, will immediately burst into song. One of them may have a guitar or harmonica. Perhaps a seller of pistachio nuts will enter the bus, anxious certainly to sell his wares but quite prepared, if no one seems willing to buy, to engage instead in a conversation about the price of food or the prospects of the present government. (*Views of Attica*, 1950)

Another British visitor, Osbert Lancaster (his book, *Classical Landscape with Figures*, was published in 1947), provides a vivid picture of the Athenian scene, enlivened by his deft and humorous drawings. His eye for architecture is apparent in the description of Kifissia Street (Vas. Sofias Avenue):

Opposite the gardens the street is lined by a series of imposing public buildings in a variety of interesting styles. The Foreign Office, strict neo-classic; the Ministry of War, Greek traditional; The French Embassy, pure Deuxième Empire; the Egyptian Legation, a Cairene version of Italian renaissance; the palace of Princess Nicholas, very Othonian, and most remarkable of all, the Skaramanga House used during the Regency as the official residence of his Beatitude.. [a] perfect example of Hollywood Balkan.

The home of the Duchess de Plaisance, further up the street, had in 1930 become the Byzantine Museum, and the British Embassy remained notable for its pink stucco. Lancaster also admired Leoforos Syngrou, but not the buildings that line it! The rapid growth of Athens, now a city of two million people, took place largely without planning, 'in the Attic way', as the architectural historian John Travlos resignedly called it. Many buildings were funded by the system of *antiparochi*: an owner would sell his plot or house in exchange for the right to occupy one of the apartments that were to be built on it. This enabled building to take place without the need for substantial capital.

The development of Athens as a modern city really began in the 1950s. The rapid growth in population was the result of industrial expansion which led to a flight from the country and islands to secure employment in the capital. (Now in the 2000s increasing prosperity has enabled some to return to the countryside and make a living through tourism or boutiques, if not from farming.) Between 1949 and 1959 300,000 people migrated to Athens, and in the 1960s Athens was home to one-quarter of the population of Greece, two-thirds of its wealth and four-fifths of its industry.

The 1950s and 1960s saw much demolition in central Athens. The bulldozer claimed the buildings at the top of Ermou Street, where a new building was erected for the Ministry of the Economy. The Café Papaspyrou in Syntagma Square was also demolished, and the building that replaced it now houses McDonald's. The Café Zacharatous (built in 1888 on the corner of Stadiou by the George I Hotel) was demolished in April 1963. However, new cafés were established, including the famous Floka's (before 1950), and the delightful Zonar in Panepistimiou (1951; in 2003 the building was being gutted for renovation).

Street names also changed after the war. Smuts, for example, became Voukourestiou. Others, such as Voulis and Stadiou, were also changed, but later returned to their original appellations. Panepistimiou (University) had its name changed to Venizelou: this is still its official name, but everyone calls it Panepistimiou.

In November 1952 Karamanlis, now Minister of Public Works, enlarged the Marathon reservoir and had it linked to Lake Yliki, thus ensuring an adequate water supply for Athens. In 1953 the Athens–Piraeus roads were improved, as part of a programme of road-building throughout the country. A more controversial step was the abolition of the trams in favour of trolleys and buses. Such was the popular opposition to this move that Karamanlis personally visited the tram sheds one dark night to oversee the removal of the rails, so that they could not leave in the morning! The last tram actually ran in 1959. (In 2004 the trams will be reintroduced on the line that closed in 1959, from Zappeion to Fix, Nea Smyrni and Faliron.)

The first industrialisation projects included the establishment of Olympic Airways in collaboration with Aristotle Onassis and the establishment of the shipyard of Skaramangas in collaboration with Stavros Niarchos (both 1956). 1959 saw expansion of the University, and in 1960 television arrived in Greece. The 1950s established the present configuration of Athens, with the smart regions including Kolonaki in the west, and increasing industrial scruffiness to the east, down to the downright squalor of the oil, cement and ship factories along the road from Eleusis that destroys the beauty of the Saronic Gulf.

The most conspicuous development of the 1950s was the beginning of international tourism, as gradually increasing prosperity in Western Europe led to the discovery of the paradisaic beaches and landscape of Greece, as well as a desire to visit its incomparable antiquities. The region around the Acropolis and Philopappos Hill was landscaped in 1951–7. A *Son et Lumière* was established there in 1960. Hotels sprang up in Glyfada and in 1958 the beginning of work on the Athens Hilton (completed in 1963) signalled the arrival of Greece in the transatlantic field of vision. The aggressive modernism of the Hilton aroused predictable reactions of dismay both at home and abroad, but the influence of the style of Mies van der Rohe was pervasive in many new projects including office buildings in Athens, the National Bank of Greece in Praxitelous Street (1963), and the Fix brewery on Syngrou, a huge building which dwarfed the tiled houses surrounding it. In 1959–61 the US Embassy was built to designs by Walter Gropius.

The advance of architectural modernism continued in the 1960s with Le Corbusier-influenced buildings like the Doxiadis offices at 24 Strat. Syndesmou, the new Athens University Faculties of Divinity and of Philosophy, the new passenger terminal at Piraeus, the new fruit and vegetable market in Athens, the OTE office in Kallithea (1969–71). The foundation stone for the new university campus in Panepisti-mioupolis was laid in 1969. The University is a functionalist concrete complex with affinities to the multi-storey car park.

The new style also affected private housing: many houses were built to frame the view from the interior, while from the exterior they looked like toasters. The National Gallery (1963, opened 1976) was a less successful implementation of the Le Corbusier style in concrete and marble. In 1971–3 the first glass and steel tower was erected – the office building at Vas Sofias/Mesogeion. Other office buildings in Piraeus followed suit.

The influx of workers to Athens led to a housing boom. Whole districts were taken up by illegal developments, north into Attica. Buildings often preceded roads. People built bit by bit as the money became available. Even into the 1990s, fires were deliberately set to open protected forest land for building by unscrupulous developers, as far west as Sounion.

This was also the era of the rapid construction of numerous concrete hotels in the most beautiful parts of the Greek landscape, often with little regard for their suitability to their surroundings. All this was a part of the rapid advance of Greece to catch up with its European con-temporaries, and its change from an outpost of the Levant to a country recognisably European. Such modernisation also symbolised a defiance of the stagnant social and economic development of the communist states by which Greece was surrounded.

Archaeological activity resumed with work by the Archaeological Society (Secretary: A. Orlandos 1951–79) in 1950 at the Library of

Hadrian and in 1952–4 at Brauron in Attica. The Society moved to new offices in 1957. Further work followed at Marathon, Rhamnous and Eleusis over the next two decades. From 1979 to 1988 George Mylonas, the excavator of Eleusis and one of the most internationally prominent of Greek archaeologists, was secretary of the Society. Overshadowing all was the continued progress of the excavations of the American School in the Agora. As buildings became derelict the School was ready to buy them up, clear them, and continue investigations in what has become one of the largest and best-studied archaeological operations in Europe. Much of the agora of classical Athens has been unearthed and interpreted, and provides a draw for tourism, not equal to the neighbouring Acropolis, to be sure, but at least as evocative to those with an interest in the past.

THE ARTS IN ATHENS

The 1950s and 1960s were a time of rapid artistic developments in Athens, especially in theatre and music. Theatre had been an important element of Athenian life since the beginning of the century, and had relied very heavily on new productions of the great classics of fifth-century Athens, both tragedy and comedy. A festival of classical drama in Athens had been founded as early as 1936. Summer festivals of drama were established in Epidaurus (1954) and Athens (1955). From 1956 the National Theatre of Athens put on numerous productions under the direction of Alexis Solomos: a production of *Thesmorophiazusae* in which Euripides appeared on a motorcycle was notable. But in the 1950s the emergence of the theatre director Karolos Koun (1908–87) had a major impact on Athenian theatre. Steeped in the values of the left, who were still regarded as pariahs and subversives by the governing classes, Koun found in Aristophanes a vehicle for contemporary concerns: 'Aristophanes mirrored the new sensibilities of an upwardly mobile but often disillusioned urban audience' (Gonda van Steen, *Venom in Verse* 2000, 121). Koun's production of *Birds* in the Odeion of Herodes Atticus in 1959, with designs by the painter Tsarouchis, became a *succès de scandale*. The plot centres on the attempts of the hero Pisetairos to construct a new polity among the birds in Cloud-cuckoo-land, away from the festering strife of his home city divided after years of ruinous warfare; but the brave new world degenerates into a new dictatorship. Parallels with the contemporary scene were all too obvious, and were accentuated when the episode of a sacrifice by a priest was played by an actor dressed in full Orthodox clerical garb. Many were shocked, and the following day Konstantinos Tsatsos, a leading member of the Karamanlis government, banned the production. Intellectuals mocked the ban, and cartoonists seized on the opportunity to depict Tsatsos, with his beaky profile, ever after accompanied by a chicken. (The Greek word *Ornithes*, in ancient Greek 'Birds', in modern Greek connotes 'Chickens'.)

This typical manifestation of Cold War politics, when social criticism was perceived as dangerous opposition to a right-wing government, was mirrored two years later by the Karamanlis government's ban on playing the music of Mikis Theodorakis on the radio. Theodorakis (b. 1923), an active leftist, had married the styles and melodies of Greek popular music as it had grown out of *rebetika* to songs that were often purely lyrical or romantic, but as often deeply politically engaged, for example in settings of the communist poet Yannis Ritsos. Besides the great song cycles of the 1960s, he was known as the composer of the soundtrack for Cacoyiannis' celebrated film *Zorba the Greek*. It was a time when many creative artists all around the world had nailed their colours to a revolutionary mast; and Greece, with its memories of the Civil War still near the surface, was more sensitive than many to political protest.

Koun's style of '*laikos* expressionism' was manifested in later productions such as *Wealth* (1957) and *Frogs* (1966), but *Birds* was not produced again until 1975 (a planned production in 1967 was banned by the Colonels).

The Colonels, 1967–74

Greece in the 1960s continued to suffer from the divisions created by the Civil War, and the left-wing agitation that affected many countries in the world (and culminated in the Paris *événements* of 1968 and the anti-Vietnam war protests in the USA) led to political instability in Greece as well. Rightist activism was at least as virulent as anything on the left. George Papandreou died in 1968 but the rise of his son Andreas had begun at the beginning of the decade. He had agitated, generally with the support of the student body, for the legalisation of the still-outlawed Communist Party (KKE), and the release of political prisoners (975 Communists were still in prison, more than a decade after the Civil War had ended).

The assassination of the left-wing lawyer Grigorios Lambrakis in Salonika in 1963 became a *cause célèbre* and gave strength to the left-wing cause. (Andreas Papandreou accused Karamanlis of complicity.) A left-wing conspiracy ('Aspida') in the armed forces in 1967 was put down and led to many convictions, though attempts to implicate Andreas Papandreou were unsuccessful. The king had increasing difficulty in forming a government, and on 21 April 1967 a group of army officers conducted a military coup d'état. (Karamanlis blamed Papandreou for the 'storm of passions' he had whipped up.) Tanks rolled down the streets of Athens. Parts of the constitution were suspended and military courts were established in Athens and Salonika. George Papadopoulos emerged as the leader of the junta. The rule of 'The Colonels' had begun.

21 April 1967 was the beginning of seven years of fierce political repression, linked to considerable economic incompetence and a bizarre mixture of reactionary and quasi-religious shibboleths. Beards were declared immoral and many visiting hippies had to shave them off. The Colonels replaced the church hierarchy with nominees of their own and ordered the population to be more religious. More seriously, they persecuted artists and intellectuals. The celebrated actress Melina Mercouri was deprived of her citizenship for criticising the junta. The newspaper proprietress Helen Vlachou was placed under house arrest. The music of the composer Mikis Theodorakis was banned everywhere; Theodorakis himself was arrested in August 1967 and imprisoned in a concentration camp at Oropos; conditions were such that three months he was reported unfit to stand trial. Later (in 1970) his sentence was commuted to exile. Hundreds of alleged left-wing activists were imprisoned and tortured. The king too was sidelined and in December 1967 he fled to Rome: in 1973 the monarchy was abolished and the king has never returned to Greece.

Opportunities for resistance were limited because of repression, and in more rural parts of Greece the citizens actually felt some benefit from the Colonels' rule. Such measures as the abolition of the 'closed shop' for licences for bakeries and taxicabs in Athens eliminated a layer of profiteers from society. The Colonels had the tacit support of America and the CIA, and also established agreements with a number of the countries of communist Eastern Europe and China. To the visitor life in Athens seemed reasonably normal apart from the evident military presence, the bombastic posters of the regime, and the censorship of the press. But as the rulers gained more confidence in their ineptitude they began to over-reach themselves. The torture of political opponents by the Military Security Police under Brigadier Ioannidis became an international scandal. Some signs of liberalisation led to active protests. In March 1973 a sit-in in the Athens Law School was broken up by police. In November of the same year another sit-in took place at the Athens Polytechnic. On the night of 16–17 November, armed police and twenty tanks laid brutal siege to the Polytechnic; many were injured and twenty killed.

The atrocity was blamed on Papadopoulos whose grip was assumed to be slipping. He was deposed and replaced by the brutal Ioannidis, and martial law was re-established. The concentration camp on Gioura (Gyaros) became infamous for the torture practised there. The end came when the junta devised a plot, with CIA support, to assassinate Archbishop Makarios, the ruler of Cyprus, and reunite the island with Greece, an act which they supposed would bolster their prestige. Makarios escaped and the Colonels' nominee, Nikos Sampson, lasted only a few days as President of Cyprus. Then Turkish forces invaded Cyprus and began the division of the island which only began to show signs of collapse in 2003. The dictators threw in their hand and President Gizikis invited Constantine Karamanlis to return from exile and Paris and form a government. This was the end of the last great hiatus in the development of Greek democracy. Elections were held on 17 November, and Karamanlis' newly founded 'New Democracy' party gained 220 out of 300 seats, leaving Papandreou's newly founded socialist party, PASOK, far behind. On 8 December a plebiscite was held on the form of the constitution, and Greece embarked on a new phase as a republic. (In Greek, the words for 'democracy' and 'republic' are the same.)

Athens since 1974

The return of constitutional democracy in Greece has continued to the present day, and the alternation of conservative (New Democracy) and socialist (PASOK) governments has mirrored the pattern of other western democracies. Both these parties were founded in 1974, and in the same year the KKE was made legal: it immediately split into two parties, the KKE-Interior (a 'Eurocommunist' party) and the KKE-Exterior, which followed Moscow s line. Since 1996 PASOK has been the ruling party under Papandreou's successor Costas Simitis.

The process of 'dejuntification' was not trouble-free. 100,000 public oficials were purged. An army plot was foiled in February 1975. Thirty bombs exploded in Athens in December 1978. One hangover from the era of the Colonels which continued until the next century was the activities of the shadowy terrorist organisation November 17th (named after the date of the massacre at the Polytechnic). This organisation carried out twenty-three murders of Greeks and foreigners as well as more than 100 bombings. The motivation for the atrocities was difficult to fathom. The last murder was of Brigadier Stephen Saunders in June 2000. The involvement of Scotland Yard assisted the Greek police in at last tracking down the ringleaders, and their trial began in March 2003.

Social improvements in the 1970s included the nationalisation of Olympic Airways and the Aspropyrgos refinery. Karamanlis encouraged the development of roads and agriculture, as well as of an indigenous arms industry. Plans for a new airport at Spata, and an underground railway for Athens, began to be made in 1976. In 1979 a dam on the River Mornos secured Athens' water supply. In October 1979 the National Cultural Centre was founded.

The 1970s and 1980s saw an explosion of tourism in Greece which had begun already in the 1960s. The arts flourished. Karolos Koun put on a production of Aristophanes' *Knights* in December 1974 into which was inserted a special parabasis (the section of the play where the author addresses the audience directly, through the chorus) which reflected the widespread jubilation at the fall of the Colonels. Further productions, of *Acharnians* (1976) and *Peace* (1977) created a central figure who was modelled on the hero of the shadow puppet theatre, Karagiozis, forging fresh links between the classical heritage of Greek theatre and folk culture. In 1976 a production of *Acharnians* by Dionysios Savvopoulos in a basement club in Plaka presented an opposite political position by attacking Theodorakis and other leftists.

The music of Theodorakis was played again, and the composer continued to create ever more ambitious works, including operas based on the plays of Sophocles and Euripides, as well as lyrical song cycles. He remained involved in politics, as a parliamentary deputy from 1981–6 and 1989–93, and was also a minister in 1990 and 1992; but rumours that he might run for mayor of Athens in the 1980s led to nothing. His collaborations with the Turkish artist Zülfü Livaneli also made a political statement in a period of great tension between Greece and Turkey following the Turkish occupation of northern Cyprus and continuing territorial disputes over the waters of the Aegean.

Every art form could boast a noted Greek exponent of international reputation in the 1970s and 1980s. In film, it was Theo Angelopoulos who commanded the scene as auteur, with his series of hypnotic films from *The Travelling Players* (1975) onwards tracing the course of Greek history through the Civil War to the present. Greek cinema in the 1950s and 1960s had been largely light entertainment with the exception of the internationally renowned work of the Cypriot Cacoyannis in the 1950s. But in the mid-1960s there had been over 600 cinemas in Athens. A current Athens guide lists about 160.

The actress Melina Mercouri (Athens 1922–New York 1994) established her reputation in 1949 with her performance in *A Streetcar named Desire* (1949), directed by Karolos Koun with music by Manos Hadjidakis and in a translation by Nikos Gatsos. She performed in more than sixty plays before achieving international fame in 1960 with the film of *Never on Sunday*. Declared an 'enemy of the people' by the Colonels in 1967, she became a minister in the PASOK government of Andreas Papandreou in 1981. One of the best-known Greeks abroad, her popularity in Greece was very great. The scenes of her funeral in

Melina Mercouri

Athens on 8 March 1994 could not be compared with anything in their popular and spontaneous fervour. *Ta Nea* hailed her as 'a new Pasionaria'.

The Parthenon Marbles

She made it her ambition to effect the return of the Parthenon Marbles (the Elgin Marbles) to Greece. The Greek republic regards it as a point of honour that these, the greatest works of art from the greatest building of the greatest period of Athenian history, should be returned to Greece. Even after Mercouri's death the campaign has been continued by every Minister of Culture, and a new museum has been designed, to the south of the Acropolis in Makriyanni, to house these works of art. But the British Museum (which was so loath to purchase them from Elgin in 1801) has declared that they will never be returned.

One cloud that has (literally) hung over the campaign for their return is the serious problem of atmospheric pollution in Athens. The city, which now houses more than 3 million people (nearly a third of the population of Greece), produces a formidable amount of chemical emissions from its factories, the oil refineries of Eleusis and private motor vehicles and central heating boilers as well as the aged public transport vehicles. The acids in the atmosphere have caused considerable damage to many of the ancient monuments. The Caryatids of the Erechtheum, for example, have had to be taken indoors for their protection and replaced with replicas. The one caryatid that Lord Elgin removed to the British Museum is now in much better condition than those in Athens. Major works of restoration have taken place on the Acropolis in the 1980s and 1990s to protect and stabilise the monuments. Environmental problems have also been belatedly recognised, though Greeks are not in general fond of nature for its own sake.

On 28 May 1979 Greece signed the Treaty of Accession to the European Community (after negotiations which began in 1962). The embrace of Greece by its western neighbours acts as a guarantee of political stability. Athens has come to resemble much more a city of Western Europe, shaking off its Levantine traits. In April 2003 Athens was also host to the group of European Ministers who signed the accord for the extension of the EU to a number of other states. Another sign of progress is that Athens elected its first ever female mayor, Dora Bakoyianni, in January 2003. (She was widowed by November 17th and narrowly escaped assassination herself in December 2002, when she bent down to open her handbag just as the bullet was fired.)

Architecture in Athens in the 1980s and (especially) 1990s has reflected the rapid economic advance of Greece. No notable building was erected during the rule of the Colonels, when Athens resembled Beirut more than a western city. In 1983 a master plan for Athens by Tsitsis was actually made law, following some planning reforms and initial pedestrianisation in 1979. Successive mayors, Dimitris Beis, Miltiades Evert and Dimitris Avramopoulos, have pursued noble plans for the city, but it has proved difficult to get local government to co-operate. The introduction of the general Building Regulations in 1985 accelerated urban sprawl in violation of the Tsitsis plan.

But if planning has been difficult, restoration work has been extensive. The National Bank and other banks have been in the forefront of such work. Plaka has been transformed into a freshly painted jewel, a neo-classical village in the heart of Athens. The Triangle bounded by Ermou, Athinas and Akadimias – the neo-classical heart of Athens – has been extensively refurbished. Even Omonoia Square is much less run down than in the 1970s, and there is another

A refurbished balcony in Plaka

new plan for its landscaping under way. A facelift is planned for Athinas Street over the next few years. The pedestrianisation of a large area south of the Acropolis and west to the Theseion, completed in 2002, has created a magnificent archaeological park. The list could be continued.

New architecture is notable. The Goulandris Museum (1982–5) is a postmodern exercise in free style classicism. A similar style characterises the HQ of the Credit Bank at 40 Stadiou. In 1984–8 the Karolos Koun theatre at 14 Frynichou was created from an old timber store and won a gold medal in 1991. The German Embassy (1983) is another fine building. The renowned concert hall, the Megaron Mousikis, opened in 1994.

In the 1990s one of the most important commissions was for the New Acropolis Museum at Makriyanni. The plan is that this area will see the erection of a building of marble and masonry with a view that frames the Acropolis itself as a background for the exhibits. However, agitation in July 2002 about damage to the archaeology underneath, as well as by the inhabitants of the buildings overlooking the site, has slowed progress; and in May 2003 the Supreme Court ruled that building was forbidden on the site because of the archaeological remains underneath. The outcome remains uncertain. The success of the building also depends on the Parthenon Marbles being returned to Athens.

Other new buildings include the Glaxo Wellcome building with geometric forms (1992–5), the new University Library (1996–8), the Museum of the History of Hellenism (1999) with its cones, whorls and non-parallel planes. Even the Detroit Motors and Allen Furniture showrooms in Maroussi purvey clean lines and a quality of openness to the landscape though the plentiful use of glass. Hotels like the Astir Beach in Glyfada and the Megali Akti in Vouliagmeni convey much greater sensitivity to setting than the hotels of the 1960s; such buildings complement and exploit the beauty of the Greek landscape but do not disturb it.

Though prices rose as a result of entry to the EU, Greece has also reaped many economic benefits. Notable among these are the investment that has been made in the extension of the Athens Metro in the 1990s. The minimal service of the previous public railway to Piraeus and Kifissia now links all parts of central Athens and extends to the major suburbs, though it has not yet reached the new airport. The airport at Ellinikon, familiar to generations of holiday makers as one of the most uncomfortable in Europe, has been replaced by a modern and well-designed airport at Spata.

The excavations for the Metro (1992–7) proceeded at an agonisingly slow pace because every inch of the ground was an archaeological treasure trove. Finds and information had to be preserved and recorded before the building could progress. The building of the Metro has proved to be one of the greatest advances in the understanding of the topography of ancient Athens since American work began at the Agora in 1881. The total surface area excavated was 70,000 sq.m. and more than 30,000 artefacts were found. All discoveries have been carefully excavated and recorded, and several of the Metro stations (Syntagma, Evangelismos, Panepistimio and in 2004 Monastiraki) have been laid out as museums in their own right. The major discoveries were set out in a magnificent exhibition, 'The City beneath the City', at the Goulandris Museum in 2000–1.

Much of the restoration work of the 1990s received a setback with a severe earthquake in September 1999. Damage was caused to many buildings including the Gennadeion, and the National Theatre, but repairs have proceeded apace.

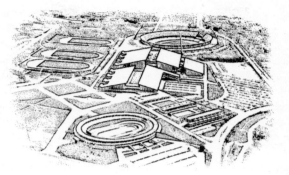

The Olympic Stadium

The culmination of Athens' (and Greece's) march to international centre stage is the celebration of the Olympic Games in Athens in 2004. This is the first time the Games have been celebrated in Greece since their foundation in 1896. Athens failed to secure the Games for the centenary in 1996 because of the problems of pollution and poor infrastructure. Hence the determination to solve the transport crisis. The completion of the Metro and the airport were key stages in the build-up to the Games, as was the hoped-for Acropolis Museum for the Parthenon Marbles. In 2004 some 16,000 athletes will be housed in the Olympic Village and will take part in over 300 events in 28 different sports. Besides these, some 20,000 media people are expected, and some 45,000 security and other staff will be employed. 120 km of new roads have been built and 90 km upgraded. The infrastructure of Athens has been transformed. Concern was shown by the International Olympic Committee in 2003 that the facilities would not be completed on time: one opposition spokesman described the preparations as 'a theatre of the absurd'. But there is every sign that the Games will be a resounding success. Athens looks forward to its future with greater confidence than has been possible for centuries.

Major Buildings of Athens

1. Classical Athens

The Acropolis

The Acropolis dominates the city from most directions, and can be seen from afar when approaching the city from north or west. This remarkable rock was first fortified in Mycenaean times when it was perhaps the residence of the shadowy early kings. A concealed spring on the north side made it defensible against siege. After the Pisistratid period it became a sanctuary occupied exclusively by sacred buildings. The ancient sanctity of the rock was symbolised by the salt spring of Poseidon close to the Erechtheum, next to which was planted an olive tree, sacred to Athena. These two gods were the twin protectors of the city, and Athena, a virgin goddess of wisdom and of war, was pre-eminent. The Erechtheum itself was named for one of the early kings, and the legend of the daughters of Cecrops was also associated with the Acropolis (Chapter 1)

After the sack by the Persians in 479 BC the temples were rebuilt in a tremendous explosion of building activity associated with the age of Pericles, from 448. (For a detailed account of the buildings see Chapter 3.) The Parthenon was completed in 438 and the Propylaea, Temple of Nike, and Erechtheum also belong to this period, though the Erechtheum was only completed in 395 BC. Though Demetrius Poliorcetes shocked Athenian opinion by making his home in the Parthenon (307–287), there was no new building until Athens became part of the Roman Empire. The base for an equestrian statue at the SW corner was originally erected for a chariot group incorporating King Eumenes II of Pergamon; in 27 BC this was replaced by a statue of Marcus Agrippa. The Temple of Rome and Augustus east of the Parthenon dates from 27 BC.

Entrance to the Acropolis was through the Propylaea, the monumental gateway erected as part of the rebuilding programme under Pericles. The monumental staircase was added in the reign of Claudius (AD 52). Before the staircase is the so-calle Beulé Gate, built around AD 267 in response to the barbarian invasions and named after its excavator, Ernest Beulé (1853).

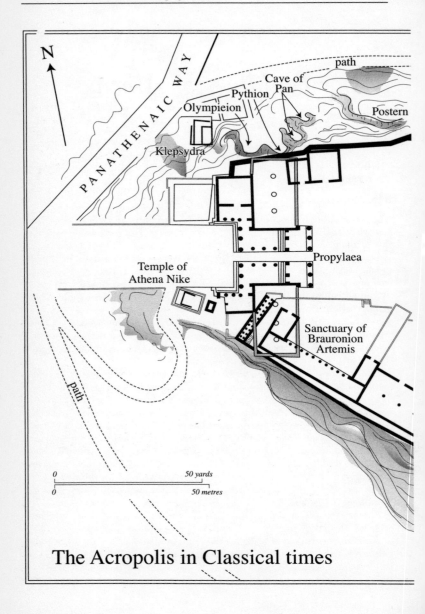

The Acropolis in Classical times

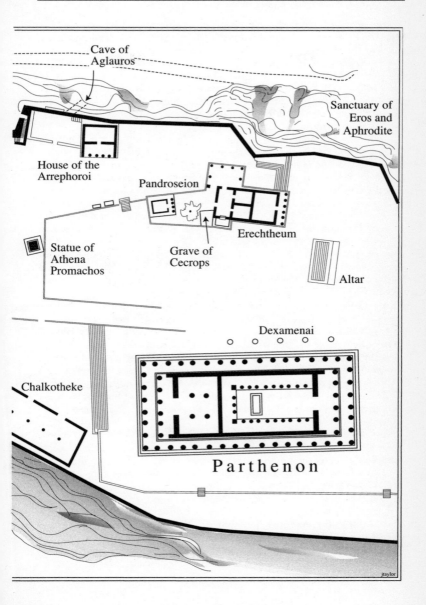

Cave of
Aglauros

Sanctuary of
Eros and
Aphrodite

House of the
Arrephoroi

Pandroseion

Erechtheum

Statue of
Athena
Promachos

Grave of
Cecrops

Altar

Dexamenai

Chalkotheke

Parthenon

' The Acropolis reverted to its function of defence against siege in the Macedonian wars of the second century BC, during Sulla's sack in 86, and in the attack by the Heruli in AD 267. With the abolition of paganism by Theodosius in 429 the temples ceased to be used and some were turned into Christian churches, as were those in the agora. The Parthenon became the Church of Our Lady of the Rock. In 1018 the Byzantine Emperor Basil the Bulgar Slayer celebrated his defeat of the Bulgars here. The statue of Athena Promachos was removed in the early Middle Ages to Constantinople, and was destroyed during the sack of that city by the Crusaders in 1204.

In 1204 the Acropolis was captured by Otho de la Roche, first of the Dukes of Athens. At the end of the Catalan period it was captured by the Florentine merchant Nerio Acciauoli, and his son Antonio built a palace in the walls of the Propylaea. The Italian scholar–merchant Cyriac of Ancona stayed with Nerio in the palace and made precious drawings (the originals are now lost and are known through copies) of the Parthenon pediments (see Chapter 9). Also under the Dukes (though some believe it to be Catalan) was erected the Frankish Tower next to the Propylaea; this was demolished at the expense of Heinrich Schliemann in 1874, as part of the restoration of the Acropolis to its classical state.

In 1458 Athens and the Acropolis fell to the Turks. The Acropolis immediately became the seat of the Turkish garrison. The Parthenon, which had been the Cathedral of the Virgin Mary throughout the Frankish period, now became a mosque. The Erechtheum became the harem of the Turkish commander (*disdar*). The surface of the rock filled up with Turkish houses and other buildings, and access was forbidden to all non-Turks. Lightning struck a powder magazine in the Propylaea in 1640 or 1656 and caused serious damage. In 1684 the temple of Athena Nike was demolished to erect a gun emplacement. In September 1687 the Venetian army led by Morosini commenced a bombardment of the Turkish forces on the Acropolis. One of the shells fell on the Parthenon and caused the explosion of the powder magazine in its interior. All the central columns on the north and south sides were blown out and the Parthenon was more heavily damaged by this event than at any time in the previous two thousand years.

Turkish rule and habitation continued until 1827. Early travellers to Athens in the seventeenth and eighteenth centuries were occasionally able to secure permission to enter the fortress and draw the remains. Precious accounts from these visits include the drawings of the Parthenon pediments by Jacques Carrey who accompanied the Marquis de Nointel in 1674; the description by Jacob Spon in 1686; the drawings and watercolours by James Stuart of the 1750s; and topographical paintings from the early nineteenth century by William Page and others. In 1814 the 'entasis' of the columns of the Parthenon was first observed by C.R. Cockerell: none of the lines of the Parthenon is entirely straight, but a slight bulge gives a feeling of fluidity and motion to the columns and horizontal surfaces: 'a rod or line stretched down from the top of the columns begins to

The Acropolis 1801 after a painting by Edward Dodwell

depart from the shaft at the height of 17'7" and leaves 2" at the base of the column'.

In 1801 Lord Elgin, newly appointed ambassador to Constantinople, sent agents to see if they could acquire some marbles to decorate his newly built home at Broomhall near Dunfermline. By the time Elgin came to see what they were up to, most of the pedimental sculptures and the frieze had been removed. These were sent to Britain and, after a long campaign, were bought by the British Museum (Chapter 10). This was the second greatest despoliation of the Acropolis in history, but it preserved the marbles from the ravages of the Civil War and the pollution of the twentieth century.

In 1822 the Turkish garrison surrendered to the insurgent Greeks and it became the base of operations for a time of Odysseus Androutsos, one of the commanders in the War of Independence. He walled up one of his enemies, a priest, in a masonry column on the rock. In February 1825 he decided to join the Turkish side but was seized by the commander of the Acropolis, his former lieutenant Iannis Gouras, and was himself imprisoned in the Frankish Tower. One day he was found dead at the foot of the tower, allegedly after attempting to escape from his prison. In 1827 after a long siege Reshid Pasha recaptured the Acropolis for the Turks, and the Turks only departed with the official end of the war in 1833 (Chapter 10).

With the establishment of the kingdom in 1834 restoration and archaeology began apace on the Acropolis. This was fortunately not disturbed by a plan devised by the architect Karl Friedrich Schinkel to convert the whole Acropolis into a palace for King Otho. Most of the medieval and Ottoman buildings were demolished. The temple of Nike was re-erected. (It has now – 2003 – been demolished again for a new re-erection.) Ludwig Ross and Leo von Klenze were the directors of this work (Chapter 11).

In 1853 Beulé discovered the gate that bears his name, and in 1874 Burnouf discovered the Klepsydra spring. The Greek Archaeological Society excavated from 1876 to 1885, and work has continued ever since. In the first years of the twentieth century many of the stones were stabilised with iron clamps under the direction of K. Balanos; but these have now corroded causing more damage to the stones. In the 1980s and 1990s work was undertaken to secure the north face with retaining netting. Cranes are usually in evidence, engaged in the process of restoration. The heavy atmospheric pollution of Athens has led to severe damage to the fabric and protective measures have had to be applied. The Caryatids of the Erechtheum were removed in the 1980s on their own train to the Acropolis museum, and their place taken by replicas.

The Theatre of Dionysus

The Theatre is only the most conspicuous part of the Sanctuary of Dionysus, which dates from the Archaic period: the small temple of Dionysus Eleuthereus (the Liberator) was built about 530 BC and rebuilt about 480 BC. In the fifth century Alcamenes created a new gold and ivory statue of the god to replace the original wooden cult figure. A new temple was built in the fourth century.

The theatre faced this cult centre from further up the slope. In the late sixth century it was predominantly a wooden structure, and was used for the first dramatic performances in Athens when Thespis invented the art form. The existing marble theatre was begun in 360 BC and completed by Lycurgus (390–324 BC). It can seat about 17,000 people. Seats for dignitaries and the Priest of Dionysus were installed at this time. The round area, the orchestra, was used by the chorus who danced there; the actors performed on the elevated stage which had a building with doors for entrance and exits. A crane was used for appearances of gods and the like: the arrival of Oceanus in a flying chariot in the *Prometheus Bound* attributed to Aeschylus must have been particularly spectacular. Action all took place off stage: a trolley (the *ekkyklema*) was used to display tableaux such as the pile of corpses that appears at the climax of Aeschylus' *Agamemnon*.

Plays were presented as part of a competition at the festival of the Great Dionysia in March. The winning playwright received a prize, while the *choregos* (in effect the producer, who financed the production as a public service or *liturgy*) received a bronze tripod or similar monument. Surviving choregic monuments include that of Thrasyllus (320/19 BC), on the cliff face above the theatre, and the Monument of Lysicrates (335 BC) in Plaka, to the north-east of the Acropolis. In 278/7 BC a long inscription was erected in the theatre listing all the victorious poets and actors from 485/4 to 278/7 BC. From the late third century AD the theatre was used for public assemblies as the agora now lay outside the city wall. In late antiquity a Christian church was built in the east entrance of the theatre.

The Odeion of Herodes Atticus

This conspicuous building was put up by the wealthy orator and sophist Herodes Atticus (Chapter 8) in honour of his deceased wife Regilla, between AD 160 and 170. Unlike a Greek theatre, the stage building is three storeys high. In addition, the building was roofed – the essential difference between an odeion, or concert hall, and a theatre. The beams of cedar of Lebanon had to span a width of 38 metres.

The building remained visible throughout the Middle Ages, and many travellers supposed that this was the Theatre of Dionysus, the actual theatre being buried under the earth. Excavation was followed by restoration in the 1950s, so that the Odeion is now regularly used for dramatic performances on summer evenings.

The Monument of Philopappus

Conspicuous from the Acropolis to the south-west is the monument crowning the Hill of the Muses. This was erected to commemorate C. Julius Antiochus

Philopappus, the last descendant of the kings of Commagene, who was exiled to Athens by the Emperor Vespasian in AD 72. A great benefactor of the city (and consul in 109), his monument was erected in AD 114–16. Niches contained statues of the deceased and two of his ancestors. The right hand portion of the façade, with a statue of Seleucus I Nicator (301–280 BC), was still standing when Cyriac of Ancona visited Athens in 1436/7 and drew the monument; a surviving copy of his drawing gives valuable information about its original appearance.

Demetrius Poliorcetes built a fortification wall around this hill, part of which can still be seen.

The Pnyx

The Pnyx, on the Hill of the Nymphs, is separated from the Hill of the Muses by a valley in which substantial remains of an ancient road can still be seen. In the fifth century BC this was a pleasant suburban area of Athens. Cimon had his house in this area, as well as his orchards, which were famously unwalled so that everybody could come in and help themselves to fruit.

The centre of the Pnyx is the bema, the speaker's platform of the Attic democracy. The *Ekklesia* (Assembly) met here from the sixth to the third century BC. The citizens assembled facing the speaker's platform, with a view of the Acropolis behind. In the late fifth century, as a result of the rule of the Thirty in 404/3, the orientation was reversed, and the citizens sat with their backs to the Acropolis. Large retaining walls were built to uphold the new audience area.

A third stage about 340 BC, possibly associated with Lycurgus, resulted in the enlargement of the audience area: this is what is visible today.

In Roman times, probably in the first century, after the abandonment of the Assembly, a healing cult of Zeus Hypsistos was established on the east side of the bema: some votive niches are still visible, but the plaques they contained are in the British Museum.

The Pnyx is now used as an auditorium for *Son et Lumière* performances on the Acropolis.

The Areopagus

North-east of the Pnyx is the rock of the Areopagus or Hill of Ares. This was the site of the major court of ancient Athens; the plot of Aeschylus' *Eumenides* (458) turns on its conversion into a homicide court as a result of the reforms of Ephialtes in 462. The Furies (the 'Kindly Ones' of the title) are supposed to have taken up their abode below the rock as guardians of justice.

St Paul appeared before the court of the Areopagus (AD 50/1) to preach the new religion of Christianity, but there are scant remains of any building apart from traces of a temple base.

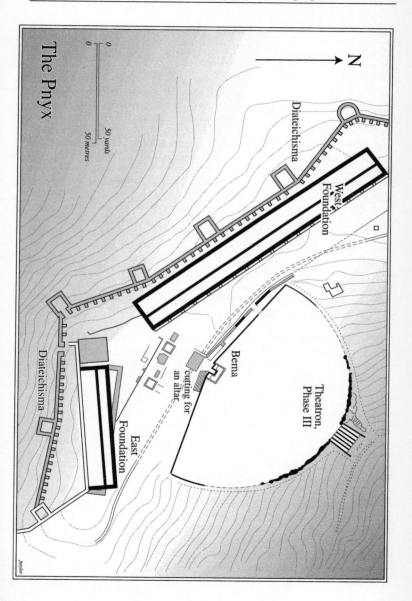

The Pnyx

N

0
0

50 yards
50 metres

Diateichisma

West
Foundation

Diateichisma

Bema

cutting for
an altar

East
Foundation

Theatron,
Phase III

Jupiter

The Supreme Court of the modern Greek state still bears the name of the Areopagus.

The Classical Agora

The word 'agora' means place of assembly and is connected with the verb *agoreuo,* 'speak in public'. The first agora of Athens was to the north-east of the Acropolis, but after Pisistratus had come to power in about 566 BC, a new agora was laid out (from ca 530) in the present position, on a site which had formerly been partly residential and partly a burial ground (Chapter 2). Boundary stones were set up, several of which survive, bearing the inscription 'I am the boundary of the agora'. The earliest buildings, on the west side of the agora, date from this time: the altar of the twelve gods, the *Enneakrounos* or fountain house (ca 530–20), the *Heliaea* (courts), the old *Bouleuterion* (Council House, the meeting place of the ruling body of Athens) and the little *Metroon* (the shrine of the Mother of the Gods which housed the archives) (all ca 508). To the south-west a large building, under the later *tholos,* was perhaps the assembly place for the *Prytanies,* the administrative officials of Athens. In the north-west corner of the agora was the *Stoa Basileios,* the office of the *Archon Basileus,* the chief religious official of the city. A water supply and drain were built by Cleisthenes.

After damage during the Persian Wars, repairs were carried out. The Painted Stoa (colonnade) on the north side of the square was established by Cimon and housed paintings by Polygnotus, notably a series depicting the battles of the Persian Wars. Cimon also beautified the agora and other areas of Athens with shade trees. The *tholos* was built for the *Prytanies,* and a new Council House was built for the Council which had now been enlarged from 400 to 500 members.

Through the fifth and fourth centuries the agora became more and more crowded with public buildings, temples and shrines. The Temple of Hephaestus (known erroneously as the Theseion) was erected ca 449–4 on the Kolonos Agoraios: the architect was Alcamenes, who also built the Temple of Poseidon at Sounion. The Stoa of Zeus Eleutherios was erected in 429 BC, overshadowing the *Stoa Basileios* next to it. The Temple of Apollo Patroos dates from ca 350, as do those of Zeus Phratrios and Athena Phratria. Around 300 the philosopher Zeno began to lecture to students in the Painted Stoa, which led to his school being given the name of Stoics. Other stoas include the Stoa of the Herms and the South Stoa. To the south of the agora were private houses and shops, including a cobbler's shop which may be the one where Socrates instructed the youth of Athens.

In the Hellenistic period the generosity of Attalus the king of Pergamon led to the erection of the Stoa of Attalus along the east side of the agora. Because this has been reconstructed by the American School to function as a museum and administrative offices for the agora excavations, it is one of the most conspicuous buildings in the agora. Further building on the west side of the agora unified the elevation with a colonnade linking the *Metroon* and *Bouleuterion*; the two buildings shared a *Propylon*.

The agora was damaged by the Macedonian invasion of 200 BC but repaired; Sulla's invasion in 86 BC seems to have caused damage only to the fringes of the area. Under Roman rule the agora became cluttered with further grandiose buildings, most notably the Odeion of Agrippa, a large roofed concert hall in the middle of the open area (27–12 BC) which will have dominated the entire agora by its height and bulk. The sculptured giant from its portal which still stands gives some idea of its scale. Augustus seems to have pursued a policy of centralising Attic cults in Athens, and the temple of Ares was removed from Pallene and re-erected just north of the Odeion. Architectural materials from Thorikos and Sounion were also built into two new temples in south-west and south-east corners of the agora.

The next major building was the Library of Pantaenus (early second century AD) south of the Stoa of Attalus. A colonnaded street runs past it linking the Panathenaic Way to the new Roman Agora. A *Nymphaeum* was also erected as part of the imperial project to improve the city's water supply.

The attack of the Heruli in AD 267 resulted in the construction of a new defensive wall (wrongly called the Valerian Wall) in which many materials from ruined agora buildings were used. This wall enclosed only a small part of the ancient city and the agora lay outside the wall. It thus lost its civic function. Assemblies were now held instead in the Theatre of Dionysus. The slopes of the Areopagus became a residential area, and some of the schools of philosophy established themselves here (Chapter 8).

In the Middle Ages the area was largely uninhabited and in the Ottoman period it became built over with dwellings. An extensive fire in the bazaar area (over the Roman agora) in 1884 resulted in the destruction of many buildings here and opened the opportunity for extensive ground clearance and archaeological excavations. Digging for the construction of the Piraeus Railway also brought to light many archaeological remains. From 1931 the American school of Classical Studies began to purchase buildings in the area as they came on the market, and demolished them to continue the excavations. The work of the American School has continued ever since (except for 1942–5) and every season brings new knowledge about the civic heart of classical Athens.

The Ceramicus

The name means the Potters' Quarter, after the region just beyond to which the ancient road led. This tranquil area in the valley of the Eridanus was used from the 11th century BC until well into the Christian era as a cemetery. The Sacred Way to Eleusis ran alongside the Eridanus and was lined at the western end with tombs – first tumuli or rock piles, sometimes crowned with vases;

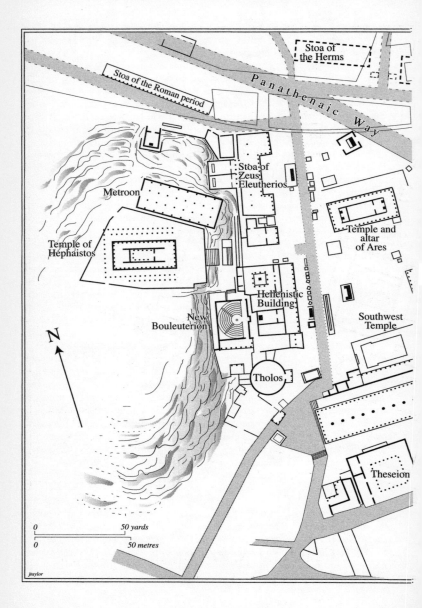

Stoa of
the Herms

Stoa of the Roman period

P a n a t h e n a i c   W a y

Metroon

Stoa of
Zeus
Eleutherios

Temple of
Hephaistos

Temple and
altar
of Ares

Hellenistic
Building

New
Bouleuterion

Southwest
Temple

N

Tholos

Theseion

| 0 | | 50 yards |
| 0 | | 50 metres |

jtaylor

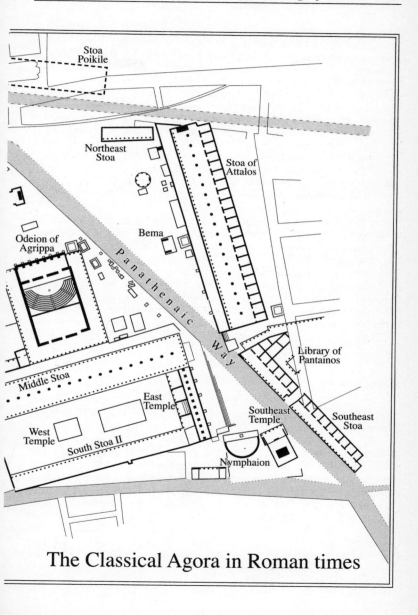

Stoa
Poikile

Northeast
Stoa

Stoa of
Attalos

Odeion of
Agrippa

Bema

Panathenaic Way

Library of
Pantainos

Middle Stoa

East
Temple

Southeast
Temple

Southeast
Stoa

West
Temple

South Stoa II

Nymphaion

The Classical Agora in Roman times

later, masonry monuments were built, often surmounted by sphinxes, sirens or lions. The war dead were honoured by public monuments, e.g. the Tomb of the Lacedaemonians, and the Demosion Sema (Public Memorial). According to Pausanias (1.2.4), this road was also lined with bronze statues of the great men of Athens; these have left no trace. Under Demetrius of Phaleron (317–07) elaborate monuments were forbidden; many simple tombstones were unearthed in the German excavations, and are assembled just below the museum. The classical monuments are in the National Museum but a number of casts have been erected in the Ceramicus, which enable the visitor to enjoy the elegiac atmosphere of the ancient cemetery.

At the eastern end of the archaeological area is the Dipylon Gate, through which Pausanias entered Athens: the road led directly from here to the agora. The gate is part of the city wall built by Themistocles in 479 BC. Immediately to the south, between this gate and the Sacred Gate, is the *Pompeion*, where the equipment needed for the annual Panathenaic procession was stored. The Sacred Gate was the gate by which the Sacred Way left Athens for Eleusis.

The *Pompeion* and other buildings around the Sacred Gate were destroyed in Sulla's sack in 86 BC, and Plutarch describes how 'the slaughter in the agora alone overflowed the area up to the Dipylon with blood, and much blood flowed through the gates into the outer city'.

After being used by potters through late antiquity (up to the sixth century), the area disappeared under the earth until 1863 when a building worker digging sand came upon one of the grave stelae. The German Archaeological Society commenced excavations in 1871, and the German Archaeological Institute took over the work in 1913; it continues to this day. In 2003 the Ceramicus was closed to the public for an extended period.

Plato's Academy and the Hill of Colonus

By following the road from the Dipylon Gate for about a mile, the ancient traveller would come by a peaceful rural route to the Sanctuary of Hekademos, adopted by Plato in the fourth century BC as his 'school'. (The modern traveller will not enjoy this walk; it is better to take the Metro to the Larissa station and walk westwards to the site, a pleasant park bounded by Alexandrias and Monastiriou Streets.) The Academy was one of three major gymnasia of ancient Athens. Young men came here to exercise and compete in sports, and also to sit at the feet of wise and learned men for instruction and intellectual training. In the sixth century BC Hipparchus diverted the R. Cephisus to run through it, and a century later Cimon beautified what was a dusty spot by the planting of trees and the installation of paths and running tracks. Plato taught here from about 388. In 86 BC Sulla cut down the trees of the Academy to build siege engines. Cicero appreciated the spot and described it in his *De Finibus* (Chapter 7). The existing remains are slight.

Half a mile east of the Academy is the Hill of Colonus, celebrated by Sophocles in his *Oedipus at Colonus* as the haunt of nightingales and a sward of flowers. Schoolboys' slates of the fifth and fourth centuries BC have been excavated here, some bearing the names of Sophocles and Demosthenes. The archaeological remains are minimal, but the hill is crowned by the tombs of two great archaeologists, Carl Otfried Müller (1797–1840), who died at Athens of heatstroke, and Charles Lenormant (1802–59).

2. Roman Athens

The Roman Agora and Library of Hadrian

Construction of the Roman market place was begun by Julius Caesar and substantially completed by Augustus. It was connected to the classical Agora by a colonnaded street which ended at the imposing Market Gate (first century BC). Hadrian's law regarding oil and fish sales was inscribed on the jamb of this gate: the lettering is now very faint. On the east there is a second gate of the second century AD. Colonnades of the second century AD line the south and west sides. The large open area used for trading also contained some notable buildings.

The 'Tower of the Winds' (Monument of Andronicus Kyrrhestes) incorporates a weather vane in the form of a bronze Triton (lost), sculptures of personifications of the eight winds and a water clock whose mechanism remains obscure. Its date of construction is uncertain: it is usually put in the Triumviral period (55–31 BC) but may be a century earlier. In the Middle Ages the area became heavily earthed up, and in the Ottoman period the tower was converted into a *tekke* of the Whirling Dervishes, whose displays impressed western travellers such as Edward Dodwell. There is a fine painting of the Tower at this time by James Stuart.

South of the Tower of the Winds, an arcuated building has been thought to be the office of the Agoranomoi (market supervisors) but may have been the temple of the Imperial Cult established by Augustus: it bears a dedicatory inscription to the Emperor Claudius.

The most impressive building in the Roman Agora is the Library of Hadrian: for a full description see pp. 139–141. This building, actually more like a forum or market place than a mere library, bears comparison with the Forum of Trajan in Rome. In the Ottoman period the whole area of the Roman Agora and the Library became the bazaar of the city (see map in Chapter 10). The *voyvode* had his office in the western part of the Library and the area around Tower of the Winds was the grain bazaar. The Turks erected the Fethiye Mosque, which still stands here, and there were also two Turkish baths close by (one survives, in Kirristou Street). The Turks also established the *Medrese* or theological school opposite the Tower of the Winds: its gateway still stands, but the rest of the building, which was used as a prison in the early nineteenth century, has been demolished.

The clock tower erected by Lord Elgin as a recompense for the removal of the Parthenon Marbles stood within the area of the Library; it was demolished after a fire in 1884 destroyed the whole area and opened up the site for archaeological excavation.

The Arch of Hadrian and the Temple of Olympian Zeus

Following Lysikratous Street from the Lysicrates Monument, one comes in view of a large arch, the Arch of Hadrian, on the far side of Leoforos Amalias. This Arch was erected in about AD 13 to mark the limits of the 'new' city of Athens.built by Hadrian. The inscriptions on its façades read (on the west), 'This is the ancient city of Theseus,' and on the east, 'This is the city of Hadrian, not of Theseus.' The gate lies to the west of the line of the Themistoclean Wall.

To the left a path leads through pleasant wooded gardens to the Zappeion, the exhibition hall commissioned by Constantine Zappas and begun in 1874 by the French architect F.R. Boulanger but finished after his death by the Dane Theophilus Hansen. It was completed in 1888.

To the right lies the Temple of Olympian Zeus, the largest temple in Greece, of which Livy wrote that 'it is the only temple on earth of a size adequate to the greatness of the god'. Work was begun on a temple on this site by Pisistratus in the sixth century BC, but work was abandoned and the masonry used in the city walls. A new design was begun in 174 BC at the expense of Antiochus Epiphanes of Syria, with Corinthian instead of Doric columns; many of these were carried off by Sulla in 86 BC for use in the Capitoline temple at Rome. The temple was finally completed and dedicated by the Emperor Hadrian on his second visit to Athens in about AD 130. A copy of Phidias' chryselephantine statue of Zeus at Olympia was erected in the cella, and also a colossal statue of Hadrian himself.

The peribolos of the temple was four stades, or nearly one kilometre. Cyriac of Ancona, on his visit in 1450, observed 21 columns still standing with their architraves. There were 17 left in 1676. In 1760 another was torn for use in the construction of a mosque by the Voyvode Tzistaraki (pp. 210, 214). In 1801 the traveller E.D. Clarke reported 'upon the top of the entablature, on the western side of the principal group, is shewn the dwelling of a hermit, who fixed his solitary abode on this eminence, and dedicated his life entirely to the contemplation of the sublime objects by which his mansion was everywhere surrounded'. This hut can still be seen in some of the early nineteenth-century paintings of the ruins.

3. Churches

After the abolition of paganism many of the temples and other buildings of classical Athens were converted into churches. A number of new churches were

Temple of Olympian Zeus with hermit's hut

also built as early as the sixth century, but the only remains of this period are those of the Megali Panagia in the grounds of the Library of Hadrian. Others may have been incorporated in now existing churches, but the earliest buildings that can be visited are of the eleventh century. Most churches are open daily from 7 am to noon and some from 15.30 to 19.30.

Agioi Apostoloi (Ancient Agora). This early eleventh-century church in the south-east corner of the ancient Agora was built on the foundations of a sec-ond-century temple of the Nymphs. The usual ground plan of a cross-in-square, plus triple arched narthex, is here enhanced by eight apsidal niches which both strengthen the walls and make for more visual interest in the interior. The cloisonné brickwork on the exterior is an indicator of an early date. The church survived the attack of Leon Sgouros on the lower town in 1204, and in Ottoman times it was known as the Solaki Church, presumably after the family who owned the land. The church was restored in 1954–7.

Metamorphosis (Sotiraki) (Theorias St, near Kanellopoulos Museum, Plaka). This small church may be as early as the late twelfth century, but much of the fabric is of the fourteenth. It has four disengaged columns supporting the dome, and no narthex; traces of the cloisonné brickwork are visible around the drum of the dome. The grave of Odysseus Androutsos is in front of the building, as he fell close to here after his 'fall' from his prison on the Acropolis in 1825.

Nikolaos Rangavas (Prytaneiou/Epicharmou Sts, Plaka). This church was built in the eleventh century by St Paul of Xiropotamou, grandson of the Emperor Michael I Rangavas. It probably stands on the site of a ninth-century church built by the son of the same emperor, a monk named Theophylact. A number of ancient blocks are incorporated in the fabric. It has the usual cruciform plan and brickwork patterning around the windows.

The church was the first to be fitted with bells in 1821: bells were banned under Turkish rule. On 12 October 1944 those bells sounded the city's liberation from German occupation. It was rebuilt and expanded in the early twentieth century, and restored in 1978, when the north wall was again laid bare.

Nearby are the seventeenth-century churches of St George of the Rock and the Dormition or St Spyridon: the women of Athens are said to have leapt from the Acropolis here to escape the invading Turks in 1456, but were saved by the miraculous icon of the Virgin. No such miraculous intervention awaited the guardian of the Acropolis who leapt to his death by St George of the Rock when the Germans marched into Athens in 1941.

Ag. Ioannis Theologos (Erotokritou/Erechtheos Sts, Plaka). This church may be as early as the late ninth century but is more likely to be of the eleventh or twelfth century; it lies just within the Late Roman fortification wall and is orientated north–south because of the restrictions of the site. Its dome is supported by only two piers instead of the usual four, and the columns incorporate reworked classical capitals. In 1687, some of Morosini's cannons were set up in the square here for the bombardment of the Acropolis.

Ag. Anargyroi (The Penniless Saints) (Prytaneiou/Erotokritou Sts, Plaka). Tradition records that this was one of the churches established by the Athenian-born Empress Irene in the late ninth century. The Penniless Saints are the doctor-heroes SS Cosmas and Damian. The church was rebuilt (or possibly founded for the first time) in 1651 by a wealthy Athenian Demetrios Kolokynthis. In 1760 the church became a dependency of the Church of the Holy Sepulchre in Jerusalem, and the adjacent offices are those of the Exarch of Jerusalem, the emissary of the Patriarch to the Archbishopric of Athens.

Ag. Ekaterini (Plat Ekaterini, Plaka). This church was probably built in the eleventh or twelfth century. Parts of a Roman building stand nearby, and columns are probably remains of a sixth-century church. In Ottoman times it became a dependency of the Monastery of St Catherine on Mt Sinai. In 1882 it was re-established as a parish church.

The Saviour, 'Kottaki' (Kydathenaion St, Plaka). This church of the Transfiguration, probably eleventh–twelfth century, was the parish church of the Russian community until 1847. It has a cross-in-square plan and there is more recent work on the north and west sides.

The Saviour Lykodemou (Filellinon St, Plaka). This is an eleventh-century church. Most of the adjoining monastery was demolished by Haseki in 1780. The bell-tower was built in 1847 and the church contains wall paintings of the same year by Ludwig Thiersch.

Panaghia Gorgoepekoos or Little Metropolis (Mitropoleos Sq). This twelfth-century church takes the usual cross-in-square form; it is supposed to stand on the site of a church founded by the Empress Irene in 787. What makes it a delight is the plentiful re-use of earlier sculptural materials on the exterior: these include a frieze recording the state festivals of Attica, from the second or third century AD, classical triglyphs, a twelfth-century relief of an eagle with a hare, as well as the lintel with lions flanking a cross. The north side incorporates further classical stelae and reliefs. This abundance of classical detail (safely christianised by the inclusion of crosses, one of them directly over a depiction of the Panathenaic ship: the wheels are still visible) may reflect the love of the twelfth-century Archbishop of Athens, Michael Acominatus, for classical antiquity.

After the expulsion of King Otho it was known for a time as Ag. Eleutherios.

Kapnikarea (Kapnikareas Sq, in Ermou St). The church dates to about 1060/70. The ground plan is relatively complex, with a cruciform core, a three-conch apse on the west and a further apse on the east surrounded by two smaller ones. The exonarthex (exterior porch) at the west end, and the *parekklision* of St Barbara on the north side, are probably of the twelfth century. The occasional cloisonné brickwork reflects an older tradition. The church's official dedication is to the Presentation of the Virgin, and the meaning of its common name is unknown. It is sometimes also known as the Panagiatis Vasilopoulas (Church of the King's Daughter) and attributed to the Empresse Irene (late eighth century). It was listed for demolition by the planners of the new city of Athens in 1834, who wanted an uninterrupted run for Ermou St, but was saved by the personal intervention of King Ludwig I of Bavaria, father of King Otho. It later became the official church of the University of Athens, which paid for its restoration.

Monastiraki (Pantanassa) (Monastiraki Square). The original church was built in the tenth century. This one dates from around 1678 and was a gift of Nicholas Bonefaccio. It preserves the basilica form of the original church, and excavations for the Metro station uncovered a building of similar plan, with arcades and a mosaic floor, dating back to the fifth century AD. In the eleventh century it was a dependency of the Monastery of Kaisariani. The extensive buildings occupied by the nuns who lived there were destroyed during the excavations in 1885 and later for the Piraeus Railway (1896). The church was restored in 1911, the bell-tower was added and the rest of the monastic buildings demolished, but the name 'Little Monastery' has remained.

Ag. Paraskevi (Ag. Anargyron/Agatharchou, Psyrri). This small cruciform eleventh-century church is a well-preserved little gem with decorations of cloisonné masonry and a band of terracotta tiles.

Ag. Anargyroi tou Psyrri (Penniless Saints, Psyrri) (Ag. Anargyron Sq, Psyrri). This eleventh-century church on a basilica plan has been heavily reworked and its appearance was substantially altered in 1908 when the exterior was stuccoed to look like ashlar masonry.

Ag. Asomatoi (The Holy Bodiless Ones, i.e. the Archangels) (Ag. Asomaton Sq, in Ermou St towards Ceramicus). This eleventh-century church, islanded amid the roar of traffic along this busy intersection, is a cross-in-square with three apses and its decoration resembles that of Ag. Apostoloi in the agora. Its façade incorporates two terracotta plaques with inscriptions in Arabic script. It was rebuilt in 1880, and more sensitively restored in 1955.

Ag. Thedoroi (Klafthmonos Square). This attractive church was founded in 1049 or 1065 (inscription in west wall) and rebuilt in stone with brick courses and Cufic decoration in the twelfth century by Nikolaos Kalomanos, a Byzantine court official. It is a three-aisled basilica with a large three-bayed narthex and an octagonal dome supported by the interior walls.

The final Byzantine church in Athens, the **Omorfoklissia (Beautiful Church, officially Ag. Georgios)** lies some way out of the centre in Galatsi (bus 608 from Panepistimiou and then a fifteen-minute walk): it is usually locked and stands on a busy dual carriageway. The elegance of the building and its landscaped surroundings ensure that it lives up to its popular name. It probably belongs substantially to the twelfth century, though the rib-vaulting in the chapel has been taken to imply a knowledge of western building methods and thus a thirteenth-century date. The narthex is probably sixteenth century. The frescoes in the interior are of the thirteenth or fourteenth century, and are lively though badly damaged.

4. *The Modern City, 1833–1913*

The Parliament Building/Old Royal Palace

Begun in 1836 to plans by Friedrich von Gärtner, the palace was completed in 1842. Its simple classical design overlooked open countryside but was soon incorporated in the street grid of the newly founded city. The palace remained the royal residence until 1909 when it was gutted by fire, and King George and his family moved permanently to their newly acquired summer palace at Tatoi (ancient Decelea). After being used as a shelter for refugees in 1923, it was converted to a parliament building in 1930 and came into use in July 1935. The Memorial of the Unknown Soldier was constructed in front of the building in 1929.

The Academy, National Library and University

These three imposing neo-classical complexes dominate the north side of Panepistimiou Street. The easternmost and most recent is the National Library, established in the reign of Otho, though the present building is the work of Theophilus Hansen (1887–1902). The twin wings in the style of Roman temples contain the book stacks, and the reading room is in the central section whose interior resembles the cella of a temple. The façade was renovated by Ernst Ziller in 1906. The collection numbers over three million books as well as 4,500 manuscripts, and other items.

The central position is occupied by the old building of the University of Athens. This is still used for ceremonies but the main university campus lies to the east at Panepistimioupolis in the suburb of Zografou. After the original university was established in Stamatios Kleanthes' house in Plaka (now the museum of the university), this building was erected by Christian Hansen between 1839

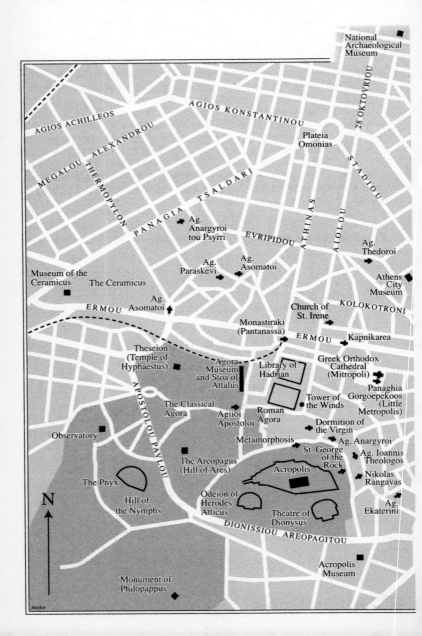

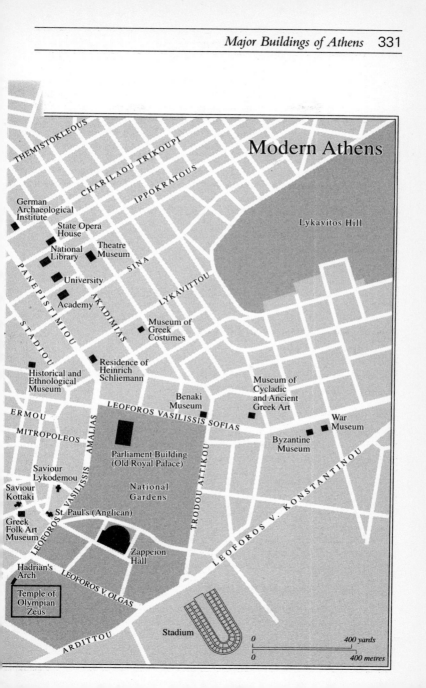

Modern Athens

THEMISTOKLEOUS
CHARILAOU TRIKOUPI
IPPOKRATOUS

German Archaeological Institute

State Opera House

National Library

Theatre Museum

University

PANEPISTIMIOU

SINA

Academy

AKADIMIAS

LYKAVITTOU

Lykavitos Hill

STADIOU

Museum of Greek Costumes

Historical and Ethnological Museum

Residence of Heinrich Schliemann

Museum of Cycladic and Ancient Greek Art

ERMOU

MITROPOLEOS

AMALIAS

LEOFOROS VASILISSIS SOFIAS

Benaki Museum

TRODOU ATTIKOU

War Museum

Byzantine Museum

Saviour Lykodemou

Saviour Kottaki

Parliament Building (Old Royal Palace)

LEOFOROS VASILISSIS V. KONSTANTINOU

National Gardens

St. Paul's (Anglican)

Greek Folk Art Museum

Zappeion Hall

Hadrian's Arch

Temple of Olympian Zeus

LEOFOROS V. OLGAS

ARDITTOU

Stadium

0   400 yards
0   400 metres

and 1842. In front of the simple façade stand statues of the British Prime Minister William Gladstone (1886); Rhigas Pherraios (1757–98, killed by Ottoman authorities in Belgrade; statue 1869–71); Patriarch Gregorios V (hanged at the gates of the Patriarchate in Constantinople in 1821; statue 1869–72); Count John Capodistria, President of Greece 1829–31, assassinated 1831 (statue 1875); Adamantios Korais (1748–1833), the intellect behind the reawakening of Greek national consciousness at the end of Ottoman rule (statue 1875).

The third building is the Academy, begun in 1859 by Theophilus Hansen with funding from Baron Sinas. It closely resembles Hansen's Parliament in Vienna. Ernst Ziller, who oversaw the construction, made some modifications to the design. Sinas withdrew his funding after the expulsion of King Otho in 1863, and it was only completed in 1887. There is a statue of Sinas in the entrance hall, and the frescoes depict a Battle of the Gods and Giants, a traditional symbol of the victory of civilisation over barbarism.

The Eye Hospital

Also in Panepistimiou is the neo-Byzantine Eye Hospital of Christian Hansen (1857), substantially altered after his departure from Greece by the Constantinopolitan architect Lysandros Kaftanzoglou. A second storey was added in 1869. It still continues in its original function.

Iliou Melathron

Also in Panepistimiou is Heinrich Schliemann's mansion, which after several changes of use is now the Numismatic Museum: see under Museums.

The Observatory

This building on the Hill of the Nymphs was funded by Baron Sinas and designed by Theophilus Hansen. It attractively dominates the top of its hill; the new observatory of 1905 is a little lower down.

The Anglican Church

This rather improbable Gothic building in granite imported from Scotland was designed in 1838 by Charles Robert Cockerell but taken over by Christian Hansen and consecrated in 1843. These architects, both talented in the neo-classical style, abandoned their forte to create this dull building of which Robert Byron mordantly remarked, 'there is no salvation in marble'. A stained glass window commemorates the victims of the Dilessi Murders (1870).

The Greek Orthodox Cathedral

This large building, the largest church in Athens, was begun in 1840. The cornerstone was laid by King Otho and Queen Amalia on 25 December 1842.

It incorporates masonry from 72 Byzantine churches which were demolished in the course of the building of modern Athens. Four architects were involved in different parts of it: Theophilus Hansen, Franz Boulanger, Dimitrios Zezos and Panagiotis Kalkos. The statue in front of the cathedral is of Archbishop Damaskinos (1891–1949), who accepted appointment under German rule when his predecessor refused to swear in the puppet government. He made considerable efforts to ameliorate the lot of the population during the occupation by his influence with the German rulers. Nearby is a statue of the last emperor of Constantinople, Constantine XI Palaiologos.

Church of St Irene (corner of Eolou/Athinaidos)

Built in 1847 by Lysandros Kaftanzoglou, it has a basilica-style interior and a façade which blends neo-classical arches and pediment with a Byzantine-style narthex.

The Polytechnic (Patision/28 October St)

Founded in 1836, the institution was funded by several benefactors: George Averoff (1818–99), Michael Tositsas (1787–1856) and Nikolaos Stournaras (1806–53), all of whom were wealthy merchants and community leaders in Alexandria. The architect was Lysandros Kaftanzoglou, and the building, completed in 1862–80, is of Pentelic marble with two Doric pavilions flanking an Ionic entrance portico. In 1973 a student occupation at Polytechnic was brutally put down by the army with tanks, resulting in a number of deaths of students. The protest became a symbol of resistance to the rule of the Colonels, and international shock at the massacre contributed to the fall of their regime.

Subjects taught include Engineering, Architecture and Fine Art.

The Archaeological Schools and Institutes

The many mansions and embassies of nineteenth- and early twentieth-century Athens are too numerous to describe in detail, but the foreign archaeological schools deserve particular attention. The British, American, French and German schools are all old-established and interesting buildings. The **American School of Archaeology** dates from 1881 and the **British School of Archaeology** from 1886. The two buildings are neighbours at 52 and 54 Souedias Street in Kolonaki, and share a tennis court. The American School is probably the best general research library on classical studies in Athens, while the British School has many rare and early holdings. The **German Archaeological Institute** in Trikoupi Street is a work of Ernst Ziller of 1887, and has been well restored, though it suffered damage in the earthquake of September 1999. In the early 2000s efforts were made by the Greek government to sequester the building as war reparations, but these came to nothing.

The **French School**, originally established in 1846 in a neo-classical house, transferred in the 1960s to a simple modernist structure at Didotou and Sina Streets, Kolonaki. **The Danish Institute** in a renovated house in Plaka is a model of sensitive architectural restoration. The **Swedish Institute** in Makriyanni is another example of intelligent re-use of a historic building that had suffered neglect, while the **Finnish Institute** close by is a fine modern building.

All the schools have excellent libraries. Outstanding among these is the **Gennadeion**, which was built for the American School in 1926 to house the book collection of John Gennadius, former Greek Minister in London. The collection is unrivalled in its holdings on early travel in Greece, on modern Greek history and arts, and also includes a large collection of paintings by early travellers including William Haygarth and Edward Lear.

Mention should be made of some important buildings of the late twentieth century.

The University

University expansion after the Second World War led to the transfer of the university's activities from the neo-classical building in Panepistimiou Street to a purpose-built campus in Zografou known as Panepistimioupolis (University City). Largely built of concrete in the 1960s, several of the faculty buildings have claims to attention for their architecture. The School of Theology (1965) was a prize-winning entry in the competitions to design the buildings; arranged on several levels on its hillside site, it echoes features of Byzantine architecture in modern materials. The courtyard shows signs of neglect, however. The School of Philosophy (1982) focuses around a multi-storey interior passage and an atrium with a glass pyramid: all corridors and stairs lead off from the central passage, and 'a walk through the school is like a journey through the history of philosophy' (Errica Protestou, *Athens: A Guide to Recent Architecture* 1998). Other buildings use similar materials and approaches, and though individual parts of the campus are fine, neglect of weeds and the unfinished state of electrical fixtures and the like means that the overall effect is bleak. The new library (1996–8) is housed in the north wing of the 1936 administration building. Entered by an underground passage, it concentrates reading areas on the window side and the clean lines of its metal staircases add to the feeling of space.

The Megaron Mousikis (1994)

This imposing building of white marble with its colonnaded front, consisting of eight pairs of rectangular pillars that echo the effect of a classical temple in utterly modern terms, is a landmark in the city. A Metro stop bearing its name is very close to the entrance. The Megaron was begun in 1975 but the design was modified and it was completed in 1994. It incorporates, besides a renowned concert hall, exhibition spaces, a restaurant and bookshop, and other cultural venues. The spacious interior in two storeys, with magnificent lighting, is an exhilarating place to visit. The musical programme includes concerts of classical music and opera of all periods.

The Airport

Planning for a new airport began in 1974 under Constantine Karamanlis, following the fall of the Colonels. Seasoned travellers to Athens will remember the old two-terminal airport at Hellenikon, whose facilities and buildings were probably the worst in Europe, and which struggled to cope with the explosion of package holiday flights in the 1970s, whose unfortunate customers might often be condemned to spend an entire night 'sleeping' on the bare floor of the terminal. The new airport at Spata, in the arid centre of Attica, opened in 2000, is a spacious, state-of-the-art building with good facilities and air conditioning, reasonable restaurants, shopping facilities and efficient luggage carousels and flight displays. The only thing it lacks at the time of writing is a public transport link to Athens. The only reasonable route to Athens is by taxi. However, the Metro will in due course be extended to the airport, and this will simplify communications enormously.

The Olympic Venues

The main Olympic stadium for the 2004 Games is in the suburb of Maroussi, close to the Metro stop Iraklio. Originally built for the 1982 European athletics championships, it was completely overhauled for 2004. The stadium dome is designed by the Spanish architect Santiago Calatrava, noted for his imaginative buildings such as the Milwaukee Art Museum. The huge amphitheatre is encircled with tiers of seating which were assembled separately and wheeled into place. In early 2003 the opposition spokesman for the Olympics described the preparations as 'a theatre of the absurd'; but the progress of work throughout the year was impressive.

A second venue is the Karaiskaki football stadium in Piraeus, damaged in the 1999 earthquake but now thoroughly renovated.

Many events, including basketball, softball and baseball, take place on new grounds on the site of the Hellenikon airport. Work in 2003 ran behind schedule so that many test events had to be scrapped, but the works were completed on time.

An artificial lake was constructed for sailing and rowing events in 2003 on the Plain of Marathon near Nea Makri, to the indignation of archaeologists who protested at the destruction of part of the historic battlefield of Marathon. (The government, it turned out, thought the battle had taken place at sea.) Tests in summer 2003 resulted in serious accidents among the athletes, prompting speculation that the ghosts of Marathon were still unquiet.

The Metro

Athens' Metropolitan Railway traces its beginnings to the horse-drawn bus established for the run from Piraeus to Athens soon after the formation of the modern state in 1834. The major fire in the bazaar area in 1884 gave the opportunity for demolition and for the construction of an underground railway line through the area, from Monastiraki to Piraeus. These excavations also led to the first finds of the classical agora. The underground railway line was inaugurated in May 1895, with steam trains at first, becoming electric in 1904. A steam train also ran from Viktoria Square to Kifissia, beginning in February 1885: it was known as The Beast (*To Thirio*), and continued to run until 1938. In 1925 Omonoia Square was remodelled, and in the process a tunnel was constructed linking the Monastiraki–Piraeus railway to the Kifissia line. This single line, eventually electrified throughout, was Athens' only urban railway until the 1990s.

A network of trams linked other parts of Athens from the 1880s; originally these were horse-drawn, but these were soon replaced by steam trams. After one of the latter exploded in May 1907, killing five passengers, they were upgraded to electricity. The sixteen tram lines continued to run until they were closed down by Karamanlis as Minister of Transport in the 1950s. The Phaliron tram will however be reintroduced in 2004.

In 1974 Karamanlis as President embarked on plans for the construction of an extended rapid transit system, but it was only in the 1990s, with the imminence of the 2004 Olympics, and the availability of EU funds for the improvement of Athens' infrastructure, that the dream became a reality. Two further lines were constructed, from Sepolia to Daphni (not the monastery but the homonymous suburb in south-east Athens) and from Syntagma Square to Ethniki Amyna; the latter line will eventually be extended to the airport. Progress on the excavation of the new lines was immensely slow, as every step of the way uncovered priceless archaeological information about the history of the city. The archaeological service was involved from the start, often working under extreme pressure of time, and the results of their work were made public in a magnificent exhibition at the Goulandris Museum in 2000–1, 'The City beneath the City'. The finds have in many cases transformed our understanding of the urban development of Athens from earliest times to the early medieval period.

Several of the new stations incorporate display cases making them virtually small museums in their own right: there are exhibits at Syntagma, Panepistimio and Akropoli stations, and a particularly illuminating one is planned for Monastiraki station in 2004. The new stations, with their cool atmosphere, clean lines and fine materials (mainly marble) have transformed the experience of getting across Athens from a sweaty struggle with the buses to a pleasurable experience. The older stations on the Piraeus line have also been upgraded in

Akropoli Metro station

2000–3: with the needs of the Olympics in mind, they accommodate longer trains and improved shelter for passengers. The 1930s station for the Piraeus line at Monastiraki has been given a facelift, and other stations such as Maroussi have been transformed into modern works of art.

5. Cemeteries, Parks and Gardens

The National Garden on Vas Amalias Avenue, behind the former Royal Palace, was laid out by Queen Amalia in 1839–60, and became the National Gardens in 1927. Its pleasant surroundings can be a welcome relief from an Athens summer day; they include a small zoo, a playground, a library and a café. Memories of sniper fire in the dangerous days of winter 1944–5 are a world away.

The more formal Zappeion gardens surround the Zappeion Hall founded by E. Zappas and built to designs by Hansen between 1874 and 1888.

The First Necropolis (entrance on Anapafseos, a street lined with the showrooms of funerary sculptors and masons) is both a tranquil retreat among cypresses and other trees, and a showplace of neo-classical sculpture of the nineteenth century. It was established in the first years of the kingdom, and the earliest grave dates from 1834. It has since been enlarged several times, and the gate (1939) is a century later than the cemetery. Famous citizens and heroes of Greek history are buried here, including (from the War of Independence) Theodore Kolokotronis (1770–1843), General Makriyannis (1797–1864), Odysseus Androutsos (ca 1790–1825), Sir Richard Church (1784–1873), George Finlay (1799–1875), and Melina Mercouri (1922–94). Poets, politicians and wealthy benefactors such as George Averoff (1818–99) and Antonios

Benaki (1873–1954) also rest here, as do the archaeologists Heinrich Schliemann (1822–90), in an imposing tomb decorated with scenes of the Trojan War, and Adolf Furtwängler (1853–1907), the excavator of the Temple of Aphaia on Aigina. There is also a memorial to the 40,000 who died of starvation in Athens in World War II.

6. Museums of Athens

The most important museum is the **National Archaeological Museum** (Patission St). The building by Ludwig Lange, completed in 1889 and extended in 1925–39, houses the most extensive collection of Greek art in the country. Prehistory is well represented with the haunting Cycladic figurines; the gold masks and other finds from Schliemann's excavations at Mycenae; and the Minoan frescoes from Spyridon Marinatos' excavations at Akrotiri on Thera. The collection includes major works of sculpture from the archaic, classical, Hellenistic and Roman periods; and a huge collection of Geometric, black-figure and red-figure pottery. No visitor to Athens can afford to miss this collection.

A separate entrance in Tositsa Street leads to the **Epigraphic Museum** which is housed in the same building. All major public documents in ancient Greece were inscribed on stone. This important collection of ancient inscriptions is of interest primarily to scholars.

The **Numismatic Museum** is housed (since the late 1990s) in the **Schliemann Mansion**, 'Iliou Megaron' in Panepistimiou Street (officially Venizelou). Heinrich Schliemann built this palace in the Renaissance style for himself after his successful excavations at Mycenae, Troy and Orchomenos. The interior of marble paving and Pompeian style wall decoration is rather cavernous and bleak, but the display of the coin collection is a triumph of instruction quite apart from the intrinsic beauty of the exhibits.

The other major museums of classical art are the **Acropolis Museum** (finds from the Acropolis), the **Agora Museum** (finds from the Agora), and the **Ceramicus Museum** (finds from the Ceramicus, all situated on the relevant site). The Agora Museum occupies part of the reconstructed Stoa of Attalos. There are plans for a new Acropolis Museum, to be built on a site beyond Dionysiou Areopagitou Street facing the Acropolis to the north: this is intended mainly to house the 'Elgin Marbles' when (if ever) the British Museum returns them to Greece.

There are a number of other very rewarding museums in Athens. The **National Historical Museum** in the Old Parliament (Kolokotroni Square) houses exhibits, including some paintings, relating to the post-classical history of Greece, notably of the War of Independence. The **Museum of the City Athens** (Klafthmonos Square), a neo-classical mansion, was originally the home of King Otho. Displays and models illustrating the growth of the city are enhanced by a very fine collection of topographical paintings, mainly from the nineteenth century.

The **Benaki Museum** (Vas Sofias and Koumbari), formerly the home of Antonios Benaki (1873–1954), was given to the state in 1931 to house his collection of antiquities, Byzantine art, Muslim and Ottoman pottery, metalwork and textiles, paintings and other treasures. After a ten-year closure and complete remodelling of the interior, the museum re-opened in 2001. The collections are displayed in well-designed spaces and there is a constant rotation of temporary exhibitions. Perhaps more than any other, this museum breathes the atmosphere of Romiosyni of all ages with its exhibits reflecting all aspects of Orthodox and Ottoman Greece.

Almost next door (Neofitou Douka St) is the newest museum in Athens, the **Goulandris Museum of Cycladic and Ancient Greek Art** (opened 1986); it is connected by a passage to Ziller's Stathatos House of 1886 which houses further collections including a series of watercolours by James Skene.

The **Byzantine Museum** (Vas Sofias) occupies a Florentine-style villa built by Kleanthes for the Duchesse de Plaisance. The historical arrangement of the galleries, and the design of some rooms as Byzantine buildings, make for a very instructive survey of the riches of a thousand years of Byzantine art.

Next door is the **War Museum**, with extensive displays of weaponry, uniforms and (on the first floor) finds from antiquity up to the War of Independence and beyond.

The **National Art Gallery** (corner of Konstantinou and Alexandrou, opposite the Hilton), established in 1954, contains mainly nineteenth- and twentieth-century Greek painting, and the visitor will soon learn that these painters are the equal of their better-known equivalents in Western Europe.

Smaller but intriguing museums include the **Kanellopoulos Museum** in Plaka (Panos and Theorias) with ancient and Byzantine objects as well as Coptic textiles and Egyptian mummies; the **Museum of the University of Athens** in the original home of the University in Plaka (Tholou 5), having previously been the home of Kleanthes; the **Venizelos Museum**; and the **Jewish Museum** (Amalias 36).

Excursions outside Athens

The closest excursion from Athens is to the port of **Piraeus**. From an archaeological point of view this is a disappointment as there is little of antiquity to see; and the distinguished buildings of the nineteenth century that made the Piraeus waterfront a place to see and be seen have fallen into sad and often catastrophic disrepair. But the **Archaeological Museum** (Kh Trikoupi 38), not far from remains of the Themistoclean Wall at Zea and of a Hellenistic theatre, is home to an important small collection of finds from Attica, the Saronic Gulf and Kithira. These include the large bronze Piraeus kouros, and other bronze statues. It is rare for bronze statues to survive as they were often melted down for their metal: these statues may have been part of Sulla's spoils after the devastation of 86 BC, which somehow were never shipped to Rome. Some archaising marble reliefs of Amazons illustrate the Roman fashion for imitations of fifth-century Attic style.

A favourite excursion is to **Sounion** to the ruins of the Temple of Poseidon. Pausanias begins his description of Greece at Sounion, but the landmark temple he describes is the temple of Athena, a sixth-century temple on a low eminence above the neck of the isthmus, 500m NE of the standing temple. The blocks of the temple of Athena were removed in the first century AD for a temple in the agora at Athens. In the Middle Ages the ruins were sometime known as 'the palace of Alexander'.

The Doric peripteral temple of Poseidon was built ca 444 BC on the foundations of an earlier one of ca 490. It is contemporary with the Parthenon. Its architect was probably responsible also for the Theseion in Athens and the temple of Nemesis at Rhamnous. The frieze depicted exploits of Theseus, the Athenian hero.

Lord Byron was nearly abducted by bandits here, though not before he had carved his name prominently on one of the blocks (the right-hand anta as you enter). Excavations were begun by Wilhelm Dörpfeld in 1884, continued by the Greek Archaeological Society in 1897–1915. The finds, including several kouroi reflecting the wealth of the region's inhabitants in archaic times, are in the National Archaeological Museum.

Marathon   The modern village is approx 42 km NW of Athens. It was here that in legend Theseus killed the Bull of Marathon which was terrorising Attica.

In 490 the important Battle of Marathon was fought between the Greeks and the invading Persians on the bay between Marathon and New Makri. The Greek camp was near the present-day church of Ag. Demetrios (where the museum and the Mycenaean tombs are) and the Persian camp was on the stream Charadros near Panagia Mesosporitissa.

Miltiades' army caught the Persians in a pincer movement and forced them back to their ships. The soldier who carried the news of the victory to Athens fell dead on arrival after giving his message: his run is commemorated in the name of the modern long-distance race, the Marathon.

The Athenian grave mound (soros) stands 550 m E of the modern road; the Plataean burial mound is a little further inland. The stele of Aristion which marked it is now in the National Archaeological Museum and has been replaced by a copy. In antiquity the battlefield was surrounded by legend and the soldiers received heroic cult. Sir John Boardman has suggested that the number of figures on the Parthenon frieze (192 by some calculations) is intended to commemorate those who fell at Marathon.

'Here every night you can hear the noise of whinnying horses and of men fighting. It has never done any man good to wait there and observe this closely, but if it happens against his will the anger of the daemonic spirits will not follow him' (Pausanias 1.32.3).

In 2001–2 plans by the Greek government to develop part of the site as a venue for some of the events of the 2004 Olympics met with strong protest from the archaeological community, and were abandoned.

Brauron   38 km north of Athens on the east coast of Attica is Brauron. One version of the legend of Agamemnon's sacrifice of his daughter to obtain a fair wind for Troy had her spirited away by the goddess at the moment of sacrifice and replaced by a deer; the girl arrived at Tauris (Crimea) where she became priestess of a savage cult of Artemis involving human sacrifice. Her brother Orestes rescued her and brought her, with the cult statue, to Brauron.

This was the most important shrine of Artemis in Attica. From the eighth century cult focused around a cleft 30m SE of the present temple (remains of the so-called 'Temple of Iphigeneia'). By the fifth century a quadrennial festival, the Brauronia, was celebrated in March–April: the particular feature of this festival was the shedding by young girls aged 5–10, who were known as 'bears', of their saffron robes. This was the final act of their childhood religious duties. The service as bears lasted for the year preceding the festival. Their dedication to Artemis was a rite of passage at puberty (menarche being assumed to occur at the age of ten), but because the festival only took place every four years, some girls as young as five took part rather than be missed out altogether.

Participation was something to boast of afterwards: 'I was only seven when I carried the sacred vessels; at ten I bore the temple mill; then, in yellow I acted the little bear at Brauron, and as I grew taller and lovelier, I took care of the holy basket' (Aristophanes, *Lysistrata* 641–7).

Though the inscriptions here remain largely unpublished, a sense of the cult's atmosphere can be gained from the charming dedicatory statues of young girls with their pets, and of processions to Artemis, which have been collected in the museum.

The site was flooded in the fourth century BC and abandoned by AD 40. Past the chapel of Ag. Giorgios one comes to the foundations of the fifth-century temple of Artemis and the Grotto of Iphigeneia. To the north lies the court complex (ca 425 BC), including a three-sided stoa with small rooms, with eleven couches, where the girls met to dine. Behind the N wall is the colonnade where the dedicatory statues stood, and to the W of this the only surviving bridge from classical Greece.

The Amphiareion, Oropos   The sanctuary of the prophet Amphiaraus lies near Markopoulo, just SW of Skala Oropou. During the siege of Thebes by the Seven, Amphiaraus as pursued by Periclymenus, and to save him Zeus opened the earth so that he was swallowed up. The Amphiareion marks the place where he re-emerged from the ground in a spring. He was revered here as a healing divinity. Cures were sought by 'incubation' on the fleece of a ram sacrificed to the god. The spring itself had healing properties.

Excavations were begun by Sp. Phindikles in 1884 and concluded by B. Leonardos in 1929. The fourth-century remains include, first, the Doric temple of Amphiaraus, with the base of the cult statue still in position. The altar stands 10 m before the temple, and beyond it is the sacred spring. Above the museum is a terrace with Roman statue bases, and beyond the museum is the Enkoi-meterion where suppliants slept on their fleeces, a long stoa of ca 387 BC; it had 44 Doric columns along the façade, with two long galleries within, divided by 17 Ionic columns. To the NW is the theatre, and across the stream accommodation for patients, doctors and priests, and remains of a klepsydra or water clock.

Monastery of Kaisariani   The monastery lies to the east of the city below Mt Hymettos (bus 224 from Akadimias and half an hour's walk).

The *katholikon* was founded in the eleventh century and dedicated to the Presentation of the Virgin. It follows the usual cross-in-square plan with a dome and three apses. Classical fragments are incorporated in the walls. The narthex is of the fifteenth century and the parekklision on the north side is often said to be of Frankish date but is probably later. A number of the domestic buildings of the monastery still survive, including a bath and an olive press, and cells for the monks. A five minute walk leads to a three-aisled basilica probably of the tenth century which was built on top of a sixth-century one of similar plan.

In Turkish times the monastery was known as Kozbaşı,

> Because of a sheep's head engraven on a marble sepulchre, now made use of for a cistern to the fountain arising there, whose stream falls into the Ilissos. . . . This mountain is celebrated for the best honey in all Greece, of which it makes a great quantity to send to Constantinople, where it is much esteemed for making sorbets. . . . We ate of it very freely; and were not at all incommodated with any gripings after it. (George Wheler, *A Journey into Greece*, 1682)

In antiquity there was a temple of Aphrodite here, and the legend of Cephalus and Procris was localised in this spot, accurately described by Ovid:

> Near the purple of variegated Hymettos is a sacred fountain, where the contiguous turf by its soft verdure invites the traveller to repose. Here no lofty trees are condensed into a forest shade; but the arbutus, the rosemary, the laurel, and the dark myrtle, cover the ground, and perfume the air. Nor does the sequestered scene want the thick foliage of the box, of the tender tamarisk, or the elegant pine. (*Ars Amatoria* III)

In 1801 William Gell and Edward Dodwell found the convent temporarily deserted, and climbed the walls to enjoy the hospitality and the pretty garden of their absent hosts:

> We took complete possession of the place, and feasted on the produce of the deserted mansion, which seemed to have been prepared for our reception. We barricaded the doors with great poles; and, as it grew dark, expected to hear the astonished monks demanding admittance; but they did not come; and no noise during the night disturbed the tranquillity of our solitary abode. We slept in a room, to which we ascended by a ladder, which we pulled up after us. (Edward Dodwell, *A Classical and Topographical Tour in Greece*)

Imitation is not recommended.

West of Athens, the Sacred Way (Iera Odos) leads from the site of Ceramicus towards Eleusis. The modern road largely follows the route of the ancient processional way. The Monastery of **Daphni** lies alongside the road. It was founded in the fifth or sixth century AD on top of a former sanctuary of Apollo (to whom the laurel, daphne, was sacred) which was destroyed ca 395. The present buildings date from the eleventh century. There is a strong fortification wall but the monastic buildings have largely disappeared.

In 1211 Otho de la Roche gave Daphni to the Cistercians, and they occupied it until 1458. Several antique columns were used in the construction of the Gothic exonarthex added by the Cistercians, but only one remains, the others having been removed, allegedly by Lord Elgin at the beginning of the nineteenth century. Both Otho himself and a later Duke of Athens, Walter de Brienne, who fell at the Battle of the Cephisus in 1311, were buried here. In the sixteenth century it was taken over by Orthodox monks but abandoned during the War of Independence. It became a barracks, then a lunatic asylum (1883–5) and then a mere sheepfold.

The mosaics of the interior are one of the high points of the classic period of Byzantine art (ca 1080). The frontal and hieratic style of earlier Byzantine art has given place to a softer humanistic style, still very dependent on symmetry and without the exaggerated gestures of fourteenth-century mosaic and painting. The Pantocrator in the dome has all the majesty of the Apollo of Olympia. The colours are largely naturalistic (whereas colour is used with symbolic values in Palaeologan art). The traditional iconographic programme depicts scenes from the Lives of the Virgin and of the Saviour.

Eleusis   The Mysteries of Eleusis celebrated the myth of Persephone, the daughter of Demeter the corn goddess, who was abducted by Hades the god of the Underworld while gathering flowers. While in the Underworld she made the mistake of swallowing part of a pomegranate. When her sorrowing mother eventually negotiated her return to earth, it was on the basis that for six months of the year (one for each pomegranate seed she had swallowed) she should remain below the earth: for the remaining six months life would return to earth, the crops would grow, and trees bear fruit. The myth of Demeter's search for her daughter through the long months of famine while Persephone was in Hades was believed to have ended at the palace of Celeus, King of Eleusis, where she sat and wept by the Well of the Maiden, and was appointed nurse to the young prince Demophon. She started to make him immortal by bathing him in fire, but a house servant caught her in the act and prevented her. So Demophon remained mortal, and Demeter established the Mysteries in his memory. She also taught the arts of agriculture to another prince (or perhaps the same one under another name), Triptolemus.

The Mysteries, whose content remained secret, offered new life to the initiates on the model of the return of life to earth. The central mystery was said to involve the showing of an ear of corn; but the secret has been well kept, and what little information we do have derives in large part from Christian authors who attacked a ceremony that seemed in some ways a dangerous rival to the eucharist.

Aspirants were first supposed to undergo initiation at the Lesser Mysteries held at Agrai in the month Anthesterion (February–March). The Greater Mysteries, which took place in September, began on 13–14 Boedromion with a procession from Eleusis, along the Sacred Way, to escort the 'Sacred Objects' to the Eleusinion north-west of the Acropolis. The festival proper began on 15 Boedromion and lasted six days. The candidates set out in carriages for Phaleron

– where piglets were sacrificed on the beach and purificatory bathing took place – and then returned to Athens. Further rites were followed by a quiet retreat on the fourth day. On the fifth day the Sacred Objects were escorted back to Eleusis, a distance of fourteen miles: at the bridge on the Sacred Way men gathered to hurl ribald insults at the initiates. The culminating ritual or *telete* took place on the sixth day in the *telesterion*, a large square-columned hall quite unlike the usual Greek temple. A terracotta tablet in the National Museum seems to represent some of the rites. They included 'things said', 'things done', and 'things revealed'; but their nature has remained a secret.

The Mysteries continued until the suppression of paganism in 396, and constituted a major draw for pilgrims to Athens. Many Roman emperors made a point of being initiated.

In 1801 the Cambridge don Edward Daniell Clarke removed a large Caryatid (the counterpart of a much finer one now in the Eleusis Museum), against the protests of the villages who saw in it the goddess Demeter herself. It was buried in a dunghill and intended to ensure the fertility of the fields. It is now in the Fitzwilliam Museum.

In 1811 the Society of Dilettanti excavated here, and from 1882 the Greek Archaeological Service began a programme of excavations that went on for over fifty years. George Mylonas, for many years the leader of the excavations, became the most noted authority on the Mysteries.

Aigina   Aigina is a popular excursion from Athens, by ferry or by hydrofoil ('Flying Dolphin') from Piraeus. The boats are very crowded on Sundays.

The settlement of the island began in prehistoric times and was traced to the legendary Aeacus. Greece had been withering under a drought, and the Delphic oracle instructed Aeacus to ascend Mount Panhellenion and pray to Zeus for rain. The island was then peopled by ants who became human beings and bore the name of Myrmidons (from the Greek myrmex, an ant). Aeacus' son Peleus was the father of Achilles, who led his people, the Myrmidons (by then located in Phthia) against Troy.

Aigina became a flourishing Dorian port and trading station in the seventh century BC. Silver was imported from Spain, and was used to mint the Aeginetan 'tortoises', the first coinage of Greece (from 656 BC). Aeginetan bronze was also of high quality. The wealth of the island enabled many of its noble families to compete at the Great Games of Greece; the poet Pindar had a 'special relationship' with the island's aristocracy, writing more odes for Aeginetan victors than for any other city.

This Dorian island was perceived by Ionian Athens as – in Pericles' words – 'the eyesore of the Piraeus'. It was conquered by Athens in 455 BC and became a part of the Athenian Empire. In 431 the inhabitants were expelled and replaced by Athenian colonists. It became a base of pirates in the fourth century. After the Macedonian conquest of Athens, Aigina also came under

Macedonian rule until the Roman conquest in 211. Rome presented it to the Aetolians, who then sold it to King Attalus II of Pergamum. On Attalus III's death in 133 it passed to Rome by the terms of his will. Mark Antony gave the island to Athens but Augustus took it away again, after which it remained an independent polity.

In medieval times the island shared the fate of its neighbours. It was ravaged by Khaireddin Barbarossa in 1537, when all the male inhabitants were killed and six thousand women and children enslaved. In 1715 the Turks took it from the Venetians, and after the liberation from the Turks in 1828 it became the capital of Capodistria's government. In 1829 the first National Museum of Antiquities was housed on Aigina, in the former sanatorium on the waterfront; the collection was transferred to Nauplia when it became the capital of the new Greek kingdom in 1834, and finally to Athens on the completion of the National Archaeological Museum in 1889.

Near the harbour are the temples of Apollo, Aphrodite and Dionysus, as well as the Aiakeion (the hero shrine of Aeacus) and the tomb of Phocus. Pausanias gives a detailed description, but the remains are exiguous. Pausanias does not however describe the finest building on the island, the still largely intact temple of Aphaia inland, with its outstanding view of the Saronic Gulf. This was founded in 480 BC and adorned with pediments depicting the Greeks' two expeditions against Troy. In modern times travellers generally took this for the temple of Zeus Panhellenios, which Pausanias does describe; but this was on top of the highest peak of the island, and not much now remains. Its identity was first established by Adolf Furtwängler in 1901.

The story of the excavation of the Temple of Aphaia is one of the finest in the annals of Greek archaeology. It was visited by the young architect Charles Robert Cockerell in 1811, accompanied by a group of friends. They began to dig around the temple, and

> On the second day one of the excavators, working in the interior portico, struck on a piece of Parian marble which, as the building itself is of stone, arrested his attention. It turned out to be the head of a helmeted warrior, perfect in every feature. It lay with the face turned upwards, and as the features came out by degrees you can imagine nothing like the state of rapture and excitement to which we were wrought. Here was altogether a new interest, which set us to work with a will. Soon another head was turned up, the a leg and a foot, and finally, to make a long story short, we found under the fallen portions of the tympanum and the cornice of the eastern and western pediments no less than sixteen statues and thirteen heads, legs, arms &c, all in the highest preservation, not 3 feet below the surface of the ground. It seems incredible, considering the number of travellers who have visited the temple, that they should have remained so long undisturbed. (C.R. Cockerell, *Travels*)

The acquisition of the marbles became an international competition, but in the end the British Museum bid too low and lost them to King Ludwig of Bavaria. The Glyptothek in Munich was built to designs by Leo von Klenze to house the sculptures, along with the rest of his collection of antiquities.

Chronological Table

BC

4000–3000	Neolithic settlement on Acropolis
3000–2000	Early Helladic period
2000–1600	Middle Helladic period
1600–1100	Late Helladic Period
	Mycenaean remains on Acropolis
1100–1025	Sub Mycenaean period
1025–900	Protogeometric period } Dark Ages
900–710	Geometric period
710–600	Archaic period
624	Draco's Laws
594	Solon's reforms
566	Panathenaea instituted. First temple of Athena Nike
561	Pisistratus (d. 527)
521	Altar of Twelve Gods
514	Hipparchus assassinated
510	Hippias retires to Sigeum
507	Cleisthenes' reforms
499–3	Ionian Revolt

Classical Athens

493–72	Career of Themistocles (d. 459)
490	Battle of Marathon
480	Battles of Thermopylae and Salamis
479	Battle of Plataea. Themistoclean Wall
478/7	Delian League founded
470	Tholos built
ca 462	Reforms of Ephialtes
460–29	Career of Pericles
459–46	First Peloponnesian War
447–32	Parthenon built

437–2	Propylaea built
431–04	Peloponnesian War
427–4	Temple of Nike
421	Peace of Nicias
421–03	Erechtheum
415–13	Sicilian expedition
412	Revolt of Athens' allies
411	The Four Hundred
404	The Thirty
377	Second Athenian Confederacy
366–2	Career of Callistratus
338	Battle of Chaeronea
336	Accession of Alexander the Great
334	Lysicrates Monument
323	Death of Alexander; beginning of

Hellenistic Age

322	Lamian War
317–07	Demetrius of Phalerum rules Athens
307	Demetrius Poliorcetes liberates Athens
266–2	Chremonidean War
229	Demetrius II d, Athens free until 88; Piraeus becomes independent city
200	Philip V burns down Cynosarges and Lyceum
197	Battle of Cynoscephalae
168	Battle of Pydna
150	Stoa of Attalus
146	Mummius takes Corinth
133	Slave rebellion in Attic silver mines

Roman Rule

88–6	Sack of Athens by Sulla
ca 50	'Tower of the Winds'
21	Athens deprived of jurisdiction over Eretria and Aigina
15	Odeion of Agrippa

AD

66–67	Nero in Greece
100	Library of Pantaenus
101	Birth of Herodes Atticus
114–16	Philopappus Monument
122, 125, 129, 135	Hadrian visits Athens
130	Library of Hadrian
135	Gate of Hadrian; Temple of Olympian Zeus

143	Herodes Atticus consul
140–4	Panathenaic Stadium built by Herodes Atticus
168	Disgrace of Herodes Atticus?
176	Marcus Aurelius visits Athens
177	Death of Herodes Atticus
267	Heruli attack Athens
274	'Valerian Wall' built by Probus
348–58	Gregory of Nazianzus studies in Athens
355	The future Emperor Julian studies in Athens
396	Visit of Synesius
400	Academy rebuilt
408–50	Edicts of Theodosius outlawing paganism
421	Athenais becomes Empress Eudocia
429	Statue of Athena Parthenos removed by Christians; never seen again
450–60	Temple of Hephaestus and Asclepius converted into churches. Theatre of Dionysus likewise
529	Justinian closes philosophical schools
Early 6th c	Erechtheum converted into church

Middle Ages: Byzantine Empire

539	Bulgar and Slav invasions. Justinian restores walls of Athens
578	Slavs at Thermopylae
653	Visit of Constans II
662–3	Constans II visits Athens
722–3	Willibald in Argolid
752	Birth of Empress Irene (an Athenian); r. 780–802, d.803
807	Theophano of Athens marries son of Byzantine Emperor
915	Stoning of Byzantine official, Chases
1018	Basil II visits Athens
1033–43	Harald's graffito (?)
1040	Bulgar invasion. Athenian revolt against Zoe?
11th c	Churches of Ag. Apostoloi and Soteira Lykodemou
1050–75	Kapnikarea. Ag. Theodoroi. Daphni
1102	Icelandic pilgrim Saewulf
1130	Normans in Boeotia; ? and Attica
1160	Benjamin of Tudela bypasses Athens
1175–1205	Michael Acominatus bishop of Athens
1187	Normans conquer Thessaloniki
1202	Athenian 'philosophers' at court of King John of England. John of Basingstoke studies in Athens
1204	Leon Sgouros attacks Athens and Thebes

Frankish Rule

1204	Sack of Constantinople. Boniface enters Athens, defeats Sgouros
1205	Boniface beheaded
1205–25	Otho de la Roche, megaskyr
1208	death of Sgouros
1217	Michael Acominatus' last visit to Athens
1220	Death of Michael Acominatus
1225–60	Guy I de la Roche moves home to Thebes
1260–3	Guy I becomes Duke of Athens
1261	Constantinople recaptured
1263–80	Duke John
1278	John of Athens reconquers Euboea
1280–7	Duke William
1287–1308	Guy II
1309	Walter of Brienne arrives in Glarentza

Catalan Rule

1311	15 March, Battle of the Cephisus: Catalan Company becomes ruler of Athens until 1385

Florentine Rule

1385	Nerio I Accaiuoli seizes Athens; Duke of Athens 1394
14th c	Frankish Tower on Acropolis (possibly Catalan) Metamorphosis (on site of Temple of Dioscuri)
1392	Turks lay waste Attica and Boeotia
1394	Niccolo Martoni visits Athens
1396	Turks in the Peloponnese
1402	Antonio takes Athens, Euboea
1402	Battle of Angora delays Turkish advance
1405	Antonio I
1423	Plague in Athens
1430	Turks take Thessaloniki
1435–9	Nerio II
1436–7	Cyriac of Ancona's first visit to Athens
1439–41	Antonio II
1441–51	Nerio II returns from Florence to Athens
1444	Battle of Varna; Turks secure Greece
1446	Battle of the Isthmus, 10–14 Dec
1451	Accession of Mehmet II; death of Nerio II
1453	Ottoman Conquest of Constantinople
1458	Omar conquers Athens

Ottoman Period: 'Tourkokratia'

1450–1500	Fethiye Camii
1460	Mehmet II visits Athens, August. Turks conquer Peloponnese. Franco Acciaiuoli killed
1466	Turks take Negroponte
1571	Battle of Lepanto
1610	William Lithgow in Greece
1640	Propylaea damaged by explosion in powder magazine
1658	Capuchin mission established
1669	Turks take Candia; Capuchins acquire Lysicrates monument
1674	J.P. Babin's map of Athens
Mid 17th c.	Yeni Camii; Hamam of Hajji Ali; Church of Ypapandi
1674	Nov, Marquis de Nointel visits Athens
1676	Jan–Feb, Jacob Spon and George Wheler in Athens
1687	26 Sept, bombardment of Parthenon by Morosini
1699	Treaty of Carlowitz
1706	Paul Lucas visits Athens
1721	Medrese gate in Roman agora
1751–3	Stuart and Revett
1759	Syntrivani mosque
1778	Ionic temple by Ilissus destroyed. Wall of Haseki built
1801–2	Lord Elgin's agents remove Parthenon Marbles
1805	Edward Dodwell in Athens
1809	Lord Byron arrives in Athens
1810–13	C.R. Cockerell, Carl Haller von Hallerstein and J-O. Brøndsted excavate the Temple of Aphaia on Aigina
1811	William Haygarth visits Athens
1813	Philomousos Etaireia founded
1821–9	Greek War of Independence
1826–7	Siege of Acropolis
1827	20 Oct, Battle of Navarino

Independent Modern Greece

1828	President Capodistria arrives
1831	9 Oct, Capodistria assassinated
1832	Ludwig Ross assumes responsibility for archaeology
1833–62	KING OTHO
1834	Klenze's plan for new capital
1835–	Megaron Rallis (Kleanthes)
1836	Royal Palace (Friedrich von Gärtner)
1837	Arkhaiologike Etaireia founded

1838–41	University (Christian Hansen)
1839–62	Cathedral (Ed. Schaubert)
1839–41	Anglican Church (Christian Hansen/Kleanthes)
1842–6	Observatory (Theophilus Hansen)
1842–3	Demetri house (Th. Hansen; later the Grande Bretagne Hotel)
1846	Ecole Française founded
1850–4	Eye Clinic (Chr. and Th. Hansen)
1859–87	Academy (Chr. and Th. Hansen)
1862–1913	KING GEORGE (new constitution)
1862–80	Polytechnic (Kaftanzoglou)
1885–92	National Library (Chr. and Th. Hansen)
1874–88	Zappeion (Th. Hansen and F. Boulanger)
1853–	Catholic Church of St Dionysius (Klenze)
1874	German Archaeological Institute founded; Frankish Tower removed from Acropolis
1878	Schliemann Mansion, 'Iliou Melathron'
1882	American School founded
1883	Evangelismos Hospital founded by Queen Olga
1886	British School founded
1889	National Museum
1893	Corinth Canal opened
1895	Piraeus Railway completed
1896	Olympic Games re-established in Athens; Stadium rebuilt
1899	Spyros Mercouris mayor; cleans up Athens
1901	Public lavatories established
1902	Electric street lighting
1905	Theodore Deligiannis assassinated
1910	Oct, Eleftherios Venizelos become PM (b.1864)
1911–13	Balkan Wars
1913	King George assassinated. CONSTANTINE 1913–17
1916	Greek railway linked to Europe
1917–20	ALEXANDER
1920–2	CONSTANTINE (again)
1922	Smyrna burnt by Turks
1922–3	GEORGE II
1925–6	Dictatorship of Pangalos
1926	Presidency of Koundouriotes. Richard Strauss in Athens
1928	Psychiko built. Corinth earthquake
1929	New Kifissia settled
1930s	Venizelos mansion (becomes British Embassy 1936)
1932	Revival of Theatre. Unknown Soldier unveiled. Beautification of National Garden and Zappeion

1935–41	GEORGE II (again; then exiled until 1946)
1936	18 Mar, Venizelos d
1937	Dictatorship of Metaxas
1938	Attiki–Kifissia railway electrified. National Theatre demolished
1940	28 Oct, Metaxas says *Ochi* to the Italians
1941–4	German occupation
1946	March, Anastylosis of Parthenon
1946–9	Greek Civil War
1947–64	PAUL
1948	1 May, Murder of Christos Lada
	December, votes for women
1950	Cyprus votes for Enosis
1964–73	CONSTANTINE II
1967–74	Military dictatorship: 'The Colonels'
1974	Presidency of Karamanlis
1992–7	Metro excavations
2000	Metro extensions opened. New airport
2003	May, trials of November 17 terrorists begin
2004	Olympic Games

The Attic Calendar and Major Festivals

The year begins in mid-summer, at the new moon before the summer solstice

1.	*Hecatombaeon*	early June–mid July	Panathenaea
2.	*Metageitnion*	July–August	
3.	*Boedromion*	August–September	Boedromia Artemis Agrotera Eleusinian Mysteries (7 days)
4.	*Pyanopsion*	September–October	Apaturia, Thesmophoria (3 days)
5.	*Maimakterion*	October–November	
6.	*Poseideon*	November–December	Country Dionysia
7.	*Gamelion*	December–January	Lenaea (5 days), Gamelia
8.	*Anthesterion*	January–February	Anthesteria (3 days)
9.	*Elaphebolion*	February–March	Elaphebolia, City Dionysia (5 days)
10.	*Munichion*	March–April	Delphinia, Munichia, Brauronia
11.	*Thargelion*	April–May	Thargelia, Bendideia, Plynteria
12.	*Scirophorion*	May–June	Dipolieia

Guide to Further Reading

General Studies, and Early Athens

JOHN CAMP, *The Archaeology of Athens* (Yale 2001)
GEORGE FINLAY, *History of Greece BC 146–AD 1864* ed. H.F. Tozer (8 volumes, 1877)
JEFFREY HURWIT, *The Athenian Acropolis* (Cambridge 1999)
LIANA PARLAMA and N. CHR. STAMPOLIDIS, *The City beneath the City* (Athens 2000)
ATHINA SCHINA et al., *Athens the Famed City* (Athens: Miletos n.d. but 2002) – in Greek and English
JOHN TRAVLOS, *Urban development of Athens* (2nd edn Athens 1993) – in Greek
JOHN TRAVLOS, *Pictorial Dictionary of Ancient Athens* (1971)
HENRY WALKER, *Theseus and Athens* (Oxford 1995)

Classical Athens

V.J. BRUNO, *The Parthenon* (New York 1974)
PHILIP DE SOUZA, *The Peloponnesian War* (London 2002)
ROBERT GARLAND, *The Piraeus* (2nd edn London 2001)
C. HIGNETT, *Xerxes' Invasion of Greece* (Oxford 1963)
SIMON HORNBLOWER, *The Greek World 479–323* (London 2002)
SIAN LEWIS, *The Athenian Woman* (London 2002)
CHRISTIAN MEIER, *Athens: a portrait of the city in its Golden Age* (New York 1998)
RUSSELL MEIGGS, *The Athenian Empire* (Oxford 1972; 1995)
P.J. RHODES, *The Athenian Empire* (Greece and Rome pamphlet 1993)
P.J. RHODES, *A Commentary on the Aristotelian Athenaion Politeia* (2nd edn Oxford 1993)
RAPHAEL SEALEY, *Demosthenes and his time* (California 1993)
G.E.M. DE STE CROIX, *The Origins of the Peloponnesian War* (London 1972)
I.F. STONE, *The Trial of Socrates* (New York 1988)

The Fourth Century and the Hellenistic Period

CHRISTIAN HABICHT, *Athens from Alexander to Antony* (1997)
JON D. MIKALSON, *Religion in Hellenistic Athens* (1998)

Roman Athens

W. AMELING, *Herodes Atticus* (Hildesheim 1983) – in German
MARY T. BOATWRIGHT, *Hadrian and the Cities of the Roman Empire* (Princeton 2000)
J. DAY, *Economic History of Athens under Roman Domination* (New York 1942)
DANIEL GEAGAN, *The Athenian Constitution after Sulla* (*Hesperia Suppl.* xii 1967)
PAUL GRAINDOR, *Athenes sous Auguste* (1927), *Athenes de Tibere à Trajan* (1931), *Athenes sous Hadrien* (1934)
MICHAEL HOFF and SUSAN ROTROFF, *The Romanization of Athens* (Oxford: 1997)
LESLIE T. SHEAR, 'Athens: from City State to Provincial Town', *Hesperia* 50 (1981), 356–77

Medieval Athens

MICHAEL ACOMINATUS, *Letters*, ed Sp. Lambros (1899) – in Greek; and there is a more modern edition by Photeini Kolovou (Berlin 2001)
BERNARD ASHMOLE, 'Cyriac of Ancona', *Proceedings of the British Academy* 45 (1959), 25–41, and *Journal of the Warburg and Courtauld Institute* 19 (1956), 179–99
E.W. BODNAR, *Cyriacus of Ancona and Athens* (Latomus 43) (Brussels 1966)
ROBERT BROWNING, *Byzantium and Bulgaria* (London 1975)
NICHOLAS CHEETHAM, *Medieval Greece* (Yale 1981)
FERDINAND GREGOROVIUS, *Geschcihte der Stadt Athen im Mittelalter* (1889)
WILLIAM MILLER, *The Latins in the Levant* (1908)
NICETAS CHONIATES, *O City of Byzantium: Annals of Nicetas Choniates*, tr. Harry J. Magoulias (Detroit: Wayne State 1984)
JAMES MORTON PATON, *Medieval and Renaissance Visitors to Greek Lands* (Princeton 1951)
K.M. SETTON, *Catalan Domination of Athens, 1311–88* (Cambridge, Mass. 1948)

Ottoman Athens

EVLIYA CELEBI, *Ta Attika tou Evliya Chelebi* (a Greek translation by K. Biris)
MOLLY MACKENZIE, *Turkish Athens* (Reading: Ithaca Press 1992)
LIZA MICHELI, *Monastiraki: from Corn market to Yousouroum* (Okeanida 1986) – in Greek)

LIZA MICHELI, *Piraeus: from Porto Leone to the Manchester of the Orient* (Dromena 1989) – in English

Nineteenth-Century Athens

ELENI S. BASTEA, *The Creation of Modern Athens* (Cambridge 2000)
DAVID BREWER, *The Greek War of Independence* (London 2001)
RICHARD CLOGG, *A Concise History of Greece* (Cambridge 1992)
DOUGLAS DAKIN, *The Greek War of Independence* (London 1975)
ROMILLY JENKINS, *The Dilessi Murders* (London 1961)
WOLF SEIDL, *Bayern in Griechenland: Die Geburt des griechischen Nationalstaats und die Regierung König Ottos* (Munich: Prestel 1981)

Twentieth-Century Athens

DOROS ALASTOS, *Venizelos* (London 1942)
MARJORIE HOUSEPIAN DOBKIN, *Smyrna 1922* (London 1972)
K.M. KAIROPHYLAS, *Athens of the Belle Epoque, Athens between the Wars, Athens during the 40s and the Occupation, Athens in the 50s, Athens in the 60s* (Athens: Philippotis n.d.) – all in Greek
MARK MAZOWER, *Inside Hitler's Greece* (Yale 1993)
ERRICA PROTESTOU, *Athens: a guide to modern architecture* (London 1998)
GONDA VAN STEEN, *Venom in Verse: Aristophanes in Modern Greece* (Princeton 2000).
C.M. WOODHOUSE, *Modern Greece: a short history* (London 1968, last updated 1991)
C.M. WOODHOUSE, *Karamanlis* (Oxford 1982)

Guidebooks

ROBIN BARBER, *Blue Guide to Athens* (London 1999)
HANS R. GOETTE, *Athens, Attica and the Megarid* (London 2001)
DAVID RUPP, *Peripatoi* (Athens: ROAD 2002)

Classical Sources

AELIUS ARISTIDES, orations tr. C.A. Behr (Leiden 1981–6)
ARISTOTLE, *The Constitution of Athens* (tr. P.J. Rhodes, Harmondsworth 1984)
FGrH = *Die Fragmente der griechischen Historiker* (F. Jacoby, 1923–)
HERODOTUS, *Histories* (tr. G. Rawlinson, 1910, reissued Everyman, London 1992)
JOHN MALALAS, *Chronicle* (tr. E. Jeffreys et al., Melbourne 1986)
PAUSANIAS, *Guide to Greece* book I, Attica (tr. Peter Levi, Harmondsworth, Penguin 1971)

PHILOSTRATUS and EUNAPIUS, *Lives of the Sophists* (tr. W.C. Wright, Cambridge Mass & London, Loeb Classical Library 1968)

PLUTARCH, *Greek Lives* (Solon, Themistocles, Cimon, Pericles, Nicias, Alcibiades) (tr. Robin Waterfield, Oxford 1998); *The Age of Alexander* (Demosthenes, Phocion (tr. Ian Scott-Kilvert, Harmondsworth 1973), Sulla (in *Lives* IV, tr. B Perrin, Loeb Classical Library 1986)

SYNESIUS, *Letters* (tr. A. Fitzgerald, Cambridge, Mass & London 1926)

THUCYDIDES, *History of the Peloponnesian War* (tr. Rex Warner, Harmondsworth 1954)

XENOPHON, *A History of My Times* (tr. Rex Warner, Harmondsworth 1966)

Anthologies

KEVIN ANDREWS, *Athens Alive!* (Athens 1979)

RICHARD STONEMAN, *A Literary Companion to Travel in Greece* (Malibu 1994)

Some Modern Travel Accounts

COMPTON MACKENZIE, *First Athenian Memories* (1931)

OSBERT LANCASTER, *Classical Landscape with Figures* (1947)

HENRY MILLER, *The Colossus of Maroussi* (1941)

PATRICIA STORACE, *Dinner with Persephone* (1996)

Index